Muslim responses to Christianity down the ages have been shaped by diverse factors. One of the primary stumbling blocks has been Muslim misperceptions of Christian core beliefs about the person of Jesus and the nature of God.

In this study, Martin Parsons seeks to present Jesus to Muslims in a way which is harmonised with Muslim cultural realities. He argues that previous attempts by Christian scholars to do so have been typically based on a misreading by the Christians concerned of what would be understandable to a Muslim audience. Parsons proposes instead an approach which draws heavily on that used by early Christian writers in presenting Jesus to Jewish audiences. This study includes a practical example of contextualisation which should provide great insights to Christians who are trying to explain their faith to Muslims in diverse contexts.

The study thus makes a most valuable contribution to the task of seeking greater understanding between Christians and Muslims. In a context of increased tension between the West and Islam in the early 21st century, such a skilful and insightful study should be warmly welcomed by Christians and Muslims alike.

Peter G. Riddell
Professor of Islamics
and Director, Centre for Muslim-Christian Relations
London School of Theology

This book focuses on an enlightening comparison of the "mindset of Islamic cultures" with the mindset of "second temple Judaism." The author suggests that there is a model to be derived from the New Testament for conveying the idea that Christ might be presented to humankind as divine "from above" as it were, rather than expecting humans to work out "from below" that Jesus is more than a man. The book issues in some suggested "cantos" for public affirmation and worship that depend upon this more "theocentric" approach to declaring who Jesus Christ is. It is a fascinating and creative contribution to the delicate task of contextualising Christology for Muslim cultures.

Dr. Bill Musk
Author, *The Unseen Face of Islam*
and *Touching The Soul of Islam*

Parsons had shown how fresh appreciation of the Jewish monotheistic context of New Testament christology can assist the contextualization of christology in Islamic contexts today. This is an important book not only for Christians in dialogue with Muslims, but also for all who wrestle with the relationship between belief in the one God and the Christian confession of the deity of Jesus Christ.

Professor Richard Bauckham, FBA, FRSE
Professor of New Testament Studies
and Bishop Wardlaw Professor
University of St. Andrews

UNVEILING *GOD*

CONTEXTUALISING CHRISTOLOGY FOR ISLAMIC CULTURE

MARTIN PARSONS

Unveiling God: Contextualizing Christology for Islamic Culture

Copyright © 2005 by Martin D. Parsons

Permission to use extended quotations from the following works is gratefully acknowledged:
English translation of the poetry of Hafiz by the late Arthur J. Arberry, by kind permission of his daughter, Mrs. Anna Evans.
J. Enevoldsen, The Nightingale of Peshawar Selections From Rahman Baba. [Peshawar: InterLit, 1993].InterLit Foundation.

The Greek New Testament, Fourth Revised Edition, edited by Barbara Aland, Kurt Aland, Johannes Karavidopoulos, Carlo M. Martini, and Bruce M. Metzger in cooperation with the Institute for New Testament Textual Research, Münster/Westphalia © 1993 Deutsche Bibelgesellschaft, Stuttgart.

All Scripture quotations in this publication are from the HOLY BIBLE, NEW INTERNATIONAL VERSION®. NIV®. © 1973,1978,1984 by International Bible Society. All rights reserved.

Report of the 1980 Pattaya Consultation Christian Witness to Muslims Lausanne Occasional Paper No.13, Lausanne Committee for World Evangelization.

Cover design & typesetting: Amanda Valloza

Published by William Carey Library
1605 E. Elizabeth Street
Pasadena, California 91104
www.WCLBooks.com

William Carey Library is a Ministry of the U.S. Center for World Mission,
Pasadena, California.

ISBN 0-87808-454-1

Printed in the United States of America

This book is dedicated to the persecuted church in the Islamic world and to the memory of former Muslims who have given their lives rather than deny the divinity of Christ.

They overcame…by the blood of the Lamb and by the word of their testimony,
they did not love their lives
so much as to shrink from death.

Revelation 12:11

Acknowledgements

A study such as this inevitably involves the encouragement and assistance of a number of people and organisations, without whom this research project would not have been possible. In particular, thanks are due to Professor Peter Riddell, Dr Steve Motyer and Dr Peter Cotterell who together supervised my doctorate of which this book is the outcome. I am also grateful to friends at church who have continued to support my wife and I during the time that this study has been undertaken, and a particular debt of gratitude is due to Dick and Janice Pedlar who graciously and freely provided my family with accommodation during much of the time that this study was undertaken. Thanks are also due to the following bodies for specific funding towards the cost of the research: The Daily Prayer Union Charitable Trust Ltd; the Laing Trust; the Ogle Trust; and the Whitfield Institute.

The assistance of Andrew Willemsen and Chris Booth, who freely gave of their time and expertise to assist with the aftermath of a computer crash and the preparation of computer diagrams is gratefully acknowledged. Thanks are also due to Dr Phil Duce who helpfully commented on the final chapter from a systematic theology perspective and a large debt of thanks must be expressed to Dr Steve Wheatley Price who, during the course of his own academic sabbatical, took time both to scan lost chapters into the computer and proof-read the draft.

However, the largest acknowledgement must go to my wife, Lesley, who has patiently endured the progress of this research with all its trials and frustrations, prayed for its progress, encouraged me and somehow managed to keep two small children relatively quiet and largely out of Daddy's study! I am also grateful for the lessons in life that our children have given me – in particular that there is far more to life than writing up a research study!

Contents

ABBREVIATIONS – MODERN ACADEMIC

AB	*Anchor Bible.*
AFS	*Asian Folklore Studies.*
AH	After Hijira date (Islamic lunar calendar).
AH{P}	Persian (Solar) Islamic calendar.
AM	*Al-Mushir.*
ANE	Ancient Near East.
BCE	Before Christian Era.
BDCM	*Biographical Dictionary of Christian Mission* ed. G.H. Anderson [Cambridge:Eerdmans,1998].
BMS	Baptist Missionary Society.
Bull.HMI	*Bulletin of the Henry Martyn Institute.*
BT	*The Bible Translator.*
CE	Christian Era calendar.
CEOI	*Concise Encyclopaedia of Islam* by C. Glassé [San Francisco:Harper & Row,1989].
CISN	*Centre for Islamic Studies Newsletter*
	London Bible College (now 'London School of Theology').
CMS	Church Missionary Society (now 'Church Mission Society').
CSC	Christian Study Centre, Rawalpindi, Pakistan.
CTIS	*Contributions to Indian Sociology.*
CWC	'Currents in World Christianity' Project, University of Cambridge.
DJG	*Dictionary of Jesus and the Gospels* ed. J.B. Green & S. McKnight [Leicester:IVP,1992].
DNTB	*Dictionary of New Testament Background* ed. C.A. Evans & S.E. Porter [Leicester:IVP,2000].

EDWM	*Evangelical Dictionary of World Missions* ed. A.S. Moreau, H. Netland & C. Van Engen [Carlisle: Paternoster,2000].
EGGNT	*Exegetical Guide to the Greek New Testament.*
EI²	*Encyclopaedia of Islam* (revised edition) ed. H.A.R. Gibb et al (initial editorial committee) [Leiden: Brill,1979-].
EVV	English versions of the Bible.
IBMR	*International Bulletin of Missionary Research.*
ICC	*International Critical Commentary.*
ICh	*Islamo-Christiana.*
IRM	*International Review of Missions.*
JTS	*Journal of Theological Studies.*
JSNT	*Journal for the Study of the New Testament.*
JSOT	*Journal for the Study of the Old Testament.*
KJV	King James Version (1611).
LCWE	Lausanne Committee For World Evangelisation.
LXX	Septuagint.
ML	*Mission Legacies* – Papers previously published in *IBMR* ed. G.H. Anderson, R.T. Coote, N.A. Horner & J.M. Phillips [Maryknoll:Orbis,1994].
MW	*Muslim World* (formerly *Moslem World*).
NBD²	*New Bible Dictionary* ed. J.D. Douglas, N. Hillyer, F.F. Bruce, D. Guthrie, A.R. Millard , J.I. Packer & D.J. Wiseman [Leicester IVP,2nd edn,1982].
NDT	*New Dictionary of Theology* ed. S.B. Ferguson, D.F. Wright & J.I. Packer [Leicester: IVP,1988].
NIBC	*New International Biblical Commentary.*
NICNT	*New International Commentary on the New Testament.*

NIDNTT	*New International Dictionary of New Testament Theology* ed. C. Brown [Carlisle:Paternoster,1986]. 4 vols.
NIDOTTE	*New International Dictionary of Old Testament Theology and Exegesis* ed. W.A. VanGemeren [Carlisle:Paternoster,1997].
NIGTC	*New International Greek Testament Commentary.*
NIV	*New International Version.*
NT	New Testament.
NTS	*New Testament Studies.*
OT	Old Testament.
PA	*Practical Anthropology* (now *Missiology*).
QA	*Qessas al-anbiya.*
SPG	Society for the Propagation of the Gospel (now 'United Society for the Propagation of the Gospel').
TAB	*The Aramaic Bible* (English translations of Aramaic targums).
2TJ	Second temple Judaism.
TynBul	*Tyndale Bulletin* (formerly *Tyndale House Bulletin*).
TDNT	*Theological Dictionary of the New Testament* ed. G. Kittel & G. Friedrich [Grand Rapids: Eerdmans,1964-76] 10 vols. ET from German of *Theologisches Wörterbuch Zum Neun Testament.*
TDOT	*Theological Dictionary of the Old Testament* ed. G.J. Botterweck, H. Ringgren & H.-J. Fabry [Grand Rapids; Eerdmans,1974-98] ET from German of *Theologisches Wörterbuch Zum Alten Testament.*
TNTC	*Tyndale New Testament Commentary.*
TOTC	*Tyndale Old Testament Commentary.*
UBS	United Bible Societies.
WBC	*Word Biblical Commentary.*

ABBREVIATIONS – ANCIENT SOURCES

Add.Est.	Additions to Esther.
Agr.	Philo: De Agricultura ('On Husbandry').
Ant.	Josephus: Jewish Antiquities.
Apoc.Abr.	Apocalypse of Abraham.
Apoc.Zeph.(A& B)	Apocalypse of Zephaniah (Recensions A & B).
2 Bar.	2 Baruch.
3 Bar. (Sl & Gk)	3 Baruch (Slavonic and Greek recensions).
Conf.	Philo: De Confusione Linguarum ('On the Confusion of Tongues').
Decal.	Philo: De Decalogo ('On the Decalogue').
1En.	1 Enoch.
2 En. (J & A)	2 Enoch – longer (J) and shorter (A) recensions.
3 En.	3 Enoch.
Exagoge	Ezekiel the Tragedian.
4 Ezra	4 Ezra.
Fug.	Philo: De Fuga et Inventione ('On Flight and Finding').
G. Barn.	Gospel of Barnabas (pseudonymous but presumed to be medieval).
Jos.Asen.	Joseph and Aseneth.
Jub.	Jubilees.
Lad.Jac.	Ladder of Jacob.
LAE	Life of Adam and Eve.
Leg.	Philo: De Legatione ad Gaium ('On the Embassy to Gaius').
Leg. All.	Philo: Legum Allegoriarum ('Allegorical Interpretation').
2 Macc.	2 Maccabees.
3 Macc.	3 Maccabees.
Mos.	Philo: De Vita Mosis ('The Life of Moses').
Op.	Philo: De Opificio Mundi ('On the Creation of the World').

Orphica.(E&T)	Orpihca.
Post.	Philo: De Posteritate Caini ('On the Posterity of Cain').
Pr.Jac.	Prayer of Jacob.
Pr.Man.	Prayer of Manasseh.
Ps.Philo	Pseudo-Philo: Biblical Antiquities.
Ps.Sol.	Psalms of Solomon.
Quod Deus	Philo: Quod Deus sit Immutabilis ('On the Unchangeablenessof God').
Quod Omn. Prob	Philo: Quod Omnis Probus Liber sit ('Every Good Man is Free').
Sib.Or.	Sibylline Oracles.
Sir.	Ecclesiasticus (Wisdom of Jesus Ben Sirach).
Tg. Chron.	Targum of Chronicles.
Tg. Ezek.	Targum of Ezekiel.
Tg. Isa.	Targum of Isaiah.
Tg. Minor Prophets	Targum of the Minor Prophets.
Tg. Job	Targum of Job (11Q10).
Tg. Neofiti	Targum Neofiti.
Tg. Onqelos	Targum Onqelos.
Tg. Ps.-J.	Targum Pseudo-Jonathan.
T.Abr. (A & B)	Testament of Abraham – longer (A) and shorter (B) recensions.
T.Amram	Testament of Amram (4Q543-8).
T.Job	Testament of Job.
T.Mos.	Testament of Moses.
T.Sol.	Testament of Solomon.
T.Qahat	Testament of Qahat (4Q542).
Tob.	Tobit.
Vit. Cont.	Philo: De Vita Contemplatiea ('On the Contemplative Life').
Wis.	Wisdom of Solomon.

Qumran texts are given in the standard format. They are identified by the letter 'Q' preceded by the cave number (e.g. '1Q' is a text found in cave 1), followed by a numerical serial number (e.g. '1Q20'). The abbreviation 'Fr' indicates the numerical serial number of a particular fragment of a text, where more than one fragment exists. More precise identification of references is provided by the versification system used in G. Vermes *The Complete Dead Sea Scrolls in English* [London:Penguin,1997].

Hebrew text is cited from: *Biblia Hebraica Stuttgartensia* ed. K. Ellinger & W. Rudoph [Stuttgart: Deutsche Bibelgesellschaft, 4th Corrected edn,1990].

LXX text is cited from: *LXX Septuaginta* ed. A. Rahlfs [Stuttgart: Deutsche Bibelgesellschaft,1935].

Greek New Testament text cited is from: *The Greek New Testament,* Fourth Revised Edition, edited by Barbara Aland, Kurt Aland, Johannes Karavidopoulos, Carlo M. Martini, and Bruce M. Metzger in cooperation with the Institute for New Testament Textual Research, Münster/Westphalia, © 1993 Deutsche Bibelgesellschaft, Stuttgart. Used by permission.

OT and NT citations: Unless otherwise indicated, all Scripture quotations in this publication are from the HOLY BIBLE, NEW INTERNATIONAL VERSION®. NIV®. COPYRIGHT© 1973,1978,1984 by International Bible Society. All rights reserved. However, for the sake of clarity the Hebrew יהוה, which the NIV indicates by the capitalisation 'LORD', is transliterated as 'YHWH'.

Bible references cited are based on the verse numbering system of the NIV, where this differs from either the Hebrew or the LXX verse numbering, the latter is given in brackets e.g. Gen.30:24[25] refers to Gen.30:24 in the NIV, which is Gen.30:25 in the Hebrew text. LXX references are specifically labelled as being such.

Qur'anic citations are unless otherwise indicated from: *The Meaning of the Glorious Qur'an* ET by A. Yusuf Ali [1934, reprinted Lahore: Sheikh Muhammad Ashraf, 1975].

Ahadith citations are from: *Al-Hadis – an English Translation & Commentary of Mishkat-ul-Masabih* by al-Haj Maulana Fazlul Karim [Lahore: Sheikh Muhammad Ashraf,1938 – no date of reprint], 4 volumes.

Qur'anic verse references are given according to the verse numbering system followed by A.Yusuf Ali's translation of the Qur'an and are prefaced by the letter 'Q' e.g. 'Q7:54' etc.

Ahadith referencing system: Due to the existence of various versions of the *Mishkat al-Masabih* with different chapter and section ordering systems, Ahadith references are given with both the chapter and section reference of the individual Hadith in Fazul Karim's translation and a summary reference to the section heading.

Calendar dates: All dates referred to are Christian Era (CE) dates, unless specifically stated to be years 'Before Christian Era' (BCE), according to the Islamic lunar calendar (AH), or according to the Persian (Solar) Islamic calendar (AH {P}).

SYSTEM OF TRANSLITERATION

Alphabet letter	Arabic	Persian	Urdu
أ	-	a	a
ا	-	a	a
ب	b	b	b
پ	-	p	p
ت	t	t	t
ٹ	-	-	th
ث	th	s	s
ج	j	j	j
چ	-	ch	ch
ح	h	h	h
خ	kh	kh	kh
د	d	d	d
ڈ	-	-	dh
ذ	dh	z	z
ر	r	r	r
ڑ	-	-	rh
ز	z	z	z
ژ	-	zh	zh
س	s	s	s

Alphabet letter	Arabic	Persian	Urdu
ش	sh	sh	sh
ص	s	s	s
ض	d	z	z
ط	t	t	t
ظ	z	z	z
ع	ʿ	ʿ	ʿ
غ	gh	gh	gh
ف	f	f	f
ق	q	q	q
ک	k	k	k
گ	-	g	g
ل	l	l	l
م	m	m	m
ن	n	n	n
و	w	w	w
ه	h	h	h
ی	y	i	i
ے	-	-	e

VOWELS AND DIPHTHONGS

Alphabet letter	Arabic	Persian	Urdu
ا	a	a	a
و	u	u	u
ا ی	a	ai	ai
ا و	aw	aw	aw
ا ی	ay	ai	ai
Short vowels			
َ	a	a	a
ِ	i	i	i
ُ	u	u	u

NOTES

1. Hamza is omitted in the transliteration.

2. Alef [ا] preceding yeh [ی] is omitted in the transliteration of Persian and Urdu.

3. Vav [و] is the consonant 'w' in word initial position, and the long close rounded vowel 'u' when occurring elsewhere.

4. The genitive form *ezafe*, which is spoken but not transcribed in Persian, is phonetically transliterated as '-i-'.

5. The following Arabic letters are not distinguished in transliteration:

    a) [ا] and the short vowel [ٰ] both of which are transliterated as 'a'.

    b) [د] and [ض] both of which are transliterated as 'd'.

    c) [س] and [ص] both of which are transliterated as 's'.

    d) [ذ] and [ظ] both of which are transliterated as 'z'.

FOREWORD

The missionary statesman to Cairo, Temple Gairdner, speaking at the Pan-Anglican Congress in London in 1908, said:

> Who shall gauge the debt we may yet have to confess to Islam if that great antagonist prove finally to have compelled us to explore unknown depths of the riches of the revelation of the Triune God.[1]

The present study is such an exploration occasioned by the difficulty Muslims have of accepting the divinity of Christ while holding to the unity of God.

The early Jewish Church in the New Testament with a similar monotheism found ways to express such a high Christology, and the Lausanne Committee for World Evangelization in their Consultation on Reaching Muslims in Pattaya, Thailand, in 1980 highlighted the potential of this approach in Christian interpretation to Muslims. Christian apologetics for Muslims, however, have commonly focused on trying to explain the wording of the ecumenical creeds of the Church to them while failing to take sufficient account of the fact that these creeds utilize the concepts of the Graeco-Roman world which are further removed from the understanding of the majority of Muslims than the concepts used by the first Jewish believers in the New Testament.

Martin Parsons' approach has been facilitated by New Testament scholarship which has turned its attention in recent years to an investigation of how the early Jewish Church understood and expressed a high Christology within a high monotheism. Parsons has built on this foundation in his interpretation of the divinity of Christ using concepts that Muslims can more easily understand and accept. Happily, other studies are complementing his work arguing, for example, that the Jewish background of the early Church provides the best base for interpreting a broad spectrum of Christian beliefs.[2] And, although Parsons sidesteps Muslim speculative theology as not having a major impact on the common Muslim, it is worth nothing that once Muslim theologians adopted Western ways of reasoning the emerging orthodoxy ended up explaining the relationship of the One God to his Word and Spirit in terms reminiscent of those used by Trinitarian Christian theologians.[3]

Parsons, by dealing with arguably the greatest theological problem that the common Muslim faces in comprehending a biblical view of God in Christ has, as his title suggests, contributed to the task of "unveiling God" for the Muslim, and the Christian too. And to that extent he has taken a step toward fulfilling Temple Gairdner's dream that Islam would "compel us to explore unknown depths of the riches of the revelation of the Triune God."

J. Dudley Woodberry
Dean Emeritus
and Professor of Islamic Studies
School of Intercultural Studies
Fuller Theological Seminary

---

1 Constance E. Padwick, *Temple Gairdner of Cairo* (London: Society for the Promotion of Christian Knowledge, 1929), 179-180.

2 Mark Harlan, "A Model for Theologizing in Arab Muslim Contexts" (Ph.D. diss., School of Intercultural Studies, Fuller Theological Seminary, 2005).

3 H.A. Wolfson, "The Muslim Attributes and the Christian Trinity," *The Philosophy of the Kalam* (Cambridge, MA: Havard Univ. Press, 1976), 112-132; Joseph Cumming, "Sifat al-Dhat in al-Ashari's Doctrine of God and Possible Christian Parallels" (Unpublished paper, Yale University, May 2001).

INTRODUCTION

'If we recognise that the first disciples were brought up as orthodox Jews and therefore convinced monotheists who rejected every kind of idolatry as vehemently as the Muslim does, we may be able to approach the difficult question of the Oneness of God and the Trinity through the experience of the first disciples. If we can see how they were able to relate and identify the man Jesus with the One Eternal God without rejecting their belief in the Oneness of God, and without being guilty of the sin of idolatry, we may be able to redefine the Oneness of God in a way that the Muslim mind can accept it.'

Report of the LCWE Consultation on Reaching Muslims, Pattaya, Thailand, 1980

The Need for a Christology Specifically Contextualised for Islamic Culture

During the last 200 years the christologies used in Islamic contexts have closely reflected western contextualisations of christology, particularly those derived from Greek patristic creeds. Christology in such contexts has been interpreted through the filter of western christological formulations i.e. fig.1:

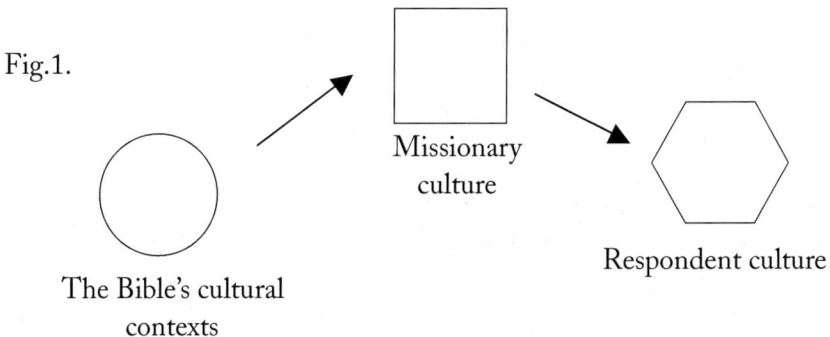

Fig.1.

The Bible's cultural contexts

Missionary culture

Respondent culture

There has been no significant attempt to develop a contextualised christology directly from the Biblical text itself i.e. fig.2:

Fig.2.

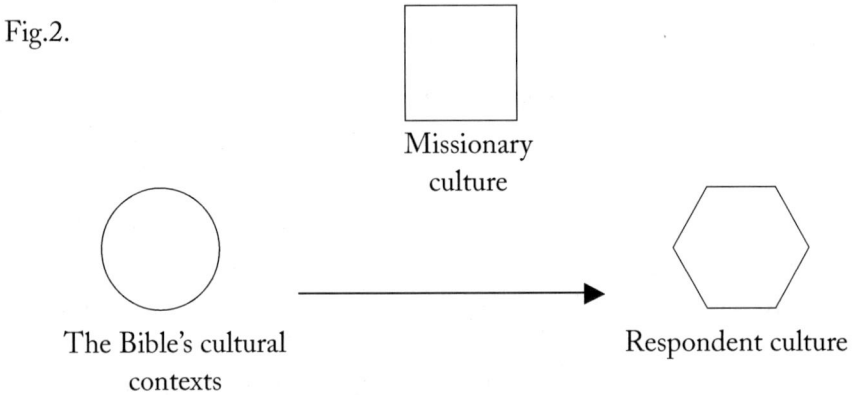

Missionary culture

The Bible's cultural contexts

Respondent culture

However, the considerable differences between Islamic contexts and those addressed by both modern western christologies and the patristic creeds[1] suggests the need for a specific contextualisation of christology being developed that, in so far as is possible, is derived directly from the NT. One of the unique contributions this study makes is in seeking to develop a christology that starts directly from the final form of the Biblical text.

A further issue that arises in Islamic contexts is that the concept of 'personhood' frequently used in western christologies to explain the relationships within the Godhead is widely misunderstood by Muslims as implying tri-theism.[2] This study will therefore seek to find alternative ways of conceptualising these relationships, whilst remaining faithful to the Biblical christology that historic creedal formulations have themselves been derived from. This does not negate the importance of other christologies, including historic creeds. These have a vital role as a hermeneutical check of the biblical orthodoxy of a contextualised christology. However, it must also be recognised that even patristic creedal formulations were themselves contextualisations addressed to specific contexts that were very different from Islamic contexts.[3]

The christology that we propose therefore goes back behind western and patristic formulations to the christology of the early Jewish church expressed in the NT.

Aim of Study

This study aims to establish a basic framework for the contextualisation of christological monotheism in an Islamic culture, that in so far as is possible, uses conceptual categories, forms and symbolic motifs commonly used in that culture.

Whilst christology involves more than explanation of christological monotheism, it is this aspect of Christian belief which is most contested in Islamic contexts, due to the Qur'anic denials of Jesus' divinity and widespread misunderstanding of the trinity as tri-theism.

This study will undertake this task by examining the way in which the early church contextualised its christology against the background of Jewish monotheism. It will then compare this context with that of a present day Islamic culture, in order to assess a) the validity of re-applying the early church's contextualisation of christology in a context influenced by Islamic monotheism and b) the changes to that contextualisation of christology that differences between the two contexts will require.

Within this general aim, this study will specifically seek to:

- express christological monotheism using the *emic* conceptual categories that are widely used in the Islamic context to conceive of God's unique identity.[4]

- develop a contextualisation of christological monotheism that avoids using the concept of divine 'personhood', as in the Islamic context this has frequently resulted in Christian belief being misunderstood as tri-theism.

Whilst the final form of any contextualised christology can ultimately only be determined by the local Christian church, this study will seek to establish a basic framework which will lay a foundation for that process.

This study draws on Islamic texts that are widely used by Sunni Muslims in the Indo-Persian world.[5] However, many of these texts such as the *Qur'an*, *Ahadith* and classical *tafsir* are widely used across the Islamic world. Whilst other texts are less widely known outside of this region, they are representative of polarities and trends that are much more widely spread across the Islamic world, traditionalist, reformist, radical Islamist, mystical and so forth. Thus whilst this contextualisation of christology will likely require adaptation to take account of local particularities, it is anticipated that the basic framework we are proposing will be relevant to much of the Islamic world.

Limitations of time and space have required this study to restrict itself to texts used by Sunni Muslims. Although Shi'a Islam raises additional issues that the church in such contexts must grapple with, I believe that much in this study will also be of relevance to Christians living in such contexts.

Methodology

Although this study draws on the insights of a number of academic disciplines, its methodological basis is determined by the study as a whole being set within missiology as an academic discipline.[6]

As a study in contextual theology our aim is to make the theology contained in the Christian scriptures comprehensible in a particular cultural context. We will do this by re-expressing biblical theology using the local culture's symbolic motifs and in so far as possible, its conceptual categories.

The process of contextualisation therefore starts from the final form of the biblical text. This does not negate the work of biblical historians in seeking to verify the historicity of the biblical text, it simply means starting at a point slightly further along the line by treating the OT/NT as a sacred text.

Although our engagement is with biblical theology, it is necessary to start from the different emphasis and modes of expression of the various biblical writers. We will then seek to draw together these features into a biblical theology, paying particular attention to those aspects of theology that are common to various biblical writers, even though sometimes expressed in different ways.

In order to re-express biblical theology within a different cultural setting, it is necessary to undertake a rigorous analysis of the conceptual categories used in both the culture which the contextualisation is being developed for, and the context which the biblical text relates to. This critical engagement with the historical setting of the biblical text is necessary both to determine its original meaning and as far as possible avoid interpreting the text in the light of concepts derived from other cultures or later church history. Only when this has been done can an attempt be made to re-express this biblical theology using concepts drawn from another culture.

A critical realist epistemology is foundational to this process.[7] This recognises that the interpreter's understanding of the text can at best only be a perspective approximating to reality, rather than an exact mirror image of the reality itself. This is so because the interpreter's understanding of the text is inevitably influenced by their own presuppositions, including the conceptual categories used to conceive of reality in their own culture. However, recognition that an initial frame of reference has a degree of provisionality allows it to be challenged by critical reflection on the text.

Critical realism highlights the danger of interpreting the biblical text in the light of conceptual categories drawn from the interpreter's own culture. It also recognises that the theology contained in the biblical text may be expressed in different ways in different cultures. Moreover, as interpreters from different cultures are likely to ask different questions of the biblical text, this engagement of scripture with different cultures is likely to bring new perspectives that have not been raised in other cultural contexts.

The development of a contextualised christology does not negate the importance of other christologies, such as those contained in the historic Christian creeds. These creeds, along with christologies developed in other cultural settings, function as a hermeneutical check of a contextualised christology's compatibility with scripture.[8] Moreover, the complimentary perspectives of these different christologies are likely to represent a closer approximation to reality, than any individual christology. In this sense the development of a contextualised christology can be viewed as a contribution towards the development of a 'global theology'.[9]

Analysis and Comparison of the Second Temple Jewish and Islamic Contexts

Approach to Comparison

In order to develop a contextualised christology, it is important to compare the context of Jewish monotheism in which the earliest christology emerged, with the present day Islamic context.

Potentially there are two approaches that could be utilised for the examination of how monotheism is understood in a particular Islamic context: either an examination of contemporary Islamic praxis in the region, or, of representative texts that illustrate and potentially inculcate local beliefs about God. However, because of the paucity of non-literary evidence from second temple Judaism,[10] analysis of how monotheism was understood in that context can only be approached through extant literature.[11] We will therefore approach the analysis of both contexts through an examination of a series of texts that different groups within each context have engaged with:

The Second Temple Jewish Context:

a) The Hebrew Bible and Septuagint translation of it into Greek (LXX).

b) Targums (Aramaic paraphrases) which provide evidence of synagogue and Pharisee interpretation of the Hebrew Bible.

c) Qumran texts as evidence of the interpretations used by one radically conservative Jewish group.

d) Pseudepigrapha and apocrypha, representing mystical and popular Jewish literature loosely based around the OT.

e) The work of the Jewish apologist Philo of Alexandria which NT scholars have often attached significance to.[12]

The Islamic Context:

a) The canonical scriptures: An indigenous translation of the *Qur'an* and *Ahadith*.

b) Classical Islamic *tafsir* (commentaries), which are used in *madrasas* (Islamic theological schools) as evidence of how the *Qur'an* is interpreted by the *ulema* who preach in mosques.[13]

c) The modern Islamist *tafsir* of Mawdudi and Sayyid Qutb, that are popular among radical conservative groups.

d) Mystical poetry including Sufi texts; and popular Islamic literature such as *Qessas al-anbiya*, (Stories of the Prophets), that are the source from which many popular Islamic stories are transmitted.

The comparable nature of the two sets of texts suggests that a certain degree of similarity may exist between the two contexts in respect of the typology of religious groups found in each. However, comparison of these contexts is not dependent on the existence of exact parallels.

Texts and Community

The relationship between texts and community has been the subject of significant debate by both anthropologists and Biblical scholars.[14] However, we may affirm the following: 1) After due account has been taken of genre, the texts provide a direct window into the beliefs of the writer, and by extension, of any community that the writer is representative of. 2) The circulation of the texts normally indicates that the readers have at least a degree of sympathy for the beliefs that they find in the texts.

Texts also fulfil two other roles. Firstly, either directly or indirectly they act as agents of enculturation by which a worldview is imposed upon the young of a society;[15] secondly, the meta-narratives contained in texts are, as Malinowski observed, charters for belief that serve to legitimate actions.[16]

Core and Marginal Beliefs

Anthropological analysis of diverse cultures has suggested that cultures are frequently characterised by a single set of central ideological beliefs, but also have peripheral ideologies that diverge from this mainstream.[17] This perspective is potentially very helpful in understanding both the context from which early Christianity emerged, that of 'second temple Judaism', and the Islamic culture that is the focus of this study.

Islamic anthropologist Akbar Ahmed, argues that the five pillars of Islam are core aspects of Islam, and claims that Islamic custom is largely derived from them.[18] Although the latter claim is probably too all encompassing,[19] the five pillars do appear to be relatively central to Islamic self-identity, with the most revered of these pillars, the *Shadada*, forming the most prominent marker of self-identity.

Biblical scholars have also increasingly recognised the diversity within early Judaism. Some scholars have even referred to second temple 'Judaisms' (plural),[20] in reaction to an earlier period of scholarship that saw Judaism largely in monolithic terms. However, recently a number of scholars have sought to paint a more balanced picture of second temple Judaism as whole. They have emphasised the need to give greater weight to beliefs which were regarded as central to Jewish self-identity by the majority of Jews, rather than placing them on a par with more peripheral beliefs that may have been held by certain marginal groups.[21]

NT scholar J.D.G. Dunn has in fact drawn a deliberate parallel with Islam by suggesting that second temple Jews understood the unifying core of Judaism to be defined by four pillars. These were 1) adherence to monotheism; 2) election - the belief that they were God's chosen people; 3) Torah - particularly as expressed in obedience to the law of Moses; and 4) possession of the promised land central to which was the temple.[22] Although not all scholars agree with the entirety of Dunn's list, monotheism is universally accepted as one of the most prominent Jewish identity markers.[23] N.T. Wright and R. Bauckham have gone further and argued that second temple Judaism was characterised by a core set of beliefs about monotheism itself. These core beliefs included the belief that YHWH was uniquely the sole creator and sovereign ruler of all things, and therefore alone worthy to be worshipped.[24] Bauckham in particular, strongly criticises the work of scholars whose analysis of second temple Judaism has focused on a few marginal texts that might possibly portray Jewish belief in semi-divine figures.[25]

Our purpose is to analyse how the early church contextualised its christology in the context of Judaism as a whole, and from that develop an appropriate contextualisation for an Islamic culture. It is therefore particularly important that our analysis and comparison of the contexts of second temple Jewish and Islamic monotheism should focus on beliefs that were most widespread across the various representative texts that we shall examine. Any other approach would be in danger of demonstrating the possibility of contextualisation with only marginal groups within the society, rather than with the society as a whole.

Specific Issues to be Compared in the Second Temple Jewish and Islamic Contexts:

Our analysis of these two contexts will examine five issues related to christological monotheism. Some of these issues are raised by the Islamic context, others by current NT scholarship. However, in order to properly compare the two contexts it is important that the same questions are asked of both:

1. The conceptual framework used to describe monotheism. We will use a metacultural grid of anthropological categories to determine whether monotheism is primarily depicted in bounded or unbounded, extrinsic or intrinsic terms.[26]

2. Monolatry. Can only God legitimately be worshipped, adored or invoked? This is an issue significantly contributing to the traditionalist-reformist divide in the Islamic context, as well as having been raised by NT scholars of the revisionist school in relation to the Jewish origins of early Christian worship of Jesus. In analysing both contexts our primary concern is not with the existence of various practices *per se*, but rather to use the texts as indicators of the degree of legitimacy attached to such activities.[27]

3. Theophany. Can mortal men and women ever see God? This is an issue of some debate in the Islamic *Ahadith* and which has also been seen as significant by some NT scholars.[28]

4. Epiphany. Can God locally manifest his presence on earth? This is an issue central to the Christian doctrine of incarnation.

5. Christological monotheism. What specific antecedents to christological monotheism existed in second temple Judaism? These will later be compared with the attitude towards christological monotheism found in the Islamic context.

These questions are primarily determined by the interaction of Biblical theology with the Islamic context. However, our use of these particular questions to compare the monotheistic context of second temple Judaism from which the earliest christology emerged, with present day Islamic monotheism, is an approach that has hitherto been largely ignored by NT scholars and may therefore in itself make a modest contribution to the study of NT christology.[29] Two aspects of this study in particular that may make some incidental contribution to understanding of NT christology are: Firstly, this study of the comparative relationship of NT christology to Jewish and Islamic monotheism highlights the importance of OT epiphany as a conceptual building block for understanding NT christology. This is an issue which has been largely ignored in recent studies of the relationship between NT christology and its Jewish background. Secondly, the use of the metacultural grid to determine how divine identity and uniqueness were understood by second temple Jews provides an important methodological tool for assessing the relationship between NT christology and its Jewish background. This is potentially significant because, as we have outlined in Appendix B, the main scholarly hypotheses concerning the origins of NT christology are based on different assumptions concerning the nature of Jewish monotheism.

Definitions

The Jewish Context

In this study we will use the terms 'Judaism', 'Jewish' and 'the Jewish context', solely to refer to the context of second temple Judaism in which the early church first contextualised its christology.

The Islamic Context

We will similarly use the term 'the Islamic context' to refer to those areas of the Islamic world where Sunni Islam is a dominant influence, and in particular the Indo-Persian world from which the Islamic texts we have utilised in this study are derived.

Christology

In this study, unless otherwise stated, we use the term christology primarily to refer to the teaching of the NT concerning Christ. Where the term christology is used in a secondary sense in reference to the articulations and analyses of this developed by various scholars, this is explicitly stated. In the latter context we use the term 'christology from above' to denote discussions of biblical christology that begin from the identity of God, and the term 'christology from below' to denote discussions of christology that start from the NT portraits of Jesus on earth.

For the sake of clarity, we restrict the use of the term 'christology' to discussion of the portrait of Christ contained in Christian texts, and refer in other ways to the depiction of Christ in Islamic texts such as the *Qur'an*.

God

In discussing Jewish, Christian and Islamic texts we use the noun 'God' to designate the supreme creator being as understood by the writers of those texts. This use of authorial intention does not in itself imply any judgement as to whether these texts refer to a common ontological being. However, this course of action is necessitated by two factors:

Firstly, as far as Islamic texts such as the *Qur'an* are concerned, Allah is the same God as the God of the Jewish and Christian scriptures.[30] However this claim is viewed, contextualisation has to engage with the understanding of God that already exists in the culture, no matter how dim, distorted or incomplete individual Christians may believe that understanding to be. Whilst this engagement will certainly not be uncritical, wholesale rejection of all notions of 'God' found in the Islamic context will leave very little basis on which to develop a contextualisation. It is therefore necessary to reserve expressing judgement on the ontology behind the linguistic form, in order to avoid a complete disjunction with the culture, and allow the possibility of some bridge to communication of Biblical christology existing.[31] This accords with Paul's use of ὁ θεὸς to refer to the God who made the world and everything in it, without implying any identification with pagan gods such as Zeus.[32]

Secondly, in the the Islamic texts we will survey there is no single word used for God. In the Indo-Persian speaking world the Persian *Khuda* and its derivatives such as *Khudarvand* (Lord) are the most widely used terms both in common speech and in Persian and Urdu literature. However, in the *Qur'an* and *Ahadith* the Islamic term *Allah* is used. Many Muslims also commonly use *Allah* in various proverbial expressions. However, in Islamic countries such as Pakistan, its use in printed and broadcast media is often seen as symbolic of the political Islamicisation process, which is viewed with differing degrees of sympathy. The English word 'God', which is used in many Islamic texts to translate both of these terms, therefore provides the most useful designation for us to use in this study to refer to belief in the supreme creator being within the Islamic context.

Contextualisation

The term 'contextualisation' has been used in a variety of different ways by Missiologists.[33] In this study we use the term to designate a process of critical engagement with a culture that starts directly from the Christian scriptures, rather than any later expression of the theology contained in them.[34] This process brings the biblical metanarrative into critical relationship with the narratives of other places and groups, yet without compromising the biblical particularity of God's own narrative identity.[35] In doing so, it aims to make theology as comprehensible and meaningful as possible in any given context. This process must therefore express the teaching of the Christian scriptures, in so far as possible, within the culture's conceptual categories, forms, and symbolic motifs,[36] whilst at the same time critically assessing each individual aspect of the culture according to its compatibility with scripture.[37] This process of contextualisation is ultimately based on the example of the incarnation.[38] In this God entered the narrative history of a particular people and expressed himself through the concepts and forms of their culture,[39] without in any sense uncritically endorsing every aspect of that culture.[40] Whilst this process might perhaps be more adequately expressed by a term such as 'incarnational theology', in this study we will refer to it as 'contextualisation' both to maintain continuity with existing scholarship, and to avoid any potential confusion that might arise when the incarnation itself is part of the theology we are seeking to develop a contextualisation for.

Finally we may note that contextualisation largely confines itself to the expression and communication of biblical theology. Christian theology holds that convincing people of the truth of these theological claims is ultimately the work of the Holy Spirit.[41]

Emic and Etic

Anthropologists categorise descriptions of cultures into two categories: *emic* categories are concepts commonly used by the people themselves in contrast to *etic* categories, which are those used by outsiders.[42] Any attempt to develop a contextualised local theology must as far as possible be based on *emic* categories. However, if these are inadequate for the expression of Biblical theology it may also be necessary to either expand or supplement them.

It is therefore of crucial importance that both the conceptual categories used in the original Biblical revelation and those used within the recipient culture are properly understood. It is particularly important that the contextual theologian does not unconsciously or otherwise interpret either in the light of conceptual categories drawn from their own culture.

Bounded and Unbounded; Extrinsic and Intrinsic

In order to facilitate this *emic* understanding we will use a series of anthropological conceptual categories as a metacultural grid[43] to assist in determining how monotheism was conceived of both by second temple Jews i.e. Jews at the time of Jesus and the early church; and by Sunni Muslims. These anthropological categories are of course ultimately still *etic* categories. However, their use will hopefully enable us to identify at least the broad parameters of the appropriate *emic* categories.

Essentially there are four basic ways in which monotheism can be understood, which we have illustrated in fig.3.[44]

Fig. 3. The Metacultural Grid

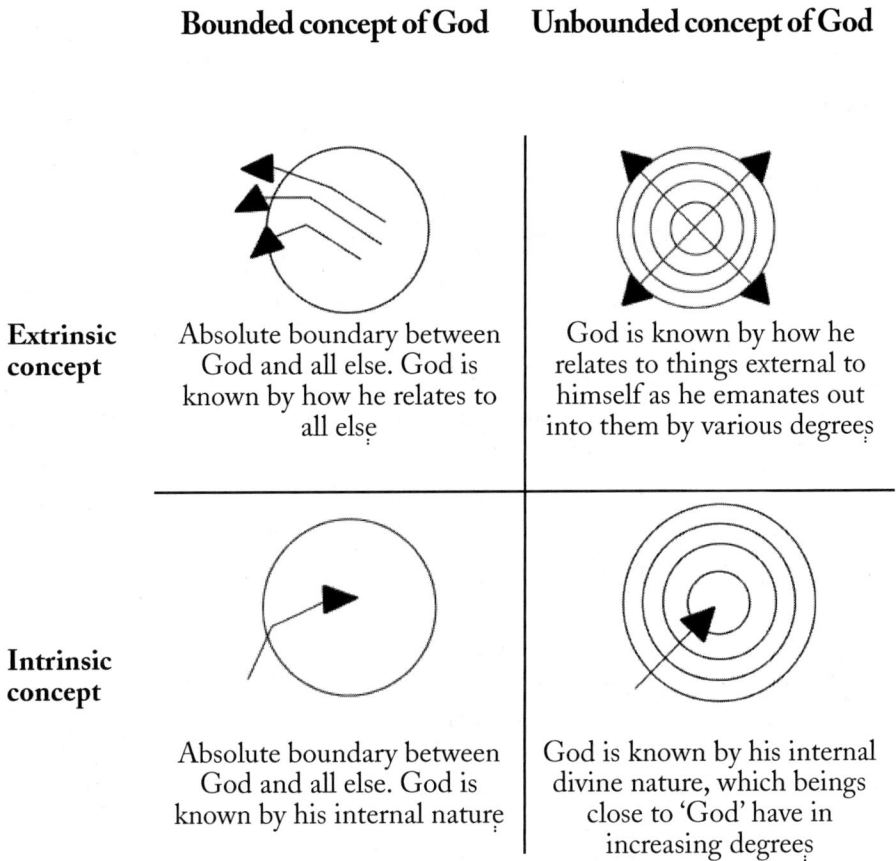

	Bounded concept of God	**Unbounded concept of God**
Extrinsic concept	Absolute boundary between God and all else. God is known by how he relates to all else	God is known by how he relates to things external to himself as he emanates out into them by various degrees
Intrinsic concept	Absolute boundary between God and all else. God is known by his internal nature	God is known by his internal divine nature, which beings close to 'God' have in increasing degrees

1. Bounded Monotheism

This draws a clear and absolute boundary between God and all else. There are two basic conceptions of bounded monotheism:

a) 'Bounded extrinsic conceptions': A bounded extrinsic concept of monotheism emphatically distinguishes between God and all else, and conceives of who God is by the identity which is revealed as he relates to 'non-God' e.g. as creator, ruler and judge. God is therefore known in functional, rather than ontological terms. Although God's existence (ontological nature) is assumed, it does not form the basis by which he is known.

One important corollary of this is that where God is primarily known in bounded extrinsic terms, it is not possible for anyone other than God to take on the major functions that define the identity of God without making God unknowable. Any divine chief agent assuming such functions would in effect become indistinguishable from God.

b) 'Bounded intrinsic conceptions': A bounded intrinsic concept of monotheism also emphatically distinguishes between God and all else. However, God is primarily known not by how he relates to all else, but by his internal (ontological) nature. This understanding of monotheism can be seen in the Nicene creed which speaks of Jesus being of one 'substance' (οὐσία) with the Father. Potentially an intrinsic bounded conception of monotheism allows a distinction to be made between divine function and ontology, thereby allowing a 'divine chief agent' to carry out divine functions on God's behalf. However, in practice if God is conceived of solely in intrinsic terms i.e. in terms of his divine nature (ontology), rather than by how he relates to all else (divine functions), then it becomes impossible to know anything about the identity of God. Because of this, most cultures that have intrinsic conceptions of monotheism in practice can only do so by adding this on to an existing extrinsic conception of who God is, as can be seen in the Nicene creed.

2. Unbounded Monotheism

This does not draw a sharp distinction between God and all else. It is therefore possible to conceive of semi-divine beings who have various degrees of divinity. As with bounded monotheism, unbounded monotheism can be conceived of in either intrinsic or extrinsic terms:

a) 'Unbounded intrinsic conceptions': Here God is known by his internal nature, rather than by how he relates to all else. However, because God is not sharply distinguished from all else, it is possible to conceive of individuals having increasing degrees of divinity. Religions that believe in apotheosis i.e. human beings becoming God, such as traditional Greek and Roman religion during the NT era, are typical of unbounded intrinsic conceptions of God.

b) 'Unbounded extrinsic conceptions': Here God is known by how he relates in an unbounded way to things external to himself. Whilst unbounded intrinsic concepts of God conceive of beings having increasing degrees of divinity, unbounded extrinsic concepts conceive of God by decreasing degrees emanating out into things external to himself. Monistic religions based on the idea of one life force pervading all things to various degrees are typical of unbounded extrinsic concepts of God.[45]

Other Definitions

A glossary of key Islamic terms referred to in this study is provided at the end of the book.

Endnotes

[1] The attempts by theologians such as K. Koyama to develop an 'Asian' christology do not satisfy the need for a specific contextualisation of christology for Islamic cultures, for as Koyama himself argues 'The Asian Approach to Christ' *Missiology* 12:4 (1984) 435-47, Islam is even more distant from Asian religions than it is from western expressions of Christianity.

[2] So, E. Nida 'Are We Really Monotheists?' *PA* 6:2 (1959) 49-54 reprinted in W.A. Smalley *Readings in Missionary Anthropology* [New York:Practical Anthropology,1967] 223-28 and C.H. Kraft *Christianity in Culture: A Study in Dynamic Biblical Theologizing in Cross-Cultural Perspective* [Maryknoll:Orbis,1979] 303-04.

[3] So, J.I. Packer 'The Gospel: Its Content and Communication – a Theological Perspective' 97-114 in J.R.W. Stott & R.T. Coote (eds) *Down to Earth: Studies in Christianity and Culture: The Papers of the Lausanne Consultation on Gospel and Culture* [London:Hodder & Stoughton,1980] 100-103 who claims this with respect to *all* theologies, wherever and whenever produced.

[4] cf. the following 'Definitions' section for discussion of *emic* and *etic* categories.

[5] cf. Appendix C for a fuller description of these texts.

[6] i.e. it draws on the insights and methodologies of disciplines such as anthropology, biblical studies, historical theology and Islamic studies insofar as they are compatible with its own ethos as an academic discipline. This ethos exemplified in the statement of D.J. Bosch *Transforming Mission* [Maryknoll: Orbis,1991] 497 that 'missiology consciously pursues its task from a faith perspective.'

[7] So, P. Hiebert *Anthropological Reflections on Missiological Issues* [Grand Rapids:Baker,1994] 19-103 esp. 29-31,69-71. Hiebert observes that critical realism has now largely replaced instrumentalism in anthropology (66-69). In biblical studies critical realism has been championed by B.F. Meyer *Critical Realism and the New Testament* [Alison Park:Pickwick,1989].

[8] Hiebert *Reflections* 30-31,103 speaks of the cultural biases of local churches needing to be checked for their compatibility with scripture by the international community of churches drawn from many cultures. As theologies developed in specific cultural contexts the historic Christian creeds can similarly contribute to this process.

[9] So, Hiebert *Reflections* 102-103 who terms this a 'Supracultural Theology'.

[10] Hereafter abbreviated as '2TJ' in footnotes.

[11] So, N.T. Wright *The New Testament and the People of God* [London:SPCK,1992] 47.

[12] Philo's use of Greek philosophy to explain Judaism is to some extent paralleled by the use of western philosophy by Islamic liberals. However, because Islamic liberals are confined to the educated elite they represent only a very small peripheral group within the Islamic context, and are therefore of only marginal significance in assessing the Islamic context as a whole. Our inclusion of Philo's works is therefore driven solely by the importance attached to them by NT scholarship, which has recognised that his works reflect not only engagement with Greek philosophy, but also first century CE Jewish interpretations of Scripture, for which our extant evidence is otherwise limited.

[13] Here we use *ulema* simply to denote those preaching in mosques who have previously attended *madrasas*, rather than the narrower sense of those who have graduated from the most advanced classes.

[14] For concise summaries of the debate amongst anthropologists and Biblical scholars respectively cf. P. Hiebert *Cultural Anthropology* [Grand Rapids:Baker,1976,1983] 372-74 and Wright *NTPG* 50-54.

[15] cf. Kraft's observation (*Christianity* 53) that a worldview is imposed on the young of a society through the teaching and learning process.

[16] Cited without reference by Hiebert *Cultural* 373.

[17] So, A.P. Cheater *Social Anthropology: An Alternative Introduction* [London:Routledge,1986,1989] 243-44.

[18] A.S. Ahmed *Islam Today* [London:Taurus,1999] 7,20-21,32-38.

[19] Ahmed here defines Islamic custom as including food, clothing and language (7).

[20] cf. e.g. J. Neusner, W.S. Green & E. Frerichs (eds) *Judaisms and Their Messiahs at the Turn of the Christian Era* [Cambridge:CUP,1987].

[21] e.g. R. Bauckham *God Crucified* [Carlisle:Paternoster,1998] 5; J.D.G. Dunn *The Partings of the Ways* [London:SCM,1991] 18-36; Wright *NTPG* 244-45.

[22] Dunn *Partings* 18-36 who rightly observes that the Qumran community's rejection of the Jerusalem cultus was a rejection of a corrupted temple, not of the temple *per se* (34).

[23] e.g. P.M. Casey *From Jewish Prophet to Gentile God* [Cambridge:James Clarke,1991] passim but cf. esp. 12-13, gives 8 identity markers of which he claims ethnicity was the most important.

[24] Bauckham *Crucified* passim but cf. especially 9-13; 70-71; Wright *NTPG* 248-252 who describes 2TJ monotheism as creational monotheism, providential monotheism and covenantal monotheism - categories that approximate to those of Bauckham. Wright (244-45) specifically criticises Neusner for losing sight of the unity of Judaism in the midst of its diversity.

[25] Bauckham *Crucified* 2-5. Wright *NTPG* 248 similarly describes focus on anything other than what he terms 'basic beliefs'- such as the *shema* – 'misleading' (248).

[26] cf. following 'Definitions' section for a description of these conceptual categories.

[27] cf. the observation of T.W. Dye 'Towards a Cross-Cultural Definition of Sin' 439-54 in C.H. Kraft & T.N. Wisley (eds) *Readings in Dynamic Indigeneity* [Pasadena:William Carey,1979] that in analysing a culture it is essential to distinguish between behaviour that is practised and that which is approved of (442).

[28] Here we use 'theophany' to mean any visible appearance of God to people, whether in the form of a vision or an actual appearance on earth. We use 'epiphany' solely to designate the latter. Although this distinction is not always made by Biblical scholars our engagement with the Islamic context makes it a helpful distinction, as at least in eschatological terms theophanic vision is much more strongly affirmed than epiphany.

[29] Although some NT scholars such as Dunn *Partings* 19,285 n.8 have seen the potential for such comparison to shed light on the relationship between NT christology and the context of Jewish monotheism that it emerged from, there has to date been no significant analysis of this.

[30] cf. Q2:139; 3:81; 43:46-64.

[31] So, Kraft *Christianity* 370 who observes that the greater the difference in worldview, the smaller the number of mutually accepted presuppositions, the greater will be the difficulty in adequately and effectively communicating the Christian message.

[32] Acts 17:24ff. That Paul is deliberately using the general word for God ὁ θεὸς and specifically avoiding the any identification with pagan gods can be seen by comparing his Athens speech with a similar speech that Josephus attributes to Aristeas (Ant.12:22). In this Aristeas states that Jews and Greek worship the same God, the God who created the universe, and he is appropriately called Zeus because he breathes life (ζωή) into creatures.

[33] For concise summaries of different models of 'contextualisation' cf. S. Bevans 'Models of Contextual Theology' *Missiology* 13:2 (1985) 185-202 and D. Gilliland 'Contextualisation' *EDWM* 225-27.

[34] Following the lead of Kraft *Christianity* passim, but cf. esp. 310.

[35] So, R. Bauckham *Mission as a Hermeneutic for Scriptural Interpretation* CWC Position Paper 106 [Cambridge: Faculty of Divinity, University of Cambridge,1999] 16-17.

[36] So, C. Taber 'Contextualisation: Indiginization and/or Transformation' 143-54 in D.M. McCurry (ed.) *The Gospel and Islam: A 1978 Compendium* [Monrovia:MARC,1979] 146.

[37] This approximates to what Gilliland terms the 'Critical model' though also draws on the 'Semiotic model'.

[38] So, C.H. Kraft 'Dynamic Equivalence Churches: An Ethnological Approach to Indigenity' 87-111 in Kraft and Wisley *Indigeneity* 104.

[39] So, Kraft *Christianity* 300.

[40] Contra. Kraft who claims that the 'functions' served by cultural forms are 'with few exceptions...neutral' (*Christianity* 113). However, his caveat indicates a prior evaluation of these in the light of scripture.

[41] So, L. Newbigin *Trinitarian Doctrine for Today's Mission* [1963 – reprinted Carlisle:Paternoster,1998] 53-55; P. Cotterell *Mission and Meaninglessness* [London:SPCK,1990] 164-66 and D.J. Bosch *Transforming Mission* [Maryknoll:Orbis,1991] 10 (cf. also 389-93) who distinguishes between 'God's mission' and 'missions'. J.H. Bavinck *An Introduction to the Science of Missions* [Phillipsburg:Presbyterian & Reformed Publishing Co.,1960] 221-22 ET from Dutch by D.H. Freeman of *Inleiding in de Zendingswetenschap*, similarly observes that whilst the verb ἐλέγχω is used in the NT with both human and divine subjects, ultimately 'only the Holy Spirit can do this' (222).

[42] The *emic/etic* distinction was first articulated by pioneering missionary linguist and Nobel laureate K. Pike who drew an analogy with the linguistic distinction between phonemes (sounds recognised as distinct by native speakers) and phonetics (sounds recognised as distinct by outside linguists).

[43] cf. P.G. Hiebert *Anthropological Reflections on Missiological Issues* [Grand Rapids:Baker,1994] 69-71, 87-88, 92 for a discussion of metacultural grids and their importance for contextualisation.

[44] Both Fig.3 and the following description are largely based on Hiebert *Reflections* 110-133 although only in 124-25 does Hiebert specifically apply this to monotheism. Hiebert's categorisation of anthropological categories is based by analogy on mathematical set theory (intrinsic and extrinsic bounded sets, and intrinsic and extrinsic unbounded 'fuzzy' sets). However, it is important to note that because this metacultural grid of anthropological categories is based on analyses of various cultures, its application to concepts of monotheism is not dependent on God being defined as a mathematical set of one. Its relationship to the mathematical theory is analogical and therefore accidental.

[45] cf. Hiebert *Reflections* 131-320.

CHAPTER 1

CHRISTOLOGIES USED IN ISLAMIC CONTEXTS

Holy, Holy, Holy! Merciful and Mighty!
*God in **three** persons, blessed **trinity**.*[1]

Introduction

In this chapter we review the main christologies that have been used in Islamic contexts from the commencement of the modern missionary movement to the present day.[2]

Although there have been several histories produced of Christian engagement with Islam during this period,[3] little attention has been paid to the christologies advocated by the most influential figures during this period. This chapter will attempt to assess the extent to which these christologies were appropriately contextualised to the Islamic context, and conversely the extent to which they simply translated western christologies.

It must be stated at the outset that there has been little real attempt to develop a coherent contextualised christology for the Islamic world. In 1945 J.W. Sweetman lamented this lack saying

> We have been great writers of tracts, but where are the standard works on Christian doctrine?[4]

Our survey in this chapter suggests that little has changed since then.[5] A prophetic note was however sounded at the 1980 Pattaya consultation *Christian Witness to Muslims*, which after lamenting

How difficult it is to express ourselves in a way that Muslims understand added that

> If we recognise that the first disciples were brought up as orthodox Jews and therefore convinced monotheists who rejected every kind of idolatry as vehemently as the Muslim does, we may be able to approach the difficult question of the Oneness of God and the Trinity through the experience of the first disciples. If we can see how they were able to relate and identify the man Jesus with the One Eternal God without rejecting their belief in the Oneness of

God, and without being guilty of the sin of idolatry, we may be able to redefine the Oneness of God in a way that the Muslim mind can accept it.[6]

This is precisely what this present study sets out to do.

As this chapter will demonstrate, to date there has been no specific attempt to develop a contextualised christology for an Islamic culture. In large measure, the best that can be said is that the scholarly writings of Christian leaders who have been most influential in engaging with Muslims do in various places deal with christological issues.

We will therefore attempt to draw together these various strands of christology from works whose primary purpose has been either as guides for intending missionaries, apologetic works intended for Muslims or comparative studies of Islam and Christianity. The almost total lack of any existing scholarship surveying this field will require us to treat these works as primary sources, which will inevitably lengthen our treatment somewhat. However, this in itself may be a modest contribution to current scholarship.[7]

Patristic Creeds

In this chapter we will see that western missionaries have frequently simply translated patristic creeds into the vernaculars spoken in Islamic contexts. Patristic creedal formulations have also had a generative and lasting impact on the western christological writings, which have influenced western missionaries working in Islamic cultures and through them, the local church they have sought to establish. It is therefore important to briefly discuss the context such creeds originally sought to address, and its critical distance from Islamic culture, in order to assess the relevance for an Islamic context of christologies based on these creeds.

In Chapters 2-4 we will demonstrate that both the early church and the Jewish context out of which it arose primarily conceived of God in extrinsic terms; i.e. God's unique identity was primarily known by how he related to all else, rather than by his internal nature. Because of this, the christology which we find in the latest books of the NT is explicitly a Logos christology; i.e. one that identifies Jesus as how God reveals himself to his creation as creator, ruler, judge and so forth.[8]

However, when the Gospel spread to regions where Hellenistic philosophy was a dominant influence, it had to relate to a context radically different from Jewish monotheism. In the OT God is portrayed as intimately involved in the life of his people, even personally appearing to them in theophanic visions, and on rare occasions in epiphanies on earth. However, where Platonism influenced Hellenistic culture, God was seen as a distant being, who could not be defiled by having anything to do with the world, even in the act of creation.[9] Consequently God could not be conceived of by means of his relationship to the world (i.e. extrinsically), but only in his presumed ontological being itself (i.e. intrinsically).[10] The claim that Jesus was God himself relating to his creation was therefore liable to be either rejected, or remoulded to mean that Jesus must be a lesser god who had been created by God as a means of relating to his creation. The early church heresy of Arianism was essentially an expression of the latter belief. In order to safeguard the full divinity of Christ in the face of the Arian claim that Jesus was only a created being, it was therefore necessary for the fourth century church to express their christology in ways that were somewhat different from the Logos christology they had inherited. This 're-contextualisation' was accomplished by talking about God in his internal nature (i.e. intrinsically), rather than simply by how he related to all else (i.e. extrinsically). The use of this intrinsic conceptual category was an appropriate contextualisation, because it was the way that God was primarily conceived of within cultures dominated by Platonism. Its use enabled the church to say that there was one divine *essence or substance* (οὐσία), but within it were three *persons* (ʿυπόστασις), concepts which although not used in the NT, safeguarded the full divinity of Jesus in the face of Arian claims.[11]

However, as we will demonstrate in chapter 5, in the Islamic context being studied, God's identity is not primarily conceived of in intrinsic terms (i.e. in his internal nature), but in extrinsic terms (i.e. by how he relates to his creation). To this extent at least, it more closely parallels the Jewish context out of which NT christology emerged than the Hellenistic context in which the patristic creeds were formulated.[12] It must therefore be seriously questioned whether a christology based on an intrinsic conception of God would be an appropriate contextualisation for an Islamic context. In fact, at least one prominent Islamic writer has gone out of his way to stress the differences between the Greek view of God's transcendence and the Islamic view of God being immanently involved in his creation.[13]

A further issue arises from a change in the meaning of 'person'. When the concept of 'personhood' (Greek ʿυπόστασις / Latin: *persona*) was used in the patristic creeds, its range of meaning included the mask that an actor used when acting as different persons. The word emphasised the oneness of God, who appeared in different roles. The creedal writers therefore had to speak of the eternal relations between the persons in order to safeguard against the heresy of *modalism*.[14] However, throughout the period covered by this chapter, in both the western world and the Islamic world, the concept of personhood has normally meant an individual (human) being. When personhood has this meaning, the emphasis given by the patristic writers is in fact reversed, with the description of God as existing in three persons, actually emphasising the distinctions within the godhead, rather than its unity. It is therefore perhaps unsurprising that when descriptions of God as being three persons have been used in Islamic contexts, they have almost by default been understood by many Muslims as meaning tri-theism. Moreover, even those who have attempted to understand otherwise, have often concluded that such Christian claims are neither rational nor intelligible.[15]

Henry Martyn

Henry Martyn (1781-1812)[16] may fairly be regarded as the inspiration for the commencement of modern missionary work specifically focused on Muslims.[17] Martyn, a chaplain of the East India Company, was posted to Dinapore in Bihar,[18] and Cawnpore in the Muslim heartland of North India. While in India he translated the Anglican Book of Common Prayer into Urdu, and the NT into Urdu, Persian and Arabic. His work still forms the basis for the current Urdu and Persian Bible translations.[19] It was reading Martyn's Urdu NT that finally led a prominent Muslim *'alim*, Shaikh Salih (c.1772-1827)[20] to embrace the Christian faith, and follow Martyn's example in devoting his life to evangelism in North India. After 4 years in India, Martyn went to Persia to test and revise his Persian NT. While in Shiraz, he was persuaded to exchange tracts with Mirza Ibrahim, a leading Imam. These tracts set out to answer the Mirza's five main proofs of the truth of Islam,[21] but also provide the fullest statement of Martyn's christology. After the completion of the Persian NT and arranging for its presentation to the Shah of Persia, Martyn set out for England via Turkey, but died en route in Tocat in 1812, after only 6 years as a missionary. Martyn's influence on later generations of missionaries to Muslims was chiefly due to the publication of a biography based on his journals and letters by his Cambridge friend John Sargent in 1819,[22] and by the translation and publication of his Persian tracts by Samuel Lee, the CMS orientalist in 1824.[23]

Martyn's christology was emphatically a christology from above.[24] Even when talking with Sufis, he appears to have stressed the absolute boundary between the Creator and the creature.[25] He asserted that Christ was the Creator, rather than a creature, though admitting that his manhood was created.[26] When

Martyn was asked for his opinion about Christ, he generally began by saying that he was the Son of God.[27] When required to recite the Islamic *Kalima* in a *munzara* debate, he began 'God is God', but instead of 'Muhammad is the prophet of God' substituted 'and Jesus is the Son of God', [28] although this expression gained a much more negative response than his earlier identification of Christ as the Creator.[29]

Martyn's apologetic for the trinity is based on explaining the intrinsic concept of personhood, by drawing an analogy between men being known by the words they utter, and God being known by his Word. However, whatever the usefulness of this analogy, his reference to God as being three persons, still left him having to add a caveat, that this does not mean three gods:

> If it be asked how it can be possible that three persons can be possessed of a dignity which belongs to none but God, we answer; the Spirit of God and the Word of God have the same relation to God himself, as the spirit and word of a man have to him, which in fact constitute the same person; but which when considered with respect to others, are more than one. It is not however, our intention to speak of more than one God.[30]

Martyn's Word analogy is stated more clearly in his final tract, where he states that Jesus is

> called "the Word of God": for the word of anyone is that by which his thoughts, hitherto latent, are presented to the perceptions of others.[31]

This philosophical analogy of Christ as the self-revelation of God became a standard part of Christian apologetics to Muslims in the next century.[32]

Karl G. Pfander

Karl Pfander (1803-1865)[33] spent most of his missionary life in North West India, being based at Agra (1840-53), and pioneering new work in Peshawar (1853-56), before moving to Constantinople (1858-64). However, he initially worked among Armenian Christians in Georgia and Persia, as part of the 'Great Experiment' of seeking to revive the ancient Eastern churches, in the hope that they would reach out to the surrounding Muslim majority.[34] The initial publication of his most renowned work, the *Mizan al-Haqq* ('The Balance of Truth') in Armenian (1829), a language only spoken by this historic Christian community, clearly indicates that its original intention was to train Armenian Christians to engage with the Muslim community among whom they lived. However, an 1835 translation into Persian made it accessible to Muslims, and

Pfander's subsequent revisions in Persian and later Urdu, were clearly intended for direct reading by Muslims.[35] Pfander subsequently produced a number of other apologetic works, including the *Miftah al-Asrar* ('The Key of Mysteries') which dealt specifically with the Christian doctrine of the trinity.[36] However it was the *Mizan al-Haqq* which had the greatest impact both on Muslims, amongst whom 30,000 copies had been distributed by the time of Pfander's death,[37] and on subsequent generations of missionaries. The latter was largely due to the publication of R.H. Weakley's English translation in 1867, and W. St Clair Tisdall's revision and enlargement in 1910.[38]

Vander Werff, in his history of Christian mission to Muslims in India and the Near East, speaks of all subsequent Christian apologetics to Muslims being either an admiration of, in reaction to, or a modification of Pfander's approach.[39] Although this is particularly true in respect of his use of 'necessary controversy' as an aspect of evangelism, the extensive circulation of his books inevitably gave his christology a lasting impact, an influence that has been almost entirely ignored by scholarship to date. Pfander's books dealt with a defence of the integrity of the Bible, the presentation of christology, and a response to the five traditional proofs of Islam advanced by the *ulema*.[40] Pfander significantly influenced later generations of Christian workers in Islamic countries, including T.V. French,[41] Imad ud-Din Lahiz,[42] W. St Clair Tisdall,[43] and even in the mid twentieth century was still warmly regarded by Samuel Zwemer.[44] Unfortunately the concentration of some later missionaries and much recent scholarship on attacking his critique of traditional Islamic proofs makes it difficult to assess the impact of his christology.[45] The limited evidence we do have, does however point to a longstanding impact on later generations of missionaries. In 1905 E.M. Wherry, spoke of it as a strong argument for the doctrine of Christ's divine sonship and the trinity,[46] while W. St Clair Tisdall, who revised both the *Mizan al-Haqq* and the *Miftah al-Asrar*, largely left Pfander's christology intact. However, Muslims clearly found Pfander's christology somewhat hard to comprehend. Powell speaks of Pfander's constant difficulties during the 1853 Agra debate 'in defining the Godhead, and the "mystery" of the Incarnation in terms which would at least be comprehensible, if not acceptable to his Muslim opponents.'[47] Similar difficulties are evident in Pfander's discussions with Kazi Najib Khan,[48] one of the leading mullahs of Peshawar, who after receiving copies of the *Mizan al-Haqq* and the *Miftah al-Asrar* had invited Pfander to discuss christology over breakfast. Pfander's own account of the discussion suggests that the area of his theology Najib struggled most to comprehend was the concept of three persons in one Godhead.[49]

Monotheism is absolutely central to Pfander's christology, and he speaks of man having been 'created only that he might render perpetual service to God.'[50] His explanation of christology combines both extrinsic and intrinsic concepts: he states that God has revealed himself in scripture as the holy and loving Father who from all eternity ordained the salvation of men; as the Saviour-Son who through his incarnation and suffering provided salvation for sinners, and as the Holy Spirit who enlightens the hearts of men. However, he then goes on to explain that 'these manifestations of the Divine Being, Christians call *the Three Persons*, or the *Trinity in Unity*.'[51]

Pfander also echoes Martyn's earlier apologetic that, just as speech is both united to and yet also distinct from the thought it came from, so the Son whilst being united with the Father has also 'with a peculiar distinction, come forth and been begotten from Him from all eternity.'[52]

Pfander also stresses that God must show his justice by punishing sinners. However, as man is a creature of God, He is obligated to render complete and absolute service to God all of his days. Therefore, no matter how great his devotions, they are simply his duty to God, and he simply cannot accomplish anything extra which could atone for his sins. Man is therefore in need of a saviour and mediator, and because all men are sinners, such a saviour cannot be merely a man.[53]

Thomas Valpy French

Thomas Valpy French (1825-1891) worked with the CMS in North West India, first at Agra in 1851 where Pfander was then based, before in 1862 founding the Derajat mission in the Afghan border region. After several years convalescence in England, French returned to the region in 1869 to found St John's Divinity School in Lahore, before in 1877 becoming the first Bishop of the newly created Lahore diocese which included the entire North West Frontier region, where he continued to engage in bazaar preaching during diocesan visitations. French retired to England in 1887 as a result of ill health. However in 1891 at the age of 66, he responded to a hitherto unanswered call by the CMS for missionaries to Arabia, becoming the first missionary to Muscat, where he died three months later.[54] French, whose own contribution to the church in the Islamic world was considerable, saw himself as being greatly indebted to the foundational work of Martyn, whose biography he continued to read throughout his life,[55] as well as Pfander whose books he greatly valued.[56] He spoke of Pfander as having left

> a rich legacy to other ages of the church, in his clear, strong, unembellished statements of Christian truth and refutation of Mohammedan error. It was no small privilege I had in being the disciple of Pfander in my youth, a worthy successor of the heroic Henry Martyn.[57]

Significantly, Zwemer was later to compare French himself to Martyn.[58]

Many aspects of French's understanding of contextualisation anticipated later missiological thought. He stressed the need for a simple lifestyle, was offended at the grandeur of some missionary buildings,[59] and at one point himself desired to live like a member of an Afghan tribe.[60] He urged the use of Christian poetry and song to 'carry the Gospel wider and fix it deeper' in the minds of ordinary people. His understanding of the need for contextualisation to a limited extent even included theology. His plan for the theological college at Lahore spoke of it being a place where

> Christianity should be domesticated on the Indian soil....(where) men who, by a severe and close attention bestowed on Mohammedan and Hindu literature, can express the delicate shades, the nice distinctions of thought, which some at least of our standard works of theology involve.[61]

However, as the final clause hints, this indigenous theology would essentially be western theology carefully expressed through Indian languages. The Lahore curriculum in fact was largely based around several western theological texts including Liddon's *Bampton Lectures* on christology, Owen on the Holy Spirit, and Butler's *Analogy,* which were used to teach the various articles of the Nicene Creed.[62] This was despite the fact that no lesser person than B.F. Westcott, then Regius Professor of Divinity at Cambridge and an active supporter of the college, had urged French that among the lessons the West had to learn from the East would be hearing Biblical truth 'as it is apprehended by Eastern minds.'[63] French's Anglican ecclesiology appears to have been one of the principal influences that prevented him from allowing the possibility of the Indian church developing its own indigenous theology. He understood adherence to the historic creeds, together with apostolic succession and rejection of Roman Catholicism, to be the defining points of the Anglican communion.[64] This made it impossible for French to countenance any formal expression of christology other than the existing Anglican theology based on patristic creeds. French's understanding of the Anglican communion as the historic and true church led him to describe any movement by the Indian church towards independence of the patristic creeds as not only removing historic safeguards against heresy, but also cutting itself off from the church of antiquity, thereby 'substituting an institution of man for the church of Christ.'[65] For French the main articles of the Christian faith, including the articulation of christology, had been once and for all settled in the creeds. He regarded contextualisation as applying only to such lesser matters as customs of worship and church discipline.[66] Interestingly French also rejected the use of the Islamic name 'Isa, as unlike the Syriac *Yezu (Yeshu)*, it did not mean 'Saviour'.[67] However, this argument had earlier been refuted by French's colleague Lowenthal, who had demonstrated that not only did 'Isa probably originate in pre-Islamic Christian circles, but as a phonemic assimilation of the Hebrew/Syriac *Yeshua*, it paralleled the NT Greek Ἰησοῦς, as neither *Isa* nor Ἰησοῦς in themselves mean 'Saviour' or for that matter anything else.[68]

French's own explanation of christology to Muslims, emphasised both the emphatically bounded concept by which most Muslims thought of God, and utilised the intrinsic conception of monotheism contained in patristic creeds. French's own description of his approach, which was later more widely disseminated by St Clair Tisdall, stated:

> I begin…by asking the Muhammadan to define the nature of the Unity of God. In many respects one accepts his definition and lays stress on the Unity – *in the sense of entire distinction from all created being.* Then I say, 'Now here we have the Divine Nature on one side, by itself (so to speak), and all else on the other: we see how wholly distinct and unique it is. But we have not yet touched the question of what mysteries it may contain in itself.' I go on to point out how inevitable it is that there should be *some* great mystery in that Supreme Nature…whether we hold to a sterile monotheism or a Plurality of hypostases in one Essence – *in either case* it does not conflict with the Unity, for we are dealing simply with *the inner Nature* of that *Essence* which we have already, in accepting the Unity, separated off and posited wholly by itself.[69]

Like Pfander, French also stressed the necessity of Christ's divine nature in order to effect redemption. In evangelistic contexts he spoke of Christ as the mediator between God and man.[70] He was however careful to stress that there was no mixing of human and divine natures in the person of Christ, but both met unchanged and unaltered.[71] In speaking with Muslims, he identified Christ with OT theophanies including the figure wrestling with Jacob and the angel accompanying the exodus in whom the divine name dwelt.[72] Like Pfander he identified Christ as the pre-existent word and wisdom in Proverbs 8, an argument which was later to be rejected by St Clair Tisdall.[73]

French's lifelong predilection for patristic theology[74] led him at one point to question whether the focus of nineteenth century christology on the divinity of Christ had insufficiently stressed Christ as the means of access to the Father. However, French's fear of expressing Christology in anything other than creedal formulae prevented him from publicly expressing even this modest shift of emphasis towards a Logos christology.[75]

Imad ud-Din Lahiz

Imad ud-Din (c.1830-1899) was a member of an important family of Islamic scholars in the Punjab that claimed descent from Qutub Jamal, a renowned pir belonging to the Persian royal family. After a traditional Islamic education, Imad ud-Din was appointed as a preacher in the Central Mosque in Agra, where he was a participant in the famous 1853 debate, opposing Pfander and French. He later became a wandering ascetic, before eventually embracing the Christian faith. After Anglican ordination, he became chaplain to Bishop Thomas Valpy French, with whom he shared a common approach to Muslim evangelism. His apologetic writings, which laid the foundation for Urdu Christian literature,[76] were primarily critiques of Islam or defences of the Bible. However, he also wrote two works that dealt in some measure with christology,[77] both of which are largely unobtainable today.[78] Imad ud-Din was much influenced by Pfander's writings, although his *Tauzin al-Aqwal* ('The Weigher of Opinions') develops a slightly more original approach, justifying trinitarian monotheism by means of divine pneumatology. Imad ud-Din wrote this particular book in response to the recently emerged Ahmadiyya movement centred on the teachings of Mirza Ghulam Ahmad of Qadian who claimed to be 'the spirit of the Prophet and the Messiah', referring to Moses and Jesus, respectively. The Mirza, who was influenced in his Qur'anic interpretation both by Sufism and by the rationalism of Sir Syed Ahmad Khan, asserted that Christ was the Son of God only in a mystical sense, comparable to a disciple's relation to his master, and explained the trinity as 'the three fold forms of divine love'. Imad ud-Din responded to these claims firstly by setting out the doctrine of the trinity in the Athanasian Creed, and secondly by asserting that the Bible teaches the doctrine of the trinity from Genesis to Revelation. In particular, he identified the OT angel of the covenant as the second person of the trinity; thirdly, he claimed that Islamic teaching implied the existence of a distinction within the Godhead between Allah and the divine Spirit. In support of this, he cited various Islamic writers, including commentators, who had spoken of the Holy Spirit in ways that imply he is divine. In particular, he quotes from *Insan-i-Kamil* ('The Perfect Man') of Abdul Karim Jilani (b.c.1365), which developed Ibn Arabi's *wahdat al-wujud* Sufism:

> The Spirit of God is the Spirit of all spirits, who was not created, but who has subsisted in God from all eternity…It is not lawful to call Him a creature. He is one of the 'mouths' of God, and by Him all things were created. He breathed into Adam, and all human and finite spirits were created, wherefore He is the Spirit of all spirits.[79]

In this way, Imad ud-Din used the avenue of pneumatology to open the door to the idea of there being distinctions within the Godhead, thereby allowing the possibility of Trinitarian monotheism. This approach has much to commend it, and although formulated in response to Ahmadiyya claims, potentially has at least a degree of relevance to some Sunni Muslims. However, it must be questioned whether the particular view of pneumatology it is based on is really widespread among ordinary Muslims.

William St Clair Tisdall

William St Clair Tisdall (1859-1928) joined the CMS in 1884 initially being sent to work with T.V. French in Lahore and then at Bombay, before moving to Persia and eventually lecturing at the CMS training college in Islington, London.[80] His most important contribution to the development of christology in the Islamic world was his revisions of Pfander's works the *Mizan al-Haqq* (1910)[81] and *the Miftah al-Asrar* (1912).[82] Indeed, it is largely through Tisdall's revisions that Pfander's writings became available during the twentieth century.[83] However his own original *A Manual of the Leading Mohammadanian Objections to Christianity* (1904)[84] also deals at some length with christology.

Tisdall's conception of monotheism is central to his christology. He speaks of the *shema* as the foundation stone of all true religion,[85] and is emphatic that there is an absolute boundary between God and all else, arguing that this is one of eight key Christian doctrines that all orthodox Muslims accept.[86] He therefore, unequivocally speaks of God in bounded terms. However, he is equally insistent that for this doctrine to be of any value to man, it is necessary for God to reveal himself.[87] He argues that God the creator has therefore entered into a relation with his creatures, which does not breach the creator/creature divide. God did so by creating the universe, sending inspired men and ultimately in the incarnation. Tisdall argues that just as the God-man relationship inherent in creation and prophetic commissioning did not lead to any change in or loss of God's nature, neither did the incarnation do so, or in any way alter God's nature by compounding it with human nature.[88]

Tisdall regarded it as noteworthy that the doctrine of the trinity and the deity of Jesus originated in Palestine and among Jews, 'who were then as ardent asserters of the Unity of God as Muhammadans now are.'[89] He advocated following the example of the apostles by first teaching the unity of God, then letting the doctrine of the trinity evolve itself in the minds of converts.[90] However, he did not make any real attempt to demonstrate what aspects of the early church's preaching to monotheistic Jews might be applied in an Islamic context.[91]

He did however use this bounded conception of monotheism to demonstrate the necessity for Jesus' divinity. Like Pfander, he argued that God's law teaches that man owes him a duty of perfect devotion and man's failure to attain this results in him being in debt to God. However, as every creature owes a duty of absolute obedience to its creator, no creature can have any surplus merit, to pay the debt of another creature. Therefore only God can be the saviour, for only he can pay another's debt. This is one of the strongest points of Tisdall's christology, as he has used the common ground of the creator/creature distinction to introduce the concept of God the saviour, which is largely absent in the Islamic concept.[92]

Tisdall frequently quotes from the creeds, and appears to regard them as transcultural definitions of theology. He did recognise that the concept of 'personhood' in formulations of the trinity lent itself to being misunderstood by Muslims as implying Christian belief in three gods. However, his solution was simply to use technical language to express this, even though such language was not easily understood by most Muslims. He replies to a hypothetical Muslim objector:

> Your difficulty probably arises from your not understanding the technical sense of the word "Person." [In Arabic, Urdu, and Persian we use the Syriac word (Aqnum), Ar. pl. Aqanim to express "Person" or "Hypostasis" in its theological sense in reference to the Godhead, explaining it by the Persian word (hasti) existence.][93]

However, even if the Muslim has grasped the meaning of the Syriac vocabulary, the use of the Persian *hasti* still lends itself to being understood as three separate gods.[94] The basic problem is in fact not one of vocabulary but of conceptuality.

Tisdall's discussion of the relationships within the trinity is heavily determined by Patristic and later western theology. His assumption that Biblical and western theology were entirely identical is well illustrated by his claim that Christians have always believed that:

> The Bible teaches that the Father is the Fountain of Deity [πηγή θεότητος] and in this sense is greater than the Son [n.2 Jn 14:28], though in nature (*zat*) they are One [n.3 Jn 10:30].[95]

Tisdall's Greek citation here is not from the NT at all, but is almost certainly patristic. Not only does the NT never use the fountain (πηγή) motif to describe the intrinsic relationships within the trinity, its only application of this motif to God is to describe the Spirit's extrinsic relationship to God's people as the source of the salvific water of life.[96]

However, a more promising aspect of Tisdall's christology is his view of theophany. He claims that any visible appearance of God must be Christ, because the Father himself is invisible.[97] As such, Tisdall interprets the OT appearances of 'the angel of the Lord' and the shekinah in the cloud accompanying the exodus, as pre-incarnate appearances of Christ.[98] Although he regarded Pfander's identification of personified divine wisdom with Christ as somewhat forced exegesis that was inappropriate in Islamic contexts,[99] he regarded all revelation between God and man as taking place through the agency of Christ, stating:

> Whenever, therefore, it is stated in the Old Testament that God revealed Himself to Adam, the father of mankind, to Noah, Abraham, Isaac, Jacob, to Moses and other prophets, and spoke to them, it is evident that the Divine Speaker was the eternal *(azle)* Word of God *(Kalima'llah)*...For only through Him who is the one true Manifestation *(mazhar)* of God has God Most High ever spoken unto men.[100]

Although this appears to ignore the role of the Spirit, this Logos christology is one of the strongest points of Tisdall's christology. It is therefore all the more surprising that he makes so little of it. It is only explicitly articulated in one short section of his revision of Pfander's fairly lengthy treatise on the trinity and not at all in his even lengthier revision of the *Mizan al-Haqq*.[101]

W.A. Rice

W.A. Rice was a CMS contemporary of St Clair Tisdall's, working initially in the Punjab, Sindh and Peshawar from 1888, before transferring to Persia in 1894 where he worked until 1910. In the introduction to his handbook for missionaries working among Muslims, he suggested that much theology was too moulded to a western audience to be readily grasped by Muslims. He therefore states his own motive for writing as an attempt to address 'the apparent want of definite, constructive views of Christian truth stated in the manner best calculated to recommend them to Oriental minds.'[102]

Rice viewed the problem of explaining the nature of the trinity in the light of *tawhid* as the most difficult of all problems faced by the Christian in Islamic contexts.[103] Like French, he felt that the trinity was an advanced topic, which needed to be explained after an initial foundation had been laid in terms of teaching on the character and work of the individual persons of the trinity.[104]

Rice almost appears to be a man ahead of his time, in his recognition that the creeds of the church were merely 'symbols' used to express this sacred mystery and that a Christian might possess saving faith in the triune God without knowledge of these dogmatic forms, although adding that no true believer would reject them either.[105] However, despite this promising start, he makes only a limited attempt to reformulate Biblical theology using symbols current in the Islamic world.

Interestingly, Rice saw nothing in the Qur'anic and *Ahadith* accounts of Jesus that could be usefully used in presenting Biblical Christianity. He claimed that 'there is no one cardinal fact concerning the Life, Person and Work of the Lord Jesus Christ, which is not either denied, perverted, misrepresented or at least ignored in Muhammadan theology.'[106] He observed that even the Qur'anic titles of Jesus that correspond to NT christological titles, such as 'the Word from Him' and 'a Spirit from Him', whilst being echoes of Gospel truth, have their Christian sense categorically denied in the *Qur'an*.[107]

The christology Rice advocated for Islamic contexts is quite emphatically a christology from above. He states:

> We do *not* affirm that there are more gods than one. We do *not* say that man is God, but that the Deity clothed Himself with a human body and nature.[108]

However, his actual description of christology is set in intrinsic terms, emphasising the internal *nature* of God:

By calling Jesus God, we do not mean to say that there was any division, or separation *(infisal)* between *the divine Nature (zat) of Jesus and that of God,* from which the existence of a plurality *(ta'addud)* of gods would necessarily follow: but that Jesus' divine Nature shone forth *(jilweh kard)* from this robe of humanity. There is no division of *substance* implied here, so that *the essence (zat) of God the Father should be separate from that of the Son.* On one side Jesus was connected with the world of Divinity, and on the other with the world of humanity.[109]

This intrinsic description of the relationship between Jesus and the Father closely reflects patristic formulations such as the Athanasian Creed. Rice argued that the latter was of 'special value' for Islamic contexts,[110] even though he recognised that Muslims found it immensely difficult to reconcile belief in one God with belief in three divine persons. However, like Tisdall, his solution was an attempted explanation of what divine personhood meant, rather than searching for alternative ways of expressing theology that might be less liable to such misunderstanding.[111]

Samuel Zwemer

Samuel Zwemer (1867-1952) worked in Arabia and Egypt for 38 years. As well as founding the American Arabian Mission, he also organised the Cairo (1905) and Lucknow (1911) conferences on Mission in the Muslim world, wrote 29 books, co-authoring a further 9, founded, and for 37 years edited, *The Moslem World.*[112]

His approach to presenting christology in Islamic contexts is somewhat different from earlier writers such as Pfander and Tisdall. However, his advocacy of their works[113] and public acknowledgement of his use of them in preparing his own books,[114] suggests that he saw a degree of complementarity between his approach and theirs.[115]

Zwemer, who saw appropriate contextualisation as essential to Christian ministry in Islamic contexts, looked for features common to Islam and Christianity that were more fully expressed in Christianity, a position advocated in the report of the 1910 Edinburgh World Missionary conference.[116] He saw the foremost of these as the accolades given to Christ in Islam, stating:

Of all the common features on which we can seize as a point of vital contact with Moslems there is none superior to *the fact of Christ*...His coming, His supernatural birth, His high office as the Bringer of a special revelation from God, His sinlessness, His compassion, and His power to work miracles. His very names afford so many points of departure to lead from the Koran and tradition to the Gospels.[117]

The latter sentence makes clear that although Zwemer viewed Islamic depictions of Christ much more positively than Rice did, he still only saw it as essentially a jumping-off point. He realised that 'all this does not distinguish His person in any way as to its nature from other prophets who came before Him.'[118] However, this approach to contextualisation creates a christology from below; i.e. it starts from the earthly identity of Jesus and tries to explain how he is God.[119] Whilst any crossing of the creator/creature divide will inevitably be problematic for Muslims, a christology from below is almost certainly the path of most resistance. As such Zwemer has laid his christology open to the common Muslim accusation that Christians try to make a man (Jesus) into God.[120] Zwemer's approach of looking for common themes that were more fully expressed in Christianity did however yield slightly better results when applied to the atonement. His most outstanding contribution in this area was his observation that the words ascribed to Jesus in Q19:33, 'Peace is on me the day I was born, the day that I die, and the day I shall be raised up', reflect the three most important Christian festivals i.e. Christmas, Good Friday and Easter Sunday.[121]

However, despite these positive aspects of Zwemer's christology, he failed to recognise the need to contextualise the actual concepts that christology is expressed in. He concludes his discussion of how christology might best be presented in an Islamic context, with a recitation of the Nicene Creed, which he introduces by affirming the words of D.B. MacDonald that:

> The presentation that still expresses most adequately the mystery behind our lives is that in the Christian Trinity, *and words that come the nearest are those of the Nicene Creed.*[122]

W.H.T. (Temple) Gairdner

Temple Gairdner (1873-1928) worked with the CMS in Cairo from 1899 to 1928. He interacted with a range of prominent missionaries including St Clair Tisdall and Zwemer, partly as a result of attending missionary summits such as Edinburgh 1910 for which he wrote the official report, but also in the context of the Cairo Study Centre for Missionaries to Muslims, which he founded with Zwemer in 1912. He produced a significant number of publications about Islam, most notably *The Reproach of Islam*,[123] as well as apologetic works for Muslims. [124]

Gairdner clearly believed in contextualisation. He analysed Egyptian music in order to produce hymns with indigenous tunes.[125] He wrote plays on Biblical themes that communicated the Gospel in a largely oral culture,[126] and produced Arabic biblical commentaries in the style of the classical Islamic *tafsir* of al-Baidawi (d. c.1286). He also saw the need for theology to be explained in different ways according to the context being addressed, although it is less clear whether he thought theological concepts themselves needed to be contextualised. His most significant move in this direction appears to have been two passing references in the Arabic evangelistic magazine *Orient and Occident* to Christ as 'the *Wakeel* of unseen Deity', and 'the *Wakeel* of God on earth'.[127] He suggested that 'al-Wakeel' might function as an equivalent to 'Son of God', which Jews understood to be designating Jesus as the Messiah-King. However, Gairdner only uses 'Wakeel' to explain 'Son of God', and makes it clear that he does not intend it to identify Jesus as God,[128] despite *al-Wakeel* being an Islamic name of God. Moreover, the complete absence of this idea from his paper prepared for the Jerusalem conference of the International Missionary Council (IMC), summarising his lifetime's reflection on the presentation of the Gospel to Muslims,[129] suggests that he himself did not see it as a particularly significant part of his christology.[130]

Gairdner did however respond to the call of the 1910 Edinburgh conference for a treatment of the Christian conception of God in a manner more acceptable to Muslims, producing a paper on how the trinity might be explained to Muslims. Although this is set in a narrative framework, it is heavily philosophical and essentially makes a bridge between Islamic *kalam* and early twentieth century western philosophy, such as the concept that higher order beings are more complex than lower ones.[131]

This paper does however, reveal what he considered to be the limits to theological contextualisation. In it he admitted that terms such as 'Son of God' were only used at first to 'shadow forth the ineffable substance of eternal truth',[132] and recognised that in an Islamic context they may do 'the exact reverse of this'.[133] Nevertheless, although he acknowledged that such terms should be avoided in initial communication of the Gospel, he refused to look for alternative expressions that might express meaning more clearly to Muslims, stating:

> We have no right to play fast and loose with expressions that GOD sanctioned with such tremendous emphasis; because their continued existence in Holy Writ and use by His church are like the preservation and employment of a standard which we cannot afford to lose.[134]

The weakness of Gairdner's approach here is his apparent failure to distinguish between Scripture and the theology of the church. He is almost certainly right in thinking that expressions such as 'Son of God' must be retained in Scripture translation; however their use by the later church to express theology is another issue. Gairdner in fact largely sticks with patristic terminology, that as we have seen, was itself a recontextualisation of biblical descriptions. Therefore, his articulation of the trinity largely falls back on a long explanation of the members of the trinity sharing one indivisible 'essence', yet being distinct as 'persons'.[135]

Like Zwemer, he spoke of Christ fulfilling the highest aspirations of Muslims and all that Islam claimed for Muhammad,[136] and of vital elements of Christian theology being preserved in Islam 'although dimly perceived and neglected or distorted'.[137] Gairdner identified three particular bridges to the communication of Christian theology to Muslims:

Firstly, like Imad-ud-Din, he observed that the Qur'anic designation 'The Spirit of Allah' had led a few Muslim scholars even to admit that the Holy Spirit was uncreated.[138] Gairdner spoke of using the Bible 'to clarify and vitalise the Islamic teaching about the Spirit'.[139]

Secondly, 'the Muslim version of the Logos doctrine'.[140] By this he meant the problems Islamic theologians have wrestled with concerning the eternal divine attribute of God's Word, and the temporal book with a divine message which it became. He argued that the existence of this theological conundrum, enabled the Christian doctrine of the Logos to be presented to Muslims.[141]

However, in both of these cases Gairdner seems to be in danger of contextualising to the beliefs of a tiny minority, rather than to the beliefs of the ordinary Muslim. In discussing the Logos doctrine however, he touched on a potential point of contact with a wider range of Muslims, when he observed that Islamic ideas of a special real presence of God locally in the burning bush, and the lowest heaven, could be used to introduce the idea of the real presence of Christ.[142]

Thirdly, although Gairdner saw much of the Islamic portrait of Jesus as 'distorted and worse than useless',[143] he saw two aspects that were potential bridges for the communication of christology. These were Christ's sinlessness and the description of him as 'living' in high heaven, where he is an intercessor *(wagih)* for men.[144] However, neither gives Jesus any higher status than various *Ahadith* claim for Muhammad.

Elsewhere though, he emphasises a christology from above, his book *God as Triune, Creator, Incarnate, Atoner* expressing this as a Logos christology:

> The Father designs each act and wills it and shares in the spiritual emotion consequent on it – in a word, does it, while the actual execution is the Word's. There is no contradiction in terms here; the brain does an act, which a member executes for example.[145]

He then used this as a basis for explaining the incarnation:

> This incarnation was willed and planned by the Father, and carried out by the inspiration of the Spirit. We can, therefore, say that God was incarnate, without saying that the Father was, or that the Spirit was, in the same sense as the Son...the Godhead was not limited by the Man Jesus...the fullness of the Godhead was in Christ, yet was not bounded by the Man Jesus.[146]

This is one of the most significant points of Gairdner's christology. Here he has moved towards an extrinsic description of the relationships within the trinity that both stresses their unity of purpose, yet also differentiates them by the roles played in fulfilling that purpose.[147] By doing so he has avoided the concept of three divine persons, derived from intrinsic descriptions of the trinity, which has proved so problematic in Islamic contexts. However, despite the usefulness of this approach, Gairdner did not theologically develop this any further, but left it in this latent form.

L. Bevan Jones

Bevan Jones (1880-1960), the son of a Baptist missionary in India, was born in Agra, the scene of Pfander's and French's earlier labours. After training in England with the Baptist Missionary Society (BMS), he was sent back to Agra in 1907, before transferring to Dhakka in East Bengal[148] in 1909. After attending the 1911 Lucknow conference for missionaries to Muslims, he began to specialise in Muslim evangelism, being officially designated for this work by the BMS in 1914. In 1917 he spent 6 months learning Arabic at the Cairo study centre run by W.H.T. Gairdner, and in 1924 attended the Jerusalem conference of missionaries to Muslims. He was therefore exposed to a range of influences from other leading missionaries to Muslims. Jones taught at Serampore College, Bishop's College, Calcutta, and then as principal of the ecumenical school of Islamic studies in Lahore, which he renamed the Henry Martyn School. On his retirement to England he became chairman of the Fellowship of Faith for Muslims (FFM), which Zwemer had earlier founded.[149] He wrote a number of books, of which *The People of the Mosque*

(1932)[150] and *Christianity Explained to Muslims* (1938)[151] originally contained sections dealing with christology. The latter work was intended to replace Tisdall's *Christian Reply,* and Rice's *Crusaders of the Twentieth Century,* the former of which Jones regarded as no longer appropriate.[152] The question of Jones' orthodoxy has been raised as a result of his writing sometimes entertaining doubts raised by the liberal theology[153] of his day. However, a careful reading of his works suggests that he himself almost certainly held to an orthodox view of the main christological beliefs, although he at times doubted the historicity of the Biblical text they were based on.[154] Moreover, as we shall subsequently demonstrate, contemporary liberal theology does appear to have influenced the way that he suggested christology should be presented to Muslims.

Jones claimed that the longstanding Muslim prejudice against Christianity was directed against certain doctrines, rather than the Christian message itself. He therefore urged in *The People of the Mosque* that:

> We ought to re-think and, if need be, restate our Christian beliefs so as to remove from their minds any possible cause of misunderstanding or offence.[155]

Despite this, Jones himself never attempted to restate christology in a manner that might be less offensive to Muslims, and in his later work *Christianity Explained to Muslims* modified these comments by adding:

> But having done this we must be prepared to find that with many a Muslim the chief stumbling-block is the familiar one of the offence of Christ Himself, i.e. the offence of the Cross. That is something which only the grace of God can remove.[156]

In fact, Jones appears to have regarded any attempt to explain christology to Muslims as almost pointless. He argued on the basis of 1 Cor.12:3 that Muslims cannot appreciate Christ's divinity until they experience moral regeneration. Consequently, the title 'Son of God' should not needlessly be applied to Christ 'as though it were the foundation, rather than the fruit, of faith in Christ.'[157] Jones advocated starting with aspects of truth that are in Islam as well as Christianity, and from this leading on to a statement of the fuller truth found in Christ.[158] However, for Jones this common ground was pre-eminently the person of Christ during his earthly life. Moreover, Jones went further than this and claimed that the early church came to recognise who Jesus was, because

> Not (sic) his teaching particularly, but His character, His personal dealings with them, proclaimed Him to be related to God.[159]

Jones' christology – insofar as he advocated one – was therefore very much a christology from below, that stressed the ethical quality of Jesus' character. This emphasis, which has had a significant impact on subsequent Christian engagement in Islamic contexts, appears to derive from two particular influences.

Firstly, Jones responded to the intense antagonism to Christianity and in particular the person of Christ that he saw among Indian Muslims. He very precisely dated the origins of this 'new polemic' to the founding of the Ahmadiyya movement in 1875, which he claimed immediately led to a significant escalation of Muslim attempts to discredit Christ by means of European works of higher criticism.[160] He claimed that this movement

> was part of the reaction in the body of Indian Islam to the upheaval of thought and feeling caused by the exposure of Islam and Muhammad in the public debates initiated by Dr Pfander.[161]

Jones' scholarship is somewhat questionable here, not merely because of the twenty two year gap between Pfander's 1853 Agra debate and the very precise date given by Jones for the emergence of this new polemic. In reality, the emergence of Muslim anti-Christian polemic in India predated Pfander, and indeed, almost all missionary work in India, by a considerable period. Pfander in fact, only participated in one public debate, which was initiated not by him, but by the Muslim side. The chief Muslim protagonist in this debate, Rahmat Allah Kairanawi, had already written three books against Christianity, and in a fourth, finalised immediately after the debate, acknowledged his dependence on a stream of anti-Christian polemic written in India over the previous half century. Moreover, there is no evidence that even in agreeing the subjects for the Agra debate, Pfander ever did more than follow the example of Henry Martyn in making an apologetic critique of the main proofs that the *ulema* had historically advanced in support of Muhammad and the *Qur'an*.[162] There is little, if any evidence that Pfander himself initiated polemical debate.[163] It is clear that the use of European works of historical criticism by the Muslim 'new polemic' does lie in the Agra debate. There the Muslim side attacked biblical christology using D.F. Strauss' *The Life of Jesus,* the very first work of European historical criticism, which had recently been translated into English.[164] Pfander was wholly unprepared for an attack in these terms and the jubilant Muslim claims of victory that ensued suggest that the *ulema* involved viewed themselves as having finally found a weapon that could mount a successful ambush, and that gave them at least the semblance of a public victory in their longstanding polemic against Christianity. However, it was not until nearly fifty years later, which, according to the date given by Jones, was a full twenty five years after the 'new polemic' against Christianity started, that missionaries even began to write critiques of Muhammad and the *Qur'an* using similar historical-critical methods.[165]

However, although Jones' analysis was in many respects inaccurate, this reaction against Pfander's approach led him to adopt a somewhat different emphasis. Jones stressed Christian piety and the character of Christ[166] to the extent that he even appears to have rejected the appropriateness of the apologetic christologies that earlier writers such as Pfander and Tisdall had developed.[167]

The second major influence on Jones' christology appears to have been western theologians such as C. Gore (1853-1932), P.T. Forsyth (1848-1921), and H.R. Mackintosh (1870-1936),[168] who followed the lead of the prominent nineteenth century liberal Albrecht Ritschl (1822-89)[169] in trying to build a christology based on the ethical character of the human Jesus. Gore had attempted to reconcile contemporary critical scholarship with the Gospel portrait of Jesus, by claiming that Jesus' full humanity involved a voluntary self-emptying (kenosis) of divine knowledge, and a resultant human ignorance. Jones reflects this when he affirms Forsyth's term 'a Godhead self-reduced' and claims that God 'could not put more into humanity than humanity will hold'.[170] The limitation this entailed meant that Jesus is known to be God by the ethical quality of his life, rather than by divine functions and attributes, which Jones regarded as largely absent from him.[171]

The influence of these nineteenth and early twentieth century 'ethical' christologies is apparent in Jones' explanation of Jesus' divine sonship in the face of Muslim misunderstandings of this title. He argues that because God is supremely *Holy Love*:

> The highest category which we can apply to the Divine "essence" is ethical. Beholding as we do the love and trust and obedience which mark the life of the Son, we infer that Holy Will and Loving Purpose are of the very essence of God Himself. *Beyond this it is profitless to discuss whether Jesus shared the "substance" of God. Here is all that ultimately matters – the will of Jesus, as "Son", was one with the Will of God;* not partially, nor intermittently, nor yet in a metaphor, but identically one.[172]

It is hard to see how Jones' affirmation that Jesus perfectly fulfilled the will of God points to Jesus' divinity. In itself it does not place Jesus in any higher category than pre-fall Adam, whom the *Qur'an* explicitly compares Christ to, or for that matter angelic beings who serve God. Jones' christology here appears to closely parallel that of Ritschl, who rejected traditional views of the knowledge of God, but claimed that God was known through the Gospel witness to Jesus as the one who uniquely fulfilled God's will for the world.[173] However, Ritschl's concept of Jesus' divine sonship was somewhat different from the one that Jones' was trying to present to Muslims, for as A.N.S. Lane observes:

> Ritschl can speak of Jesus' deity, but by this he means his perfect humanity. He was God in the sense that he had a perfect knowledge of God and was united to him in moral obedience.[174]

It is however unclear whether Jones fully appreciated that such were the implications of this christology, or whether he simply repeated it without adequate understanding.

Jens Christensen

Bishop Jens Christensen was a Danish Lutheran missionary who worked in the North West Frontier Province of Pakistan for more than forty years, latterly as Bishop of Peshawar. During this time he was involved in producing a revised Pushtu translation of the NT. His major missiological work *The Practical Approach to Muslims*[175] was the result of lectures initially given to the West Pakistan Christian Council between 1949 and 1960. The work's subsequent publication by the North Africa Mission[176] made it available across the wider context of the Muslim world.[177]

Despite its title, Christensen's book is quite a complex piece of theology. This is well illustrated by his attitude to contextualisation, which he terms 'adaptation'.[178] Although Christensen holds this up as an ideal, he appears to reject it as a practical possibility.[179] Instead he falls back on the patristic creeds, particularly the Nicene and Athanasian Creeds, which he equates directly with the teaching of the NT claiming that they are 'confessions of the faith once for all delivered to the saints in the Bible'.[180] Although he admits that elements of the language in these creeds address issues specific to their cultural context,[181] he nonetheless regards them as confessions of the church 'universal'.[182]

Despite this he admits that the creedal term 'substance' is a 'poor word' as it implies something physical, and that 'personhood' is 'utterly inadequate' to express christology. He notes that although personhood was used by the creedal authors to express the oneness of God,[183] the modern change in meaning of this word to 'individuality' actually implies the exact opposite, and so renders description of the trinity in terms of personhood liable to misunderstanding as tri-theism. However, despite this Christensen argues that the creeds should not, and indeed cannot, be either improved or modernised.[184]

Significantly, Christensen's writing has noteworthy parallels with the neo-orthodox theology of Karl Barth.[185] Like Barth, Christensen rejects all forms of natural theology. He therefore explicitly rejects both Gairdner's philosophical approach and the use of Qur'anic titles of Jesus that Zwemer had advocated because these would appear to imply that there was a source of revelation outside the Bible.[186] Like Barth's, his christology focuses on the once for all event of Christ as the sole locus of God's self-revelation.[187] He argues that only God can reveal God, stating that 'no created thing could be the Revelation of God. The very fact of its creatureliness would make that utterly impossible'.[188] This argument is based on the presupposition that God is wholly other, and by implication unapproachable. It is only as he is revealed in the Logos that he can be known, and this Logos has to be God in order to reveal God.[189] As a christology for an Islamic context, this argument has the merit of being a christology from above that emphasises the absolute boundary between God and all else. However, its weakness is that it so emphasises God's self revelation in Christ that it ignores other forms of divine self revelation in the OT, such as the Holy Spirit coming upon the prophets and OT theophany and epiphany narratives.[190] In fact, Christensen goes so far as to suggest that the idea of God taking actual, visible form was a novel idea to Jews at the time of Jesus.[191]

Christensen occasionally speaks of God in extrinsic terms, describing him as Creator-Redeemer-Judge.[192] However, as Christensen emphasises the patristic creeds as the foundation for theology in the Muslim world, the christology he advocates tends to emphasise intrinsic descriptions of the relationship between God and Jesus, such as personhood and substance, that he himself admitted were liable to be seriously misunderstood in an Islamic context. Christensen's emphasis on the Nicene and Apostles' creeds does at least have the merit of presenting a christology from above. However, he makes the extraordinary claim that because the creeds were developed for Christians rather than non-Christians, when Christ is presented to Muslims, it must be in the form of a christology from below. He argues that Muslims 'MUST see Him in all His pure humanity', until the idea slowly grows that there is something more than humanity there.[193]

Kenneth Cragg

Kenneth Cragg (1913-) has been one of the most influential writers in the field of Christian engagement with Islam in the second half of the twentieth century. Cragg was born into a devout evangelical home, and after training for the Anglican ministry, went to Lebanon as a missionary with the British Syria Mission in 1939. He returned to England in 1947 to research a doctorate on the relevance of Christian theology and mission to developments in the Muslim world.[194] Thereafter he held a series of academic posts in theological colleges and universities in America, England and Nigeria, which were interspersed with returns to the Middle East in 1956-59 as canon of St George's cathedral in Jerusalem, and 1970-73 as assistant Bishop of Jerusalem based in Cairo. He has co-edited the *Muslim World* and written more than thirty books.[195]

Cragg's work is highly eclectic and draws on a wide range of theological traditions. Although, according to his biographer Chris Lamb, Cragg abandoned conservative evangelicalism prior to going to Lebanon, he has retained an evangelical commitment to evangelism throughout his life, insisting even in his later writing that 'the Christian gospel is conversionist through and through'.[196] However, in practice dialogue appears to have assumed a more prominent place during the latter part of his life.[197]

Most of Cragg's writings are essentially attempts to explain Islam to Christians and Christianity to Muslims. In undertaking the latter, he has primarily focused on describing Jesus as contemporary NT scholarship then saw him, and the meaning of NT terms, rather than specifically seeking to contextualise christology for Muslims. He has also called for 'genuine theological and spiritual "embassy"', representing Christ in a way that is subject to 'local presentation'.[198] Cragg's specific contribution was to suggest the term 'filiality' as a substitute for divine sonship, although he leaves this idea largely undeveloped.[199]

However a number of general criticisms may be levelled at the validity of Cragg's approach to explaining Christianity to Muslims. He has been criticised for failing to make clear what particular form of Christianity he is presenting to Muslims, and how distinctive that version is to himself.[200] Cragg's own form of Christianity appears to be a mixture of traditional orthodoxy infused with liberal elements. In his doctoral thesis, Cragg spoke of the need for Christian engagement with Islam in 'the spirit and form of Christian "liberalism"',[201] and commended the approach of Bishop Gore, whose kenotic theory gave legitimacy to contemporary critical scholarship remoulding the Gospel portrait of Jesus, as one whose sayings were sometimes spoken in ignorance and error.[202] Cragg endorsed this position even though it was clearly difficult for him to argue for its potential missiological significance, when it appeared to validate a number of Muslim arguments against Christianity.[203]

Cragg's presentation of christology to Muslims, therefore, starts not so much from the final form of the Biblical text itself, as from the conclusions of contemporary critical scholarship concerning its historical reliability.[204] The distinction is of some significance for contextualisation, as the former is a fixed point from which the bridge of ChristianMuslim encounter can start, while the latter is at least to some degree always in a state of flux. The impact of this can be seen in Cragg's christology. In his 1986 *Jesus and the Muslim* Cragg focused on portraying Jesus primarily in terms of his perfect filial obedience to his father *Abba*.[205] This emphasis appears to be largely determined by the christological debate in NT Studies during the 1970s, where the dominance of theories of evolutionary christology[206] meant that the Aramaic *Abba* was one of the few sayings of Jesus that NT scholars felt confident in ascribing back to the earliest Palestinian church.[207] However, this inevitably created a christology that was much more narrowly constrained than that of the NT canon. It is this that makes Cragg's use of it to address the Islamic context highly questionable. The weakness of Cragg's approach is highlighted by the subsequent disavowal of evolutionary christology by many biblical scholars, coupled with a greater confidence in the historicity of other NT christological texts resulting in a focus on other christological themes. In short, Cragg appears to have failed to make the crucial missiological distinction between the task of establishing the historical authenticity of the Biblical text, and the task of making the theology contained in what the church holds to be a sacred text understandable to adherents of another faith.[208]

Cragg does however view christology as the most fundamental distinction between Islamic and Christian descriptions of God. He argues that

> Whereas, in Christian thought, theology and Christology are mutually necessary and mutually definitive, in Islam theology is largely defined by the exclusion of Christology. The person of Jesus is where the contrast proceeds.[209]

He urges that christology must be from above as:

> We only properly broach the questions that belong with Jesus from the perspectives that belong with God.[210]

Cragg's approach to explaining christology to Muslims therefore starts from the doctrine of God.[211] He sees an extrinsic understanding of God, in which God is known by how he relates to the human situation, as a common theme of Judaism, Christianity and Islam. Developing this extrinsic view of God is central to his christology, and at least in some measure fulfils the call he has made elsewhere for the church urgently to

> break free of "substance" metaphors that set Christology/theology in the realm of abstract metaphysics, and bring it firmly into the concrete "operation" of divine energy to save.[212]

Cragg argues that the doctrine of creation shared by Islam and Christianity suggests that God has initiated a relationship with humanity that opens God to a kind of vulnerability to his creatures. He contends that God's relation to man implies a degree of *kenosis*, in that God limits himself by letting man choose to fulfil his obligation to be *muslim* to God. When man rejects this, God's response ultimately culminates in Jesus.[213] Cragg then argues that 'what happened in Jesus takes God to explain - indeed takes God to achieve.'[214] Cragg's argument here is similar to Tisdall's, who argued that as every creature owed a duty of perfect obedience to God, no mere creature could have any surplus merit to pay another's debt.[215] However, Cragg leaves out this stage from his argument and simply argues that Christian theology lifts Christ's perfect obedience of his messianic vocation into creedal formulations of divine ontology.[216] One cannot help feeling that at this point Cragg is simply assuming too many conceptual leaps on the part of his readers. It must also be questioned whether Cragg has really broken free of substance metaphors, as his christology appears to culminate in creedal formulations. Moreover, although Cragg argues that Jesus' apostles declared him to be divine, because his significance 'demanded to be fitted into the unity of God in Whom they unswervingly believed,'[217] Cragg simply fails to explain the vital question of *how* it was so incorporated.

Phil Parshall

Phil Parshall (19??-)has been one of the most significant missiologists to write about Christian engagement with Islam in the second half of the twentieth century. Since 1962 he has been a missionary with International Christian Fellowship (now merged with SIM International) and has lived and worked in Bangladesh and more recently in the Philippines, where he is presently director of SIM's East Asia research centre in Manila.

He obtained a D.Miss from Fuller Theological Seminary, and has held fellowships at both Harvard and Yale universities, as well as writing six books including *New Paths in Muslim Evangelism: Evangelical Approaches to Contextualization.* The latter became paradigmatic as an approach to Christian mission to Muslims that asked 'how much of a Muslim's cultural background can they biblically retain on becoming a Christian?'[218]

The focus of Parshall's writing on contextualisation has primarily been on the external barriers to communication such as dress, prayer forms, days of worship and so forth, rather than on contextualisation of theology.[219] Parshall does however move some way in the direction of theological contextualisation. He notes similarities between Islamic names of God and Biblical ones,[220] and looks for NT passages that could form bridges to key aspects of Islamic theology. For example he suggests that the 'confession' of 1 Tim. 3:16 is a Christian counterpart to the Islamic *shahada.*[221] Moreover, he goes further than this and affirms that:

> Contextualization must be carried out with emic methodology. Theological formulations should be made after coming to grips with emic concepts.[222]

Parshall sees the trinity as one aspect of Christian theology that needs to be addressed in this respect. He urges that:

> Our efforts should be directed toward exploring the potential to bridge differences between Islam and Christianity. Let us develop a meaningful theological statement on the Trinity that can clear away some of the fog in Muslim minds...and perhaps in Christian minds as well![223]

Parshall himself does not do this, although he affirmatively cites the work of two earlier missionary writers who moved to a very limited extent in this direction. Firstly, Calverley,[224] who proposed changing a number of creedal terms, in order to communicate the trinity more effectively to Muslims:

> Changes in terminology may be suggested in presenting the Trinity to the Muslim mind. Our conventional theological vocabulary uses the word Person for each of the Divine Beings. This is a word that has corporeal, physical, concrete, human connotations. Would not the abstract term "personality" preserve better the immaterial ideas associated with God?...A statement of Christian theology about God for Muslim thinkers could say: "God is the one and only Divine, eternal and infinite Spirit with Unity of Essence in a Trinity of Personalities..."[225]

However, this does not resolve the basic problem, which is that the present day denotative meaning of 'person' appears to emphasise the three-ness of God. This issue can only be tackled by finding an alternative to the *intrinsic* description of God's *essence* that the concept of three divine persons derives from.

Secondly, Parshall cites from James Barton, an early twentieth century mission writer.[226] Barton perceived the problematic nature of using western christological formulations in Islamic contexts, and observed that:

> If the Trinitarian conception of God is taught simply as a revealed metaphysics (sic), it may easily degenerate, as Mohammed thought that it had done, into tri-theism. If it does not do this, it may become to the mind a mere mathematical paradox...[227]

However, Barton's solution to this problem was a christology from below, that like many early twentieth century writers focused on the ethical Jesus:[228]

> Let the doctrine not be dissociated from the person of Jesus of Nazareth as he lived in Palestine. Let it always palpitate with the pulses of that love for men that spoke so eloquently in him. Let it not be regarded as the final expression of all that can be known of God, but as a symbol of elements in the constitution of the nature of God that are of vital importance to religion, to human experience, and to human hopes.'[229]

It is hard to see how portraying the earthly Jesus as the supreme expression of love towards fellow men, and symbol of divine religion, actually identifies him as God, still less deals with Muslim misconceptions of Christians as tri-theists.

Although Parshall's own christology, insofar as he articulates one, clearly does portray Jesus as fully divine, it is still a christology that starts from below. Even though he considers the small amount of Christian exposure in Islamic scriptures as infinitely more harmful than beneficial,[230] he nonetheless argues on the basis of Paul's Mars Hill sermon that it is biblically justified to use Qur'anic christology as a bridge in presenting Jesus to Muslims.[231] He sees the designation of Jesus as 'God's Word', as the most important Qur'anic title given to Jesus,[232] and argues that 'this designation can be a launching pad to show the Muslim that Jesus is God's eternal Word of redemption, rather than just another prophet.'[233] He also refers to other Qur'anic titles of Jesus, including 'Spirit', 'Prophet', 'Apostle', 'Pre-eminent One', 'Sign', 'Mercy' and 'Servant' as other ways that may help bridge the gap. However, the problem with all of these is not whether Paul's 'as even your own poets' address, provides Biblical justification for them, as it undoubtedly does, but whether this is really the path of least resistance in presenting divine christology to Muslims. In chapter 5 we will demonstrate that the *Qur'an* emphasises the existence of an emphatic boundary between God the creator and his creation.[234] It may therefore be somewhat harder to explain to Muslims how the Jesus they know of was actually God, than how the God they know of humbled himself to become man.

Michael Nazir Ali

Michael Nazir Ali (1949-) was born in Pakistan, but went to England to study at Oxford and Cambridge universities. He was ordained into the Anglican Church of Pakistan, eventually becoming Bishop of Raiwind. In 1986 he moved to England, where he became director of the Oxford Centre for Mission Studies, general secretary of the Church Mission Society and more recently Bishop of Rochester.

As a Christian from an Islamic country he has a distinctive perspective. He regards much of Islamic culture as a God-given inheritance of Eastern Christians, by virtue of the fact that many Islamic forms were originally derived from the historic Eastern churches.[235] However, this acceptance is not universal, as he regards other aspects of Islamic culture as coming under the judgement of the Gospel. He therefore speaks of Christians living in Islamic contexts having to work out 'how to accept Muhammad as the founder of their culture without necessarily accepting him as authoritative in matters of faith.'[236] He strongly urges that there are 'valid and necessary limits to inculturation', particularly the God given 'norm' of Scripture and apostolic tradition, the latter ensuring continuity of the local church with the church in history and throughout the contemporary world. However, he allows the creative and radical reinterpretation of both Scripture and apostolic tradition in the light of the church's context.[237]

He recognises that the creeds are formulations of scriptural faith, developed in a particular *sitz im leben* and therefore 'requiring reinterpretation and reformulation in our own context.'[238] In particular, he admits that the traditional expression of three persons sharing in the one substance of the Godhead, 'is not easily understood by the Muslim,'[239] and asks whether in Islamic contexts a more dynamic approach might be possible than traditional christologies, whether Chalcedonian or non-Chalcedonian.

Nazir Ali's own contribution to this is to suggest that the traditional christological language relating to the Son's generation from the Father could be re-expressed in terms of the Son's 'procession' from the Father. He observes that this is both the NT usage and that 'the Muslim would be less offended by the language of procession than by the language of generation which is completely alien to his whole tradition'.[240]

He also suggests two possible points of departure that might be used in explaining christology to Muslims: firstly, the titles 'Word' and 'Spirit', which unlike other Qur'anic christological titles are uniquely applied to Jesus, and secondly, the human demand to see God. He observes that if, according to the Qur'an, 'God can show himself to Moses in the burning bush, can he not show himself to us in the man Jesus?'[241] The latter point particularly has much to commend it, and is capable of being developed much further than this bare question.

Nazir Ali warns against two approaches to christology that he has observed Christians in Islamic contexts adopting.[242]

Firstly, a *modalist* christology in which Jesus becomes simply 'the particular manifestation *(Tajalli)* of God at that particular time'.[243]

Secondly, a radically Nestorian christology, whereby, in attempting to explain Christ to Muslims, some Christians claim that wherever in the *Qur'an* 'the divinity of Christ is denied, only the human Jesus is meant.'[244] He observes that one consequence of this is that:

> …much preaching on the passion of our Lord in Pakistan claims that only the human Jesus suffered on the cross and that the divinity abandoned him in order to preserve its impassibility…Christians thus tend to lose sight of the important truth that God has, in Christ, suffered for us, that he has given up his transcendence and omnipotence in order that he might identify himself with us in our weakness, poverty and death.[245]

Conclusions

In this chapter we have evaluated the various christologies that different scholars have advocated for Islamic contexts, in terms of the appropriateness of the conceptual categories they use. It is noteworthy that this survey had been dominated by the christologies of expatriate missionaries.[246] To a certain extent it is to be anticipated that missionary christologies would have had a generative impact on a church which at least initially emerged in response to western missionary endeavour. However, this under representation is itself suggestive of the dominant influence of western theology on the church in regions dominated by Islam, and points to the need for theological contextualisation.

Most scholars have recognised that in Islam an emphatic boundary is typically understood to exist between God and all else, with God being far above all of his creation. The implication of this is that for christology to be comprehensible in an Islamic context, the path of least resistance lies in a christology from above, that seeks to explain how God became man, rather than a christology from below that seeks to explain how the human Jesus is God. However, some scholars have paid insufficient attention to this and, influenced by apparent parallels between certain aspects of Qur'anic and NT christology, have advocated christologies from below. We have also shown that sometimes, as in the case of Bevan Jones, a further reason for the adoption of christologies from below appears to have been the influence of early twentieth century neo-orthodox western theologians, whose christology emphasised the human ethical Jesus at the expense of his divinity.

We have also seen the dominant influence of western theology in the conceptual categories used to describe the relationship between Jesus and the Father. This has been dominated by intrinsic descriptions of God, derived from the patristic creeds, even when some attempt has been made to describe God in other terms. This intrinsic focus on the internal nature of God has inevitably resulted in relationships within the Godhead being described in terms of personhood. Although, there has been widespread recognition that it is difficult for Muslims to comprehend this concept, without misunderstanding it as tritheism, there has until recently been a strong reluctance to move away from it. This has been due in part to an assumption that the creeds were a pure, culture-free Christian theology, rather than being contextualisations of christology addressing specific contexts.

A further factor with a number of writers, especially French, St Clair Tisdall and Gairdner, has been that their commitment to Anglican ecclesiology has made it difficult for them to envisage any alternative expression of christology than those found in patristic creedal formulae.

A number of more recent writers, Cragg, Parshall and Nazir Ali, have recognised the urgent need for a contextualisation of christology to be developed in terms that would be more readily understandable in the Islamic world. However, as yet the small steps that have been taken in this direction are at best embryonic, and have mainly focused on finding new terms in which to express creedal concepts, rather than finding alternatives to those concepts themselves.

It is this area that this present study specifically seeks to address.

Endnotes

[1] Hymn by Reginald Heber (1783-1826) Bishop of Calcutta, who ordained the first Indian clergy in the Anglican church. Source of hymn: *Hymns Ancient and Modern* [London:Clowes,1916].

[2] M. Nazir Ali *Islam: A Christian Perspective* [Exeter:Paternoster,1983] 145 has criticised western writers for unjustifiably understanding Christianity's encounter with other religions in terms of the modern West's encounter with these faiths, a criticism which is certainly valid in those areas of the Islamic world where ancient churches exist. However, it has already been well documented that where the ancient churches do exist in the Islamic world, they have clung tenaciously to the liturgical forms and creedal expressions such as the Nicene Creed that were in use prior to the advent of Islam with little attempt at any form of contextualisation (cf. D.P Teague (ed) *Turning Over a New Leaf: Protestant Missions and the Orthodox Churches of the Middle East* [London:Interserve/Lynnwood:Middle East Media,2nd edn 1992] passim cf. esp. the paper by J. Napper 'The Divine Liturgy: The Heart of Worship in the Orthodox Church' 46-54). This present chapter therefore seeks to explore the christologies that have been used in churches that owe their origins to the modern missionary movement, a subject which to date has not been subject to any significant scholarly investigation.

[3] cf. especially L.L. Vander Werff *Christian Mission to Muslims: The Record, Anglican and Reformed Approaches in India and the Near East 1800-1938* [Pasadena:William Carey,1977]; A.A. Powell *Muslims and Missionaries in Pre-Mutiny India* [Richmond:Curzon,1993]; E. Stock *The History of the Church Missionary Society vols 1-4* [London:CMS,1899-1916]; and K.S. Latourette *A History of the Expansion of Christianity* [3rd edn – reprinted Exeter:Paternoster,1971] – especially vols 6 (North Africa and Asia 1800-1914) and 7 (1914-).

[4] *Islam and Christian Theology: A Study in the Interpretation of the Theological Ideas in the Two Religions* [London:Lutterworth,1945-67] 1:1:viii. Sweetman's work is an important comparative study of Christian and Islamic theology. However, its concentration on the philosophical aspects of Islamic *kalam* and scholastic theology limits its relevance to the study we are seeking to undertake which has to engage with the Islamic beliefs that are most widely held in the Islamic context, rather than simply those of the educated *ulema*.

[5] R.M. Speight 'Some Bases for a Christian Apologetic to Islam' *IRM* 54:2 (1965) 193-205 is not untypical of later emphases. Speight urged that apologetics should be less focused on dogma, replacing this with an emphasis on thankfulness, interiority and Islamic culture. Speight did also advocate using biblical presentations of God's mighty acts of redemption; however, the limited emphasis he gave this resulted in Daud Rahbar ('Christian Apologetic to Muslims' *IRM* 54:3 (1965) 353-59) appearing to understand Speight's position ONLY in terms of thankfulness, interiority and culture (cf. 358).

[6] Report of the 1980 Pattaya Consultation *Christian Witness to Muslims* Lausanne Occasional Paper No.13, *www.gospelcom.net/lcwe/LOP/lop13.htm* reproduced here and in 'Introduction' by permission of LCWE.

[7] Vander Werff's historical survey occasionally and briefly touches on the various missionaries' theology since 1800. However, there has been no survey of the theology used in Islamic contexts, let alone more specifically of christology. C. Lamb *The Call to Retrieval: Kenneth Cragg's Christian Vocation to Islam.* [London:Grey Seal,1997] is the only scholarly analysis of any of these theologies and even this only briefly discusses Cragg's christology.

[8] cf. Jn 1:1-3; Rev.19:11-15.

[9] For a concise overview of the various forms of Platonism cf. D.F. Wright 'Platonism' *NDT* 517-19.

[10] Middle Platonism so heightened God's transcendence that he could only be described negatively (i.e. apophatic theology), while the later Neoplatonism of Plotinus spoke of God as the One who was beyond both description and being itself.

[11] cf. the discussion of Nicene theology in Bauckham *Crucified* 77-79.

[12] Although Greek philosophy did have a major impact on the development of Islamic *Kalam* (i.e. systematic theology), our concern is with how ordinary Muslims conceive of God. Significantly, Muslim writers speak of *Kalam* having become inaccessible to ordinary Muslims (cf. chapter 5 n.4). Western scholars have also seen the influence of Neo-Platonism on Islamic Sufism. However, as we will subsequently demonstrate, in the Islamic context Sufi descriptions of God normally only supplement more widely held bounded extrinsic descriptions of God (cf. discussion of 'Sufism' in chapter 5 section 'Conceptual framework of monotheism').

[13] cf. the comments of Sayyid Qutb to this effect cited in chapter 5 section 'Sole creator, ruler and judge'.

[14] *Modalism* understood the Father, the Son and the Holy Spirit as simply different modes of being temporarily adopted at various times by the one God.

[15] For Mawdudi's reaction in this respect cf chapter 5 section 'Titles and decriptions of Jesus'.

[16] For concise biographies cf. Vander Werff *Record 30-36*; C. Bennett 'Martyn, Henry' BDCM 438-9 and 'Henry Martyn 1781-1812 Scholarship in the Service of Mission' in ML 264-70. The standard biography is J. Sargent *The Life and Letters of Henry Martyn* [1819,1862 – reprinted Edinburgh:Banner of Truth,1985].

[17] Nearly a century later, G. Smith's biography was entitled *Henry Martyn, Saint and Scholar: First Modern Missionary to the Mohammedans,*1781-1812 [London:RTS,1892].

[18] Now part of Bangladesh.

[19] So, V. Stacey *Life of Henry Martyn* [Hyderabad:Henry Martyn Institute,1980] 1,70.

[20] Later baptised as Abdul Masih, for a concise biography of whom cf. D.A. Kerr 'Abdul Masih, Salih' BDCM 1.

[21] 1) Earlier prophecies of Muhammad's coming 2) Muhammad's miracles 3) The Spread of Islam 4) The Character of Muhammad 5) The inimitable language and style of the Qur'an. Answering the same five questions later formed the basis of the third section of Pfander's *Mizan al-Haqq* (cf. subsequent section 'Karl.G. Pfander' esp. n.40).

[22] cf. n.16.

[23] S. Lee *Controversial Tracts on Christianity and Mohammedanism by the Late Rev. Henry Martyn,* B.D. [Cambridge:no publisher cited in book,1824]. Lee who was professor of Arabic at Cambridge 1819-31, also became professor at the CMS training college from 1825 where he was involved in the training of new missionaries.

[24] i.e. a christology that starts from the identity of God, as opposed to a 'christology from below' that starts from the NT depiction of the earthly Jesus.

[25] cf. Martyn's journal Sept 29th 1811 cited in Sargent *Life* 332.

[26] Journal 23rd February 1812, 8th -12th June 1812 cited in Sargent *Life* 355,365.

[27] cf. Martyn's own comment on this cited in Sargent *Life* 329, 354.

[28] Journal June 12th 1812 cited in Sargent *Life* 368.

[29] cf. n.26 above.

[30] 'Translation of the Second Persian Tract of Mr Martyn In Reply to Mirza Ibrahim' 102-23 in Lee *Tracts* 117-18.

[31] 'Mr Martyn's Third Tract on the Vanity of the Sofee System, and on the Truth of the Religion of Moses and Jesus' in Lee Tracts 150.

[32] cf. e.g. its occurrence in W. St Clair Tisdall's revision of K.G. Pfander's *Miftah al-Asrar* [London: Christian Literature Society for India,1912] 93 and use by W.A. Rice in *Crusaders of the Twentieth Century* [Published by author – but supplied London:CMS,1910] 271.

[33] Also known as *C.G. Pfander*, the designation of his first name as 'Charles' on his memorial tablet in All Saints Church, Peshawar suggests that he may have anglicised his name to 'Charles' while working with the British CMS.

[34] The scholarly literature on the 'Great Experiment' is limited. Discussion in relation to specific regions occurs in R. Blincoe *Ethnic Realities and the Church: Lessons from Kurdistan* [Pasadena: Presbyterian Centre for Mission Studies,1998]:passim; Latourette *Expansion* 6:113-14; W. Shenk 'Claudius Buchanan 1766-1815 - Laying the Foundation for an Indian church' in ML 255-263 and Vander Werff *Record* 97-167. For a concise overview, cf. my earlier pseudonnymous (D. Edwards) '200 Years of Missions to Muslims Part 2. Claudius Buchanan and the Great Experiment' CISN 7 (1999) 8-9.

[35] *Kitab Mizan al-Haqq* (= 'The Book of the Balance of Truth') [Agra:no publisher stated, 3rd rev'd edn,1849] (Persian); *Kitab Mizan al-Haqq* [Agra:Agra Religious Tract Society, 2nd rev'd edn,1850] (Urdu).

[36] *Miftah al-Asrar* [Agra:no publisher stated,1850] (Persian); *Miftah al-Asrar* [Agra:Agra Religious Tract Society, 2nd rev'd edn,1850] (Urdu); *Tariq al-Hayat* (='The Path of Life') [Lahore:Punjab Religious Book Society,1847] (Urdu) and *Hal al-Ishkal da Jawab Kashf al-Astar wa Kitab Istifsar* (='Solution of difficulties in answer to the 'Kashf al-Astar' and the 'Kitab Istifsar') [Agra:no publisher stated,1847]. The books replied to were respectively by Maulvie Muhammad Hadi of Lucknow (Lucknow:1845 – published at the direction of the Mujtahid of Lucknow] which sought to refute Pfander's *Miftah al-Asrar*, and by Maulvie Ali Hasan [Lucknow:1846].

[37] So, H. Birks *The Life and Correspondence of Thomas Valpy French* [London:Murray,1895] 1:70.

[38] We shall therefore base our analysis of Pfander's christology principally on Weakley's translation of the *Mizan ul Haqq* [London:CMS,1867] as this had by far the largest circulation and was the only work relating to Pfander's christology translated into English. The *Miftah al-Asrar*, which was published in Urdu, Turkish and Arabic is now largely unobtainable in the West, other than in the form of St Clair Tisdall's 1912 revision which we will discuss in relation to Tisdall's own christology.

[39] Vander Werff *Record* 43-44.

[40] The three sections of Pfander's *Mizan al-Haqq* and also the subject of Martyn's earlier tracts cf. n.21.

[41] So, Vander Werff *Record* 43-46. cf. Birks *Life* 1:70.

[42] So, E.M. Wherry *The Muslim Controversy* [London: Christian Literature Society,1905] 15.

[43] C. Bennett *Victorian Images of Islam* [London:Grey Seal,1992] 128-29 implies influence via French. However, in the area of christology, the influence was clearly more direct as Tisdall revised Pfander's *Mizan al-Haqq and Miftah al-Asrar*.

[44] Note his laudatory biography defending Pfander's methods: 'Karl Gottlieb Pfander 1841-1941' *MW* 31:3 (1941) 217-26.

[45] This tendency appears to have begun with L.B. Jones *The People of the Mosque* [Calcutta: Baptist Mission Press, 1932 3rd rev'd edn,1959] 283 and has been followed by more recent writers such as C. Chapman 'Rethinking the Gospel for Muslims' 107-125 in J.D. Woodberry (ed.) *Muslims and Christians on the Emmaus Road* [Monrovia:MARC,1989] 117-18. We will subsequently discuss the validity of Jones' argument in our subsequent section 'L.Bevan Jones'. However, here we will simply note that even Pfander's *Mizan al-Haq* simply provides an apologetic critique of traditional Islamic proofs, just as Martyn had earlier done in Persia. This fact alone significantly undermines both the assumption of such writers that Pfander 'initiated' polemics, and the more recent suggestion based on Edward Said's analysis of 'Orientalism' that missionary works such as the *Mizan al-Haq* should be seen as an attempt by the West to dominate and have authority over the Orient. (cf. D.A. Kerr 'The Problem of Christianity in Muslim Perspective: Implications for Christian Mission' *IBMR* 5:4 (1981) 152-62 who gives a sympathetic appraisal of this modern Islamic perspective).

[46] Wherry *Controversy* 13. Wherry was a missionary in North India from 1868-1922 and later became an associate editor of the *Moslem World.*

[47] Powell *Pre-Mutiny* 228.

[48] Presumably the transliteration *Kazi* indicates that he was a Muslim judge (*Qazi*).

[49] Pfander's own account is contained in the *First Report of the Church Missionary Society's Mission to the Afghans at Peshawur for the Years 1855 and 1856* [Agra,1857] 11-16.

[50] *Mizan* iii.

[51] *Mizan* 51 (italics original).

[52] *Mizan* 52.

[53] *Mizan* 36-38.

[54] For concise summaries of French's life cf. D.A. Kerr 'French, Thomas Valpy' *BDCM* 227 and V. Stacey 'The Legacy of Thomas Valpy French 1825-1891' *ML* 277-82 and *Thomas Valpy French First Bishop of Lahore* [Rawalpindi:Christian Study Centre, 2nd edn,1993]. For a more comprehensive account cf. Birks' 2 volume *Life and Correspondence of Thomas.Valpy French (op. cit.)* which contains a considerable volume of primary source material. All subsequent biographies draw extensively on Birks's *Life.*

[55] French refers to this under various titles including 'Henry Martyn's *Life and Memoirs'* (e.g. 2:53-54,58,84,). However, the page number (380) cited in French's correspondence (2:66) clearly indicates that this is J. Sargent's *Life and Letters of Henry Martyn (op. cit.)* first published in 1819 and reprinted in 1862.

[56] Birks *Life* 1:70-71,293.

[57] Birks *Life* 1 :70.

[58] S. Zwemer in an early paper of the Arabian Mission cited from without further reference in Birks *Life* 1:xxii.

[59] Birks *Life* 1:194,213.

[60] Birks *Life* 1:143.

[61] T.V. French 'Proposed Plan for a Training College of Native Evangelists, Pastors and Teachers for North-West India and the Punjab' [London:CMS,1867], cited in Birks *Life* 161.

[62] Birks *Life* 1:247-48.

[63] B.F. Westcott forwarding an offertory from the terminal meeting of B.D.s and D.D.s at Cambridge cited in Birks *Life* 1:232.

[64] cf. French's addresses to first synod convened in the diocese of Lahore (1878) cited in Birks *Life* 1:367; and at conferment of Lambeth D.D. on Imad ud-Din (1884) cited in Birks *Life* 2:115.

[65] Cited in Birks *Life* 1:252.

[66] Cited in Birks *Life* 1:251,253.

[67] Birks *Life* 2:229 gives French's own account of him disputing this point whilst reading the NT with a Muslim in Iraq in 1888. The 1890 revision of the Pushtu NT (*Kitab da Nui Ahed* [London:B&FBS,1890]) and the introductory pages to the Pushtu Pentateuch (*Kalam Allah* [London:B&FBS,1890]) in which French appears to have had a significant if not dominating hand (cf. Birks *Life* 2:135-36) followed the pattern of Martyn's Urdu NT in using *Yeshua* rather than *'Isa.*

[68] I. Loewenthal *The Name 'Isa* paper read at the American (Presbyterian) Mission meeting at Subathu, November 1860 and subsequently published [Calcutta:Baptist Mission Press,1861]. The paper was later reprinted in *MW* 1:3 (1911) 265-82 with an introduction by S.M. Zwemer. A précis of the paper has more recently been reprinted in J.P. Dretke *A Christian Approach to Muslims* [Pasadena:William Carey,1979] Appendix B 207-12. Lowenthal was an outstanding Semitic scholar who was a missionary in Peshawar and translator of the Pushtu NT until his death in 1864.

[69] Unreferenced verbatim citation in W. St Clair Tisdall *A Manual of the Leading Mohammadanian* (sic) *Objections to Christianity* [London:SPCK,1904] subsequently republished under the title *Christian Reply to Muslim Objections* [Villach:Light of Life,1980] 165 n.1 (italics - emphasis added; underlining – Tisdall's emphasis).

[70] Birks *Life* 1:69.

[71] Birks *Life* 1:198.

[72] Birks *Life* 2:57,68,283.

[73] Birks *Life* 2:68 cf. St Clair Tisdall's comments in the preface to his revision of Pfander's *Miftahu'l-Asrar* that he omitted this argument as being both 'very doubtful' and inappropriate for Muslim readers (x-xi).

[74] So, Birks *Life* 1:378-79 who notes his particular predilection for the works of Hilary of Poitiers and Chrysostom.

[75] Letter to Mr Frost 1856 whom he asked to keep these thoughts confidential, in case 'I might be supposed to be infringing the glory of the Saviour's Divinity' - cited in Birks *Life* 1:84-5. Perhaps significantly, the issue was raised by French's reading of Irenaeus, one of the very earliest patristic writers, whose own teacher had possibly been taught by the apostle John.

[76] So, D.A. Kerr 'Imad ud-Din' *BDCM* 317-18, and Wherry *Controversy* 15-16.

[77] *The Divinity of Christ* and *Tauzin al-Aqwal*.

[78] However, Wherry *Controversy* 57-66 provided a chapter by chapter summary of the *Tauzin al-Aqwal* on the basis of which the following analysis is made.

[79] Cited in Wherry *Controversy* 63-64.

[80] For a critical appraisal of Tisdall cf. Bennett *Victorian* 128-149, Bennett also provides a summary biography 'Tisdall, William St Clair' in *BDCM* 673.

[81] [London:1910 – reprinted Villach:Light of Life,1986].

[82] cf. n.32.

[83] H. Goddard *Muslim Perceptions of Christianity* [London:Grey Seal,1996] 67 n.25 reports finding Arabic and English editions of Tisdall's revision in the Sudan in 1977. It is in fact exceedingly difficult to find copies of Pfander's original editions today, even in academic libraries.

[84] Reprinted as *Christian Reply to Muslim Objections* [Villach:Light of Life,1980].

[85] *Mizan* 132.

[86] *Objections* 20-21,165 n.1.

[87] *Mizan* 132.

[88] e.g. *Miftah* 96-98.

[89] *Objections* 145 n.2 affirming the comments of an unnamed contributor to *Objections*.

[90] *Objections* 8.

[91] In fact the model advocated by Tisdall is more easily discernible in the early church's preaching to pagans (e.g. Acts 17:22ff) than to monotheistic Jews.

[92] cf. discussion of bounded monotheism in chapter 5 section 'Conceptual framework of monotheism' esp. discussion of the boundary markers distinguishing the creator from the creature.

[93] *Objections* 160 n.1.

[94] *Hasti* is the noun form of the verb *hast* ('to be'). Although this is applied to God in the Persian phrase *Khuda hast* ('God is'), this is understood to mean that there is one God who really exists. It is therefore hard to see how speaking of three divine *hasti* is any less likely to be misunderstood as tri-theism, than speaking of three divine 'persons'.

[95] *Mizan* 179, the sentence is repeated in *Miftah* 138 verbatim, except for the omission of the footnotes.

[96] Jn 4:14; Rev.21:6 and possibly 7:17.

[97] *Miftah* 107-08.

[98] *Miftah* 117-18; 124-26.

[99] *Miftah* preface x-xi.

[100] *Miftah* 129.

[101] Even when Tisdall expanded this section of the *Miftah* it only amounted to six of its 213 pages (123-129). The closest the 370pp *Mizan al-Haqq* comes to an explicit articulation of a Logos christology is a passing reference to Christ as the effulgence of God's glory (175).

[102] *Crusaders of the Twentieth Century* [*op.cit.*] xlvi.

[103] *Twentieth* 216.

[104] *Twentieth* 220 citing Birks *Life* 1:57.

[105] *Twentieth* 217. Rice is here affirmatively citing a passage from Arnold's *Ishmael, or a Natural History of Islamism* 444.

[106] *Twentieth* 244. This argument is developed in 244-316.

[107] *Twentieth* 270.

[108] *Twentieth* 289.

[109] *Twentieth* 289 (emphasis added). NB vocabulary bracketed by Rice is Persian.

[110] *Twentieth* 298, crediting Rev. Worthington Jukes of Peshawar for first observing this.

[111] *Twentieth* 227-28.

[112] For a concise biography cf. A. Neely 'Zwemer, Samuel Marinus' *BDCM* 763. For a fuller treatment cf. J.C. Wilson Snr *Apostle to Islam: A Biography of Samuel M. Zwemer* [Grand Rapids:Baker,1952].

[113] In *Islam: A Challenge to Faith* [New York:SVM,1907] 213-14 (+ inset) he described Tisdall's *Manual* as 'indispensable for the missionary', and included Pfander's *Mizan al-Haqq* in a list of 12 apologetic works for Muslims, while his brief biography of Pfander in the *Moslem World* [*op.cit.* n.44] cited affirmatively the words of Julius Richter that the *Mizan* was 'almost indispensable to every missionary among Mohammedans' (222), and lamented its decline in popularity (223-224).

[114] This acknowledgement is made in the heading of the bibliography in his *The Moslem Christ* [Edinburgh: Oliphant, Anderson & Ferrier,1912] – reprinted as *The Muslim Christ* [Moseley,Birmingham:The Message for Muslims Trust,n.d.] 195.

[115] L. Vander Werff 'Our Muslim Neighbours: The Contribution of Samuel M. Zwemer to Christian Mission' *Missiology* 10:2 (1982) 185-97 claims that from 1890-1916 Zwemer reflected nineteenth century practice that pitted Christianity over against non-Christian systems, but from 1916-1938 wrote empathetically of the Muslim as a person seeking God. However, Zwemer's praise of Pfander's approach in his 1941 reflection in the *Moslem World* (cf. n.44) suggests that Zwemer simply focused on what he saw as a complementary perspective, rather than rejecting earlier approaches.

[116] Zwemer *Christ* 181 n.1 cites the 1910 *Edinburgh Conference Report* 4:141. This is presumably a pre-publication report as the final published report edited by W.H.T. Gairdner was only one volume.

[117] Christ 181(italics- Zwemer's).

[118] S. Zwemer *The Moslem Doctrine of God* [Boston:American Tract Society,1905 – reprinted Moseley: The Message for Muslims Trust,1981] 86.

[119] As opposed to a christology from above that starts from the identity of God.

[120] The weakness of Zwemer's christology in this respect is emphasised by the fact that when he presented christology to a Western audience, he did so very much in the form of a christology from above (cf. his chapter 'The Changeless Christ' in S. Zwemer *Dynamic Christianity and the World Today* [London: IVF,1939] 35-46).

[121] *Christ* 181-82.

[122] *Christ* 192 citing D.B. MacDonald's 1909 annual address at Hartford Seminary entitled 'One Phase of the Doctrine of the Unity of God' (emphasis added).

[123] [Edinburgh:Church of Scotland/United Free church,1909].

[124] For concise biographies of Gairdner cf. L. Poston 'Gairdner, William Henry Temple' *EDWM* 383-84 and K. Cragg 'Gairdner, W(illiam) H(enry) Temple' *BDCM*:233-34. The fullest account of Gairdner's life is that by his Cairo colleague C.E. Padwick *Temple Gairdner of Cairo* [London:SPCK,1929] written shortly after his death, portraying him as an exemplar of missionary life. Vander Werff *Record* 184-224 appraises Gairdner's missiology within its historical context, while Cragg presents a more personal evaluation of his missiological contribution that reflects on the present state of the church in Cairo, in 'Temple Gairdner's Legacy' *IBMR*:5:4 (1981) 164-67. Both Padwick (327-30) and Vander Werff (279-82) provide comprehensive lists of Gairdner's publications.

[125] Padwick *Gairdner* 288-89 reproduces the musical MSS of a dervish funeral dirge Gairdner transcribed as the procession passed, and later harmonised for a four verse hymn.

[126] cf. Padwick *Gairdner* 256-60.

[127] ET posthumously published as 'The Essentiality of the Cross' *MW* 33:3 (1933) 230-51, citations 236,238 (published emphases).

[128] 'Essentiality' 236 n.4.

[129] W.H.T. Gairdner 'Christianity and Islam' in *The Christian Life and Message in Relation to Non-Christian Systems – Report of the Jerusalem Meeting of the International Missionary Council March 24th-April 8th 1928* [London:OUP,1928]:1:235-83. Gairdner, who died six weeks after the conference, was too ill to attend.

[130] This somewhat negates Cragg's claim in 'Gairdner's Legacy' that Gairdner's designation of Christ as God's '*Wakil*' (sic) was prophetic of the present urgency to set christology free of substance metaphors. Cragg is being overgenerous and perhaps deserves more credit for this embryonic idea himself.

[131] W.H.T. Gairdner 'The Doctrine of the Trinity in Unity' *MW*:1 (1911) 381-407.

[132] 'Trinity' 385.

[133] 'Trinity' 385.

[134] 'Trinity' 166. Contra. Cragg 'Gairdner's Legacy' who speaks of Gairdner being 'ready to concede that terms like *Ibn Allah* "Son of God," must be replaced as long as their meaning is opaque or frustrating'. However, the basis of this claim is unclear as no specific references are cited.

[135] 'Trinity' 402-03.

[136] cf. W.H.T. Gairdner *The Muslim Idea of God* [London:The Christian Literature Society,1909] 31 and *Jerusalem Report* 1:241,249-50.

[137] *Jerusalem Report* 1:260.

[138] *Jerusalem Report* 1:239-41.

[139] *Jerusalem Report* 1:264.

[140] *Jerusalem Report* 1:241-42 cf. also *Reproach* 158-59.

[141] *Jerusalem Report* 1:242.

[142] cf. our discussion of the Moses epiphanies in a range of Islamic literature in chapter 5 section 'Epiphany prior to the Last Day'.

[143] *Jerusalem Report* 1:243.

[144] *Jerusalem Report* 1:243.

[145] W.H.T. Gairdner *God as Triune, Creator Incarnate, Atoner* [Madras:Christian Literature Society for India,1916] 40.

[146] *Triune* 40-41.

[147] i.e. that which Systematic Theology terms 'the economic trinity'.

[148] Now Bangladesh.

[149] For concise biographies cf. C. Bennett 'Jones, Lewis Bevan' in *BDCM* 342; and 'Lewis Bevan Jones 1880-1960 Striving to Touch Muslim Hearts' *ML* 283-89.

[150] *Op cit.* (n.45).

[151] [Calcutta:YMCA,1938].

[152] Both were then out of print. However, Jones (*Christianity*:xi) referred to the Rice's work as 'excellent', but stated that Tisdall's work though 'valuable', was no longer appropriate.

[153] In this chapter we will use terms such as 'liberal', 'liberal evangelical' and 'neo orthodox' in the purely descriptive sense in which they are used by historical theologians. Many early twentieth century writers themselves accepted such terms as self-designations.

[154] e.g. his discussion of the virgin birth strongly affirms the claim of Bishop Gore that 'the Virgin Birth was certainly not part of the original Apostolic message' (*Christianity* 162), and appears to raise questions about the Biblical text relating it (163-64). However, despite this, Jones' conclusion makes clear that he affirms this doctrine. C. Bennett *Jones* 286 claims him for the liberal tradition, though admits his affinity with the evangelical constituency.

[155] *Mosque* 266.

[156] *Christianity* x - appended to the above comment first written in *Mosque* six years earlier.

[157] *Christianity* 79-80.

[158] Although he emphatically rejected the fulfilment concept advocated by J.N. Farquhar, stating that 'Truth can never be the fulfilment of error' (*From Islam to Christ: How a Sufi Found His Lord* [Brighton: FFM,1952] 21.

[159] *Christianity* 91.

[160] *Mosque* 279ff.

[161] *Mosque* 283.

[162] cf. n.21,40. Tisdall clearly states this in his 1910 revision of Pfander's *Mizan al-Haqq* (225-26), and a perusal of the main subjects dealt with in section 3 of Pfander's original (76-134) clearly justifies this, cf. also n.45.

[163] The *First Report of the CMS at Peshawar* 16-21 suggests that Pfander's street preaching primarily consisted of the exposition of Gospel passages, although he was sometimes 'obliged' to respond apologetically to Muslim heckling – including that relating to traditional proofs of Islam such as the inimitability of the Qur'an.

[164] C. Schirrmacher 'Muslim Apologetics and the Agra Debates of 1854: A Nineteenth Century Turning Point' *Bull.HMI* 13:1 (1994) 74-84 raises the possibility that Kairanawi also introduced the 'Gospel of Barnabas' to the Islamic world as a result of reading the works of the English rationalist deist John Toland (1670-1722) who referred to the Gospel of Barnabas foretelling the coming of Muhammad. Schirrmacher observes that Kairanawi appears to refer to this in both his 1854 *I'jaz-i-Isawi* and his later *Izhar al-Haq*.

[165] Tisdall's *Yanabi' al-Islam* published in Persian in 1900, subsequently translated into English and abridged by Sir W. Muir as *The Sources of Islam* published in 1900 [Edinburgh:T&T Clark,1905]. Muir, a colonial administrator who later became principal of Edinburgh University, had himself written a number of

books in English based on the earliest Islamic sources, including *The Life of Mahomet and History of Islam to the Era of the Hegira* [London:Smith Elder,1858]; Although Muir was a friend and supporter of missionaries he was not himself a missionary and may be more accurately described as an oriental scholar, indeed he later became president of the Royal Asiatic Society of Great Britain and Ireland. Moreover, such works on Islam were not translated into Muslim languages and missionaries appear to have been reticent to use them even for those Muslims capable of reading weighty academic tomes in English. Wherry for example in his survey of available literature for Muslims (*Controversy* 130-31) merely included Muir's book in an appendix of books 'useful to the student of Islam'.

[166] cf. *Mosque* 303-10; *Christianity* 70.

[167] cf. Jones' comments cited on this page.

[168] Jones both cites from and commends for further reading reference works by Forsyth, Gore and Mackintosh in his chapter on 'The Person of Jesus Christ' in *Christianity* 55-81. For concise summaries of these writers' theologies cf. *NDT* articles: R. Brown 'Forsyth, Peter Taylor' (260-61); C.D. Hancock 'Gore, Charles' (278); J.D. Douglas 'Mackintosh, Hugh Ross' (409) and B.E. Foster 'Kenoticism' (364).

[169] For concise summaries of Ritschl's theology cf. P.N. Hillyer 'Ritschl, Albrecht' *NDT* 595-6 and (T) A.N.S. Lane *The Lion Book of Christian Thought* [Oxford:Lion,2nd edn 1992] 185-86.

[170] *Christianity* 74.

[171] *Christianity* 74f.

[172] *Christianity* 70 emphasis added.

[173] Detailed discussion of the influence of Ritschl and other liberal theologians on Jones is beyond the scope of this study. However, it appears probable that the influence of Ritschl's ideas on Jones came via Mackintosh who translated his works into English, as Jones both cites from and recommends his christological writing. In this context it may also be significant that Mackintosh also translated the works of Schleiermacher into English, as Jones' explicit rejection of any discussion of Jesus sharing the Divine substance closely parallels Schleiermacher's rejection of classical christological formulations concerning distinctions within the Godhead. The influence of liberal theology on Jones clearly merits further study.

[174] Lane *Thought* 186.

[175] [Marseille:NAM,1977].

[176] Now renamed *Arab World Ministries*.

[177] Although including a disclaimer that the book's theology does not necessarily reflect that of the mission.

[178] The term is used on p 47.

[179] *Approach* 47-49.

[180] *Approach* 420 cf. also 634.

[181] On p 635 he concedes that the creedal writers changed the NT phrase 'resurrection of the dead', to 'resurrection of the flesh' in order to counter ideas current in the Greek philosophical and religious context.

[182] *Approach* 634.

[183] 386, 387 observing that 'person' then meant one actor wearing several different masks.

[184] *Approach* 420.

[185] Christensen does not cite Barth directly, possibly because this would have offended the evangelical constituency he was writing for. However, a number of his major emphases significantly parallel those of Barth. e.g. emphatic rejection of all natural theology (272,384); emphatic assertion that the Bible is not itself revelation, but its words and sentences which are only of 'various degrees of worth', when preached 'become the Word of God' (445 cf. also 272,316, 422-23, 494-5); the event of Christ as the sole locus of God's self revelation, with

an apparent downplaying of the work of the Spirit (385). Christensen also several times appears to echo Barth's famous dictum 'Let God be God' (326) and in other more incidental ways appears to reflect Barthian theology, such as his affirmation of 'salvation time' in preference to linear time (327). For a concise overview of the main emphases of K. Barth's theology cf. J.B. Webster 'Barth, Karl' *NDT* 76-80 and Lane *Thought* 200-204.

[186] *Approach* 390-91, 621.

[187] *Approach* 327.

[188] *Approach* 328.

[189] *Approach* 328.

[190] A similar position is adopted by Christensen's missionary colleague and fellow Pakistani Bishop Arne Rudwin, 'Islam – An Absolutely Different Ethos?' *IRM* 71:1 (1987) 59-65. Rudwin, who wrote the preface to Christensen's book, speaks of Jesus as 'the objective possibility of revelation', but the Spirit as only 'the subjective possibility of revelation', in both cases explicitly citing Barth (59,62).

[191] *Approach* 434f. OT theophany and epiphany narratives and second temple Jewish understandings of these will be discussed in Chapter 2. Elsewhere (428) Christensen also erroneously suggests that Jews at the time of Jesus had no concept of the Spirit of God as a personal being.

[192] *Approach* 642-43. He argues that the order of these terms is important, because man cannot properly conceive of his own sin or God as judge without first understanding God's act of redemption in Christ, an emphasis strikingly similar to Barth's.

[193] *Approach* 425-26 cf. also 385.

[194] A.K. Cragg *Islam in the Twentieth Century: The Relevance of Christian Theology and the Relation of Christian Mission to its Problems.* Unpublished D.Phil thesis Oxford University,1950.

[195] For a concise biography of Cragg cf. D.A. Kerr 'Cragg, Albert Kenneth' *BDCM* 157. For more detailed and critical appraisals of his life and work cf. A. D'Souza 'Christian Approaches to the Study of Islam. An Analysis of the Writings of Watt and Cragg' *Bull.HMI* 11:2 (1992) 33-80 and particularly Lamb *Retrieval* passim.

[196] *The Christ and the Faiths: Theology in Cross-Reference* [London: SPCK, 1986] 17.

[197] i.e. dialogue that does not see conversion as a principal aim. Lamb *Retrieval* 118 cites from the privately published memoir of former Muslim intellectual Daud Rahbar, who in 1958 asked Cragg for baptism. Rahbar states that Cragg 'was startled by my request for baptism…He had started counting on me as a liberal participant in the dialogue between Christians and Muslims. (He said:) "I was hoping you would take part in the dialogue as a Muslim". The request for baptism was too sudden for his ears'.

[198] *Christianity in World Perspective* [London:Lutterworth,1968] 198.

[199] *Jesus and the Muslim:An Exploration* [London:Allen & Unwin,1985] 197f.

[200] So, Lamb *Retrieval* 52 who draws attention to this particularly in respect of Cragg's version of theodicy.

[201] Thesis pt 2:263-64 cited in Lamb *Retrieval* 13.

[202] So, Lamb *Retrieval* 12ff.

[203] So, Lamb *Retrieval* 13.

[204] Interestingly Cragg also speaks of NT scholarship as 'a discipline in need of discipline' and avers that 'its more radical practitioners will have to be radically countered if confusions, especially in the Muslim direction, are not to be wantonly increased.' (*Jesus* 8). However, it is far from clear on what basis he so strongly rejects some aspects of critical scholarship, whilst endorsing others. This must at least add to the suspicion that the version of Christianity he presents to Muslims is in some measure idiosyncratic.

[205] *Jesus* 125-65 (esp. 149),291-93. Although Cragg does emphasise Jesus as the Messiah (Chapter 5), he interprets this as synonymous with 'Son of God' (197), which he appears to understand primarily in terms of filial obedience (cf. 30, 149ff;197).

[206] cf. Appendix A for description of this hypothesis.

[207] A response to evolutionary christology was J. Jeremias *The Prayers of Jesus* [London:SCM,1967]11-65 ET from German of *Studien zue neutestamentlichen Theologie und Zeitgeschichte*. Jeremias drew attention to the NT references to Jesus addressing God as *Abba*, which as an Aramaic word undeniably went back to the earliest Christian community, and implied a unique filial relationship between Jesus and God. Although this was a helpful and appropriate corrective, because it responded to the radical form critics by their own rules, it inevitably resulted in a christology that was much more constrained than that of the final form of the NT. Although Cragg strongly rejects the work of radical NT scholars (*Jesus* 8), and regards the negative use of the criterion of dissimilarity as risky (83), his presentation to Muslims of Jeremias' christology fails to appreciate the fact that Jeremias had been obliged to work from the same negative use of the criterion of dissimilarity as the radical critics, thereby developing a christology based on one very narrow aspect of NT christology. For a concise summary of NT christological debate at this time cf. I.H. Marshall *The Origins of New Testament Christology* [Leicester:Apollos,2nd edn 1990] esp. 11-31.

[208] By using the state of academic opinion as the foundation for the church's communication of its faith to Muslims, Cragg has in philosophical terms shifted the terms of the church's engagement with the academy from an 'accidental' relationship to an 'essential' one.

[209] *Jesus* 45.

[210] *Jesus* 11.

[211] *Jesus* 11.

[212] 'Gairdner's Legacy' citation 166.

[213] So, Lamb *Retrieval* 50.

[214] *Jesus* 219 cf. also 194-6.

[215] cf. earlier section discussing Tisdall's christology.

[216] *Jesus* 291.

[217] *Jesus* 195.

[218] [Grand Rapids:Baker,1980] cf. also *The Fortress and the Fire* [Bombay:Gospel Literature Service,1975]; *Beyond the Mosque* [Grand Rapids:Baker,1985]; *Bridges to Islam* [Grand Rapids:Baker,1983]; *The Cross and the Crescent* [Wheaton:Tyndale House,1989/Amersham:Scripture Press,1990] and *Inside the Community* [Grand Rapids:Baker,1994].

[219] cf. especially *Paths* 85-89. This is well illustrated by Parshall's diagram fig 4 (86) which draws a box around 'Theological Basics', focusing on external factors that hinder the communication of what is internal to this box.

[220] *Bridges* 123-26.

[221] Paths 58. Parshall is correct in understanding ὁμολογουμένως as 'confession' although some EVV including the NIV do not bring out this sense.

[222] Paths 42.

[223] Mosque 13.

[224] Edwin Calverley (1882-1971) was a missionary in Arabia with the Reformed Church of America (1909-30), who later succeeded D.B. McDonald as professor of Arabic and Islamic Studies at the Kennedy School of Mission, and co-edited the *Moslem World* with Zwemer. For a summary biography cf. D.A. Kerr 'Calverley, Edwin Elliot' BDCM 110.

[225] E.E. Calverley 'Christian Theology and the Qur'an' *MW*:47 (1957) 289 cited by Parshall in *Paths* 144.

[226] James L. Barton (1855-1936) an educational missionary in Turkey, who later became foreign secretary of the American Board of Commissioners for Foreign Missions. For a summary biography cf. D.M. Stowe 'Barton, James Levi' *BDCM* 46.

[227] J.L. Barton *The Christian Approach to Islam* [Boston:The Pilgrim Press,1918] 165 cited in Parshall *Fortress* 15-16.

[228] cf. section 'L. Bevan Jones' above. The impact of liberal theology on Barton's missiology merits further attention. However, any such influence on Parshall's writing is clearly unintentional, as he very specifically disavows the presuppositions of such theology (cf. *Paths* 32ff;133).

[229] Barton ibid cited in Parshall *Fortress* 16.

[230] *Fortress* 7.

[231] *Paths* 136-37 in which Parshall appears to affirm Don McCurry's comments in this respect.

[232] *Paths* 139-40 and *Community*:18,164 referring to similar designation of Jesus in *Ahadith*.

[233] *Paths* 140.

[234] cf. chapter 5 section 'Conceptual framework of monotheism' esp. discussion of 'Boundary markers distinguishing God from all else'.

[235] *Perspective* 7-8; *Frontiers in Muslim-Christian Encounter* [Oxford:Regnum,1987] 80-81.

[236] *Perspective* 8.

[237] M. Nazir Ali 'Directions in Mission: Christian Worship, Witness and Work in Islamic Contexts' *IRM* 76:1 (1987) 33-37 (citation 36).

[238] *Frontiers* 96.

[239] *Frontiers* 26.

[240] *Frontiers* 29-33 (Citation 33).

[241] *Frontiers* 127.

[242] Nazir Ali does not suggest that these christologies have necessarily been advocated by scholars, and, at least in respect of the second approach, illustrates it with reference to Christian preaching in Pakistan.

[243] *Frontiers* 27.

[244] *Frontiers* 27.

[245] *Frontiers* 28.

[246] Wherry *Controversy* passim notes a number of scholarly works by Indian evangelists. However, with the exception of the works of Imad ud-Din which we have discussed, they do not deal with christology.

CHAPTER 2

MONOTHEISM IN FIRST CENTURY JUDAISM

Holy, Holy, Holy! Though the darkness hide thee,
Though the eye of sinful man thy glory may not see.[1]

Introduction

In this chapter we will examine the context of Jewish monotheism that formed the background to the early church's contextualisation of christology. This will enable us subsequently to compare the Jewish context faced by the early church with that faced by the church in the Islamic context, thereby enabling us to make the necessary adaptations to the early church's contextualisation of christology.

We will examine five issues relating to Jewish beliefs about monotheism: firstly, how monotheism was primarily understood, whether in bounded or unbounded, extrinsic or intrinsic terms; secondly, monolatry – whether Jews regarded it as legitimate to invoke or venerate beings other than God; thirdly, theophany – whether Jews believed that God could be seen by mortals; fourthly, the related though distinct concept of epiphany - whether it was believed that God could locally manifest a form of his presence on earth; and fifthly, whether any second temple Jewish beliefs provided specific antecedents to christological monotheism. In order to do this we will examine not only the OT, but also the interpretations of the OT found in a range of second temple Jewish texts, the Septuagint (LXX), Aramaic targums which provide some evidence of synagogue interpretation, pseudepigrapha and apocrypha, Qumran texts and the writings of Philo of Alexandria.

How Jews Thought About God: The Conceptual Framework Used to Describe Monotheism

Bounded Monotheism

The OT makes an absolute distinction between God and all else. YHWH alone is declared to be the only creator, ruler of all things, judge and saviour. Not only does the OT never apply any of these titles to any heavenly beings other than YHWH, but the subject/object distinction inherent in them further emphasises YHWH's distinction from all else; i.e. he is the creator, all else are his creatures; he is the ruler, all else is ruled by him and so forth. Unsurprisingly, Isaiah speaks of the utter impossibility of comparing YHWH with anyone else.[2]

This distinction between God and all else is heightened in the LXX and targums with Hebrew texts comparing people to God being carefully reworked to avoid direct similes.[3] *Onqelos,* the earliest extant targum, also makes a number of interpretative insertions to assure the listener that there is an unbridgeable gap between earth and heaven.[4] Both the Qumran literature and various pseudepigrapha repeatedly refer to YHWH as the creator and ruler of 'all things' in a way that suggests this phrase had become a standard part of Jewish monotheistic rhetoric.[5] The Qumran texts repeatedly affirm that there is none beside him, or in any way comparable to him, to the extent that none can even stand in his presence.[6]

Other ways in which second temple Jews emphasised the absolute boundary between God and all else include the exclusive application to YHWH of certain titles such as 'the Holy One' and 'the First and the Last', titles that the NT later applied to Jesus;[7] and the *Shema,* whose affirmation of the oneness of God came to be came to be recited twice daily by pious Jews.[8]

Extrinsic Monotheism

An examination of the OT provides no real evidence that it ever defines God in intrinsic terms. In fact there is not even a Hebrew or Aramaic equivalent of the relevant Greek terms such as οὐσία or φύσις. Even the divine self designation in Ex 3:14 אֶהְיֶה אֲשֶׁר אֶהְיֶה, whilst acknowledging the being of God, does not even hint at any description of his internal nature.

God is however repeatedly defined in extrinsic terms. The pentateuch, psalms and prophets repeatedly and consistently refer to him as the sole creator, ruler of creation, judge and saviour.

Thus for example in the decalogue, which formed a central part of second temple piety, YHWH identifies himself, firstly, as the saviour who delivered his people out of Egyptian bondage (Exodus 20:2); as one who will judge them according to whether or not they respond to this salvific action by monolatry (:4-7); and as the creator of the heavens, the earth, the sea and all that is in them (:8-11). Although it is not explicitly stated that YHWH is sole ruler of the universe this is strongly implied both by the command to acknowledge no other lords either in heaven above or on earth below (:4-5) and by the statement that YHWH created heaven and earth and 'all things' in them (כָּל־אֲשֶׁר־בָּם) (:11). Significantly, the first five commandments of the decalogue are explicitly based on this extrinsic description of YHWH.

Similarly, Isa.40-55, one of the most polemical statements of monotheism in the OT, also bases its appeal on this extrinsic understanding of God. YHWH is repeatedly referred to as only creator who alone gives life and who as 'the First and Last' existed before all else;[9] as the judge of both Israel and the whole earth;[10] as the only 'saviour' (ישׁע) and 'redeemer' (גאל). The latter is frequently coupled with the designation 'The Holy One' and draws on the imagery of the exodus deliverance, although YHWH is now declared to be not merely the saviour of Israel, but also of the ends of the earth;[11] YHWH is also depicted as the one who alone rules the affairs of nations and creation, before whom every knee will bow.[12]

Not only the LXX and targums, but also the pseudepigrapha overwhelmingly portray YHWH as the saviour/redeemer of his people,[13] as the sole creator,[14] the ruler[15] and the final judge[16] of 'all things'. The explicit use of these extrinsic descriptions in one of the LXX additions to the Hebrew text may even indicate that these had become a Jewish monotheistic formula by this stage.[17] Although the LXX rendering of Isa.40:13-14 which portrays the Spirit as νοῦς κυρίου may conceivably give a slight hint of reflection on the intrinsic nature of God's being, the absence of any other such hints cautions against reading too much into this text.

Even Philo appears to conceive of God in something akin to bounded extrinsic terms. His arguments on this subject are complex and not always clear. However, he strongly affirms that mortals can know nothing of God's essence (οὐσία),[18] rather, God can be perceived by the evidence of creation,[19] and God's 'powers that range throughout the universe'.[20] The latter description parallels Zechariah 4's portrayal of the sevenfold Spirit as 'the eyes of the Lord which range throughout the earth.'[21] Philo goes much further than the OT and distances God from all contact with his creation, even excluding him from the act of creation. Instead, God acts through his powers, particularly the Logos, whom he describes as being like a first-born son whom a king appoints as a viceroy to govern in his stead.[22] Philo clearly does not regard these powers as being semi-divine beings as he quite categorically rejects the notion of such beings existing.[23] Rather, they are personified divine attributes that as extensions of God enable him to relate to the universe. On one level this is no different from the OT portrayal of the impossibility of God being seen by mortal men, but revealing himself to them in the forms such as the Spirit.

Some scholars have suggested that some second temple texts portray personified divine attributes such as wisdom, certain principal angels and exalted patriarchs as acting as God's 'chief agent' in the rule of the universe.[24] However, if this were the case, any figure taking on the totality of divine functions would be indistinguishable from God himself, unless God could be known in some other way than by how he acted; i.e. if his inner being (ontology) was intrinsically knowable.

However, not only do the vast majority of Jewish texts only portray God in bounded extrinsic terms, but it is extremely questionable whether any texts can be said to unequivocally depict anyone other than God carrying out the totality of divine functions. Texts such as *Ben Sirach* and the *Wisdom of Solomon* which personify divine wisdom,[25] and the latter's portrayal of wisdom as pervading and permeating all things as 'a clear effluence from the glory of the Almighty',[26] need to be understood in the light of the Jewish belief that Torah is the primary expression of divine wisdom.[27] This identification is explicitly made in *Ben Sirach's* wisdom eulogy.[28]

It has also been claimed that *Orphica* and *The Exagoge* depict semi-divine figures on God's throne.[29] However, *Orphica* emphatically distinguishes the one God from all else,[30] while the *Exagoge* itself interprets Moses sitting on the throne as simply a prophetic dream revealing Moses' sovereignty over Israel and her past, present and future role among the nations.[31]

What various Jewish texts do acknowledge is that God employs angels and even people as his servants in exercising his exclusive universal rule. However, no such being ever takes on the entirety of roles such as universal rule and judgement. For example, various texts depict God as having delegated the rule of limited areas of creation or spheres of activity to certain named angels.[32] Similarly, although *4 Ezra* and the *Testament of Abraham* speak of preliminary judgements by the Messiah and Abel plus the twelve tribes of Israel respectively, they reserve the final eschatological judgement for God. Moreover, there is no hint that any such figures are themselves able to delegate to others authority to rule or judge aspects of God's creation. This appears to be understood as an exclusively divine prerogative, a factor that we will see is of some significance when we subsequently examine the NT portrayal of Jesus as sovereign ruler and judge.[33]

The only exception to YHWH's exclusive prerogative of exercising universal rule and eschatological judgement is 1 Enoch's portrait of the son of man, a figure we shall examine more closely in our discussion of specific antecedents of christological monotheism.[34]

Monolatry: Can Only God Legitimately be Worshipped, Adored or Invoked?

Legitimate Worship

It is clear from the OT that throughout Israel's history they were surrounded by peoples who worshipped a variety of gods, and called on various spiritual beings for assistance. However, the OT is emphatic that Israel was to worship no god except YHWH. One of the clearest statements of this is the Decalogue, where YHWH decrees that monolatry is the appropriate response to his unique identity as the saviour God, who brought them out of Egypt. The Decalogue more precisely defines this response as not making an idol of any created thing, whether heavenly or earthly; and not worshipping or even bowing down to such. It is also stated that divine judgment, extending to the third and fourth generation, will be YHWH's response to those who fail to respond to him in this way.[35] Deuteronomy records still more specific details of YHWH's expectations in this respect including a general injunction not to imitate the practices of pagan religion, such as child sacrifice, divination, sorcery, interpretation of omens, witchcraft, practising as a medium or spiritist, or invoking the dead and a specific prohibition on prophecy in the name of anyone other YHWH.[36]

Such injunctions certainly do not mean that Jews never engaged in such practices. Both the OT narratives and the denunciations of the prophetic books makes it clear that Canaanite religious practices continued under the surface of Judaism as 'folk religion'[37] throughout much of OT history.[38] However, our concern is not with a study of Israelite religious practice *per se*, but rather with which aspects of Jewish religious practice were regarded as legitimate.

It must be said at the outset that the overwhelming majority of Jewish texts do not portray worship and prayer being offered to anyone other than YHWH.

Even Philo who is writing for a pagan audience is most emphatic that the foremost commandment is to worship the one God and nothing else.[39] We must therefore be careful not to give undue weight to any traditions that are only representative of less widely held Jewish beliefs.

In view of the stringency of the OT injunctions, it is perhaps unsurprising that the primary issues in relation to monolatry that arise from second temple texts concern issues not directly addressed in the Torah. Firstly, whether it was legitimate to bow before or in other ways venerate figures other than God, such as rulers, departed patriarchs or angels; secondly, whether it was legitimate to pray to such figures for assistance in time of need.

Veneration of Figures Other than God

One of the Jewish responses to being ruled by pagan nations was the development of a tradition of refusing to bow before anyone other than YHWH. This 'refusal tradition' is highlighted in a lengthy insertion into the LXX narrative of Esther (4:17). In this, Mordecai tells YHWH that even though he is tempted to bow before Haman to save Israel, he refuses to do so as this would set the glory of man above the glory of God, who alone he will worship (προσκυνέω). In the LXX, Psalm 72[71]:11's depiction of the obeisance of the gentile nations before a future Israelite king[40] formed an exception to the 'refusal tradition' precisely because it involved no hint of divinisation, in the way that bowing before pagan rulers might.[41]

One Jewish text that does run counter to the refusal tradition is the *Life of Adam and Eve*, which portrays Satan's expulsion from heaven due to his refusal to obey God's command to bow before the newly created Adam.[42] It is unclear how significant such ideas were within second temple Judaism, particularly in view of the much more widely attested Jewish refusal tradition. However, the text does have some significance for our study as an almost identical story occurs on a number of occasions in the Qur'an.[43]

It has been claimed by some scholars that in second temple Judaism angels could receive honour as subordinate beings aligned with God, and this provided a precedent for Jewish Christians honouring Jesus alongside YHWH, without fear of compromising monotheism.[44] The evidence for this is, however, somewhat limited, with even Philo specifically rejecting the worship of subordinate beings.[45]

Some texts do mention angels in thanksgivings directed to God. For example Tobit on his safe return declares 'Praise be to God, and praise to his great name and to all his holy angels'.[46] However, as Tobit at this point is unaware that God's deliverance has been achieved through the instrumentality of an angel, it is probable that this is simply a formulaic way of praising God.

The *Apocalypse of Zephaniah* underlines the need for a critical examination of texts that appear to portray angel veneration. This text not only provides evidence of the 'refusal tradition', but also of Jewish belief that God himself could appear in angelomorphic form. In this text, Zephaniah explicitly states that he prostrated himself and worshipped before the glorious angelic figure he saw, because 'I thought that the Lord Almighty had come to visit me.'[47] Similarly in *Joseph and Asenath*, the self-identification of the figure Asenath bows before, as 'the commander of the whole host (ἀρχιστράτηγος) of the Most High'[48] suggests that it is intended to represent the theophanic figure who identified himself to Joshua as the commander of the Lord's army (LXX ἀρχιστράτηγος).

Invocation of Figures Other than God

Although some Jewish invocation texts exist that call on names of YHWH's angels to deliver them, the question that concerns us is whether this was regarded as consistent with Torah, and therefore legitimate.

The book of *Tobit* is potentially significant in this respect, as it enshrines an extremely literal obedience to the Torah,[49] and its circulation was sufficiently widespread to include even the Qumran community.[50] Although Tobit is only portrayed as praying to God, the angel Raphael is depicted as able to bind the demon Asmodaeus if Tobit burns fish liver with incense.[51] The provision of such remedies is clearly attributed to God, and interestingly bears marked similarities to Islamic attempts to ward off evil spirits such as by burning rue seeds.[52]

Tobit thus presents a theology of certain angels being able to bind certain demons. This theology becomes much more developed in the *Testament of Solomon*, which although post-Christian may reflect earlier Jewish ideas. In this Solomon is given a ring by God, which enables him to imprison all demons, which leads to him discovering which angels can bind which demons.[53] However, even here, Solomon only prays to God that a particular angel might be sent, rather than directly invoking the assistance of the angel himself.[54] The text does however contain a list of formulaic sayings such as the demon

Raux admitting that, 'should I hear only, "Michael, imprison Raux," I retreat immediately'.[55] Although the author probably intended these to be the divine fiat uttered in answer to prayers such as Solomon's for angelic assistance, it is conceivable that some readers would have interpreted the text as legitimating the use of such formulaic sayings to invoke angelic assistance. This appears to have been the view of Josephus, who regarded incantations to relieve illness and demonisation as relatively commonplace, and attributed their discovery to Solomon. Josephus' comments appear to imply that such things were regarded as the gift of God.[56] Further evidence of this is provided by Luke's account of Jewish exorcists looking for a new name to invoke in order to drive out evil spirits. Luke's description of these exorcists as sons of a Jewish chief priest points to their mode of exorcism being accorded at least a degree of legitimacy in a society that strongly emphasised patrilineal authority.[57]

However, we should note that the type of invocation, which would have been acceptable to the widest range of Jews, and therefore the background against which the early church contextualised its christology, is that contained in the *Prayer of Jacob*. This invokes YHWH alone, stating that he is the one who is superior to all heavenly beings, angels or other spiritual powers,[58] a description which bears marked similarities to the contextualisations of christology found for example in Col.1:15-20.

A further issue relates to whether prophets and patriarchs were the object of Jewish veneration. The question arises because a number of second temple texts portray OT patriarchs such as Abraham and Enoch as having ascended through the various heavens to the throne of God, and as such able to dispense heavenly wisdom to men, including knowledge of the future.[59] Interestingly, Islamic *Ahadith* accounts of Muhammad's ascent *(mi'raj)* to the highest heaven closely parallel these Jewish ascent traditions.

Had such a 'cult of saints' existed, one might expect prayer to exalted patriarchs to have been centred on the tombs of such figures, as is the case with prayer offered to Islamic saints.[60] The Gospel comments on the Pharisees building the tombs of the prophets[61] may suggest that such places were indeed a focus of religious attention in the second temple era. However, the accepted belief that the two exalted patriarchs most prominent in the pseudepigrapha, Enoch and Moses, had no known tombs, probably weighs against the writers of books pseudonymously ascribed to these patriarchs, themselves intending to promote a cult of saint devotion.

It is clear however that by the first century CE, there was widespread speculation about patriarchal ascents to heaven. Evidence of this can be seen in the contextual allusion to such traditions in the NT, such as the fourth Gospel's account of Jesus' statement to Nicodemus that 'no-one' has ever gone into heaven, 'except' the Son of Man who came from heaven,[62] and the real possibility that Peter's day of Pentecost speech is modelled on the format of ascent traditions, but announces that it is Jesus rather than an OT patriarch who has ascended to the right hand of God in heaven.[63]

In the Islamic context, veneration of departed prophets and saints is frequently linked to the hope of intercession by such beings on the day of judgement or, indeed, in daily life in this world. However, whilst in the OT the living prophet's commission included interceding for the ungodly, this was at most to delay God's immediate temporal judgement to allow time for repentance.[64] Unlike the Qur'an, the OT contains no suggestion that God might give permission for any departed prophet to intercede for other human beings. Interestingly, the strand of Jewish tradition represented by *4 Ezra* specifically repudiates any idea of intercession on the day of judgement, stating that the intercession of prophets and patriarchs such as Moses, Samuel, Solomon and Elijah was simply the strong praying for the weak in this age.[65] However, the very repudiation of this in *4 Ezra* raises the question of whether some Jews did believe that prophets or patriarchs might so intercede for them.

Theophany: Can God be Seen?[66]

The Invisible God

Throughout most of the OT it is taken as axiomatic that no-one may see the face of YHWH and live,[67] a theology based on the statement of YHWH to Moses that

> You cannot see my face, for no-one may see me and live (Ex.33:20).

However, it is important to note that the import of Ex 33:20 is not that YHWH cannot be seen by mortal man, but that mortal man could not survive looking at God as he is; i.e. in his כָּבוֹד.[68] As such it affirms the immense gulf between YHWH as seen in all his glory, and even his most humble prophet. The theophany Moses actually sees is quite specifically not a sight of God's glory and beauty, but rather a description of God's goodness.[69]

Divine Self-Revelation in Visible Form

Although YHWH's transcendence means that he is hidden from man's sight, the OT affirms that he chooses to reveal certain aspects of himself.[70] This self-revelation of YHWH occurs in a variety of forms including his actions in history, through his Spirit who comes upon his prophets and through his word.[71] However, it also occurred in various visible forms such as the glory, later termed the *shekinah*, which appeared in the tabernacle and temple,[72] and in forms which, as we shall see below, may broadly be described as anthropomorphic in one way or another.

The Genesis narrative depicts Adam and Eve in the pre-fall era enjoying close communion with God, who in an apparently anthropomorphic form at certain times 'walked' (הלך) with them in the garden (3:8). This text is important as it suggests that the later fear of looking at God, and expulsion from his presence in the garden, was a direct result of man's sin (3:8-10, 23-24). The use of this motif of divine anthropomorphism at the start of Genesis, may form something of a hermeneutical key for understanding later theophanies.

Subsequent to its description of the expulsion from God's presence, the pentateuch contains a number of narratives that appear to relate YHWH taking the initiative and in an apparently anthropomorphic form visibly appearing to a few specially chosen individuals. Genesis 28 records a dream in which Jacob saw a ladder reaching to heaven, above which stood a figure who identified himself with the words 'I am YHWH, the God of your father Abraham and the God of Isaac',[73] a divine self-identification that is taken literally by both Jacob and the Genesis redactor.[74] The dream is important as it clearly indicates that God could be seen in a visible, even heavenly form, although it makes no suggestion that Jacob saw God in his full glory. Similar theophanic visions occur in texts relating later Israelite history including YHWH's reaffirmation of the davidic covenant to Solomon.[75] However, an intriguing development in later Israelite history is the emergence of visions of God on his heavenly throne.

According to the OT, the implied anthropomorphism of YHWH sitting on a throne dates back at least to the exodus,[76] although it records no such theophanic vision being seen until the time of Jehoshaphat (825BCE).[77] Even though the OT describes both this and the vision seen by Isaiah[78] as being visions of YHWH himself in heaven, it refrains from giving any physical description of God. However, the later books of Daniel and Ezekiel do not show this degree of constraint, and give cautious descriptions of the enthroned God.[79] The descriptions of both visions carefully distinguish God from all his creatures. The seers emphasise that they only saw 'a likeness' of God,[80] and only portray YHWH as seated on his throne. These visions, especially Ezekiel's, came to be of immense importance in later Judaism. However, for our purposes here we may simply note that they depict a seemingly anthropomorphic vision of God in heaven, yet at the same time set God apart from all else.[81]

This concept that God can reveal a local form of his presence at least in a vision, occurs across a wide range of second temple texts, including the LXX, targums and a range of pseudepigrapha literature. The Qumran *Genesis Apocryphon* even uses a *gezerah shawah* parallel[82] to go beyond the Hebrew text of Gen.13:14-16 and suggests that Abraham actually saw a vision of God when he was promised that his descendants would inherit the whole Jordan valley.[83] In fact, it is only Philo who really raises the question of whether God can be seen. Moreover, it is by no means certain that his insistence that anthropomorphic language in the OT should be taken figuratively reflects Jewish belief, as the pagan Hellenistic audience he is addressing believed that it was impossible for God to have anything to do with the world.[84]

Although the LXX does not make any significant alteration to the description of these theophanic visions, significant developments do occur in other texts.

Firstly, the manner in which the targums narrate theophanic visions tends to place God himself one stage removed from the actual vision of the seer, by speaking of 'the glory of the Lord', or 'the glory of the Shekinah of the Lord', being on the throne.[85] The *Targum of Ezekiel* in fact, takes great pains to clarify that Ezekiel did not see the full glory of God, stating that the enthroned figure who was of 'the likeness of the appearance of Adam' had 'an appearance of glory which the eye is unable to see, such that it is impossible to look at it'.[86] Although caution is needed in using these targums, due to the probability of their final form reflecting a relatively later date, the possibility must be considered that these trends may have begun to emerge during the second temple era.

Secondly, various pseudepigrapha texts give a high degree of prominence to heavenly visions that are often described using imagery drawn from Ezekiel's chariot throne vision. Apocalypses typically describe an ascent through the heavens to reach the dwelling of God himself,[87] and may even begin to describe God's garments, although the seer refrains from describing God's face and generally remains at a distance from God himself.[88] As with the Biblical theophanies, the climax of the vision remains the immediate environs of God himself. However, a number of developments are evident. Firstly, heaven is divided into between two and seven compartments, which results in a much more wide-ranging description of heaven than just theophany. Secondly, rather than receiving a direct vision of God, it is necessary for the seer to ascend, normally with the help of an angelic guide, through these various heavens. Both of these are developments that heighten the distance between God and mortal man.[89] Thirdly, within the lower heavens, other figures such as Abel may be portrayed as seated on heavenly thrones.[90] However, this does not imply that such figures were seen as taking on the functions of God, or in any other way blurring the distinction between God and all else.[91] Significantly, all of these developments are paralleled in *Ahadith* accounts of Muhammad's *mi'raj* to the seventh heaven.

Although most apocalypses do contain one or more of these developments, it appears probable that not all second temple Jews accepted such speculations. A more restrained trend is represented by *4 Ezra* and *2 Baruch*, in which the seers do not experience any theophanic vision. *4 Ezra* in fact specifically describes God's throne and glory as being presently beyond measure and comprehension,[92] even though it refers to God's eschatological appearance on his throne to men.[93] Both books appear to reject the claims made by other texts of heavenly knowledge gained as a result of ascent journeys.[94] Other texts appear to exclude all references to the anthropomorphic figure seen in Ezekiel's chariot vision,[95] and in 3 Baruch, the seer does not even see God, but remains in a lower heaven while Michael alone enters God's presence.[96]

However, although this restrained trend may have emerged in the second temple era, the provenance of these texts in the late first century and later necessitates caution, particularly in view of possible reaction against Christian claims of Jesus' ascent to God's right hand. Should however this 'restrained' trend have emerged in the second temple era, it would suggest that a debate existed in Judaism as to whether mortals could see God, that at least partially parallels a debate in the Islamic context concerning whether any mortal other than Moses could actually see God before the day of judgement.

Epiphany: Can God Appear on Earth? [97]

Overview

We earlier noted the depiction in the Genesis narrative of God in an apparently anthropomorphic form walking (הלך), with Adam and Eve in pre-fall Eden. The text is particularly important as at the very start of the pentateuch it implies that God could locally manifest his presence on earth in an apparently anthropomorphic form. As such it is a hermeneutical key for understanding later texts that appear to depict epiphanies.

The Genesis narratives relate at least five such appearances and imply a sixth.[98] In two of these, the figure appearing explicitly identifies himself as God Almighty אֵל שַׁדַּי.[99]

At the end of his life Jacob provides an interesting insight when he refers to this local manifestation of God's presence as:

> The God before whom my fathers Abraham and Isaac walked,
>
> The God who as been my shepherd all my life to this day,
>
> The Angel who has delivered (הַמַּלְאָךְ הַגֹּאֵל) me from all harm.[100]

Whatever the origins of the word (מַלְאָךְ), it is clear from the close parallels with Gen.28 that Jacob has in mind the heavenly figure who revealed himself as the God of his fathers Abraham and Isaac and promised to watch over him.

Theophanic revelation reaches something of a climax in the Exodus narratives. This includes the revelation of the name *YHWH* to Moses (Ex.3:1ff) and the salvific character associated with that name;[101] God coming down in terrifying theophanic glory on Sinai at the giving of the law (Ex.19:3ff), announcing that he will send ahead of the Israelites a *malak* in whom his own name dwells (Ex.23:20ff); God coming down to give out the Spirit (Num.11:25); and the direction of the ensuing conquest by a figure identifying himself as the 'commander of the army of YHWH' (שַׂר־צְבָא־יְהוָה)[102] who strikingly parallels YHWH's first appearance to Moses, and is redactionally identified as YHWH.[103] The exodus theophanies are particularly important as the whole exodus event became a paradigm of YHWH's salvific deliverance for later generations, as we earlier observed in relation to Isa.40-55.

The Malak YHWH (מַלְאַךְ יהוה).

In the pentateuch such appearances are usually, though not exclusively, redactionally termed the *malak YHWH* (מַלְאַךְ יְהוָה). Although this is normally translated into English as 'the Angel of the Lord', care must be taken to avoid imposing later NT conceptions of angels as created beings, onto earlier texts. Our concern in this chapter is rather with how second temple Jews understood these texts.

The Hebrew root מַלְאַךְ indicates the bearer of a message and thus suggests that in some way his function is revelation. We have no basis on which to press the meaning beyond this.

Modern scholarship has generally seen the *malak YHWH* as either a) a visible manifestation of God himself;[104] b) a later interpolation to soften earlier textual traditions that depicted God anthropomorphically appearing on earth;[105] or c) merely a representative speaking and functioning on behalf of God.[106] The latter view stands or falls on the assumption that divine ontology and function can be distinguished in the OT. Strangely, this premise is invariably assumed without discussion, although the OT evidence is, as we have already demonstrated, strongly to the contrary. The latter two views also rely on the Graf-Wellhausen hypothesis to remove a number of explicit divine self-identifications by the *malak YHWH* including the revelation of the divine name 'YHWH'. However, as there is little evidence that second temple Jews understood OT epiphany texts in the terms suggested by the documentary hypothesis, it is the final form of the OT text that we must deal with.

Although Jacob appears to have referred to epiphanies as the *malak* who has delivered him from all harm, it is only in the post exodus narratives that Israelites are portrayed as referring to epiphanies as the *malak YHWH*.[107] The redactional dubbing of this designation into the narrational comment, but not into the actors' speech, in earlier pentateuchal narratives,[108] suggests that reflection on the Sinai and Exodus epiphanies was central to the emergence of this whole area of theology,[109] the *malak YHWH* being seen as YHWH himself coming to earth to act as saviour and judge,[110] and occasionally as the source of prophetic commissioning and inspiration.[111]

This understanding that YHWH could visibly appear on earth when he acted as saviour is maintained and even emphasised in a range of second temple texts, including pseudepigrapha.[112] Even Philo speaks of 'God the saviour of all men' speaking to Moses from out of the burning bush.[113] The LXX translators appear to have assumed that where YHWH visibly appeared on earth, it must have been as the *malak YHWH*. Illustrative of this is the LXX rendering of 'YHWH met Moses' (Ex.4:24) as the ἄγγελος κυρίου met him.

Some second temple texts actually add a 'no other agent' formula to emphasise that epiphanies were YHWH himself, for example Isaiah 63:8-9's narration of the exodus events when God 'became their saviour....and the angel of his presence (מַלְאַךְ פָּנָיו) saved them' is rendered by the LXX as 'not an ambassador, nor a messenger (ἄγγελος), but he himself saved them'. Similarly, the *Targum of the Minor Prophets* not only retains Hosea 12:4-6's interpretation of the man wrestling with Jacob as the *malak,* YHWH the God of hosts, but actually inserts an additional clause identifying this figure both as the God of Abraham, Isaac and Jacob and as the tetragrammaton revealed to Moses at the burning bush.

This widespread acceptance of the concept of epiphany appears to have led to considerable speculation about the name of the *malak* accompanying the exodus in whom the divine name dwelt. For example a number of texts such as the *Apocalypse of Abraham* refer to *Yahoel* (a combination of *Yahweh* and *El*),[114] who is empowered by God's ineffable name in him, and is explicitly identified as the creator, the eternal One, the uncreated God.[115]

The 'commander of YHWH's hosts', (Heb. שַׂר־צְבָא־יְה וָה/LXX ἀρχιστράτηγος) encountered by Joshua was similarly either termed Sariel (Heb. 'commander of God) or identified as *Michael*. [116] The former interpretation is followed by the *Targum Neofiti*, which names the theophanic figure wrestling with Jacob (Genesis 32:22ff) as *Sariel*. At Qumran the same figure appears to have been identified as Michael, who was also known as Melichizedek (Heb. 'king of righteousness'). The Qumran texts depict him as the heavenly deliverer, call him *Elohim* and apply to him Ps.82:1 and 7:7-8's descriptions of God judging people and gods, the former being an explicitly YHWH text. They also report him as claiming that he rules over 'all things', a description that elsewhere forms part of the Qumran monotheistic rhetoric.[117] The war scroll not only claims he has a heavenly kingdom[118] but, despite its fragmentary state, clearly depicts him describing himself in language strikingly reminiscent of the monotheistic polemic of Isa.40-55:

> My glory is incomparable, and apart from me none is exalted. None shall come to me for I dwell in...in heaven, and there is no...

> ...Whom do I count as despicable, and who is comparable to me in my glory?

Who is...like me? Is there a companion who resembles me....no instruction resembles (my instruction)...Who shall summon me to be destroyed by my judgement?[119]

However, the lack of unanimity concerning the name of the epiphanic *malak* resulted in a confusing situation with some pseudepigrapha texts referring to, for example Michael, as the ἀρχιστράτηγός whilst others portray him as a created angel.[120] Similarly, even the designation ὁ ἄγγελος κυρίου could refer to either an epiphany or a created angel.[121]

Although belief in epiphany appears to have been extremely widespread, Luke's description of Sadducean belief raises just the possibility that they at least might have rejected this concept. After informing his readers that 'the Sadducees say that there is no resurrection', Luke goes on to state:

μήτε ἄγγελον μήτε πνεῦμα, Φαρισαῖοι δὲ ὁμολογοῦσιν τὰ ἀμφότερα.[122]

Whilst most scholars have taken this as a general disbelief in angels and spirits (plural),[123] this view is problematic as both ἄγγελος and πνεῦμα are singular nouns.[124] Moreover, as C.K. Barrett observes, it is hard to see how Jews who believed in the law of Moses, as Josephus tells us the Sadducees did,[125] could reject the existence of angels.[126] A grammatically less problematic reading would be to accept both as singular nouns, in which case they would most likely refer to the angel of the Lord (ἄγγελος κυρίου)[127] and the Holy Spirit, denying that either was a manifestation of the presence of God. Although the evidence does not allow us to be certain about this, it clearly does raise this possibility. If this is the case it may provide a partial parallel to Islamic belief that it was a created angel (Gabriel), rather than God himself who accompanied the Exodus. However, Josephus' comment that the Sadducees were a tiny minority, who when holding public office concealed their beliefs to avoid the antagonism of the masses,[128] indicates that their views were neither widespread, nor popular.

God Coming to Earth Eschatologically

The OT also speaks of YHWH himself eschatologically and visibly coming to earth. Isaiah 35:2-4 states:

...they will see the glory (כָּבוֹד) of YHWH, the splendour of our God....

...say to those with fearful hearts...Your God will come,

He will come with vengeance, with divine retribution

He will come to save you.[129]

Isaiah goes on to describe the results of this divine visitation as:

> Then the eyes the blind will be opened
>
> and the ears of the deaf unstopped.
>
> Then will the lame leap like a deer,
>
> And the mute tongue shout for joy.[130]

a prophecy that Matthew and Luke record Jesus claimed to have been fulfilled in his own ministry.[131]

A further accompaniment in some prophetic texts is the 'no other agent' formula - the suggestion that it is YHWH alone who will enact salvation; e.g.

> YHWH looked and....was appalled that there was no-one to intervene,
>
> so his own arm worked salvation for him, and his own righteousness sustained him...
>
> ...The redeemer will come to Zion, to those in Jacob who repent of their sins,'
> (Isa.59:15-20).[132]

Significantly the redeemer (גאל) of 59:20 has already been repeatedly and exclusively identified as YHWH in Isa.40-55,[133] an identification that continues in these latter chapters of Isaiah.[134]

Interestingly, Zechariah uses anthropomorphic language to describe this eschatological epiphany, speaking of YHWH's feet standing on the Mount of Olives, a feature that was maintained in the Septuagint.[135]

The juxtaposition of this hope of YHWH himself coming to enact salvation with prophecy relating to the universal judgement of the 'Day of YHWH'[136] may imply that YHWH's anticipated end time epiphany will in some way be a reversal of the effects of the fall, when men's sin resulted in their loss of access to the immediate presence of God which they had enjoyed in the garden.

This belief that YHWH would eschatologically come to earth is reflected in a wide range of second temple texts, including pseudepigrapha and Qumran texts.[137] Illustrative of this is the opening section of 1 Enoch:

> The God of the universe, the Holy Great One, will come forth from his dwelling. And from there he will march upon Mt Sinai and appear in his camp emerging from heaven with a mighty power. (1:3)

However, although second temple Jews clearly believed that God would eschatologically come to earth, it was widely expected that this would be the day of YHWH when God enacted judgement on Israel's enemies and salvation for his people. There is no evidence that Jews anticipated that God would appear twice, first as saviour and then as judge.[138]

The Spirit and Shekinah

The OT also portrays two other ways in which God locally manifested his presence on earth. Firstly, by the Spirit[139] who at the very start of the pentateuch is portrayed as hovering over the waters of the unformed earth,[140] and whose coming down upon the prophets is depicted throughout the OT as the means of prophetic inspiration and empowerment.[141] Secondly, by a dazzling display of His glory (כָּבוֹד) which Second temple Jews later termed the *Shekinah*. When YHWH went ahead of the departing Israelites, and when he came down at Sinai, he did so in a cloud from which his glory emanated.[142] However, the cloud itself was not the theophany, but only screened its full majesty from view.[143]

Specific Antecedents of Christological Monotheism
A Divine Messiah?

Throughout the LXX a number of pericopes are interpreted in the light of other OT passages with similar lexical items, an exegetical technique later termed *gezerah shawah* by the rabbis. A number of prophecies relating to future epiphanies appear to be interpreted in the light of *malak YHWH* narratives. Particularly significant is the messianic prophecy of Isa.9:6[5]

> his name shall be called Wonderful (פֶּלֶא יוֹעֵץ) Counsellor, Mighty God, Everlasting Father...

which the LXX interprets as

> his name shall be called the angel of great counsel (μεγάλης βουλῆς ἄγγελος).

This appears to result from a *gezerah* comparison of this text with the narrative of the *malak YHWH's* appearance to Manoah, based on the occurrence of פֶּלֶא ('wonderful') in both theophanic pericopes (cf. Jdg.13:18). This interpretation would have been strengthened by the reference in Isa.9:4[3] to 'the day of Midian's defeat', which alludes to the role of the *malak YHWH* in the Judges narratives. In fact, given the strong OT tradition that one could not see God and live, it is hard to see how such an explicitly theophanic messianic prophecy as Isa.9:6[5] could have been interpreted other than with reference to the *malak YHWH* traditions.

The motif of the coming 'branch' which in Isaiah 11:1ff is depicted as a coming Davidic king, also appears to have been subject to a similar *gezera* comparison. The motif first occurs in Isa.4:2ff where the LXX translation appears to deliberately reflect Isa.9:6[5] when it replaces the Hebrew 'in that day the Branch of YHWH shall be beautiful and glorious' by 'in that day God shall shine gloriously in counsel (βουλή) on the earth'. This *gezera* linking with the *malak YHWH* narratives was probably given additional impetus by 4:5 describing this divine appearance as being similar to the pillar of cloud and fire at the exodus.

Interestingly, Philo also indicates that some Jews believed that the coming Davidic 'branch' would be God himself. He explains the LXX translation Zech 3:8/6:12's prophecy of this coming branch as 'the rising' ('Ανατολη) saying:

> …strangest of titles, surely, if you suppose that a being composed of soul and body is here described. But if you suppose that it is that Incorporeal one, who differs not a whit from the divine image, you will agree that the name 'rising' ('Ανατολή) assigned to him quite truly describes him. For that man is the eldest son, whom the Father of all raised up and elsewhere calls him His first-born.[144]

This series of interpretations is significant as it implies that at least some Jews could conceive of a divine messiah, even though most messianic expectations at the time of Jesus clearly differed significantly from this.

Incipient Bifurcation
We shall here examine three OT themes - the portrayal of personified divine attributes, the Spirit and the *malak YHWH* - to assess whether these were understood in the second temple era to represent any degree of incipient bifurcation in the godhead.

Divine Attributes and Anthropomorphism
Much significance has been attached by some NT scholars to the role of personified divine attributes such as Word and Wisdom, as precedents for early christological development.[145] However, personification is a very widespread and longstanding ANE literary device and does not in itself imply any degree of incipient bifurcation or hypostasisation within God.[146] There are however

certain developments in the way that various Jewish texts speak about, for example, God's Word that may be more significant.

In the *Wisdom of Solomon* Wisdom is portrayed as a pure effluence from the glory of the Almighty and sitting beside God's throne, while *Ben Sirach* describes her as enduring eternally.[147] However, as Wisdom in both the OT and later Jewish writings primarily refers to God's wisdom, which is expressed through Torah, it is improbable that there is any hint of bifurcation involved in these texts. As Hurtado observes, the primary meaning of such statements is governed by the books' fundamental religious commitment to the Jewish faith.[148]

Word is similarly portrayed in personified terms, the clearest being the *Wisdom of Solomon's* statement that 'your all powerful Word leapt from your royal throne in heaven into the midst of that doomed land like a relentless warrior' (18:15). However, both the context and the content of this verse, the killing of the Egyptian firstborn (18:5-19), indicates that the Word who leapt from the throne is simply a reference to the OT depiction of God himself coming down to enact this judgement. This is, however, significant as later targums similarly refer to theophanies as the *Memra* of God, which appears to be an Aramaic equivalent of the 'Word' of God.

The targums use the terms the *Memra* (ממרה) *of YHWH* and sometimes the *Shekinah*[149] to refer to various OT appearances of God to mortals. Although some scholars have suggested that the *Memra* may refer to Jewish belief in a semi-divine being,[150] this is improbable as the targums emphasise the uniqueness of God. It is most likely a way of dealing with the tension between OT statements of the impossibility of seeing God and the existence of OT theophanies and epiphanies. This can be clearly seen in the interpretation given of Jacob's blessing by *Targum Onqelos*, the earliest extant targum:

> The Lord before whom my fathers Abraham and Isaac worshipped, *the Word of God (Memra) who has sustained me,* the *malak* who has redeemed me from all evil (Gen.48:15-16).

This 'Memra' trend is most marked in later targums, and may have been influenced by rabbinical reaction against Christianity. However, its occurrence in both targums *Onqelos* and *Neofiti* may possibly suggest that this hermeneutic began as early as the second temple era.

This concept potentially forms a very important precedent to the fourth Gospel's identification of Jesus as the eternally existing divine 'Word' who is the means by which the invisible God created the world.[151]

The Spirit of God

In the OT the Spirit is depicted as the way in which YHWH relates to his people, and mediates his immediate presence to them. Although the Spirit is consistently portrayed as God himself, the totality of God is clearly more than the Spirit, an understanding that remained essentially unchanged in second temple Judaism.[152]

The *Malak YHWH*

It is clear from our earlier discussion of the *malak YHWH* that most second temple Jews clearly understood that God could locally manifest his presence on earth in seemingly anthropomorphic form when he enacted salvation and judgement.

Although the exact relation between YHWH and the *malak* is not precisely defined in the OT, the *malak* is both clearly identified as YHWH and functions as YHWH's chief agent in dealing with men. However, the totality of YHWH is clearly depicted as somewhat more than this visible manifestation of his form.[153] The incipient bifurcation implied by this is intriguingly inferred when YHWH himself descends to Sinai in glory to announce that he will send the malak in whom his name dwells ahead of the Israelites.[154] However, the description of Moses and the seventy elders then seeing the God of Israel and the pavement of sapphire 'under his feet'[155] goes beyond previous epiphanies by implicitly raising the question of whether YHWH could concurrently assume more than one anthropomorphic form. The LXX deals with this conundrum by removing the reference to YHWH's feet, while *Targum Onqelos* changes God's command to listen to the *malak* from the Hebrew text 'because my name is in him', to the rather more ambiguous '...because his *Memra* is in my name'.[156] The change is significant as elsewhere both targums *Onqelos* and *Neofiti* repeatedly translate *malak YHWH* narratives as actual epiphanies. However, it appears the sticking point for both the LXX and targum writers was not that YHWH could appear on earth in seemingly anthropomorphic form, but rather the possible implication of bi-theism suggested by YHWH being depicted as adopting two such anthropomorphic forms concurrently.[157]

However, one text that does depict an apparently divine figure alongside God is 1 Enoch, where the figure variously termed *the Elect One, the Son of Man* and *the Righteous One* and *the First Word*,[158] is placed on the divine throne by the Lord of Spirits, where he judges both men and heavenly beings[159] and is worshipped by earthly kings as the one who rules over everything.[160] The ascription of these exclusively divine roles and worship to him implies a degree of incipient bifurcation that the LXX and targum traditions appear reluctant to countenance.

Self-Humbling and Suffering of God?

The idea of God humbling himself to the point of even appearing as an actual human being was without precedent in the second temple period. The most that can be said is that there was nothing in the Jewish scriptures that specifically repudiated such a possibility.[161] Moreover, although the OT does imply that God suffers emotionally from the waywardness of people he loves,[162] there is no indication that any Jews considered the possibility that God himself might physically suffer.

The sufferings and even violent death of God's prophets is a significant theme in both the OT and other second temple literature. However, even these were not generally seen as redemptive and Ps.49:7-9 specifically states that it is impossible for any man to pay another's debt to God.

Isaiah did speak of God as dwelling with the humble and contrite in heart,[163] although even in Isaiah the dominant image of God is that of 'the Most High', who is above all else. The closest hint the OT gives of God humbling himself to suffer is Zechariah 9-13. This speaks of YHWH himself appearing to fight for his people (9:14ff) and save Jerusalem (12:7ff), but concludes ironically by stating the inhabitants of Jerusalem will 'look on me, the one they have pierced, and mourn for him as one mourns for an only child' (12:10) - which will result in a removal of impurity from the land (13:2). However, the LXX rephrasing of this verse to read 'they will look on me because they have mocked me', illustrates the great difficulty that most Jews had with even beginning to comprehend the idea that God might suffer.

Conclusions

We have therefore seen that, in the second temple era, Jews believed there to be an absolute boundary between God and all else, and primarily thought of God in terms of his identity which was revealed as he related to his creation; i.e. as the sole creator, ruler and judge of all things and the only saviour of his people and therefore alone worthy to be worshipped. This has significant, though not exact, similarities with the way in which God's identity is primarily conceived of in the Islamic context. This degree of similarity suggests that it may be possible to utilise the early church's contextualisation of christology in the Jewish context as a basic framework for contextualisation in the Islamic context.

In the Jewish context, it was also widely held that God could locally manifest a form of his presence that was sufficiently veiled, so as to be seen by mortals, and that in times past he had even done so on earth, and was expected to do so again eschatologically. We have also seen that there were specific antecedents of christological monotheism such as the *Memra* concept and, possibly, even an acceptance by some Jews of the possibility of a divine messiah, although popular messianic expectation was clearly otherwise.

However, Jews tended to shy away from any suggestion of bifurcation within the godhead. The concept of God humbling himself to become an actual contemporary man and suffer an ignominious death for his people's sins was also clearly beyond the comprehension of most if not all Jews in the pre-Christian era.

We shall later examine Islamic beliefs in these areas in order to determine what adjustments need to be made to the early church's articulation of christology in order to take account of the differences between Jewish and Islamic monotheism.

Endnotes

[1] From the Hymn *Holy, Holy, Holy! Lord God Almighty* by Reginald Heber. Source Hymns *Ancient and Modern* [London:Clowes,1916].

[2] e.g. Neh.9:6ff; Isa.40:18-28; 44:6-8; 45:5-22.

[3] e.g. Ex.4:16f (LXX; Tg. Onqelos; Tg. Neofiti); Zech.12:8 (LXX; Tg. Minor Prophets).

[4] e.g. Tg. Onqelos Gen.11:4; 28:12.

[5] e.g. 1 En.9:5; 84:2-3; 2 En.(A & J)66:4; Sir.43:33; Wis.12:13; T.Mos.4:2-4; Add.Est.13:9; 2 Macc.1:24; 3 Macc.2:3; Jub.12:19; 31:29; 45:5; Apoc.Abr.7:10; Jos.Asen.12:1; Sib.Or.3:20; T.Abr.(A) 20:3; 20:12; T.Job.2:4; Pr.Man.:2-4; 4Q510:1-5.

[6] e.g. 1QH Hymn 16:27,33; 1QH Hymn 19:1ff; 1QH Hymn 23:10; 4Q417 Fr 1:17; 4Q381 Fr 76-77:13.

[7] Ps.22:3; Prov.9:10; Isa.40:25; 41:4; 44:6; 1QapGen 2:13, 6:4, 7:5, 12:17; 4Q163:1. Angels are referred to as 'holy ones' (plural) but the singular with a definite article is reserved for God.

[8] Based on Deut.6:4-9; 11:13-21 and Num.15:37-41. The extant evidence of the stipulation for twice daily recitation is rabbinical. However, m.Ber.1:1-4 traces debates concerning how late the evening *shema* could be recited back to Rabbi Gamaliel.

[9] e.g. Isa.40:10,15-28; 41:4; 42:5; 43:1,10ff.

[10] e.g. Isa.40:15-16,23-24; 41:1,11.

[11] e.g. Isa. 41:8-14,17; 43:3,11,15; 45:21.

[12] e.g. Isa.40:22-24; 41:1,4; 45:20-24.

[13] e.g. Ps.Sol.3:5-6; 8:33; 17:3: Apoc.Abr.17:17.

[14] e.g. 1 En.9:4-5; 84:2-3; Jub.12:4; Apoc.Abr 9:1-4;10:6.

[15] e.g. 1 En 9:4-5; 84:2-3; T.Moses 4:2-4; Apoc.Abr 13:8; 17:8; 4 Ezra.13:58.

[16] e.g. Ps.Sol.2:30.

[17] LXX Esth.4:17. cf. Earlier occurrences of this 'formula' in both the Hebrew text and LXX of the Decalogue (Ex.20:1-17) and Isa.40-55.

[18] Quod Deus.:51-68; Leg. All. 3:206; Fug.:164-65.

[19] Post.:167.

[20] Post.:167.

[21] Zech.4:10 (combining 2 Chron.16:9 and Isa.11:2's depiction of the seven fold Spirit of YHWH).

[22] Agr.:50-51.

[23] Vit.Cont.:6; Decal.60-64.

[24] e.g. L. Hurtado *One God, One Lord* [Edinburgh:T&T Clark,2nd edn.1998] passim cf. esp. 17-92.

[25] Sir.24:9; Wisd.7:25-26.

[26] Wisd.7:25.

[27] So, Hurtado *One* 42-43.

[28] Sir.24:1ff,8,21 (cf. Deut.8:3), 23ff.

[29] e.g. A. Chester 'Jewish Messianic Expectation and Mediatorial figures and Pauline christology' 17-89 in M. Hengel and U. Heckel (eds.) *Paulus und das antike Judentum* [Tubingen:Mohr,1991] 58.

[30] Orphica.(E&T):8-11,25-29.

[31] cf. Exagoge:68-89.

[32] e.g. 1 En 20:1-7; 40:1-10.

³³ cf. Matt.19:28; 1 Cor.6:2-3 and our discussion of Jesus' delegation of eschatological judgement to his disciples in chapter 3 section 'The eschatological judge - who can forgive sins'.

³⁴ cf. discussion of this figure and 'the malak YHWH' later in this chapter in section 'Incipient bifurcation'.

³⁵ Ex.20:1-6.

³⁶ Deut.18:9-22.

³⁷ cf. D. Burnett *Unearthly Powers* [Eastbourne:MARC,1988] 211-221 for an anthropological discussion of 'folk religion' in relation to both OT narratives of Israelite religion and major world religions today.

³⁸ e.g. 1 Sam.28:3ff; 2 Chron. 33:15; Isa.8:19; Jer.27:9; 29:8-9.

³⁹ Vit Cont.:6; Decal 60-64.

⁴⁰ W. Horbury *Jewish Messianism and the Cult of Christ* [London:SCM,1998] 27f demonstrates the likelihood that Ps.72 was read as unfulfilled or only partly fulfilled prophecy from the Persian period onwards.

⁴¹ So, Horbury *Messianism* 68-77,127-32 who argues it formed a counterweight to the pagan-ruler cults.

⁴² LAE:12:1-16:3.

⁴³ Q7:11ff; 15:28ff; 17:61-62; 38:71-78.

⁴⁴ e.g. L.T. Stuckenbruck *Angel Veneration and Christology* [Tubingen:Mohr,1995] passim.

⁴⁵ Vit Cont.:6; Decal. 60-64.

⁴⁶ Tob.11:14.

⁴⁷ Apoc.Zeph (B).6:11-15 (citation :13).

⁴⁸ Jos.Asen.14:8 cf. 14:10.

⁴⁹ cf. Tob.6:12; 7:13.

⁵⁰ 4Q196-200.

⁵¹ Tob.6:6-8; 8:1-3 cf. 3:7-8.

⁵² cf. discussion of prophylactic attempts to ward off evil spirits in the Islamic context in chapter 5 section 'Reformist and Traditionalist beliefs'.

⁵³ T.Sol.1:1-2:1ff.

⁵⁴ T.Sol.2:7.

⁵⁵ T.Sol 18:5.

⁵⁶ Ant.8:45-49.

⁵⁷ Acts 19:13ff. Interestingly, Matt.12:27/Lk.11:19 also refers to the sons of the Pharisees (οἱ υἱοὶ ὑμῶν) practising exorcism.

⁵⁸ Pr.Jac.:1-3.

⁵⁹ e.g. T.Abr (A & B); 1 Enoch 71ff.

⁶⁰ cf. chapter 5 section 'Reformist and Traditionalist beliefs'.

⁶¹ Matt.23:29ff/Lk.11:47-48.

⁶² Jn 3:13.

⁶³ So, M.M.B.Turner 'The Spirit of Christ in Christology' 168-90 in H.H. Rowden (ed.) *Christ The Lord* [Leicester:IVP,1982].

⁶⁴ e.g. Gen.20:7; Isa.64:9.

⁶⁵ 4 Ezra 7:102-115.

⁶⁶ Here we use 'theophany' to mean any visible appearance of God to people, whether in the form of a vision or an actual appearance on earth. We use 'epiphany' solely to designate the latter. Although this distinction is not always made by Biblical scholars our engagement with Islamic theology makes it a helpful distinction.

[67] cf. also e.g. Ex.3:6; 19:21-22; Judges 6:22-23; 13:22; Isa 6:5.

[68] So, R.A. Cole *Exodus* TOTC [Leicester:IVP,1973] 225.

[69] So, J.I. Durham *Exodus* WBC [Waco:Word, 1987] 452.

[70] cf. Deut.29:29.

[71] e.g. 1 Sam.3:21.

[72] Although the term *shekinah* itself is post-biblical the concept it refers to is not cf. Lev.9:23; Num.14:10; 1Kgs 8:11; 2 Chron.7:1-3; Ps.26:8; Ezek.3:23; 8:4; 9:3 etc.

[73] Gen.28:13.

[74] Gen.28:16ff.

[75] 2 Chron.7:12ff.

[76] Ex.17:16.

[77] 1 Kgs.22:19-23 in the year of Ahab's death.

[78] Isa.6:1-13.

[79] Dan.7:9-10; Ezek.1:1-28; 10:1-22; 43:2-11.

[80] e.g. Ezek.1:26-28; 10:1ff; Dan.7:9.

[81] So, D.I. Block *The Book of Ezekiel: Chapters 1-24* [Grand Rapids:Eerdmans,1997] 106-109.

[82] Interpreting one OT passage in the light of another that has lexical similarities.

[83] 1QapGen. 21:8.

[84] *Quod Deus*:51-68.

[85] e.g. Tg. Chron.2 Chron.18:18; Tg. Isa. 6:1.

[86] Tg. Ezek.1:26-27.

[87] 2 Baruch is an exception, although C. Rowland *The Open Heaven* [London:SPCK,1982] 81-82 convincingly argues that God's presence in a higher heaven inaccessible to the seer is clearly implied.

[88] cf. 2 En.(J & A)22:1-2.

[89] So, Rowland *Heaven* 80-81.

[90] T.Abr (A).11:1-12 (Adam near the first gate of heaven); Apoc.Zeph.(A) (angels in the fifth heaven).

[91] cf. our earlier discussion of *Orphica* and the *Exagogue* in section 'Extrinisc monotheism' of this chapter.

[92] 4 Ezra 8:21.

[93] 4 Ezra 7:33-43.

[94] So, Rowland *Heaven* 53-55,87 cf. 4 Ezra 4:7-11.

[95] So, Rowland *Heaven* 86-87.

[96] 3 Bar.(Sl & Gk)13:5-15:1 cf. 17:1.

[97] Here we use 'epiphany' to mean an actual appearance on earth, in contrast to the broader category of 'theophany', which we use to refer to any visible appearance of God to people whether visionary or an actual epiphany.

[98] Gen.11:5ff; 17:1-22; 18:1-33 (18:14 also implies an unrecorded visitation the following year); 32:24[25]-30[31]; 35:9-15.

[99] Gen.17:1; 35:11.

[100] Gen.48:15-16.

[101] So, J.A. Motyer *The Revelation of the Divine Name* [London:Tyndale,1959] passim. Although Motyer's reconciliation of Ex.6:2-3 with the use of 'YHWH' by earlier pentateuchal characters has not received unanimous support, other explanations have the inherent weakness of denigrating the intelligence of the final pentateuchal redactor.

[102] Jos.5:14.

[103] Jos.5:13-6:5.

[104] The clearest arguments for identity are made by J. Niehaus *God at Sinai* [Carlisle:Paternoster,1995] passim but cf. esp. 181-332 and C. Gieschen *Angelomorphic Christology*[Leiden:Brill,1998] passim but cf. esp. 68. Rowland *Heaven* 94-95 and 'The Vision of the Risen Christ in Rev.1:13ff.: The Debt of an Early Christology to an Aspect of Jewish Angelology' *JTS* 31 (1980) 1-11 and Dunn *Christology in the Making* [London:SCM,1980,2ndedn.1989] 149-162 also affirm this position. However, Dunn oddly entirely ignores the significance for the development of NT christology of Jewish belief that God had previously appeared on earth. The identity position is also the only position consistent with the important christological work of R. Bauckham *Crucified* passim, although as yet he has only published his work in outline.

[105] So, G. Von Rad *Genesis: A Commentary* [London: SCM,1972] 193-4 ET by J.H. Marks from German. *Das erste Buch Mose, Genesis.*

[106] So, H.-J. Fabry, D.N. Freedman & B.E. Willoughby מַלְאָךְ mal'ak' in *TDOT* 8:308-325 cf. esp. 319-320.

[107] e.g. Jdg.6:22 (by Gideon).

[108] Gen.16:7-14 (appearance to Hagar); 22:11 (to Abraham and Isaac); Ex.3:2 (to Moses); Num.22:22-35 (rebuke of Balaam) significantly all relate to God acting in salvation or judgement.

[109] So, Niehaus *Sinai* passim who argues that the Sinai theophany was central to subsequent OT theology.

[110] So, J. Niehaus 'Theophany, Theology of' *NIDOTTE* 1247-50.

[111] Jdg.6:11-23; 2 Kgs.1:3-16 and possibly Jdg.2:1-5; 5:23 cf. Ex 23:20-33; 33:7-11.

[112] e.g. 3 Bar. (Sl & Gk) 3:6 (Gen.11:5-7); Jub.15:3ff (Gen.17:1ff).

[113] Fug.:161-162.

[114] Alternative spelling *Iaoel.*

[115] Apoc.Abr.10:3(cf. 9:3-4); 17:13 (cf.:8-19); cf. also Pr.Jac.:8 *(Iao)*; Lad.Jac.2:18 *(Yao, Yaova, Yaoil).*

[116] e.g. 2 En.(J)22:6; 33:10; 71:28; 3 Bar. (Gk) 11:4,6,7,8; T.Abr.(A)1:4; 2:1,3,4,6,7,10; 3:4.

[117] 11Q13; 4Q544 Fr.2 (T.Amram) cf. 4Q542:1:1-5 – T.Qahat; 4Q510:1-9 for this monotheistic rhetoric.

[118] 1QM8:5-10.

[119] 4Q491 fr.11 (extant text fragmentary).

[120] e.g. T.Abr. (A) but not (B); 2 En.(J) but not (A).

[121] The contrasting references to Raphael in Tob.12:22[Vaticanus] as ὁ ἄγγελος κυρίου, while Sinaiticus uses the more general angelic designation ἄγγελος θεοῦ suggests that this ambiguity continued even beyond the second temple era.

[122] Acts 23:8.

[123] So, e.g. F.F. *Bruce The Acts of the Apostles* [Leicester:Apollos, 3rd rev'd. (edn,1990] 466.

[124] Whilst these could conceivably be used in an abstract sense, it would be much more natural and in keeping with the style of Luke's Greek to use a plural noun to refer to a plural subject in the abstract. cf. e.g. Lk 4:36; 10:20 (πνεῦμα); Acts 7:53 (ἄγγελος).

[125] Ant.18:16.

[126] *A Critical and Exegetical Commentary on the Acts of the Apostles* ICC [Edinburgh:T&T Clark,1998] 2:1065-66.

[127] cf. LXX translation of this anarthrously.

[128] Ant.18:17 (cf.:14-16).

[129] cf. also Zech.9:14-16.

[130] Isa.35:5.

[131] Matt.11:2-6/Lk.7:20-23 cf. discussion of this in chapter 4 section 'The eschatological appearnce of God the saviour'.

[132] cf. also Isa.62:11-63:6.

[133] Isa. 43:1,14; 44:6,22,23,24; 47:4; 48:17,20; 49:7,26; 52:9; 54:5-8.

[134] e.g. Isa. 60:16; 63:16.

[135] Zech.14:3-4.

[136] e.g. Joel 2:11; Zech.14:1-7.

[137] e.g. 4Q:530; 1 En.1:3.

[138] Although Justin Martyr *(Dialogue with Trypho the Jew:52)* claimed that Gen.49:8-12 predicted TWO epiphanies, there is no evidence that it was so interpreted by second temple Jews.

[139] cf. discussion of 'The Spirit of God' in subsequent section 'Incipient bifurcation'.

[140] Gen.1:2.

[141] e.g. Num.11:16-29; 2 Sam.23:2; Neh.9:20; Zech.4:6.

[142] Ex.16:6-10; 24:15-18.

[143] Ex.13:21ff; 14:19; 19:16-22.

[144] Conf.:62-63.

[145] cf. e.g. Hurtado *One* 41-50 or Dunn *Christology* 163-250.

[146] So, K. Kitchen 'Some Egyptian Background to the Old Testament' *TynBul* 5-6 (1960) 4-18 cf. esp.5-6 and *Ancient Orient and Old Testament* [London:Tyndale,1966] 126-127.

[147] Wisd.7:25-26; 9:4; Sir.24:9.

[148] *One* 42-3.

[149] The word *shekinah* itself is post-Biblical and probably derived from reflection on the 'dwelling' of God within the tabernacle (cf. R.A. Stewart 'Shekinah' *NBD²* 1101-1102).

[150] e.g. J.S. McIvor *The Targum of Chronicles* [Edinburgh:T&T Clark,1994] 25.

[151] cf. Jn 1:1-18.

[152] So, Fatehi *Spirit's* 65-163 who provides a detailed analysis of the second temple evidence.

[153] cf. e.g. Ex.23:20-26; 2 Sam.24:16.

[154] Ex.23:20ff cf.19:30ff; 20:21ff.

[155] Ex.24:10.

[156] Tg. Onqelos Ex.23:21.

[157] cf. A. Segal *Two Powers in Heaven* [Leiden:Brill,1977] passim for a similar rabbinic reaction.

[158] 1 En. 45:3; 49:2-4; 55:4; 61:6-7.

[159] 1 En.61:6-13 cf. also 45:3; 51:3; 55:4; 69:28-29.

[160] 1En.62:1-16 cf. also worship of the Elect One in 48:5.

[161] Even Solomon's question, 'will God really dwell on earth with men?' (2 Chron.6:18) is set in the context of God's glory immediately afterwards filling the temple where Solomon was praying (7:1-3).

[162] e.g. Hos.11:8.

[163] Isa.57:15; 66:2.

CHAPTER 3

CONTEXTUALISATION OF CHRISTOLOGY IN THE NT: USING THE EXISTING CONCEPT OF MONOTHEISM

Sooner could God change into a man than a man into God.[1]

Introduction

This chapter will demonstrate that the New Testament portrays the early Jewish church as maintaining the same conceptual framework of monotheism as second temple Judaism. In this, YHWH the one God was understood in bounded extrinsic terms as the sole creator, ruler, final eschatological judge and saviour of his people. The early church maintained a significant degree of continuity with Jewish monotheism by using these extrinsic descriptions of God, divine prerogatives and exclusively divine names to directly include Jesus within the unique identity of YHWH. We will later demonstrate in chapter 5 that Islamic conceptions of monotheism have significant elements in common with the Jewish context in which NT christology was expressed. As such there is significant potential for using the NT record of the early Jewish church's contextualisation of christology as a basis for developing a contextualised christology appropriate to an Islamic context.

Whilst this study will critically engage with the contributions of NT scholarship, the issues we will primarily focus on will be those raised by the Islamic context for which we are seeking to contextualise, rather than necessarily those on which the predominantly western academy of NT scholars has focused. An analysis of the present debate in NT scholarship relating to christology is included in Appendix B. However, here we will simply observe that the main differences between the various scholarly hypotheses that have been advanced primarily derive from whether Jewish monotheism is perceived in what approximates to *bounded intrinsic* terms (the 'strict monotheist' position), *semi-unbounded intrinsic* terms ('revisionist' hypotheses) or *bounded extrinsic* terms (the identity position). As our analysis of second temple texts has clearly shown that Jews at least primarily conceived of God in bounded extrinsic terms, it is from this perspective that we will approach an analysis of how the early church contextualised its christology against the background of Jewish monotheism.

Continuity with Second Temple Jewish Monotheism

Explicit Affirmation of Monotheism:

The NT assiduously maintains the affirmations of the OT that God is one and there is only one God. Such affirmations occur across a wide spectrum of NT books, both in terms of dating and authorship.[2] This is well illustrated by Mark's account of Jesus' affirmation of the Jewish *shema* as the most fundamental commandment. Mark's inclusion of this is highly significant as it indicates continuity in the importance given to the *shema* between the teaching of Jesus and the keys beliefs of early Christianity when Mark wrote his Gospel, probably in the seventh decade of Christian era:

> 'The most important one', answered Jesus, 'is this: Hear, O Israel, the Lord our God, the Lord is one.'[3]

However, we shall subsequently argue that the early church reformulated the Jewish *shema* to articulate its belief that Jesus was included within the unique identity of the one God.

Bounded Extrinsic Monotheism:

An important way in which the NT maintains continuity with second temple Jewish monotheism is by primarily portraying God in bounded extrinsic terms. God is explicitly understood to be the creator of all things, the ruler of all things, final eschatological judge, and divine saviour of his people, as the following texts illustrate:

Sole creator:

> 'You are worthy, our Lord and God,....*for you created all things,* and by your will they were created and have their being.' (Rev.4:11).[4]

Sole ruler:

> '*God, the blessed and only Ruler,* the King of kings and Lord of lords, who alone is immortal and who lives in unapproachable light.' (1Tim.6:15-16).[5]

Sole Judge:

> '*There is only one Lawgiver and Judge,* the one who is able to save and destroy'. (James 4:12).[6]

Sole divine saviour

> *'to the only God our Saviour,* be glory, majesty, power and authority, through Jesus Christ our Lord, before all ages, now and forever more! Amen.' (Jude:25).[7]

What is most significant about these particular texts is that they appear to affirm that God *alone* has these roles. Their ascription of these roles exclusively to God appears to exclude the possibility that the early church could have understood Jesus to be carrying out similar roles on behalf of God, without himself being God in the fullest ontological sense.

In fact, the first three of these extrinsic descriptions of God serve to sharply distinguish God from all else by means of subject/object distinctions.[8]   He is: the Creator - all other beings are his creatures;[9] Lord – all others are his servants;[10] the final eschatological Judge – all others are judged.[11]

However, we will subsequently demonstrate that the NT applies these extrinsic descriptions of God to Jesus.

Expanding Existing Jewish Concepts to Include Jesus within the Unique Identity of the One God

Jewish Monotheistic Rhetoric Applied to Jesus in the NT

The Jewish monotheistic rhetoric that God is the creator, sovereign ruler and judge of 'all things', is also employed in the NT. Descriptions of God's relationship to the cosmos are often modified by the addition of either simple adverbial phrases such as 'all things' (τα πάντα),[12] or occasionally by more complex phrases such as 'the heaven and the earth and the sea and everything in them'.[13] The existence of both types across a range of NT texts including accounts of Paul's polemic to pagans,[14] suggests that the early church took over these Jewish formulaic ways of describing God. What is most striking about the NT use of this monotheistic rhetoric is that the use of τα πάντα with a cosmic reference, hitherto reserved exclusively for statements about 'God', is now used to describe Jesus as the creator of 'all things', ruler of 'all things', judge of 'all' and so forth.[15]

Applying the Jewish Concept of Monotheism to Jesus by Identifying Him as the Creator, Ruler, Judge and Saviour

The Creator

Much debate has centred around the question of whether the NT identifies Jesus as personified Wisdom, who in Proverbs 8 and later Jewish wisdom literature is described as present with God at the creation of the world.[16] However, several other texts much more explicitly appear to include Jesus within the unique identity of the Creator-God:

> You disowned the Holy and Righteous One…You killed *the author of life*.
>
> (Acts 3:14-15).

> …for us there is but one God, the Father, from whom all things came and for whom we live; and there is but one Lord, Jesus Christ, *through whom all things came* and through whom we live. (1 Cor.8:6).

> He is the image of the invisible God, the firstborn over all creation. For *by him all things were created:* things in heaven and on earth, visible and invisible, whether thrones or powers or rulers or authorities, *all things were created by him and for him.* He is before all things, and *in him all things hold together.* (Col.1:15-17).

> …in these last days he has spoken to us by his Son, whom he appointed heir of all things, and *through whom he made the universe.* The Son is the radiance of God's glory and the exact representation of his being, sustaining all things by his powerful word. (Heb.1:2-3).

> In the beginning was the Word, and the Word was with God and the Word was God….*Through him all things were made; without him nothing was made that has been made.* (John1:1-3).

> He was in the world, and *though the world was made through him,* the world did not recognise him. (John 1:10).

It is particularly significant that in several of these texts both the Father and Jesus are included together in the activity of creation. We may summarise the various activities ascribed to each as follows:

Father	**Jesus**
Intention to create and source of creation	
through whom *he* made the universe (Heb.1:2).	
from whom all things came (1 Cor.8:6).	

Actual creation
through whom all things came (1 Cor.8:6).
by him all things were created (Col.1:16).
through whom he made the universe (Heb.1:2).
Through him all things were made (Jn 1:1-3).
though the world was made *through* him (Jn 1:10).

Sustaining of creation
sustaining all things by his powerful word (Heb. 1:3).
in him all things hold together (Col.1:17).

Regeneration of creation
through whom we live (1 Cor.8:6).

Purpose of creation	Purpose of creation
for whom we live (1 Cor.8:6).	all things were created by him and *for him* (Col.1:16).

The intention to create and the source of creation are ascribed only to the Father,[17] while the actual activity of creation is ascribed only to the Son, as is the regeneration of creation.[18] Although the actual activity of creation is ascribed to Jesus, elsewhere in the NT a further distinction in the activity of creation is made by texts that speak of the Spirit giving actual life to creation.[19] However, in the texts we have examined above, the most striking evidence of Jesus being included within the unique identity of the one Creator-God is that Colossians 1:16 ascribes the purpose of creation as being for Christ. In 1 Cor.8:6 this is only ascribed specifically to the Father, while elsewhere it is ascribed in less specific terms to God. Moreover, the language used in Colossians to ascribe the purpose of creation to Christ, is almost identical to that which Paul had used only a few years earlier in a doxology written to the Romans, that includes an OT description of YHWH.[20]

Romans 11:36 (YHWH)	**Colossians 1:16 (Christ)**
δι' αὐτοῦ καὶ εἰς αὐτὸν τὰ πάντα	τὰ πάντα δι' αὐτοῦ καὶ εἰς αὐτὸν

In fact, the only difference between the two texts is that in Colossians Paul has moved τὰ πάντα from the end of the clause to the beginning, in order to emphasise that all the thrones, dominions and so forth that he has just described were created *for* Christ.[21] This parallel is particularly significant as Rom.11:33-36 is a thoroughly Jewish doxology, that possibly reflected synagogue prayers.[22] The almost word for word application to Christ of a doxology that had only a few years earlier formed part of Paul's core description of God makes it hard to see how Colossians could have been meant to convey anything other than the inclusion of Jesus within the unique identity of YHWH.[23]

The Ruler of All Things

We earlier observed that the identification of God as the ruler of all things, was one of a number of ways commonly used by second temple Jews to sharply distinguish God from all else. It is therefore significant that a number of NT texts give titles to Jesus that appear to include him within the unique identity of God, the ruler of all things. For example:

> Jesus Christ, *who is Lord of all* (Acts 10:36).

> Jesus Christ *our only Sovereign and Lord* (Jude :4).

> These are the words of the Amen, the faithful and true witness, *the ruler of God's creation* (Rev.3:14).

> 'But the Lamb will overcome them because *he is Lord of lords and King of kings.* (Rev.17:14).

> and he has this name written *KING OF KINGS AND LORD OF LORDS* (Rev.19:16).

Jude appears to claim that Jesus Christ is the *only* sovereign and Lord (ὁ μόνος δεσπότης καὶ κύριος ἡμῶν). Although grammatically the phrase could conceivably be split with ὁ μόνος δεσπότης referring to God and only κύριος to Jesus, this is improbable. The context, those who are servants of Jesus, whether Jude (:1) or the false teachers who deny their sovereign (:4), strongly suggests that the NIV is correct in understanding that it is Jesus whom Jude calls the only Sovereign.[24]

Jude's designation of Jesus as the only sovereign and Lord is particularly significant as it excludes all possibility that Jesus is being portrayed as merely acting as a vicegerent on behalf of God the ultimate sovereign.[25]

Jude's use of ὁ μόνος in relation to Jesus' sovereignty directly parallels 1 Tim.6:15 which describes the immortal God as 'the blessed and only Ruler, the King of kings and Lord of lords' (μόνος δυνάστης, ὁ βασιλεὺς τῶν βασιλευόντων καὶ κύριος τῶν κυριευόντων), a doxology that has its roots in the Hellenistic synagogue.[26] Elsewhere in the NT other parts of this monotheistic doxology such as the description 'King of kings and Lord of lords', are also directly applied to Jesus.[27] Similarly, in Phil.2:10-11 Paul applies to Jesus an OT description of YHWH's exclusive divine sovereignty drawn from one of the most stridently monotheistic parts of the OT (Isa.45:23).[28] This suggests that these NT books are applying to Jesus the most exclusive type of God language that in second temple Judaism sharply distinguished God from all else.

The writers of both the synoptic and fourth gospels trace the portrayal of Jesus as ruler of all things back to Jesus himself, recording the resurrected Jesus teaching that all authority in heaven and on earth had been given him by the Father:

> Then Jesus came to them and said, 'All authority in heaven and on earth has been given to me...' (Matt.28:18).[29]

1 Cor.15:24-27 understands the Father to have entrusted Jesus with the mission of restoring his exclusive sovereignty over all things, which has been usurped by hostile spiritual powers. Once Jesus has destroyed these powers and regained the submission of the whole creation, he will hand the government of the universe back to the Father, 'so that God may be all in all'.[30] The latter does not imply an eschatological monism in which all distinction between God and his creation is lost; rather it describes the unchallenged reign of God over all.[31] It is the final stage of the history of God's relation to his creation, which Paul summarises in Rom.11:36 as

> For from him and through him and to him are all things.

The Eschatological Judge – Who Can Forgive Sins

We earlier observed that James 4:12 describes God as the *only* judge (εἷς ἐστιν νομοθέτης καὶ κριτής), a rephrasing of Isa.33:22 that gives additional emphasis to YHWH's uniqueness.[32] James subsequently speaks of the 'Lord's (ὁ κύριος) coming' (ἡ παρουσία) as judge (ὁ κριτής), in a manner that closely resembles OT descriptions of YHWH eschatologically coming to earth (5:7-9). The use of παρουσία twice here is significant, as in the early church it quickly became a technical term for the return of Jesus, and occurs in this sense in the gospel accounts of Jesus' teaching and in the writings of both Peter and Paul.[33] This strongly suggests that in James 5:7-9 ὁ κύριος refers to Jesus,[34] who is then referred to as 'the judge' (ὁ κριτής). In the light of James' earlier affirmation that there is only one Judge, this strongly implies that James is identifying Jesus as God the only judge, who will eschatologically come to earth. This identification is consistent with a range of other NT texts, which we shall later demonstrate identify Jesus' *parousia* with the eschatological day of YHWH.

Some strands of second temple Judaism did allow for preliminary eschatological judgements by those such as Abel and the twelve tribes of Israel.[35] However, Matthew and Luke's accounts of Jesus delegation of preliminary judgements to his followers and claim that he himself would decide the final eschatological verdict[36] makes it clear that Jesus is being identified as the final eschatological judge.[37] However, this Jewish background probably accounts for the early church in evangelistic addresses to Jews preferring to speak of Jesus being able to forgive sins, as simply describing him as 'judge' might have lacked clarity. However, Jesus' exercise of the exclusively divine prerogative of forgiving sins clearly identified him as the *final* eschatological judge.[38]

The Gospel accounts of Jesus pronouncing forgiveness of sins to a paralysed man illustrates this well.[39] Jesus is accused of blasphemy precisely because he claims that he has authority to forgive sins. I.H. Marshall observes that the basis of this accusation of blasphemy was that only God could forgive sins, as only the offended person can forgive the offender.[40] This observation is particularly significant, as the notion of justice in Palestinian Judaism appears to have been a relational one that primarily focused on the satisfaction of the aggrieved party's honour, rather than, as in western jurisprudence, on the punishment of the wrongdoer because the deed is wrong in a more abstract moral sense.[41] This focus on the injury suffered by the aggrieved party means that only they can forgive, or require judicial satisfaction from the malefactor. The need to start from this cultural hermeneutic in interpreting the significance of Jesus forgiving sins probably accounts for the Pharisees' relative clarity in believing they understood Jesus' claims, compared with that of many western scholars today.[42] For the purposes of this study however, it is significant that the Islamic culture that we are seeking to develop a contextualisation for is also one that largely focuses on relational justice.[43]

An interesting issue is raised by 1 Peter which uniquely only ascribes judgement to the Father.[44] However, this is wholly consistent with the teaching of Paul who refers to 'the day when God will judge men's secrets through Jesus Christ'.[45]

The Fourth Gospel roots a similar theology in the teaching of Jesus that 'The Father judges no-one, but has entrusted all judgement to the Son'.[46]

As the exercise of final eschatological judgement is also one of the main identity markers by which God is distinguished from all else in the Islamic context, there is the potential for a contextualised christology to use this to directly identify Jesus as God.

The Only Saviour

We earlier noted the reference in Jude's doxology 'to the only God our saviour' (μόνῳ θεῷ σωτῆρι ἡμῶν), a traditional Jewish term for God, translating the OT Hebrew אֱלֹהֵי יִשְׁעֵנוּ 'the God of our salvation'.[47] In the OT, YHWH is repeatedly identified as the saviour and sometimes as the *only* saviour. Illustrative of this is the monotheistic polemic of Hosea 13:4:

> I am YHWH your God...you shall acknowledge no God but me, no Saviour except me.[48]

Men might legitimately be spoken of as 'saviours' in a secondary sense, when they had been raised up by YHWH as his agents to enact specific temporal acts of deliverance, their evident mortality clearly differentiating them from God. However, even here, the OT is extremely cautious about applying the title 'saviour' to anyone except YHWH.[49] In neither the OT, nor inter-testamental literature is any heavenly figure except YHWH designated by the title 'saviour', nor does anyone other than God enact final eschatological salvation.[50] There are not even any instances of the messiah being specifically entitled 'saviour', even though the messianic age was widely anticipated as the time when YHWH would save Israel.[51] It therefore appears that the use of the title 'saviour' was one of the ways in which second temple Jews marked the boundary between God and all else.

It is therefore highly significant that the title 'saviour' is specifically applied to Jesus in a whole range of NT books including Paul's letters to the churches, 2 Peter, 1 John, the pastoral epistles and Luke's gospel.[52] Luke in fact, states that at Jesus' birth there was an angelic annunciation that he was the saviour.[53] Moreover, Titus and 2 Peter appear to directly describe Jesus as God the saviour.[54] The latter begins:

> ...To those who through the righteousness of our God and Saviour Jesus Christ (τοῦ θεοῦ ἡμῶν καὶ σωτῆρος Ἰησοῦ Χριστοῦ) have received a faith as precious as ours.'[55]

The majority of scholars see this as a single reference to Christ as God, on the grounds that there is no second article before σωτῆρος the similarly constructed phrase τοῦ κυρίου ἡμῶν καὶ σωτῆρος Ἰησοῦ Χριστοῦ in 1:11 and 3:18 indisputably refers to Christ alone;[56] and the use of an altogether different construction in 1:2 where the author clearly wishes to distinguish Jesus from God the Father.[57]

Interestingly, the pastoral epistles apply the title 'saviour' to both 'God' (implicitly the Father) and Jesus, sometimes in consecutive verses.[58] However, this is consistent with the OT, which refers to YHWH in general terms as 'the saviour', but also describes him as having 'become' the saviour/salvation when he enacted a particular deliverance such as the exodus.[59] This is directly paralleled by NT claims that Jesus 'became' the saviour/the source of eternal salvation,[60] i.e. the Father planned salvation, Jesus enacted it.

Other Divine Prerogatives Applied to Jesus

We have already discussed the significance of the NT's ascription to Jesus of forgiveness of sins. The NT also ascribes to Jesus other roles in second temple Judaism which were widely understood to be divine prerogatives:

Sending/Pouring Out the Holy Spirit

The OT consistently depicts the Spirit as the presence of God himself, a portrayal which is also maintained in other second temple literature.[61] It would therefore be inconceivable to second temple Jews that anyone other than God could send the Spirit, or fulfil the OT promises of God eschatologically pouring out the Spirit.[62]

The NT maintains continuity with this, speaking of the Father as the one who gives the Spirit and even referring to the Spirit as 'the Spirit of the Father' (τὸ πνεῦμα τοῦ πατρὸς).[63] However, another dimension is added in Luke's account of Peter's Pentecost speech, where the words ascribed to God in Joel 2:28 'I will pour out my Spirit' (Acts 2:16-17) are claimed to have been fulfilled by Jesus pouring out the Spirit he has received from the Father (2:33).

According to Luke, the early church understood this to be a fulfilment of the prophecy of John the Baptist that Jesus would baptise with the Holy Spirit, i.e. bring about the eschatological outpouring of the divine Spirit prophesied by Joel.[64]

However, the NT not only portrays Jesus as sending the Spirit, but also depicts the Spirit bringing the presence of Jesus in the same way that in the OT the

Spirit brought the presence of God.[65] In the Fourth Gospel Jesus states that the Father will send the Spirit 'in my (i.e. Jesus') name',[66] implying that the Spirit of God will be Jesus' own emissary.[67] Both Luke and Paul appear to express a similar idea when they refer to the divine Spirit as 'the Spirit of Jesus' (τὸ πνεῦμα Ἰησοῦ).[68] 1 Peter goes even further and refers to the Holy Spirit who spoke through the OT prophets as 'the Spirit of Christ' (πνεῦμα Χριστοῦ).[69]

The NT portrayal of Jesus as the sender of the Holy Spirit, who as Jesus' emissary may legitimately be referred to not only as 'the Spirit of God' but also as 'the Spirit of Jesus', is potentially important as in the *Qur'an* the Spirit, though not depicted as divine, is portrayed as only being sent at the command of God.[70]

Delegation to His Followers of Authority Over Evil Spirits and to Perform Miracles

A further divine prerogative ascribed to Jesus is authority over evil spirits. Although at least some second temple Jews thought that actions such as burning fish liver might have prophylactic powers against demons,[71] it appears that actual authority over evil spirits was believed to be a divine prerogative. Certain Jews did attempt to exorcise demons probably by calling on various angels or powers for assistance. However, even the *Testament of Solomon* only portrays various named angels as being matched in strength against named demons. There is no suggestion that angels have authority in themselves over evil spirits, or that they could grant such authority to others.[72]

It is against this background that the NT portrays Jesus as invested with the authority simply to order demons to leave, a practice which the synoptic Gospels describe as causing popular amazement.[73] Luke's account of Jesus' own description of this authority in fact emphasises that he did not drive out demons with the aid of rings, charms and incantations as other exorcists did, but 'by the finger of God' (11:20),[74] a designation the OT uses to emphasise the uniqueness of God.[75] Moreover, the synoptic portrayal of Jesus delegating to his disciples similar authority 'to overcome all the power of the enemy' in his own name,[76] makes it clear that Jesus' authority was located in himself, rather than something delegated to him by God, i.e. Jesus' delegation of this authority is the exercise of what most Jews understood to be a divine prerogative. The significance of this aspect of christology as an indicator of Jesus' divinity strangely appears to have been overlooked by NT scholars.[77]

Similarly, although the OT records prophets performing miracles, including raising the dead, by prayer to God,[78] Jesus not only enacted such miracles, but delegated authority to enable his disciples to do so in his own name. Both Luke and Mark speak of Jesus' disciples performing miracles 'in the name of Jesus', while the Fourth Gospel narrates Jesus telling his disciples that through prayer 'in my name' they will do even greater things than he has done, which presumably included raising the dead.[79] Narration of this delegation of authority to perform such miracles may provide an appropriate response to the Qur'anic insistence that Jesus performed miracles merely 'by God's permission'.[80]

OT Names and Descriptions of God Applied to Jesus

The NT continues to use many OT names of God such as 'the Living One' and 'the Holy One'.[81] It is therefore significant that the NT applies to Jesus similar divine titles including some which Jews appear to have reserved exclusively for God:

'The Holy One'

Illustrative of this is Peter's designation of Jesus as 'the Holy One' in his evangelistic address in the temple courts, where it is combined with another OT name of God, 'the Righteous One':[82]

> You disowned the Holy and Righteous One (τὸν ἅγιον καὶ δίκαιον) and asked that a murderer be released to you. You killed the author of life (Acts 3:14-15).

Although the adjective 'holy' was applied in a derivative sense to prophets and angels, the title 'the Holy One' appears to have been used only for God himself. There is not even any evidence that this title was ever used for the expected messiah. In the OT the title 'the Holy One' (קָדוֹשׁ) occurs forty-four times, principally in Isaiah, all of which unequivocally refer to YHWH. The LXX, which translates this divine title as ὁ ἅγιος, carefully maintains this exclusiveness, reserving this title for God alone.[83] The NT usage closely parallels this, only using it as a title for God and significantly, for Jesus.

'The First and the Last' and 'the Living One'

The titles 'the First' and 'the Last' occur in the monotheistic polemic of Isa.40-55 where they are used as a means of emphasising the incomparability of YHWH with all else,[84] illustrative of which is Isa.44:6-7:

> I am the First and I am the Last, apart from me there is no God. Who then is like me?

The NT book of Revelation maintains continuity with this by narrating God similarly describing himself as 'the Alpha and the Omega', 'the Beginning and the End'.[85] However, it also applies to Jesus both these titles and the specific OT titles 'the First and the Last' in a way that unequivocally includes him within the identity of the One God.[86] For example in Rev.1:17-18 Jesus tells John:

> I am the First and the Last. I am the Living One.

It would therefore appear that this is another example of the NT applying to Jesus the titles that in the OT most emphatically distinguished YHWH from all else.

In Rev.1:18 the title 'the Living One' (ὁ ζῶν) appears to expand epexegetically the divine title 'the First and the Last', and is therefore probably based on the OT designation 'the Living God'.[87] Although this title is only applied to Jesus in Revelation, the concept is clearly expressed in the claim of Jn.5:26 that unlike creatures which are given life by God,[88] Jesus has life in himself, in the same way that the Father does.[89] In the OT, the title 'the Living God', was primarily used as part of Jewish monotheistic polemic, distinguishing YHWH, the God who had appeared and whose voice had been heard at the exodus, from other so called 'gods'.[90] The NT provides ample evidence that both the title 'the Living God' (ὁ θεός ὁ ζῶν), and variants such as 'the living Father' (ὁ ζῶν πατὴρ) were current during the second temple era.[91] In fact, Paul actually uses this divine designation as a form of monotheistic rhetoric both against idol worship at Lystra, and in a pastoral appeal to former pagans to have no connection with idols.[92] It therefore appears that this may be another example of the NT applying to Jesus a piece of monotheistic rhetoric that second temple Jews used to emphatically distinguish YHWH from all else.

The NT's application to Jesus of the divine titles 'the First', 'the Last' and 'the Living One' is potentially significant for our purposes, as in Islam, the equivalent Arabic titles (*al-Awwal, al-Akhir,* and *al-Hai*) constitute three of the 99 names of God.

'The King of Kings' and 'The King'

In Revelation, Jesus is given the unequivocal divine title 'Lord of lords and King of kings', which we earlier observed formed part of Jewish monotheistic rhetoric. Although many second temple Jews appear to have anticipated a coming messianic king, no pre-Christian texts depict the messiah as a *heavenly* king, a designation which, as in the OT, appears to have been reserved for YHWH alone.[93]

In Matthew, Jesus describes the Son of Man as a heavenly king (ὁ βασιλεύς) who will exercise the divine prerogative of final eschatological judgement.[94] Matthew also states that the kingdom of the Son of Man will become the kingdom of the Father when all hostile elements have been removed from it,[95] an expectation similarly described in 1 Cor.15:24-28 as Christ handing back the kingdom to the Father.

This salvation-historical perspective on Jesus' divine kingship probably accounts for a range of NT books referring to the kingdom of God as the kingdom of Christ,[96] whilst Revelation portrays God and Christ sharing a single throne.[97]

Significantly, both 'King of kings' and 'the King' are Islamic names of God, the former sometimes being regarded as an exclusively divine title.

'The Bridegroom'

A number of OT prophetic books portray the relationship between Israel and YHWH as the exclusive relationship between a bride and bridegroom.[98] In Isaiah this metaphor is associated with the promise of YHWH Himself acting as the saviour of his bride, which culminates in the promise of Isa. 62:5 'as a bridegroom rejoices over his bride, so your God will rejoice over you'. Although later Judaism appears to have expected that YHWH's wedding type banquet promised in Isa.25:6 would be heralded by the appearance of the messiah,[99] there is little evidence that any heavenly figure other than YHWH was ever described as 'the bridegroom' in the second temple period.[100] It is therefore highly significant that in Matthew, Jesus' responds to criticism that his disciples do not fast by implicitly referring to himself as 'the bridegroom' who is now amongst them.[101] Matthew similarly records Jesus likening the kingdom of heaven when the Son of Man appears on the clouds to the coming of a bridegroom, describing this appearance in language drawn from OT texts relating to the appearing of God on the eschatological day of YHWH.[102] Whilst in Revelation, the final dwelling together of God and man after all hostile powers have been destroyed is described as the wedding feast of Christ and his bride, using language drawn directly from Isa.25:6.[103] However, the most significant expansion of OT bridegroom imagery occurs in Ephesians, which speaks of Christ having loved the church and given up his own life as the 'bride-price' so that she might be a beautiful bride on her wedding day.[104]

This bridegroom/bride imagery is potentially significant for our study, as it has certain parallels to the Sufi hope for reunification (wasl) with God that is expressed using similar lover/beloved imagery.[105]

'The Word of God'

The title 'the Word' (ὁ λόγος) is applied to Jesus in the prologue to the Fourth Gospel and in Revelation.[106] The title is potentially significant for our study both because it is a Qur'anic title of Jesus and because the Fourth gospel uses it to explain the title 'Son of God', which replaces it after the prologue.[107]

The Fourth Gospel describes 'the Word of God' in similar terms to the way the targums used 'the Memra of YHWH' to avoid implying that OT appearances of God constituted the totality of God, or that mortals saw the full glory of God. Although this area has not always received the scholarly attention it deserves,[108] the Fourth Gospel appears to use this concept as the basis for the development of its Logos christology, stating:

> In the beginning was the Word, and the Word was with God, and the Word was God. He was with God in the beginning. Through him all things were made; without him nothing was made that has been made (John 1:1-3).

However, the prologue develops this concept in two important ways. Firstly, although in Judaism the *Memra* was understood to refer to anthropomorphic appearances of God, including epiphanies, in verse 14 the concept is significantly expanded with the claim that God had not merely appeared in man-like form, but had actually become man:

> The Word became flesh and made his dwelling among us.

Secondly, the prologue's double claim that in the beginning 'the Word was with God, and the Word was God' makes an implicit assertion that at the very beginning there was both a single identity, and yet also some distinction between God and the Word.

'Lord'

The NT portrays both Jesus himself and the early church referring to him with the title ὁ κύριος, 'Lord'.[109] This Greek title probably reflects the early church's translation of the Aramaic *mar* meaning 'Lord', which some second temple texts used as a circumlocution for the Hebrew יְהוָה.[110] The early church's translation of *mar* as ὁ κύριος may also reflect the practice in Greek-speaking synagogues of rendering יְהוָה as κύριος when reading from the LXX.

The evidence of extant second temple texts suggests that YHWH was the only heavenly figure for whom the title ὁ κύριος was used in its unqualified form. There is no evidence that the messiah was ever referred to simply as 'the

Lord' or even the anarthrous 'Lord'. Even the *Psalms of Solomon,* which once refer to the messiah as 'the Lord Messiah', in the same pericope clearly reserve the unqualified title 'the Lord' for YHWH.[111] Whilst the title ὁ κύριος was used for human masters, it may reasonably be presumed that this was because the distinction between God and man was understood to be so immense and absolute that no confusion could possibly be engendered by this use of the title.

Significantly, the way the NT uses ὁ κύριος frequently makes it extremely difficult to tell whether God the Father or Jesus is meant. For example in Acts, forty seven occurrences definitely refer to Jesus and eighteen to God, but in thirty five instances it is simply not clear which is intended.[112] This level of ambiguity can only reasonably be explained in terms of Jesus being directly included within the unique identity of YHWH, the one God.

'God'

In the NT θεός is used 1,315 times, the vast majority of which refer to God either in general terms, or more specifically to God the Father. NT scholars have however recognised between two and ten NT passages that use the title θεός for Jesus. After an exegetical analysis of all of these, Harris narrowed down this list to seven. Of these, he recognised two in which it is 'certain' that the title θεός is applied to Jesus (John 1:1 and 20:28), four in which it is 'very probable' (Rom.9:5; Tit.2:13; Heb.1:8; 2 Pet.1:1) and one that is 'probable' (John 1:18).[113]

Illustrative of the 'very probable' texts is Titus 2:13-14, which in language reminiscent of the end time epiphany of YHWH anticipated by the OT, appears to describe Jesus as God the eschatological saviour:

> while we wait for the blessed hope - the glorious appearing of our great God and Saviour, Jesus Christ, (τὴν μακαρίαν ἐλπίδα καὶ ἐπιφάνειαν τῆς δόξης τοῦ μεγάλου θεοῦ καὶ σωτῆρος ἡμῶν Ἰησοῦ Χριστοῦ), who gave himself for us to redeem us from all wickedness.

It is extremely unlikely that two distinct persons, Jesus and God are being referred to here[114] as the following clause, 'who gave himself for us to redeem us' defines Christ's salvific work; there is no second article; and neither is there any precedent elsewhere in the NT for the idea that the Father rather than Jesus would eschatologically appear, the verb ἐπιφάνεια only ever being applied to Jesus. The most natural reading of the Greek is therefore that followed by the NIV and the majority of scholars, which is given above, i.e. designating Jesus as both Saviour and God.[115]

Since at least the time of Ellicott,[116] commentators following this view have assumed that the description 'great God' (ὁ μέγας θεός), would be superfluous if applied to the Father. However, whilst this is true, the meaning here is probably slightly more nuanced than simply designating Jesus as God. The description the 'great God' (ὁ θεὸς ὁ μέγας), is in fact applied to YHWH five times in the LXX, where it is used to emphasise the distinction between YHWH and all other 'gods'.[117] It therefore appears that Titus 2:13 is applying to Jesus the most exclusive type of God language, that in the LXX sharply distinguished God from all else, thereby categorically placing Jesus on the God side of the God/non-god divide.

Although a detailed analysis of each Jesus as θεός text is beyond the scope of this study, two observations are particularly pertinent to our study. Firstly, Harris notes that when the title θεός is applied to Jesus, the immediate context refers to his role as creator or revealer (John 1:1,18), saviour (Titus 2:13; 2 Peter 1:1) or Lord over all (John 20:28; Romans 9:5; Hebrews 1:8).[118] As such, it is likely that its primary purpose is not to make a new christological claim, but to state that when God has acted as creator, saviour and ruler of all, it has been as Jesus that he has done so. Secondly, the relative scarcity of θεός as a christological title in the NT is potentially important. Although the title is applied to Jesus in a range of NT books (the Fourth Gospel, Romans, the Pastoral epistles, Hebrews and 2 Peter), it may be significant that Paul never uses θεός as a christological title in letters to the churches he has recently planted. Had Paul done so, there would have been a very real risk that Christians from a pagan background would have wrongly understood him to mean that Jesus constituted the totality of God, in the way that Greek and Roman gods were supposed to have done when they appeared on earth.[119]

In contextualising christology for an Islamic context, equal care must be taken to avoid simplistic statements such as 'Jesus is God', that are liable to be similarly misunderstood. The Qur'anic claim that God is not the messiah[120] is in its narrowest sense an affirmation that the NT writers would agree with.

The Visible Manifestation of the Invisible God

In 2 Corinthians 4:4 Paul describes Christ as 'the image of God' (εἰκὼν τοῦ θεοῦ), a designation later expanded in Colossians 1:15 as 'the image of the invisible God'. The divine invisibility motif makes it extremely improbable that man as the image of God is being referred to.[121] Philo's repeated references to the Logos as the εἰκών of God, and description of Adam as being merely an image of this image of God (εἰκὼν εἰκόνος),[122] at the very least provides a Jewish precedent for a claim that Jesus is the visible manifestation of the invisible God.

Hebrews expresses a similar concept in describing the Son as 'the radiance of God's glory and the exact representation of his being' (ἀπαύγασμα τῆς δόξης καὶ χαρακτὴρ τῆς ὑποστάσεως αὐτοῦ).[123] The absence of any Adam connotation here, combined with the explicit affirmation of Christ as the agent of creation, suggests that at least here something akin to a Logos christology is in view.

The visible/invisible motif recurs in the Fourth Gospel which twice states that no-one has ever seen God, but God the One and only who is at the Father's side has made him known,[124] and twice explicates this by saying that anyone who had seen Jesus, had seen God.[125]

The Glory of God

The NT concept of the glory of God is rooted in the OT description of the כָּבוֹד of YHWH,[126] which appeared during the exodus and was seen in visions of the heavenly throne. However, descriptions of Jesus as having glory do not in themselves identify him as God, as even in the NT other figures including angels and Moses are similarly described, although at least in the case of Moses, this is explicitly said to be a reflection of God's glory.[127]

However, the NT indicates that Jesus is himself the source of glory. Luke implies that at the transfiguration Peter and his companions saw Jesus in his own glory;[128] Paul specifically designates Jesus as 'the Lord of glory' (ὁ κύριος τῆς δόξης), and along with 1 Peter and Revelation speaks of believers sharing in Christ's glory, in a manner that parallels Moses sharing in God's glory after God had appeared to him on Sinai.[129] Hebrews explains this theologically in terms of a Logos-type Christology:

> The Son is the radiance of God's glory and the exact representation of his being.[130]

Whilst articulating a similar theology,[131] the prologue to the Fourth Gospel uses a word play to allude to the dwelling (שָׁכֵן) of God in the exodus tabernacle (Heb. מִשְׁכָּן LXX σκηνή)[132] manifested as the cloud of glory, which in later Judaism came to be known as the *shekinah*.[133]

> The Word became flesh and made his dwelling (ἐσκήνωσεν) among us. We have seen his glory, the glory of the One and Only, who came from the Father.[134]

Discontinuity with Jewish Monotheism

Relationships within the Godhead

So far we have discussed the expansion of the Jewish concept of monotheism to include Jesus within the unique identity of the one God. However, at several points, we have discussed aspects of NT christology that point towards a new and fuller revelation of God. The application to Jesus of the extrinsic framework of God's unique identity (sole creator, ruler, judge and saviour), when combined with the ascription of different roles within this framework to Jesus and the Father points towards the existence of relationships within the Godhead.

The NT describes the purpose of creation as being both for the Father, for whom we live,[135] and Jesus, for whom all things were created.[136] However, the Father is the source of creation from whom all things came,[137] while Jesus, through whom he made the universe, carried out the actual activity of creation and is its sustainer, who sustains all things by his powerful word.[138] Jesus is also the means by which all creation will be brought back into a union of harmony with the creator.[139]

Similarly, both the Father and Jesus are described as the only sovereign ruler of all things, King of kings and Lord of lords.[140] However, because elements of God's creation have rebelled against his sovereign rule, the Father has put all things under Jesus, in order that Jesus may reign as Lord over all creation, until he has put all hostile forces including death beneath his feet.[141] When the power of these forces is completely destroyed, Jesus will hand the kingdom back to the Father, and God's rule will be exercised unchallenged in all things from the throne (singular) of God and Jesus.[142]

The NT also describes both the Father and Jesus as the one final eschatological Judge.[143] However, the Father himself judges no-one but exercises judgement through Jesus, to whom he has entrusted all judgement.[144]

Similarly, both the Father and Jesus are described as God the saviour.[145] However, it was in the death and resurrection of Jesus that God became the universal saviour.[146] The NT ascribes to the Father the planning of salvation and the sending of Jesus to become the saviour.[147] Jesus is described as having become man so that he could become the saviour and be the means of reconciling them to the Father.[148]

The Father saves those who repent of their sins and believe in Jesus, making them alive with new spiritual birth,[149] while Jesus pours out the Holy Spirit on those who have experienced this new spiritual birth in order to purify and renew them.[150]

This goes significantly further than the existing Jewish concept that God could locally manifest various forms of his presence such as the Spirit and the *malak YHWH*. The OT narratives relating to these did not generally give any hint that there might be permanent relationships within the one God.[151] Indeed, the later emergence of rabbinic polemic against the two powers in heaven speculation may indicate that any suggestion of binitarianism challenged very deeply seated assumptions held by many Jews about the nature of monotheism.[152]

However, the ascription to Jesus and the Father of different roles within the divine identity of creator, ruler, judge and saviour, clearly implies more. For example, the Father sending Jesus and Jesus being sent as the saviour cannot easily be understood simply in terms of God temporarily assuming different modes. This suggestion of a distinction within the Godhead is most explicitly expressed in the statement of the Fourth Gospel that 'In the beginning was the Word' and this Word was both '*with*' God and yet also '*was*' God. However, there is also a clear implication of this theology where, for example, it is asserted that the Father has *given* all judgement to the Son; has created all things *through* Jesus, and even in the assertion of Matthew 28:18 that all authority in heaven and on earth – an exclusively divine prerogative, has been *given* to Jesus. Interestingly however, even the Fourth Gospel's articulation of this theology does not include any intrinsic description of the inner being of God, but quickly moves on to describe the 'Word' in extrinsic terms as the way that God has related to all else, in creation and revelation of Himself.

This extrinsic description of relationships within the one God is potentially of great importance in developing a contextualised christology for an Islamic culture, because it expresses the relationship between Jesus and the Father, without using the intrinsic concept of 'personhood', which in Islamic contexts has been misunderstood to imply belief in tri-theism.

Father/Son Relationship

We earlier observed that after the prologue, the Fourth Gospel replaces the 'Word of God' motif with the 'Son of God' motif. The designation 'Son of God' is therefore used to describe how the invisible God, who dwelt in unapproachable light, whom no man had seen or could see,[153] assumed a form that was sufficiently veiled for man to see.

Although precedent exists for this in Philo's description of the Logos as God's firstborn Son, the NT goes much further than even Philo in two respects.

Firstly, especially in the Gospels, the relationship between Father and Son is expressed in terms of intimate love and knowledge of each other.[154] Both Matthew and Luke narrate Jesus' description of a unique and exclusive knowledge that he and the Father have of each other:

> All things have been committed to me by my Father. No-one knows the Son except the Father, and no-one knows the Father except the Son and those to whom the Son chooses to reveal him.[155]

The intimacy of this relationship with the Father is brought out by Jesus' prayer in John 17:24 in which he speaks of having been loved by the Father before the creation of the world.

Secondly, the NT emphasis on Jesus being the Son of God results in the NT placing a new and somewhat expanded emphasis on the fatherhood of God, which is largely absent from the OT. In fact, the entire OT contains only fifteen references to God as Father, while the NT speaks of God as Father on 245 occasions, most of which are on the lips of Jesus.

Although this whole theme of what Jesus' divine sonship means is of immense significance in Islamic contexts, we will here note two specific aspects of this that have particular significance in a contextualised christology.

Firstly, this new emphasis on the fatherhood of God is accompanied by an emphasis on God's people experiencing a more intimate relationship with him, which although in no sense identical to Jesus' relationship to the Father, is patterned after it. The Fourth Gospel records Jesus assuring his disciples that the Father himself loves them and will give them whatever they ask in his name.[156] Jesus taught his disciples to address God in corporate prayer as 'our Father'. The resurrected Jesus expressed this new relationship that his followers had with God as Father when he instructed Mary Magdalene to tell his brothers (οἱ ἀδελφοί), a term Mary understands as his disciples, that he is returning to 'my Father and *your Father*, to my God and your God'.[157] Both Galatians and Romans therefore speak of believers having become 'adopted' sons of God. The believer's relationship to God is therefore no longer characterised as one of a slave to his master, but as one who has been graciously treated as a son, and may therefore address God as 'Father' and have direct access to him without fear.[158]

This contrasts sharply with the Islamic context, where the believer[159] is typically understood to be a servant of Allah. However, the desire for a more intimate relationship with Allah, based on love rather than fear, leads many Muslims to engage in various mystical practices that are often broadly described as *Sufism*. This aspect of NT teaching may therefore in many respects be said to be the fulfilment of the highest aspirations of Islamic mysticism.

Secondly, the caution evident in Jesus' own teaching concerning his divine sonship is instructive as to how this issue should be approached in the Islamic context. In the Jewish context the title could easily have been misunderstood in terms of Jewish nationalistic hopes for a political messiah. This probably accounts for Jesus' reluctance to directly call himself 'the Son of God', preferring to speak more obliquely of God as his Father and of himself as 'the Son'. It was only when the early church was able to proclaim that Jesus had been raised to the highest heaven that the title 'Son of God' could be applied to him without risk of it being misunderstood in terms of nationalistic politics. On the occasion when Jesus was directly questioned about his divine sonship, he certainly did not deny it.[160] However, his reply to the high priest is instructive. Leon Morris paraphrases it as 'That is your word, not mine. I would not put it like that, but since you have, I cannot deny it.'[161]

Jesus' example suggests that in the Islamic context, where the title 'Son of God' is equally misunderstood, it may be best to avoid the term altogether in initial communication of Christian beliefs, where possible conveying the concept in other ways. The title should of course be affirmed in response to specific questioning, but even then only in the most carefully nuanced way.

New Name of God

At the exodus, God revealed the name, YHWH, by which his people would in future know him. This name was revealed because other designations of God were inadequate to express the new revelation of God's character, which he was about to unfold as he personally acted as the saviour of his entire people, delivering them from Egypt.[162] In a similar manner, Matthew 28:19 narrates that immediately prior to Jesus' ascension, after the disciples worshipped him and he had announced that he had been given all authority in heaven and on earth, Jesus disclosed a new name of God. This name, which the disciples were to baptise into, 'the name (singular) of the Father, the Son and the Holy Spirit' (τὸ ὄνομα τοῦ πατρὸς καὶ τοῦ υἱοῦ καὶ τοῦ ἁγίου πνεύματος), expressed a facet of the unique identity of the one God which had been newly disclosed by Jesus.[163]

Conclusions

In the course of this chapter we have demonstrated that the early church sought to directly include Jesus within the unique identity of the one God. This was done by means of the bounded extrinsic framework of monotheism, by which second temple Jews understood God's unique identity as the sole creator and ruler of all things, final eschatological judge and the only saviour, and by the ascription to Jesus of divine prerogatives and exclusively divine names.

This inclusion of Jesus within the unique identity of God is held together with affirmations of monotheism by means of a theology that finds its clearest articulation in the Logos christology of the prologue to the Fourth Gospel. This understands Jesus to be the visible manifestation of the invisible God; i.e. the way that God relates to all else as creator, ruler and restorer of his usurped rule of all things, saviour and final eschatological judge. The NT claims that it was as Jesus that God created all things, rules all things and will finally judge all things, and that it is as Jesus that God acts to save those who turn to him. Although the clearest articulation of such a theology occurs in the prologue to the Fourth Gospel, we have demonstrated that something akin to this Logos christology appears to underlie many aspects of NT christology.

In fact, the NT carefully maintains and even emphasises the Jewish bounded conception of monotheism: by the subject/object distinctions inherent in the extrinsic description of God i.e. Creator/created; Ruler/ruled; Judge/judged; by the application to Jesus of aspects of Jewish monotheistic rhetoric such as the emphasis on his rule over 'all things'; and application to him of imagery drawn from some of the most polemically monotheistic sections of the OT such as Isaiah 40-55. These, especially when viewed in conjunction with the NT's repeated affirmations that there is only one God, emphatically claim that Jesus is on the God side of the absolute boundary between God and all else.

The NT does go somewhat beyond anything known in contemporary Judaism, not only by giving a new and expanded emphasis to God as Father, but by indicating that the Father/Son motif represents actual and indeed intimate relationship within the one God. However, the NT goes no further than simply inferring the existence of such relationship, concentrating instead on describing how the Father relates to his creation through the Son and the Spirit. This new revelation of the unique identity of the one God, is however, expressed in the revelation of new name of God, the name (singular) of the Father, the Son and the Holy Spirit.

Significantly, the principal ways in which Acts, the epistles and Revelation include Jesus within the unique divine identity can be traced back to, and are most credibly seen as a development of, the teaching of Jesus and the events surrounding his life, as recorded in the synoptic gospels. The synoptic Gospels narrate Jesus claiming to have been given authority to rule all things in heaven and on earth, to be the final eschatological judge, and record an angelic annunciation at his birth that he is the saviour. They also portray Jesus exercising exclusively divine prerogatives such as delegating authority over the demonic to his followers in his own name, and record John the Baptist speaking of Jesus baptising in the Holy Spirit, implying that Jesus will pour out God's own Spirit on people. Likewise, they narrate Jesus applying to himself divine titles such as the (heavenly) King, the (heavenly) Bridegroom and the (heavenly) Lord. Both Matthew and Luke record Jesus speaking of the intimate and exclusive relationship that he and the Father have with each other, and Matthew closes his Gospel with Jesus revealing a new name of God that expresses a hitherto unrealised aspect of God's unique identity, the name (singular) of the Father, the Son and the Holy Spirit. This demonstration, that the early church's inclusion of Jesus within the unique divine identity was grounded in the life and teaching of Jesus as recorded by the synoptic Gospels, is a serious challenge that must be squarely faced by scholars who have hitherto been reluctant to admit the existence of an early high christology in the NT.

The evidence of Acts and the epistles suggests that the early church having come to a clear and unequivocal belief that Jesus was included within the unique identity of the one God, expanded the basic framework of contextualisation used by Jesus. They did this in a manner that was wholly consistent with the teaching of Jesus, but used a wider range of motifs. For example, given Jesus' inclusion within the unique divine identity by his identification of himself as the sole ruler of all things and the final eschatological judge, it was entirely appropriate for the early church to also speak of him as the sole creator of all things. Similarly, just as Jesus had applied certain OT divine titles to himself, so the early church felt justified in applying other exclusively divine titles to him such as 'the Holy One' and developing new ways of expressing who he was, such as the title 'the image of the invisible God'. In short, the core descriptions of God, which according to the Gospels Jesus applied to himself, mushroom into a much wider range of descriptions and titles in the Acts and epistles, but in a manner that is wholly consistent with the synoptic portrait of the teaching of Jesus.

This blossoming out of a range of christological expressions in the Acts and epistles potentially provides an important paradigm for the development of contextual theology. It provides a biblical precedent for the teaching of Jesus being re-expressed using new motifs and descriptions, providing that these are consistent with what is recorded in the NT.

We will also subsequently demonstrate that the bounded extrinsic conception of monotheism used by the early church to include Jesus within the unique divine identity, is also the primary way in which God's identity is characteristically described in Islamic contexts. As such the early church's use of the bounded extrinsic conception of monotheism will be an important starting point for the development of a contextualised christology.

Endnotes

[1] Philo Leg:118 satirising Emperor Gaius Caligula's claim to be a god.

[2] Matt.19:17; Mk.12:29 (cf. also :32); 1 Cor.8:6; Gal.3:20; Eph.4:5-6; 1 Tim.2:5; James 2:19.

[3] Mk.12:29-34.

[4] cf. also the designation of God as creator in Matt.19:4; Mk 13:19; Acts 4:24; 7:50; Rom.1:25; 9:20; Eph.3:9; 1 Pet.4:19; Rev.10:6; 14:7 (and Acts 14:15; 17:24 to pagans).

[5] cf. also the designation of God as ultimate ruler in 1 Cor.15:24-28; 1 Tim.1:17; Rev.11:15-18; (and Acts 17:24 - to pagans).

[6] cf. also the designation of God as judge in Rom.2:16; 3:6; 1 Cor.5:13; 2 Tim.4:8; Heb.10:30-31 (citing Deut.32:35,36); 12:23; 13:4; Jude:14-15; Rev.6:10; 11:17-18; 16:1,5; 18:8; 19:1-2; 20:11-15.

[7] cf. also the designation as saviour in Lk.1:47; 1 Tim.1:1; 2:3; 4:10; Tit.1:3; 2:10; 3:4.

[8] Unlike God's role as Creator, Ruler and Judge, his role as divine saviour does not extend to the whole of creation, but is limited to the salvation of his people. Therefore the subject/object distinction here only distinguishes between God and human beings.

[9] e.g. Rom.1:25 cf. also references to God having created 'all thing's - Eph.3:9; Rev.10:6.

[10] 1 Tim.6:15f; Rev.19:10; 22:8-9.

[11] Jas.4:12; Rev.20:10-15.

[12] e.g. Acts 17:25; Rom. 11:36; Eph.3:9; 1 Tim.6:13; Heb.2:10; Rev.4:11.

[13] e.g. Acts 4:24; Rev.10:6; 14:7.

[14] Acts 14:15; 17:24.

[15] e.g. 1 Cor.8:6; Acts 10:36; Eph.1:10; Jn 5:22.

[16] So, e.g. Dunn *Christology* 163-212 esp. 209-212.

[17] 1 Cor.8:6; Heb.1:2.

[18] Jn 1:1-3,10; 1 Cor.8:6; Col.1:16; Heb.1:2.

[19] Jn 6:63; Rom.8:11; 2 Cor.3:6 cf. also OT references to this in e.g. Job 33:4; Ps.104:29-30.

[20] The majority dating of Romans (55-57CE) and Colossians (60-61CE) places the two letters only 4-6 years apart.

[21] cf. M.J. Harris *Colossians & Philemon* EGGNT [Grand Rapids:Eerdmans,1991] 45-46 who observes that the preposition followed by the genitive used in both texts expresses ultimate cause.

[22] J.D.G. Dunn *Romans 9-16* WBC [Dallas:Word,1988] 698 observes that the style of the Romans 11:33-36 is Jewish through and through with parallels in a wide spectrum of 2T texts: OT, apocalyptic, wisdom and Hellenistic Jewish texts, including possibly the synagogue prayers that appear to have been preserved in the *Apostolic Constitutions* (e.g. 8.5.1-2).

[23] Current debates over the authorship of Colossians do not negate the force of this argument as Colossians itself evidences a strong influence of the Pauline mission on the Lycus valley churches (4:12-17 cf. also Philem.:2,23-24).

[24] So, R.J. Bauckham *Jude, 2 Peter* WBC [Waco:Word,1983] 39-40 who provides additional argument in support of this.

[25] i.e. the only options Jude gives us are that Jesus is God, the sole ruler of the universe or (rather less plausibly) he has usurped him.

[26] So, M. Dibelius & H. Conzelmann *The Pastoral Epistles* [Philadelphia:Fortress,1972] 89, n.20 ET by P. Buttolph & A. Yarbro of M. Dibelius *Die Pastoralbriefe* 4th rev'd edn by H. Conzelmann; I.H. Marshall *The*

Pastoral Epistles ICC [Edinburgh:Clark,1999] 404 and W.D. Mounce *Pastoral Epistles* WBC [Nashville: Nelson,2000] 361.

[27] Rev.17:14; 19:16.

[28] So, L.W. Hurtado *Lord Jesus Christ* [Grand Rapids:Eerdmans,2003] 73. Even Dunn *Christology* 118 concedes that this adds a new dimension to the christological claim.

[29] cf. similar statements in Lk.10:22 and Jn 3:35f.

[30] So, C.K. Barrett *A Commentary on the First Epistle to the Corinthians* [London:Black,2nd (edn,1971] 360-361. F.F. Bruce *The Epistles to the Colossians, to Philemon and to the Ephesians NICNT* [Grand Rapids: Eerdmans,1984] 74-76, 261-62 gives similar interpretations of Eph.1:10 and Col.1:20-22.

[31] So, Barrett *1 Corinthians* 360-61 and H. Conzelmann *1 Corinthians* [Philadephia:Fortress,1978] 274-75 ET by J.W. Leitch of *Der erste Brief an die Korinther*.

[32] Even the LXX does not contain this emphasis.

[33] Matt.24:3,27,37,39; 1 Cor.15:23; 1 Thess.2:19; 3:13; 5:23; 2 Thess.2:1,8; 2 Pet.1:16; and very probably also 1 Thess.4:15 and 1 Jn 2:28.

[34] So, D.J. Moo *James* TNTC [Leicester:IVP,1985] 168.

[35] cf. T.Abr.(A)12:1-13:8 and our earlier discussion of this in chapter 2 section 'Extrinsic monotheism'.

[36] Matt.25:31-46.

[37] Matt.19:28; Lk.22:29-30; cf. also 1 Cor.6:2-3.

[38] cf. Acts 2:38; 5:31; 13:38; 26:18.

[39] Matt.9:2-8/Mark 2:3-12/Luke 5:20-26.

[40] I.H. Marshall *The Gospel of Luke* NIGTC [Exeter:Paternoster,1978] 214.

[41] cf. the second temple legal axiom 'an eye for an eye and a tooth for a tooth' (Matt.5:38) based on Ex.21:24; Lev.24:17-21 and Deut.19:21. This relational concept of justice is exemplified in the OT concept of the blood avenger Num.35:19.

[42] e.g. Dunn *Partings* 175 appears to miss the point of the passage when he understands it merely as Jesus replacing the priest's pronouncement that God had forgiven sins.

[43] cf. discussion of 'Honour and shame' and 'Jurisprudence' in chapter 5 section 'Cultural themes'.

[44] 1 Pet.1:17; 2:23.

[45] Rom.2:16.

[46] Jn 5:22.

[47] So, Bauckham *Jude-2Peter* 123.

[48] cf. similarly exclusive statements in Isa.43:11; 45:21.

[49] Only Othniel and Ehud are actually called saviours and the narrative makes clear that this is only in a very secondary sense to YHWH. cf. Jdg.3:9f,15.

[50] So, G. Fohrer articles 'σωτήρ in the OT' and 'σωτήρ in Later Judaism' *TDNT* 7:1012-1013, 1013-1015; and J. Schneider & C. Brown 'σωτήρ' *NIDNTT* 3:216-223.

[51] So, Fohrer 'σωτήρ-Judaism.' Contra, Horbury *Messianism* 43. However, Horbury does not provide a single instance of a 2TJ text in which the messiah himself is specifically entitled 'saviour'. Schneider and Brown 'σωτήρ' note that even in the rabbinic literature there is only one isolated instance of the messiah being called 'saviour'.

[52] Lk.2:11; Acts 5:31; Eph.5:23; Phil.3:20; 2 Tim.1:10; Tit.1:4; 2:13; 3:6; 2 Pet.1:1,11; 2:20; 3:18; 1 Jn 4:14.

[53] Lk.2:8-11.

[54] So, M.J. Harris *Jesus as God* [Grand Rapids:Baker,1992] 178ff with respect to Tit.2:13-14.

[55] 2 Pet.1:1.

[56] As also do the slightly contracted forms of it in 2:20 and 3:2.

[57] So, Bauckham *Jude-2 Peter* 168. Contra, E. Kasemann 'An Apologia for Primitive Christian Eschatology' 169-195 in *Essays on New Testament Themes* [London:SCM,1964] ET by W.J. Montague from German *Exegetische Versuche und Besinnungen*, (183 n.2). However, Kasemann's position is somewhat undermined by his admission that 1:3 speaks of Christ as a 'divine being'.

[58] God as saviour 1 Tim.1:1; 2:3; 4:10; 2 Tim.1:8-9; Tit.1:3; 2:10; 3:4-5. Jesus as saviour 2 Tim.1:10; Tit.1:4; 2:13-14; 3:6.

[59] Ex.15:2; Ps.118:21; Isa.12:2; 63:8.

[60] Heb.5:9.

[61] So, Fatehi *Spirit's* 49-163 who presents a thorough survey of second temple evidence in this respect.

[62] So, M.M.B. Turner 'The Spirit of Christ and "Divine" Christology' 413-436 in J.B. Green & M. Turner (eds) *Jesus of Nazareth Lord and Christ* [Carlisle:Paternoster:1994].

[63] Matt.10:20 (cf. also Lk.11:13); Rom.8:11; Eph.1:17.

[64] Acts 11:15-17 cf. Matt.3:11; Mk1:8; Luke 3:16; Jn 1:33.

[65] So, Fatehi *Spirit's* passim but esp. 167-333.

[66] Jn 14:26.

[67] So, D.A. Carson *The Gospel According to John* [Leicester:IVP,1991] 505.

[68] Acts 16:7; Phil.1:19 cf. also Rom.8:9 (πνεῦμα χριστοῦ) and Gal.4:6 (τὸ πνεῦμα τοῦ υἱοῦ αὐτοῦ).

[69] 1 Pet.1:11.

[70] Q40:15 cf. also 17:85; 97:4 (and 16:2 although unlike other translations such as Arberry's and Pickthall's, Yusuf Ali translates the Arabic *ruh* as 'inspiration' rather than 'Spirit').

[71] Tob.6:1-8,15-17; 8:2-3.

[72] cf. our earlier discussion of this in chapter 2 section 'Invocation of figures other than God'.

[73] e.g. Mk.1:23-28/Lk.4:33-37.

[74] So, J.A. Fitzmeyer *The Gospel According to Luke* AB [New York:Doubleday,1985] 2:922 who also notes the following allusions (cf. n.75).

[75] Ex.8:19[15] God's power which cannot be imitated by Egyptian magicians; Ex.31:18; Deut.9:10 God writing the 10 commandments; Ps.8:3[4] God's act of creation.

[76] Lk.10:17-19.

[77] e.g. the discussion of the christological significance of the use of the name of Jesus in healing and exorcism in Hurtado's recently published magnum opus *Lord Jesus Christ* 203-206 is silent on the christological significance of Jesus delegating authority over the demonic to his disciples and merely comments on Jesus' name being regarded as uniquely authoritative and part of the publicly affirmed devotional practice of the early church.

[78] e.g. 2 Kgs.4:32-35.

[79] Acts 3:6,16; 4:10,30; Mk 9:38-39; Jn 14:12-14 (cf. 11:43-44).

[80] Q5:110 cf. our subsequent discussion of the significance of this as a divine prerogative in chapter 5 sections 'Sole creator, ruler and judge' and 'Denial of Jesus' divinity'.

[81] Rev.10:6; 16:5.

[82] Although some scholars claim the latter is messianic, the only examples of the title itself being used are for 1 Enoch's 'Elect One' and in Isa.24:16 where it specifically refers to YHWH.

[83] The issue is blurred in many EVV by NT citations of the Heb. חָסִיד and LXX ὅσιος in Ps.16:10 also being translated as 'Holy One'.

[84] Isa.41:4; 44:6; 48:12.

[85] Rev.1:8; 21:6.

[86] Rev.1:17; 2:8; 22:13.

[87] So, R.H. Mounce *The Book of Revelation* NICNT [Grand Rapids:Eerdmans, 2nd rev'd edn,1998] 61.

[88] So, Carson *John* 256-57.

[89] cf. also Jesus' claim in Jn 14:6 to be *'the* Life' (ἡ ζωή).

[90] Deut.5:26 cf. this usage in 1 Sam.17:26,36; 2 Kgs 19:4,16/Isa.37:4,17; Jer.10:10 cf. also Dan.6:20,26.

[91] Jn 6:57; Rom.9:26; 2 Cor.3:3; 6:16; 1 Tim.3:15; 4:10; Heb..3:12; 9:14; 10:31;12:22; Rev.7:2.

[92] Acts 14:15; 2 Cor.6:16 cf. also similar usage in 1 Thess.1:9.

[93] e.g. Ps.Sol. designates a Davidic messiah as king (17:21ff), but regards YHWH as the only heavenly king (17:1-46).

[94] Matt.16:27-28; 25:31-46; Rev.17:14; 19:16.

[95] Matt.13:40-43.

[96] Col.1:13; 2 Tim.4:1; 2 Pet.1:11 (cf. also similar usage in Matt.16:28). The expression ἡ βασιλεία τοῦ Χριστοῦ καὶ θεοῦ occurs in the western texts of Eph.5:5.

[97] Rev.4:2-4 cf. 5:6ff cf. also subsequent discussion of throne texts p 109

[98] Isa.54:5-8; Jer.2:2; Ezek.16:32; Hos.1:2.

[99] The only direct evidence is 3 En.48A:9ff from the 5th-6th Century CE, although even this text does not designate the messiah 'the Bridegroom'.

[100] Jn 3:28-29 cannot be pressed to infer any popular application of the bridegroom motif to the anticipated messiah as John the Baptist's discussion relates specifically to some of John's immediate circle of disciples and only links the bridegroom motif with Jesus' messiahship, rather than popular messianic expectations. John's likely awareness that the OT depicted Israel as YHWH's bride (cf. Carson *John* 211) and the the complete absence of any evidence of that second temple Jews expected a messianic bridegroom points to the most likely source of John's understanding being Jesus' own comments to John's disciples which explicitly identified himself as the bridegroom (Matt.9:14-15).

[101] Matt.9:14-15.

[102] Matt.25:1-13 (cf. 24:27-51 which applies OT day of YHWH texts [Isa.13:9-10; 34:4] to the coming of the Son of Man).

[103] Rev.19:7-9; 21:2-4ff cf. Isa.25:6-7.

[104] So, M. Barth *Ephesians* AB [New York: Doubleday,1974] 627 on Eph.5:27. Barth argues that the imagery here alludes to many elements of OT and Jewish wedding customs and has 'the highest' christological implications. He suggests that Christ's purchase of the bride with his own blood equates with the bride-price that Jewish custom demanded a bridegroom pay for the bride (670). For further discussion of the NT presentation of 'the self humbling and suffering of God' cf. the section of this name pp 117-120.

[105] Although such a contextualisation would involve a reversal of images – God being the bridegroom and his people the bride.

[106] Jn 1:1-18; Rev.19:13.

[107] So, S. Smalley *John: Evangelist and Interpreter* [Carlisle:Paternoster,rev'd edn,1998] 243-245.

[108] e.g. M. Scott *Sophia and the Johannine Jesus* JSNT Supp. series 71   [Sheffield:JSOT,1992] which despite making occasional reference to the rabbinic literature, entirely ignores the targums.

[109] Jesus: Matt.22:41-46; 24:42 (cf. :27ff); 25:37,44 (cf. :31ff) – all of which refer to a heavenly lord; Early church: Acts 2:36; 11:16.

[110] B. Witherington (iii) 'Lord' *DJG* 484-92 observes that 1QapGen uses it as a divine address, while 11Q10 (Tg. Job) uses it to translate שַׁדַּי.

[111] Ps.Sol.17:32ff cf. also Matt.20:30-31.

[112] So, B. Witherington *The Acts of the Apostles*[Grand Rapids:Eerdmans,1998] 148.

[113] Harris *God* passim but cf. esp. 271.

[114] Contra, Dibelius and Conzelmann *Pastoral Epistles* 145.

[115] cf. Harris *God* 174-83 for a discussion of the grammar of this passage and a summary of scholarship.

[116] C.J. Ellicott *The Pastoral Epistles of St. Paul* [London:Longmans,Green,Reader & Dyer,1869] 201 cf. also G.W. Knight *The Pastoral Epistles* NIGTC [Carlisle:Paternoster,1992] 322-26 for a summary of recent scholarship.

[117] Deut.10:17 (cf.11:16f); Ezra 5:8; Neh.8:6; Ps.95[94]:3; Dan.2:45.

[118] Harris *God* 290f.

[119] cf. Paul's specific repudiation of this pagan idea at Athens (Acts 17:24).

[120] Q5:72 cf. also our discussion on pp 162-68 of the widespread denial of Jesus' divinity in the Islamic context.

[121] Although Dunn *Christology* 188 agrees that Adam cannot be referred to here, he interprets the involvement in creation (16) as a reference to divine Wisdom. However, there is no evidence that any Jews thought of 'all things' being created *for* Wisdom.

[122] Op.:25.

[123] Heb.1:3.

[124] Jn 1:18; 6:46.

[125] Jn 12:44-45; 14:9.

[126] So, S. Aalen 'Glory' *NIDNTT* 2:44-48.

[127] 2 Cor.3:7-13; 2 Pet.2:10; Jude:8.

[128] Lk.9:32.

[129] 1 Cor.2:8 cf. also Rom.8:17; 2 Thess.2:14; 1 Pet.5:1; Rev.21:22-23.

[130] Heb.1:3. The possibility of an allusion to Jewish Wisdom traditions such as Wis.7:25-26 does not negate this, for as C.R. Koester *Hebrews* AB [New York:Doubleday, 2001] 187 comments Philo similarly utilised such wisdom traditions when he spoke of the Logos as the power by which God fashioned the world.

[131] So, M. Hengel *Studies in Early Christology* [Edinburgh:T&T Clark,1995] 373 who contends that 'the substantive points of contact with John's Prologue are striking'.

[132] Ex.25:8-9.

[133] So, Carson *John* 127-28.

[134] Jn 1:14.

[135] 1 Cor.8:6.

[136] Col.1:16.

[137] 1 Cor.8:6.

[138] Heb.1:2-3 cf. also Jn 1:1-3,10 and Col.1:16-17.

[139] 1 Cor.15:24-28 cf. the *wahdat al-shuhud* Sufi hope of achieving union (*wasl*) in harmony with the Creator which we discuss in relation to 'Sufism' in chapter 5 section 'Conceptual framework of monotheism'.

[140] 1 Tim.6:15; Rev.17:14;19:16.

[141] Eph.1:22; Rev.3:14; 1 Cor.15:24-28.

[142] 1 Cor.15:24-28; Eph.1:10; Rev. 22:1,3 note singular ὁ θρόνος τοῦ θεοῦ καὶ τοῦ ἀρνίου.

[143] 2 Tim.4:1; James 4:12; 5:7-9; 1 Pet.1:17; 2:23.

[144] Jn 5:22; Rom.2:16.

[145] Tit.2:13; 3:4; 2 Pet.1:1; Jude:25.

[146] Heb.5:9.

[147] 2 Cor.5:18-19; 1 Jn 4:14.

[148] Jn 1:14; Heb.2:14; cf. also Rom.5:9-11; 2 Cor.5:18-19; Col.2:15; 2 Tim.1:10.

[149] Jn 3:16-18; Eph.2:5; Tit.3:5.

[150] Acts 2:33,38; Tit.2:13-14; 3:5-6.

[151] The main possible exceptions being 1) the appearances of God on Sinai (Ex.19:20ff) announcing the *malak* in whom the divine name dwelt (Ex.23:20ff); 2) the thrones (plural) of Dan.7:9; 3) Ps.45:6[7]-7[8] 'your throne, O God, will last forever and ever...therefore God, your God, has set you above your companions'. These were subsequently used by Justin Martyr in his *Dialogue with Trypho the Jew* (:56,75,76) to demonstrate the presence of Christ in OT epiphanies.

[152] cf. Segal *Two Powers* passim. Although Segal's evidence is influenced by rabbinic reaction to Christian exegesis of the OT, he observes that these texts contain 'many hints of greater antiquity' (260).

[153] 1 Tim.6:15-16.

[154] The Father's love for Jesus: Matt.3:17/Mk 1:11/Lk.3:22; Matt.17:5/Mk 9:7; Jn 3:35; 5:20; 15:9; 17:24 cf. also Col.1:13; 2 Pet.1:17. Jesus' love for the Father: Jn 14:31.

[155] Matt.11:27/Lk.10:22 cf. also Jn 3:35; 5:20.

[156] Jn 16:23-27.

[157] Jn 20:17 cf. :18.

[158] Rom.8:14-17; Gal.3:26; 4:1-7 cf. also Eph.1:5; 3:11-12.

[159] i.e. the Muslim.

[160] Matt.26:63-64/Lk.22:70.

[161] L. Morris *The Gospel According to St.Luke* TNTC [Leicester:IVP,1974] 318. Similarly, R.T. France *The Gospel According to Matthew* TNTC [Leicester:IVP,1985] 380 following D.R. Catchpole 'The Answer of Jesus to Caiaphas (Matt. XXV1.64)' *NTS* 17 (1970-71) 213-226 describes Jesus' reply as affirmative, though 'reluctant or circumlocutory in formulation'.

[162] Ex.3:6-17; 6:1-8.

[163] So, Bauckham *Crucified* 75-77.

CHAPTER 4

CONTEXTUALISATION OF CHRISTOLOGY IN THE NEW TESTAMENT: USING JEWISH CONCEPTS OF THEOPHANY, EPIPHANY AND MONOLATRY

I know that my redeemer liveth,
and at the Last Day he shall stand upon the earth.[1]

Introduction

In this chapter, we shall examine the extent to which NT contextualisation of christology was in continuity with existing Jewish concepts of theophany, epiphany and monolatry. Later in this study we will compare the attitudes to these concepts found in the Jewish and Islamic contexts, in order to evaluate what changes the early church's contextualisation of christology will require to be re-contextualised for the Islamic context.

THEOPHANY

Continuity with Judaism

The OT emphasis that God cannot be seen by mortal man is not only repeated in the NT, but to a degree even strengthened. Some NT texts may even imply that God is not visible to any created being, 1 Timothy describing him as living in 'unapproachable light'.[2]

Expansion of Existing Jewish Concepts

Jesus as the Visible Form of God

However, in the NT this emphasis on the unapproachableness of God is combined with claims that in Jesus God has made himself known. Illustrative of this are the descriptions of Jesus in Col. 1:15ff, and Jn. 1:18:

> He is the image of the invisible God...For by him all things were created: things in heaven and on earth.

No-one has ever seen God, but God the One and Only, who is at the Father's side, has made him known.

The Fourth Gospel gives the most explicit theology of this,[3] and records Jesus as replying to Thomas' audacious request of 'Lord, show us the Father', by saying

Anyone who has seen me has seen the Father.[4]

We earlier observed two affirmations of OT theology that were seemingly in tension with each other: the existence of a number of theophany narratives and the affirmation that man cannot see God and live. The OT resolves this tension to a degree by implying that God can assume a veiled form in order to appear to people. However, in the NT, it is explicitly affirmed that God can assume a visible form that can be seen by man, and that form is Jesus.

OT Theophanies

As we have noted earlier, the Fourth Gospel portrays Jesus as the divine Logos who is the visible manifestation of the invisible God. However, it is possible that in 12:41 it actually identifies Jesus as 'the Lord' that Isaiah saw seated on the divine throne in awesome holiness. After claiming that God's throne speech concerning rejection of his message (Isaiah 6) was fulfilled in the rejection of Jesus, the evangelist states

Isaiah said this because he saw his glory and spoke about him.[5]

Scholarship is divided as to whether the evangelist simply means that Isaiah foresaw Jesus' suffering and exaltation,[6] or whether, he is additionally identifying either 'the Lord' or his glory that Isaiah saw seated on the throne as the pre-incarnate Jesus.[7] However, as the evangelist has already stated that no-one has ever seen God, except Jesus who is his visible manifestation,[8] regardless of whether or not such is the import of this verse, it is hard to see that the evangelist could have understood OT theophanies as being anything other than Jesus. As Schnackenburg observes, the idea is a natural development of the evangelist's Logos christology.[9] Similarly Gieschen observes that the claim of 1:18 that no-one has ever seen God, but God the one and only, is a profound interpretation of Jewish theophanic traditions. He comments that

This assertion implies that the Only-Begotten was *seen* before the incarnation since he is the one who makes God known, not only *in* the incarnation, but also *before* the incarnation (cf. 6:46). Therefore, he has always been the visible manifestation of God.[10]

The increasing interpretation of OT theophanies as the *Memra* of God in Aramaic targums,[11] may provide an important precedent here, as the *Memra* appears to equate quite closely with Logos christology and may even be the source from which the latter was developed.

Throne Texts

One of the ways that YHWH's exclusive rule of all things was depicted in the OT was by means of throne theophanies.[12] Although claims have been advanced that certain second temple texts place other figures on God's throne, the few texts concerned are, as we earlier argued, both marginal to mainstream Jewish belief, and easily capable of more mainstream interpretations.[13]

It is in the book of Revelation that Jesus is most clearly and unequivocally depicted as sharing the divine throne. John states that:

> I saw a Lamb, looking as if it had been slain, standing in the centre of the throne, encircled by the four living creatures and the elders (Rev. 5:6).

Although it is not absolutely clear here whether John locates the lamb in the centre of the throne and the living creatures or between them, in 7:17 the lamb is clearly at the centre of the throne:

> 'For the Lamb at the centre of the throne will be their shepherd'.

The implicit identification of Jesus as the God who appeared in OT throne theophanies is made in Revelation 22:1,3. Here the throne John saw is referred to not simply as God's throne, but rather as 'the throne of God and of the Lamb', with the singular definite article, singular form of εἰμί and singular forms of αὐτός giving added emphasis that this is one throne of one God:

> ὁ θρόνος τοῦ θεοῦ καὶ τοῦ ἀρνίου ἐν αὐτῇ ἔσται, καὶ οἱ δοῦλοι αὐτοῦ λατρεύσουσιν αὐτῷ (Rev.22:3)

The Believer's Sight of God

The NT records that a few select individuals such as John and Stephen actually saw theophanic visions of God. However, 1 Corinthians speaks of a vision of God being eschatologically experienced by all Christians:

> Now we see but a poor reflection as in a mirror, then we shall see face to face.[14]

However, prior to the *parousia*, for most Christians this dim mirror-like sight of God is an inward experience of Christ by the Spirit, who mediates God's presence. 2 Corinthians describes this:

> For God, who said, "Let light shine out of darkness", made his light shine in our hearts to give us the light of the knowledge of the glory of God in the face of Christ.[15]

The NT in fact depicts the believer being united to Christ, and the presence of Christ being brought to them by the Spirit, in a way that directly parallels the OT depiction of the Spirit bringing the presence of God to the believer.[16]

What is most significant about this for our purposes, is its remarkable similarities to the aspiration of *wahdat al-shuhud* Sufism, for *wasl* – union with God by means of a mirror-like reflection of the sight of God in the heart.[17] In the NT, this experience of God's presence is depicted as a union with Christ in the heart, mediated by the Spirit.

Discontinuity with Jewish Monotheism

There clearly were a number of discontinuities between second temple concepts of God being visibly seen and the NT claim that Jesus was the visible manifestation of God. However, as these primarily relate to the concept of epiphany we shall examine them in our discussion of that concept.

Summary

We may therefore summarise the NT teaching on theophany by saying that Jesus is depicted as the visible manifestation of the invisible God. Although on rare occasions theophanic visions of Christ might be granted to Jesus' followers, for most this hope is only to be realised eschatologically, although it is anticipated in some measure by the inward experience of Christ by the Spirit in the believer's heart.

EPIPHANY

Continuity with Judaism

In several places, the NT affirms that during OT history God himself had appeared on earth, although interestingly it does not refer to these as the *malak YHWH*. Mark records a reference by Jesus to God speaking to Moses from the burning bush, while Stephen's Sanhedrin speech refers to the God of glory appearing to Abraham and the divine appearances to Moses at the burning bush and on Sinai. The Sinai theophany is also referred to slightly more obliquely in Hebrews.[18]

Similarly, the NT also anticipates 'the Day of the Lord', although as we will subsequently demonstrate, the early church utilised this concept to identify Jesus' anticipated *parousia* as the eschatological appearing of YHWH.

The importance of these beliefs for the early church's contextualisation of christology primarily lies in the fact that they provided an existing conceptual category that God could, and indeed was, expected to appear on earth. The discontinuity between NT christology and second temple Judaism lies in the form that this epiphany took, not in the concept of epiphany *per se*.

Expansion of Existing Jewish Concepts

OT Epiphanies

We earlier observed that references in second temple texts to OT epiphanies suggest there was a widespread belief that during Israel's history God had locally manifested a form of his presence on earth. The question therefore arises as to whether, and if so how, the early church related these OT epiphany narratives to their beliefs about Jesus.

Given the prominence accorded to the *malak YHWH* motif in OT epiphany narratives, one might expect the *malak YHWH* to be used as a christological category. However, even those sections of the NT with the most highly developed christology do not directly use this motif. In fact, although the NT is not shy of OT epiphany narratives, the only direct reference to the *malak YHWH* is Stephen's reference in his Sanhedrin speech to the 'angel' (ἄγγελος) who appeared to Moses in the burning bush and on Sinai.[19] The care with which Stephen uses this concept is striking. He never simply speaks of the 'angel' but refers to it very specifically as the angel in the flames of the burning bush (ἄγγελος ἐν φλογὶ πυρὸς βάτου) and the angel who spoke to Moses on Mount Sinai (ἀγγέλου τοῦ λαλοῦντος αὐτῷ ἐν τῷ ὄρει Σινᾶ).[20] Moreover, he is careful to explain that this is God himself come down to enact salvation (Ἐγὼ ὁ θεὸς τῶν πατέρων σου...κατέβην ἐξελέσθαι αὐτούς).[21] Stephen's careful usage and explanation of the *malak YHWH* motif, probably reflects the ambiguity that had become attached to this title during the second temple era as a result of the speculations about the name of the *malak YHWH*. Although

both the OT and the LXX had carefully reserved the title (Heb. מַלְאַךְ יְהוָה /
LXX. ἄγγελος κυρίου) exclusively for theophanic appearances, this appears
to have become a lost battle by the first century CE. Some texts, possibly
including targums, applied names such as *Sariel* to *malak YHWH* epiphanies.[22]
However, as other contemporary texts, including some which were in other
ways explicitly epiphanic, used the same names and sometimes the title ἄγγελος
κυρίου for created angels, the title could as easily refer to a created angel as it
could to an actual epiphany.[23] This would have made it very difficult for the
early church to utilise it directly as a christological title.

However, 1 Cor.10:1-10 does appear to identify Christ as actually present in
OT epiphanies,[24] a theme later developed by patristic writers.[25] Paul appears to
be alluding to, and implicitly refuting, a Jewish legend that a rock shaped well
accompanied the Exodus.[26] Instead Paul claims that the 'spiritual rock' that
really accompanied the exodus was Christ, the rock being a motif applied to
God in the OT.[27] Paul's typology here, is complex and difficult to use directly
in a contextualised christology.

It is in fact hard to see how NT writers could have made the explicit references to
Christ as God that we observed in chapter 3, without the existing Jewish concept
of epiphany being a significant part of their worldview. However, although the
existing Jewish concept allowed that God could, and indeed had, appeared on earth
in anthropomorphic form, there is no evidence that it extended to God becoming an
actual contemporary man, still less one who would be crucified. Nevertheless, the very
existence of the concept of epiphany in Jewish monotheism goes some way towards
enabling us to understand how the early church's contextualisation of christology
could claim to directly include Jesus within the unique identity of the one God.

The Eschatological Appearance of God the Saviour

Isaiah spoke of the time when YHWH would eschatologically appear on earth
to enact salvation for his people. The results of YHWH's appearance would
include the blind seeing, the deaf hearing and the lame walking.[28]

Both Matthew and Luke record the questioning of Jesus by the messengers of
John as to whether he was the coming one.[29] Jesus' reply described the results
of his own ministry such as the blind seeing and lame walking, in words that
were an unmistakable allusion to Isaiah's prophecy of consequences of God's
eschatological appearance as saviour.[30] Interestingly however, Jesus' reply also
mentions good news being preached to the poor, a reference which is derived

not from these YHWH texts but from Isaiah's prophecy of a coming anointed one (61:1ff).[31] Jesus' response therefore combined a text that spoke of YHWH himself coming with one that many second temple Jews would most likely have interpreted messianically. The implication of identifying his own ministry by this combination of OT texts was to identify it as that of a divine messiah.

As well as identifying himself in terms of Isa.35:2-6, Jesus also identifies John, saying that he is the one YHWH spoke of to Malachi, saying:

> I will send my messenger, who will prepare the way before me.[32]

It is not entirely clear why both Matthew and Luke record Jesus as having changed the final personal pronoun from first to second person.[33] However, the implications of identifying John as the one who Malachi prophesied would prepare the way for the Lord himself coming to his temple, are of enormous christological significance. As R.T. France comments:

> Jesus' application of this text to John, implies that his own (Jesus') coming, for which John prepares, is the coming of God himself, an implication which is the more staggering for being so calmly assumed.[34]

THE DAY OF THE LORD – THE ESCHATOLOGICAL APPEARANCE OF GOD THE JUDGE

The NT strongly affirms the OT concept of 'the Day of YHWH', referring to it with a variety of terms including 'the day of the Lord/God',[35] 'the day he visits us',[36] or simply 'the day'.[37]

Significantly, the NT directly identifies Jesus' *parousia* with the Day of YHWH.[38] Illustrative of this is 1 Thessalonians 4:13-5:11, where Paul refers to the return of Jesus as 'the day of the Lord', describing it with language drawn from both Zechariah's and Joel's descriptions of YHWH himself coming to earth with all his holy ones.[39] Significantly, he reminds his readers that this is something that they already 'know very well', implying that this formed part of Paul's initial foundational teaching in the churches he planted.[40] Similar usage occurs elsewhere in the Pauline epistles.[41] The identification of Christ's *parousia* as the day of the Lord is not confined to Paul, as 2 Peter's assertion that the day of the Lord will come like a thief in the night almost certainly refers to the early church's anticipation of Christ's *parousia*.[42] Such texts exemplify what Kreitzer terms 'an outright *substitution* of christocentrism for theocentrism' in Pauline eschatology.[43]

The use of the thief motif in both 1 Corinthians and 2 Peter[44] strongly suggests that Jesus' description of the Son of Man's coming as being like a thief in the night was widely interpreted in the early church as referring to the day of the Lord. Jesus' descriptions of this event specifically echo other OT imagery concerning the day of YHWH, such as YHWH coming with all his holy ones and all nations being gathered before him.[45] Moreover, in both Matthew 24 and Mark 13 Jesus specifically claims that the coming of the Son of Man will fulfil the prophecies of Isaiah and Joel concerning the day of YHWH.[46]

Discontinuity with Judaism

a) God Appearing on Earth as an Actual Human Being

We have earlier demonstrated that the OT narrates a number of occasions when God had locally manifested a veiled form of his presence on earth, in human-like form. However, it appears that there was neither precedent, nor expectation, that God would appear as an actual human being. The most that can be said is that there was nothing in the Jewish scriptures that specifically repudiated such a possibility.[47]

The idea of God engaging in normal human functions such as eating and sleeping was something that was probably foreign to most second temple Jews. The Book of Judges' narrates the refusal of the *Malak YHWH* to eat food prepared by Manoah,[48] while the Psalms present a picture of YHWH neither sleeping nor needing the food offerings pagan nations assumed their gods needed. Jews believed that YHWH, as the creator who gave life and breath to all things, simply did not need such things,[49] a form of monotheistic rhetoric that Paul later used to a pagan audience in Athens.[50] The claim of the angel Raphael in *Tobit*, that he only gave the appearance of eating and drinking,[51] suggests that many second temple Jews believed that actual eating and drinking were confined to terrestrial creatures. The existence of such beliefs is at least in some measure confirmed by Luke's account of the resurrected Jesus eating, to prove to the disciples that he was not merely a spirit.[52]

The early church's claim that God had actually become a fully human man, who carried out normal human functions such as eating and sleeping, who could not only be seen, but physically touched,[53] would probably have been in such profound discontinuity with Jewish monotheism as to appear outrageous.

Moreover, the claim that God had appeared as a known contemporary man, who had recently been crucified at the instigation of the nation's religious leaders, could only have added to the scandalous nature of this claim. This was undoubtedly the greatest discontinuity between second temple Jewish and early Christian conceptions of God's identity.

The parallels between the second temple Jewish and Islamic assumptions about God on this subject are well illustrated by the Qur'anic assertion that Jesus' eating of food proves he could not be God.[54]

The Early Church's Apologetic for God Appearing as a Contemporary Man

The early church's apologetic response to the challenge of this discontinuity is therefore potentially of some significance for our study. Several aspects can be discerned in different apologetic speeches recorded in Acts:

1. OT texts relating to God himself were juxtaposed with prophecies of the anticipated Davidic messiah. In Peter's Pentecost speech, Joel's prophecy of God pouring out his Spirit on those who called on the name of the Lord was followed by reference to God's promise to set a Davidic descendant on the throne of Israel. It was then claimed that both of these had been simultaneously fulfilled in Jesus, whom God had made '*both* Lord *and* Christ' (καὶ κύριον αὐτὸν καὶ Χριστὸν).[55] The idea of a divine messiah that this implied would itself would have been discontinuous with most second temple messianic expectations, although possibly not entirely without precedent.[56] It is therefore probably significant that when Luke introduces the proclamation of Jesus as messiah in Acts, and where he gives any significant detail of the content of evangelistic speeches to Jews, the title 'Messiah' is frequently qualified by other ascriptions that more directly identify Jesus as God, thereby portraying a divine messiah.[57]

2. A further potentially significant aspect of Peter's Pentecost speech is that it alludes to the idea of Moses' ascent of Sinai to meet God. By the second temple era this tradition had developed into speculations about Moses and various other OT patriarchs making heavenly ascent journeys, that bear marked similarities to the heavenly ascent (*mi'raj*) ascribed to Muhammad in the *Qur'an* and *Ahadith*. Turner has observed that Peter's Pentecost speech, whilst not dependent on Jewish ascent traditions, alludes to them, in order to say that it is Jesus rather than Moses who has ascended to the right hand of God in heaven.[58] A similar polemic by allusion occurs in John 3:11-13, where Jesus tells Nicodemus that no-one has ascended into heaven, so as to be able to reveal

heavenly mysteries other than the Son of Man who came from heaven.[59] Turner moreover observes that while Moses' ascent resulted in him receiving the law, Jesus' ascension resulted in him receiving the very Spirit of God, whom he then bestowed on all God's people. Peter's emphatic assertion of this placed Jesus in an altogether different category to Moses and other patriarchs supposed to have ascended to heaven, because it designated Jesus as Lord of the Spirit, as only God could bestow the Spirit of God. Moreover, it met the hitherto unfulfilled aspirations of both Moses and later Judaism for the Spirit to be poured out on all of God's people,[60] thereby bringing them into intimate relationship with God.

3. The early church's presentation of Jesus to outsiders set him within, and as the climax of, a story of God's dealings with his people.[61] This 'climax of the God-story' approach can be seen clearly in both Stephen's Sanhedrin speech and Paul's address to the synagogue at Pisidian Antioch.[62]

4. Stephen in his Sanhedrin speech, begins by reiterating examples of God locally manifesting his presence in implicitly human-like form, to Abraham, Moses at the burning bush and on Sinai, and refers to the temple having been built for God's presence to dwell in. However, he then presents the conundrum that God cannot be confined to such, because all of heaven and earth cannot contain him. By doing so, Stephen has thrown the issue of Jesus being a local manifestation of the presence of God onto his opponents, saying in effect 'you believe God himself appeared to Moses at the burning bush and on Sinai: how do you think that could be when creation itself cannot contain him?'[63] This apologetic is noteworthy, as we shall subsequently demonstrate in chapter 5 that a similar conundrum exists in Islamic thought.

5. Of these apologetics, only the 'both God and Messiah' approach directly addresses the issue of God appearing as an actual human being. However, a further aspect in Pisidian Antioch is Paul's parting words to those rejecting his message, citing as paradigmatic God's words to Habakkuk, 'Look…I am going to do something in your days that you would never believe, even if someone told you'.[64] In effect, Paul is saying 'do not imagine that you know all about God, God can do things that are so radically different to what you expect, that you wouldn't believe them even if you were told in advance'.[65]

b) The Self-Humbling and Suffering of God
Although, the idea of God appearing as an actual human being was unprecedented in Jewish thought, the NT goes much further than this.

Philippians 2 holds Jesus up as an example of being prepared to take the very lowest position, that of a servant, who humbled himself to the point of obediently accepting the most ignominious death of a criminal, which according to Deuteronomy placed the participant under the curse of God.[66]

The early church recognised that Jews viewed this claim as being both scandalous and foolish.[67] However, although the church sought to avoid putting any unnecessary stumbling blocks in anyone's way, they nonetheless, saw Jesus' crucifixion as absolutely central to the Gospel.[68]

The Early Church's Apologetic for the Self-Humbling and Suffering of God

Several important facets can be seen in the way that the early church addressed this issue:

1. We have already referred to the NT's expansion of the OT divine bridegroom imagery to speak of the bridegroom giving up his own life to save the bride.[69] This is particularly significant as it predicates voluntary suffering in the very identity of God.

2. There was an emphasis on suffering being the normative experience of all the prophets, Jesus as the culmination of the prophets was no exception to this.[70] The occurrence of a similar emphasis in the *Qur'an* makes this apologetic potentially significant in the Islamic context.

3. There was an emphasis that the handing over of Jesus to his enemies was 'by God's set purpose and foreknowledge',[71] and had been prophesied by all the prophets, a belief which was traced back to the teaching of Jesus himself.[72]

According to Acts, Peter used this 'plan of God' apologetic in the early church's first evangelistic address, saying in effect that God subverted the plans of Jesus' enemies to bring about his own plan, which involved the death, resurrection and exaltation of Jesus.[73] The implication of this was that Jesus' suffering and death in no sense dishonoured him, or implied that his enemies had triumphed. Peter's use of this apologetic was probably rooted in Jesus' own teaching, particularly his insistence to Peter that the cross was so central to the plan of God that Peter's objections to it were in effect aligned with Satan, and Jesus' repeated demonstrations after the resurrection from the OT that he had to suffer.[74]

The early church came to speak of Jesus' death as not only prophesied by all the prophets, but also foreknown before the foundation of the world.[75] Revelation 13:8 appears to go even further, suggesting that the actuality of Jesus' death occurred outside the constraints of terrestrial time, Jesus being described as 'the Lamb that was slain from the creation of the world'.[76] However, in a sense this was only a fuller expression of Jesus' teaching that the kingdom of God had been prepared for his followers before the foundation of the world.[77]

4. A vindication motif was used as an apologetic. Peter's apologetic speeches recorded in Acts differ from much western theology, in that they do not emphasise the crucifixion as an act of atonement, but rather focus on God's vindication of Jesus stating 'men killed…but God raised', and not only raised him from the dead, but also exalted him to the highest point in heaven.[78] The hymn of Philippians 2:5-11, which appears to be modelled on the humiliation and subsequent exaltation of the suffering servant of Isa.52:13-53:12,[79] gives particular emphasis to this by proclaiming that because Jesus, who was in very nature God, humbled himself by becoming obedient even to crucifixion, *therefore* God exalted him to the highest heavenly place and gave him the name of Lord.[80] It is noteworthy that the sections of the NT that express the significance of the cross in terms of substitutionary atonement are addressed to Christians who have already received initial teaching.[81] It may therefore be presumed that they build on an earlier foundation in which the cross was presented as God vindicating Jesus in the face of men's sinful rejection. This may be an important example for the church in Islamic contexts to follow in articulating its christology.

Matthew's Gospel suggests that the early church saw the vindication motif as originating in the teaching of Jesus himself. Jesus spoke, both didactically and in the parable of the tenants, of suffering and rejection being the normative experience of all the prophets, of whom he was the climax. However, he also spoke of heavenly rewards for those so persecuted and ultimate judgement on their enemies.[82] The repeated references in the *Qur'an* both to previous prophets being killed, and suffering and rejection as the normative experience of the prophets,[83] creates the potential for this apologetic also being utilised in a contextualised christology.

5. The early church used prominent cultural values such as hospitality in its evangelism to underline the seriousness and corporate shame that resulted from the rejection of Jesus.[84] All three synoptic gospels relate Jesus' parable of the tenants,

who not only refuse to receive the envoys of their Lord hospitably, but actually kill his son in order to take the Lord's possessions for themselves. Peter's speech in Solomon's colonnade contains the added indictment that Jesus was actually handed over to those who would kill him, the one they killed being none other than the 'author of life' himself.[85] This motif of violated hospitality codes is stated even more emphatically in the prologue to the Fourth Gospel. This speaks of the creator himself coming to his own creation, but his own people refusing to receive him.[86] The central importance in Islamic contexts of hospitality as a cultural value and the enduring shame associated with handing over a guest to their enemies makes this a potentially significant apologetic in a contextualised christology.

6. The cross was portrayed as the triumph of Jesus over hostile evil powers that had enslaved men. Colossians speaks of men who were previously spiritually dead having been made alive by God as a result of Jesus' death on the cross cancelling their debt of disobedience, which the powers had been using as a means of controlling them. Colossians therefore describes Jesus as having disarmed the powers and authorities, making a public spectacle of them, by his triumph on the cross.[87] A similar theme occurs in the heavenly throne scene of Revelation 5, where Jesus is portrayed as a lamb looking as if it had been slain, and is worshipped 'because' by being slain, he has triumphed, purchasing with his blood, people to serve God from every tribe, language, people and nation.[88] The popular Muslim belief that the resurrected body in heaven will have the wounds and disfigurements of the earthly body, makes Revelation's portrait of the lamb looking as if it had been slain, a particularly striking image for a contextualised christology.

7. Jesus' death was portrayed as the means of effecting reconciliation between God and men. One way the NT expresses this is by depicting Jesus as a sacrificial lamb. This motif occurs in a range of NT books, but is particularly prominent in Revelation where it occurs twenty eight times, with the slain lamb being described as having ransomed people for God.[89] Although this echoes both the Passover lamb and the OT sacrificial system, it may also more specifically echo the *Aqedath Isaac* (binding of Isaac) and God's promise of a ram to be provided.[90] Schoeps has presented a range of evidence to show that the *Aqedath* was prominent in Jewish thought in the period between the first century CE and the rabbinical era, and was viewed as having atoning value for the sins of Israel.[91] Moreover, as rabbinical tradition placed the *Aqedath* on the same date as the Passover, it is likely that it was already seen as an ante-type of the Passover lamb. An extraordinary text in the *Midrash Rabbah* actually describes

Abraham carrying the wood for the burnt offering as being 'like one who bears his cross on his shoulders'.[92] The rabbinical reaction against Christian exegesis of the OT[93] makes it almost certain that this tradition originated prior to the Christian era.[94] Schoeps argues that this background made it inevitable that Paul the converted Pharisee would have had to consider whether the *Aqedath* was an ante type of Christ's sacrifice. Furthermore, the probability that Rom.8:32's 'God did not spare his own son' is a verbal allusion to the LXX text of Gen.22:16 strongly suggests that Paul saw Christ's death as a fulfilment of the *Aqedath*.[95] Longenecker, similarly suggests that the words of John the Baptist narrated by the Fourth evangelist, 'Look, the Lamb of God, who takes away the sin of the world' (Jn 1:29,36), specifically echo the *Aqedath Isaac*, and designates Jesus as the one foretold in Abraham's promise of a lamb to be provided by God himself, of which the ram Abraham sacrificed was a type.[96] This *Aqedath* motif is potentially important for us, as Abraham's attempted sacrifice of his son is both narrated in the *Qur'an*, which curiously states that God ransomed him with a 'momentous' (*azim*) sacrifice, and celebrated annually across the Islamic world in the feast of *'id al-azha* (Lit. 'feast of sacrifice'), the most important annual festival.[97]

Summary

We may therefore summarise this section by saying that the NT claims that Jesus himself identified his earthly ministry in terms of the eschatological epiphany of God the saviour, anticipated by the OT. He similarly identified his *parousia* as the anticipated day of YHWH, although it is probable that second temple Jews only anticipated one such eschatological epiphany. The NT also appears to identify Christ as actually present during OT events such as the Exodus, although this theme is not developed to any great extent. This does imply though, that Christ was understood in continuity with OT conceptions of epiphany, both in the past and those eschatologically anticipated. However, the early church's claim that God had actually become a contemporary man who had then been crucified by the national religious leaders, was almost certainly in such discontinuity with Jewish understandings of God's identity as to appear outrageous and scandalous. The apologetics that the early church developed to address this may therefore be of some significance in addressing a similar rejection of the self-humbling and suffering of God in the Islamic context.

Monolatry
Continuity with Judaism

In second temple Judaism, monotheism was not simply a theology that was articulated in the synagogue, but something that was expressed by the believing community in the forms such as prayer to, and calling on the name of YHWH, hymns of worship to YHWH, the twice daily repetition of the *Shema*,[98] and celebration of festivals such as the Passover that commemorated how YHWH the saviour had delivered them. Monolatry, therefore formed a central part of the way Jewish monotheism was expressed, and was a response to YHWH's unique identity. As Bauckham observes,

> Jews understood their practice of monolatry to be justified, indeed required, because the unique identity of YHWH was so understood as to place him, not merely at the summit of a hierarchy of divinity, but in an absolutely unique category, beyond comparison with anything else. Worship was the recognition of this unique incomparability of the one God. It was the response to YHWH's self-revelation as the sole Creator and Ruler of all.[99]

Hurtado has in fact demonstrated that the reservation of worship for God alone was a major way that many Jews emphasised the uniqueness of God.[100]

The early church maintained continuity with Judaism by strongly affirming that only God should be worshipped. Evidence of this can clearly be seen at the time when Matthew and Luke wrote their Gospel accounts, as both include Jesus' affirmation of Deuteronomy 6:13:

> Worship the Lord your God, and serve him only.[101]

This affirmation of monolatry continues in the Book of Revelation, which contains a universal command to worship the one Creator-God, and also maintains continuity with the Jewish refusal tradition[102] by its narration of John's angel guide twice refusing to accept worship.[103]

Expansion of Existing Jewish Concepts

In the light of this strong affirmation of monolatry, the NT's almost casual reference to various worship practices directed towards Jesus points to an expansion of the Jewish concept of monolatry, to include Jesus within the worship of the one God. It is not merely the individual, but also the collective impact of these devotional practices, and the early church's recognition of them as normative and legitimate that is important[104] in including Jesus within the unique identity of the one God to whom worship was offered.

Hymns

Hymns of worship both about, and specifically addressed to, YHWH were a longstanding feature of Jewish worship, dating at least from the exodus. By Davidic times these had become a formal part of temple worship and continued being so after the exile. The Qumran community used Biblical and extra Biblical compositions of Psalms, and both Matthew and Luke portray hymn singing as part of Jesus' celebration of the Passover.[105]

It is therefore highly significant that at an early stage hymns began to be sung both celebrating, and to, Christ.[106] In fact, in the NT there is much more evidence of hymns to Christ than of hymns simply addressed to 'God'.[107] Moreover, in Revelation, Christ is depicted at the centre of heavenly worship alongside the glorious figure seated on the central throne of heaven.[108] The inclusion of this christological worship alongside the refusal tradition that we earlier observed in Revelation, can only carry one import, that Christ is depicted on the God side of the God/non-God divide.[109]

Although Revelation 5 is the NT's only actual description of christological worship *per se*, it appears probable that a number of NT passages reflect similar early Christian hymns celebrating and almost certainly sung to Christ.[110] Both the didactic character of these passages and the admonition in Colossians 3:16 to 'let the word of Christ (ὁ λόγος τοῦ Χριστοῦ) dwell in you richly as you teach and admonish one another…as you sing psalms, hymns and spiritual songs' suggests that hymns were central to the articulation and inculcation of belief about who Christ was.[111]

It is significant that we have already discussed several of these hymn passages in our earlier demonstration that the early church applied to Christ the Jewish bounded extrinsic understanding of God as sole creator, ruler and saviour. Hurtado, after looking at these NT christological hymns collectively, suggested that essentially they celebrate Christ as the supreme agent of God in creation (Col.1:15-17; Heb.1:3; Jn.1:1-3); earthly obedience and redemptive suffering (Phil.2:5-8; Rev.5:9-10); and eschatological triumph (Phil.2:9-11; Col.1:20).[112] We may more specifically label Hurtado's categories by saying that they identify Christ as the way God relates to his creation as creator, saviour and in restoring his usurped rule of all things.

Prayer to Christ

In the NT, prayer is typically addressed to God the Father. However, it appears that Jesus was also addressed in prayer in two ways:

Firstly, a range of NT books including Pauline epistles, 1 Peter and Jude speak of prayer or praise being offered to God *through* Jesus Christ.[113] Illustrative of these is Jude's closing doxology:

> to the only God our Saviour be glory, majesty, power and authority, *through* Jesus Christ our Lord, before all ages, now and forevermore! Amen.[114]

However, a small number of other texts appear to indicate prayer being made directly to the heavenly Jesus:

Peter's Pentecost speech begins with a recitation of Joel's prophecy that 'everyone who calls on the name of the Lord will be saved'. However, by the end of Peter's speech, it is the name of Jesus that he urges the crowd to call on in order to be saved.[115]

Stephen's dying prayer 'Lord Jesus, receive my spirit' (Acts 7:59f) is not only unequivocally directly addressed to Jesus, but also appears deliberately to echo Jesus' dying prayer, 'Father, into your hands I commit my spirit' (Luke 23:46).[116]

Acts also records Ananias' prayer to 'the Lord', who in a vision told him to visit Saul. His subsequent comment to Saul that 'the Lord Jesus' has sent him indicates that 'the Lord' Ananias addressed in prayer was Jesus.[117]

In Paul's account of his prayers to 'the Lord' about his thorn in the flesh, 'the Lord' almost certainly refers to Jesus, as the Lord's reply 'my power is made perfect in weakness' is specifically stated in the following verse to be 'Christ's power'.[118]

The Aramaic prayer *Maran-atha* – 'come Lord', used by Paul in 1 Corinthians, is almost certainly addressed to Jesus, as the NT is consistent in only anticipating the eschatological coming to earth of Jesus. The synonymous Greek expression at the end of Revelation accords with this, by being specifically addressed to Jesus.[119] Interestingly, the NT indicates that the early church preserved two Aramaic prayers: one – *Abba,* being addressed to God the Father, while the other – *Maran-atha* - was addressed to Jesus.[120]

As well as these prayers solely addressed to Jesus, prayer was also made jointly to Jesus and the Father. In 1 Thessalonians 3:11-13 Paul asks 'our God and

Father himself and our Lord Jesus' (Αὐτὸς δὲ ὁ θεὸς καὶ πατὴρ ἡμῶν καὶ ὁ κύριος ἡμῶν Ἰησοῦς) to establish and strengthen the church, a prayer he echoes in 2 Thessalonians 2:16-17, but in reverse order, addressing it to 'our Lord Jesus Christ himself and God our Father' (Αὐτὸς δὲ ὁ κύριος ἡμῶν Ἰησοῦς Χριστὸς καὶ ὁ θεὸς ὁ πατὴρ ἡμῶν).

Interestingly, the Fourth Gospel records Jesus' teaching during the final Passover meal, that his disciples should both pray to the Father in Jesus' name, and that Jesus himself will grant them whatever they ask in his name to glorify the Father.[121] This portrays Jesus as both the means of access to the Father and the one who enacts the response to the prayer, a description that the Logos christology of the prologue makes understandable.

Significantly, Colossians 3:17 appears to echo the Fourth Gospel's account of this teaching of Jesus, when it urges that all worship practices, including thanksgiving prayer, should be done 'in the name of the Lord Jesus, giving thanks to God the Father through him'. Hurtado observes that this characteristic offering of prayer to God, through Jesus occurs both in the NT and other early Christian sources.[122]

In fact, it is hard to see how the NT's affirmation of prayer to both God and Jesus could have been held together with the explicit affirmation of monolatry, without the presupposition of something approximating to a Logos christology underlying it.

The Name of Jesus
In the OT, the worship of the one true God is referred to as 'calling on the name of the Lord'. Genesis comments, that during the time of Adam's third son Seth, men began to call on the name of YHWH. The line of patriarchs is similarly depicted as calling on the name of YHWH, and the phrase is later used to distinguish worship of YHWH from worship of other gods.[123] Isaiah, Zephaniah and Zechariah also eschatologically anticipate a time when God will act, as in the exodus, to save and purify a remnant of his people, who will then call on his name.[124]

Against this background, the early church's description of itself, as those who call on the name of the Lord, where Lord clearly means Jesus, can only be seen as a deliberate appropriation of Jewish monotheistic rhetoric.[125] This usage probably dates back to Peter's Pentecost speech that called people to fulfil Joel's prophecy of calling on the name of YHWH, by calling on the name of Jesus. Ananias for example uses this description of the church in his prayer concerning Paul, 'Lord...he has come here...to arrest all who call on your name', this name of the Lord subsequently being identified by him as the name of Jesus.[126]

The familiar manner with which this phrase is used here and elsewhere in the NT, suggests that this usage was not only widespread in the early church,[127] but was a deliberate attempt to maintain continuity between their worship of Jesus, and OT worship of YHWH.

Luke records the early church both healing the sick and continuing to exercise Jesus' authority over the demonic 'in the name of Jesus'.[128] Luke's account of other Jewish exorcists attempting to copy the disciples' use of Jesus' name implies that deliverance of the demonised 'in the name of Jesus', was both a relatively common practice in the early church and regarded by contemporary Jewish exorcists as noticeably more effective than their own attempts.[129] Significantly, prophylactic practices in Islamic contexts, such as burning rue seeds to ward off evil spirits,[130] appear to parallel attempts to deal with demonic affliction narrated in Jewish books such as *Tobit*.[131] This suggests that similar use of the name of Jesus in the face of perceived demonic affliction may generate comparable reactions to those described in the NT.

Confessing Jesus

The practice of confessing (Heb.ידה/LXX ὁμολογέω) the name of YHWH occurs in the narratives of both 1 Kings and 2 Chronicles concerning Solomon's dedicatory prayer in the temple.[132] Hence, it is perhaps unsurprising, that there is no evidence that second temple Jews ever regarded it as appropriate to confess the name of any eschatological figure other than YHWH, for whom the practice appears to have been exclusively reserved.[133]

It is therefore highly significant that both the Pauline and Johannine epistles appropriate this expression of Jewish monolatry and speak of confessing Jesus as foundational for obtaining salvation.[134] Paul tells the Romans:

> If you confess (ἐὰν ὁμολογήσῃς) with your mouth, "Jesus is Lord", and believe in your heart that God raised him from the dead, you will be saved.[135]

The origin of this practice may lie in Jesus' words concerning salvation:

> Everyone who confesses (ὁμολογήσει) me before men, I will also confess (ὁμολογήσω) him before my Father in heaven. But whoever denies me before men, I will also deny him before my Father in heaven.[136]

The universal confession of Jesus as Lord in the christological hymn of Phil.2:5-11 is directly dependent on Isa.45:23f. As the latter speaks of swearing allegiance (LXX 'ὁμολογέω) to YHWH 'alone', it appears that confessing the name of Jesus was a means of including Jesus within the unique identity of YHWH.

Prophecy

According to the NT prophecy delivered through the agency of the Spirit appears to have been a common phenomena in the early church.[137] It is highly significant that the NT records prophecy being delivered as a manifestation of the Spirit whose origin is attributed to Jesus in a similar manner to that in which the OT records prophecy being attributed to YHWH, through the agency of the Spirit.[138]

Illustrative of these is 'the Lord's' response to Paul recorded in 2 Cor.12:9 'My grace is sufficient for you, for my power is made perfect in weakness'. Paul's identification in the following verse of this power as 'Christ's power' (ἡ δύναμις τοῦ Χριστοῦ) clearly indicates that the Lord (ὁ κύριος) who spoke to him was Jesus.

In the light of the strict OT injunctions against prophecy in any name other than that of YHWH[139] it is hardly surprising that there is no parallel for this in any Jewish devotional practice of the time, other than the pattern of OT prophecy in the name of YHWH,[140] which the NT christological formula 'The Lord said' appears to be deliberately modelled on.[141] Interestingly, the only Jewish precedent for the origin of prophecy being ascribed to a figure who has previously appeared on earth is the OT narratives of prophets such as Elijah receiving prophecy from the *malak YHWH*,[142] a figure whom we earlier demonstrated was understood to be YHWH himself appearing in epiphany.[143]

The most detailed account of prophecy ascribed to Jesus is the book of Revelation, including the seven prophetic oracles sent by the exalted Jesus to various churches. In this a Logos type christology is implied that is similar to the pattern we observed in respect of NT prayer being addressed to God through Jesus. The book of Revelation describes itself as 'The revelation of Jesus Christ, which God gave him to show his servants what must soon take place', and which Jesus sent his angel to deliver. The latter clearly indicating that Jesus is the source of prophetic inspiration rather than simply the means of its delivery. A similar theology is found in Luke's account of Peter's Pentecost speech in which Peter claims that Jesus 'has received from the Father' the promised spirit of prophecy, which he has now poured out.[144]

It therefore appears that in the early church prophecy could be ascribed to both the Father and Jesus, but was often simply ascribed to 'the Lord', where this title clearly meant Jesus.

Interestingly, Matthew traces the origin of prophecy in the name of Jesus back to Jesus himself. He records Jesus both equating those who receive the followers of Jesus with those receiving prophets and also warning of false prophets who will attempt to copy the form of prophesying in Jesus' name, without genuinely seeking to do God's will.[145]

The Lord's Supper

There is no precedent in second temple Judaism for a devotional meal celebrating and conceivably communing with, any heavenly figure except YHWH.[146] However, a cultic meal dedicated to remembering the mighty acts of God the saviour was an important feature of the Jewish calendar. The NT makes clear that the antecedent on which the Lord's supper was modelled was the Passover. Although the NT depicts Christ as the type of the Passover lamb,[147] this is only part of a cluster of otherwise antithetical motifs (shepherd, sacrificial lamb, priest) applied to Jesus. The Passover lamb motif is therefore in no sense inconsistent with a number of factors suggesting that Christ was also seen as the Lord of the Passover.

Firstly, the name 'the Lord's supper' (κυριακὸν δεῖπνον) in 1 Cor.11:20, where the 'Lord' appears to be Jesus,[148] recalls the feast 'the Lord's Passover' (Heb. לַיהוָה פֶּסַח הוּא /LXX πασχα ἐστὶν κυρίῳ) in. Ex.12:11. As 1 Corinthians has earlier presented Christ as the typological fulfilment of the Passover,[149] it is hard to see that this similarity of name can be anything other than deliberate. The use of a similar name formula therefore suggests that the same 'Lord' is referred to in both feasts, which implicitly includes Jesus within the unique identity of YHWH[150]

Secondly, in 1 Corinthians, Paul uses the analogy of Israel sacrificing to demons rather than YHWH in the wilderness, to illustrate the incompatibility of participation in a cultic meal with any other object of worship than 'the Lord' (ὁ κύριος).[151] The implication is that the 'Lord' to whom OT sacrifices were offered, including those at the Passover, and the 'Lord' of the 'Lord's supper', are one and the same.

In the Islamic context, the Passover itself is not celebrated. However, the early church's typological reinterpretation of the Passover as Christ's death raises the question of whether God's ransoming of Abraham's son, which is celebrated in the annual feast of 'id al-azha, might similarly be typologically reinterpreted to celebrate Christ as the lamb of God who takes away the sin of the world.[152]

THE SHEMA

We earlier noted that Mark's inclusion of Jesus' affirmation of the Jewish *shema* as the fundamental requirement of the law suggests that this formed one of the key beliefs of the early church at the time that this Gospel was written. However, several NT texts suggest that the early church expanded the Jewish *shema* to include Jesus.[153] 1 Cor.8:6 is the clearest example of a Christianised *shema*, which appears to have been adapted to address the context in the city of Corinth where many gods and lords were worshipped:[154]

> There is no God but one. For even if there are so-called gods, whether in heaven or on earth (as indeed there are many "gods" and many "lords"), yet for us there is but one God, the Father, from whom all things came and for whom we live; and there is but one Lord, Jesus Christ, through whom all things came and through whom we live.[155]

As Jews appear to have primarily understood YHWH's identity as being uniquely the sole creator and ruler of all things, it is extremely improbable that 'one Lord, Jesus Christ' describes Jesus as less than God, but merely ruling the totality of creation on God's behalf.[156] In fact, any ascription of the rule of the entire universe to a figure other than God would inevitably have created confusion as to how such a figure could be distinguished from God himself. However, the unobtrusive way in which Paul introduces this monotheistic formula and its use as a counterweight to the 'many gods' of paganism both suggest that including Jesus within the unique identity of the one God was something Paul assumed that the Corinthians were already familiar with.

Moreover, although 1 Cor.8:6 clearly does reflect the *shema*, it is important to remember that the idea Paul is refuting is the pagan notion of there being 'many gods and many lords'. It appears unlikely that the Corinthians sharply distinguished between 'gods' and 'lords',[157] and as such the phrase cannot provide a parallel distinction between God the Father and Jesus the Lord.[158] In fact,

Paul's response to pagan belief in many gods and lords places the stress not on the Father, but on the one God,[159] who he then describes as being 'the Father' and 'Jesus Christ'.[160] He explains this in terms of 'all things' (τὰ πάντα) having come from the Father *through* Jesus Christ. This not only identifies Jesus with the act of creation, but applies to Jesus a well established piece of Jewish monotheistic rhetoric in the same breath as it has been applied to the Father.[161]

Discontinuity with Judaism

Aside from this expansion of worship to include Jesus, the main area of discontinuity between Jewish and early Christian monolatry lies in content of worship.

Firstly, there was a celebration and adoration of a newly revealed aspect of God's character. Revelation 5 describes the heavenly worship of Christ as 'a new song', a stereotypical formula used in the Psalms to indicate that previous songs are now inadequate because God has done new things.[162] The song is introduced by a statement that Jesus is worthy because he has triumphed (5:4-5), this triumph being the winning back of representatives of all the world's peoples. However, in Revelation 5 the 'new thing' celebrated by the song, addressed specifically and apparently exclusively to Jesus, is the manner in which this triumph was achieved:

> You are worthy…because you were slain, and with your blood you purchased men for God from every tribe and language and people and nation (5:9).

In the light of Revelation's explicit identification of Jesus as God,[163] it is evident that this 'new thing' is the revelation of an entirely novel aspect of the character of God the saviour. This self-humbling in order to triumph over his foes is celebrated as what makes Jesus worthy to receive the full accolade of honour, glory and praise from the totality of creation in both heaven and earth.

Secondly, there was a focus on a newly disclosed name of God, 'the name (singular) of the Father, the Son and the Holy Spirit', which Matthew 28:19 records the resurrected Jesus had commanded his disciples to baptise into. It is unclear whether baptism itself was a Christian novum.[164] However, it is evident that Christian baptism clearly did express the believer calling on the name of the newly disclosed divine identity, that of the Father, the Son and the Holy Spirit.

The worship of God as Father, Son and Holy Spirit is also strongly implied in the portrait of heavenly worship in Revelation 4:1-5:14. In chapter 4, the worship of heaven centres on the one seated on the throne around whom was a rainbow like an emerald. However, also at the centre of this worship are the seven blazing lamps representing the Spirit of God. The description of this scene is continued in chapter 5 where John additionally sees the Lamb standing in the centre of the throne receiving the worship of the entire heavenly host.[165]

Summary

We may therefore summarise the NT's expression of monolatry by saying that the early church both explicitly affirmed their belief in monolatry and also included Jesus in their worship of God. Jesus became a focus of fundamental expressions of monolatry such as prayer and worship that Jews typically reserved for God alone. Moreover, the content of both prayer and worship included the deliberate application to Jesus of some of the strongest expressions of Jewish monotheistic rhetoric. In effect, this expressed belief that Jesus was on the God side of the absolute boundary Jews understood to exist between God and all else. This expansion of the Jewish conception of monolatry can only adequately be explained in terms of Jesus being understood not merely as the means of access to God, but as God himself in a manner akin to that which the Fourth Gospel articulates as a Logos christology.

However, NT worship went further than this in two respects, both of which were entirely novel to second temple Judaism. Firstly, Jesus was regarded as worthy of worship because he had triumphed over his foes by his self-humiliation and sacrificial death, thereby disclosing a previously unrealised aspect of the character of God for which he was to be worshipped. Secondly, a further aspect of the newly disclosed identity of God, expressed in the new name (singular) of 'the Father, the Son and the Holy Spirit', became a significant focal point of worship.

CONCLUSIONS

In this chapter we have seen that Jesus was identified as the visible manifestation of the invisible God. Although the OT had narrated visions of a human-like figure on the divine throne, in the NT Jesus is seen on the divine throne, which is referred to as the throne (singular) of God and Jesus.

Similarly there was an expansion of the existing Jewish concept of epiphany, which held that God had appeared on earth in human-like form and was expected to do so again on 'the day of the Lord'. The NT expands this concept of epiphany to include the man Jesus, not merely during the time his disciples had been with him, but also eschatologically and almost certainly protologically. The NT appears to assume that Christ was in some way present during OT events such as the exodus, although this did not form a major facet of NT christology. The early church did however give a prominent focus to 'the day of the Lord', which it identified as the anticipated *parousia* of Jesus, when he would come as eschatological judge.

The implication of this for our study is that a contextualised christology needs to explain the inclusion of Jesus within the unique identity of the one God, in terms of Jesus being the visible manifestation of the invisible God, and the means by which the invisible God has related to his creation. However, the absence of any equivalent of most (although as we shall subsequently see, not all) OT epiphany narratives in the Islamic context, means that a way will need to be found of strengthening the concept of epiphany before the incarnation itself is introduced.

In this chapter we have also seen that in the Jewish context, although it was believed God would appear eschatologically as judge, there does not appear to have been any anticipation of an earlier epiphany in which God would appear not merely in human-like form, but as an actual human being who would enact salvation through a process of suffering and self-humiliation. The discontinuity between NT christology and Jewish monotheism therefore lies not in the concept of epiphany itself, but in the form that this epiphany took. The early church addressed the scandal this caused by speaking of this suffering being part of the plan of God, by which he triumphed over the hostile powers that had usurped his sovereign rule of all things, and by pointing to God's vindication of Jesus by his resurrection and exaltation to the highest place in heaven. These apologetics may be potentially useful in addressing similar discontinuities in the Islamic context.

In the previous chapter, we demonstrated that the early church contextualised its christology against the background of Jewish monotheism by directly including Jesus within the unique identity of YHWH the only God. In this chapter we have seen that the early church responded to this new understanding of the identity of God by including Jesus within the worship of the one God. In fact, monolatry provides some of the clearest evidence that the early church's christology was constructed to maintain continuity with YHWH, rather than with any other figures in second temple Judaism. No heavenly or anticipated eschatological figures except YHWH were ever the object of worship practices such as confessing Jesus, a cultic meal in his honour or a creedal statement like the *Shema*. Moreover, in the NT, the worship of God has a new justification which was previously unprecedented, Jesus is worshipped *because* he suffered and died to redeem men. Worship is also focused on a new name of God, 'the name (singular) of the Father, the Son and the Holy Spirit'.

Such emphases clearly need to be included in a contextualised christology. However, in order to assess whether christological worship in the Islamic context would as clearly express Jesus' position on the God side of the God/non-god divide, we will need to examine whether any figures other than God are the object of similar acts of worship there.

Endnotes

[1] The celebration of Christ's epiphany in *The Messiah* by G.F. Handel (1685-1759), based on the KJV text of Job 19:25.

[2] 1 Tim.6:15-16 cf. also Jn 1:18; 6:46; Col.1:15; 1 Jn 4:12.

[3] cf. Jn 1:1-18; 6:46; 14:6-11.

[4] Jn 14:9.

[5] Jn 12:41. NIV 'saw *Jesus'* glory'.

[6] So, B.M. Newman & E.A. Nida *A Translator's Handbook on the Gospel of John* [London:UBS,1980] 419-420 who believe this to be a safer translation, but do not discount the possibility of a reference to pre-incarnate Christ.

[7] So, Carson *John* 449-50; C.H. Dodd *The Interpretation of the Fourth Gospel* [Cambridge:CUP,1953] 206-7; B. Lindars *The Gospel of John NCB* [London:Oliphants,1972] 439; L. Morris *The Gospel According to John* NICNT [Grand Rapids:Eerdmans,1971] 605; and R. Schnackenburg *The Gospel According to St. John* [London:Burns & Oates,1980] 2:416-17; ET by C. Hastings, F. McDonagh, D. Smith & R. Foley of *Das Johannesevangelium.*

[8] Jn 1:18; 6:46; (cf. also 5:37).

[9] Schnackenburg *John* 2:416-17.

[10] Gieschen *Angelomorphic* 273.

[11] cf. our earlier discussion of the *Memra* in chapter 2 section 'Divine attributes and anthropomorphism'.

[12] This is particularly clear in 1 Kgs.22:19f and Dan.7:1-14.

[13] cf. our earlier discussion in the Introduction section 'Core and marginal beliefs' and subsequent discussion of *Orphica* and the *Exagogue* in chapter 2 section 'Extrinsic monotheism'.

[14] 1 Cor.13:12.

[15] 2 Cor.4:6.

[16] cf. NT references to the Spirit as the Spirit of Christ Acts 16:7; Rom.8:9; Gal.4:6; Phil.1:19 and 1 Pet.1:11. For a fuller analysis and account of this, cf. Fatehi *Spirit's* passim.

[17] cf. discussion of 'Sufism' pp 144-46, 156.

[18] Mk 12:26 (cf. also Lk.20:37); Acts 7:2f; 30-38; Heb.12:18-21.

[19] Acts 7:30-38.

[20] Acts 7:30 (cf. also :35); 7:38.

[21] Acts 7:32-34.

[22] The existence of this interpretation of Gen. 32:25 in Tg. Neofiti raises the possibility of its existence in earlier targums, although as the final form of Tg. Neofiti is later than the second temple era no certainty can be attached to this.

[23] cf. our earlier discussion of this pp 60-62.

[24] So, A.T. Hanson *Jesus Christ in the Old Testament* [London:SPCK,1965] 11-16 and, in a more nuanced form, G. Fee *The First Epistle to the Corinthians* [Grand Rapids:Eerdmans,1987] 445-49.

[25] This position was taken in the immediate post apostolic era by Clement of Rome, Polycarp, Ignatius, Justin Martyr and Theophilus of Antioch as well as later patristic writers such as Irenaeus, Tertullian and Clement of Alexandria, while in the modern period it was championed by H.P. Liddon.

[26] Ps.Philo 10:7; 11:15 cf. Fee *1 Corinthians* 448 n.34 for discussion of the development of this legend.

[27] e.g. Deut.32:4; 1 Sam.2:2; Ps.18:46.

[28] Isa.35:2-6.

29 Matt.11:2-6/Lk.7:20-23.

30 So, France *Matthew* 192-93.

31 So, France *Matthew* 192-93.

32 Mal.3:1 cf. Matt.11:10/Lk.7:27.

33 The implication appears to be that Jesus is claiming that God the Father has said these words to him.

34 So, France *Matthew* 194 cf. also his *Jesus and the Old Testament* [London:Tyndale,1971] 91-92,155.

35 Acts 2:20; 1 Cor.5:5; 1 Thess.5:2; 2 Thess.2:2; 2 Pet.3:10,12.

36 1 Pet.2:12.

37 1 Cor.3:13; Heb.10:25.

38 So, L.J. Kreitzer *Jesus and God in Paul's Eschatology* JSNT Supp. Series 19 [Sheffield:JSOT,1987] passim.

39 1 Thess.5:2; Zech.14:1-7; Joel 2:11 cf. also 1 Thess.3:13.

40 1Thess.5:2.

41 e.g. 1 Cor.1:8; Phil.1:6,10; 2:16; 2 Thess. 2:1-9.

42 So, Bauckham *Jude, 2 Peter* 289ff.

43 Kreitzer *Eschatology* passim citation 18 (emphasis his).

44 1 Thess.5:4; 2 Pet.3:10.

45 Matt.24:43; 25:31ff (cf. Obad.:15; Zech.14:1-7).

46 Matt.24:29-31/Mk 13:24-27 cf. Isa.13:9-10; 34:4; Joel 2:30-31.

47 Even Solomon's question, 'Will God really dwell on earth with men?' (2 Chron.6:18) is set in the context of God's glory immediately afterwards filling the temple where Solomon was praying (7:1-2).

48 Jdg.13:15-16.

49 Ps.50:9-13; 121:4.

50 Acts 17:24-25.

51 Tob.12:19.

52 Lk.24:37-43 cf. also Acts 10:41.

53 The Johannine epistles suggest that the disciples seeing and touching of Jesus was regarded as proof that he had indeed become a fully human man (1 Jn 1:1 cf. 4:2; 2 Jn:7).

54 Q5:75 (cf. :72-77) cf. our discussion of this in chapter 5 section 'Denial of the possibility of incarnation'.

55 Acts 2:36 as the christological climax to Peter's speech beginning in 2:14ff. Witherington Acts 149-50 both stresses the danger of underestimating the significance in Acts of the transfer of the title κύριος from YHWH to Jesus and also suggests that Χριστός is used as a functional description rather than simply as a name in speeches addressed to Jewish audiences.

56 cf. sections entitled 'Lord' pp 89-90 and 'A divine messiah?' pp 64-65.

57 Acts 2:31,36,38 (cf. 2:36); 3:6,18,20 (cf. 3:14); 4:10 (cf. 4:12); 5:42 (cf. 5:31); 10:36.

58 Turner 'Christology' in Rowden *Lord*.

59 So, Carson *John*:200-201.

60 Turner 'Christology' in Rowden *Lord* additionally notes Moses' unfulfilled desire that God would pour out his Spirit on all his people and that they would all be prophets (Num.11:29).

61 So, Witherington *Acts* 147ff.

62 Acts 7:2-53; 13:16-41 cf. also this climax of the God story approach in Heb.1:1-3 and Luke's emphasis that all the prophets looked forward to the coming of the messiah cf. Lk.24:25-27,45ff; Acts 10:43.

[63] Acts 7:2f,30-34,38,44-47,48-50. Witherington *Acts* 273 observes that point of 7:48-50 is not that God's presence can't be found in the temple, but that God's presence can't be confined there.

[64] Acts 13:41 cf. Hab.1:5.

[65] D.J. Williams *Acts* NIBC [Carlisle:Paternoster,1990] 237 observes that Paul is using the failure of Habakkuk's audience to recognise what God was doing in their day, to highlight to the synagogue audience the danger of failing to recognise what God was doing in the Jesus event of their own day.

[66] Phil.2:5-8ff; Gal.3:13 cf. Deut.21:23.

[67] 1 Cor.1:18,23.

[68] 2 Cor.6:3 cf. 1 Cor.2:2; Gal.3:1; 6:14.; 1 Tim.2:5-7.

[69] cf. section 'The bridegroom' p 88 especially discussion of Christ paying the bride-price in his own blood.

[70] Acts 7:52; 1 Thess. 2:14-15. Bruce *Acts* 208 observes that Stephen's contention that his hearers were following in the steps of those who killed the prophets is in line with the words of Jesus recorded in Matt. 23:29-37 cf. also Matt.5:12 and Lk.4:24-27.

[71] Acts 2:23. Bruce *Acts* 123 also notes a similar emphasis in Rom.8:32.

[72] Acts 2:23-24; 3:18; 4:28 cf. Matt.16:21-28/Mk 8:31-38/Lk. 9:22-27; Matt.20:17-19/Mk 10:32-34/Lk.18:31-33; Lk.24:25-27, 44-49.

[73] So, Witherington *Acts* 144 who observes that juxtaposition of God's divine plan with actions for which humans are held responsible which occurs in Acts 2:33 is also a common theme elsewhere in the NT.

[74] Matt. 16:21-23; Lk.24:25-27, 40-47.

[75] 1 Pet.1:18-20 cf. also Eph.1:4-10.

[76] So, Mounce *Revelation* 252, who observes that the alternative meaning, that believers' names were merely written rather than the Lamb actually having been slain before the foundation of the world, is unlikely as the modifying clause would then be separated from its antecedent by 12 words (n.39).

[77] Matt.25:34.

[78] Acts 3:13-15; 5:30-32 cf. also 2:22-24, 31-33; 10:39-40.

[79] So, Bauckham *Crucified* 56-61 who lists a significant number of verbal parallels between the two passages.

[80] So, L.D. Hurst 'Re-enter the Pre-existent Christ in Philippians 2:5-11?' *NTS* 32 (1986) 449-557, who emphasises a descent-exaltation pattern.

[81] e.g. Rom.3:25; 8:3-4; 2 Cor.5:21; Heb.2:17 where the concept is introduced via the high priest motif. and 1 Jn 4:10.

[82] Matt.5:10-12; 21:33-44; 23:29-39.

[83] e.g. Q2:87,91; 3:21,181-184; 4:155-58 (Jews slew previous prophets and boasted about killing Jesus).

[84] So, Witherington *Acts* 180-81 who observes that the purpose of the 'strong and polemical language' in Acts 3:13-14 is to bring people 'to the point of repentance by a "shock of recognition" technique' and then to open them up to reception of the restoration and blessings promised in Christ.

[85] Acts 3:15.

[86] Jn 1:1-11,14 cf. also Matt.21:33-46/Mk 12:1-12/Lk.20:9-19; Acts 3:13-15.

[87] So, Bruce *Colossians, Philemon, Ephesians* 108-113 on Col.2:13-15.

[88] Rev.5:5-14.

[89] cf. esp. Rev.5:6-14; 14:1-4.

[90] cf. Gen.22:1-14.

[91] H.J. Schoeps *Paul: The Theology of the Apostle in the Light of Jewish Religious History* [London: Lutterworth,1961] 141-49, ET by H. Knight of *Paulus: Die Theologie des Apostels im Lichte der Judischen Religionsgeschichte*.

[92] Cited without reference by Schoeps *Paul* 143. The source of the citation is in fact Midrash Rabbah:61(Vayera):3.

[93] This typology is explicitly stated in Ep. Barn.7:3 (c.100CE), as well as being evidenced in the writings of Clement of Alexandria, Irenaeus, Tertullian and Origen.

[94] In effect this creates a 'criterion of similarity', which lends strong plausibility to pro-Christian rabbinical traditions having originated in pre-Christian Judaism.

[95] Scheops *Paul* 141-149.

[96] So, R. Longenecker *The Christology of Early Jewish Christianity* [London:SCM,1970] 115-16, 116 n.236.

[97] Q37:100-11 cf. esp.:107.

[98] cf. Josephus Ant. 4:212; 1QS 10:9-10; The tracing to R. Gamaliel of rabbinical discussion on how late the evening *shema* may be recited (m.Ber.1:2a) suggests it was then well established.

[99] Bauckham *Crucified*:15.

[100] Hurtado *Christ* 31-32 summarising his earlier research (cf. esp. *One* 17-92). In fact, Hurtado more questionably claims it was *the* major way.

[101] Matt.4:10/Lk.4:8.

[102] cf. pp 52-53 for discussion of the refusal tradition.

[103] Rev.14:6-7; 19:10; 22:8-9.

[104] So, Hurtado 'The Binitarian Shape of Early Christian Worship' 187-213 in C.C. Newman, J.R. Davila & G.S. Lewis (eds) *The Jewish Roots of Christological Monotheism* [Brill:Leiden,1999] cf. esp. 192-94.

[105] cf. Ex.15:1-21; Jdg.5:11; 2 Sam.22:50; 1 Chr.15:16,27; Neh.7:1; Ps.40:3; 1Q36; 4Q88; 4Q380-81; 4Q400-407; 4Q427-32; Matt.26:30/Mk 14:26. M. Hengel 'Hymns and Christology' 78-96 in M. Hengel *Between Jesus and Paul* [London:SCM,1983] questions the existence of hymn singing in religious synagogues, but admits the practice was otherwise widespread in second temple Judaism.

[106] So, Hurtado *One* 102-03.

[107] So, Hengel 'Hymns' 81.

[108] Rev.5:6-14 (cf. 4:2-3).

[109] So, R. Bauckham 'The Worship of Jesus' 118-149 in R. Bauckham *The Climax of Prophecy* [Edinburgh: T&T Clark,1993].

[110] So, Hurtado *One* 101-03.

[111] So, Hengel 'Hymns' 79-81.

[112] So, Hurtado *One* 104.

[113] Rom.1:8; 5:11; 7:25; 16:27; Col.3:17; Heb.13:15; 1 Pet.2:5; 4:11; Jude:25.

[114] Jude:25.

[115] Acts 2:21,38 cf. also our earlier discussion of the NT christological title 'Lord' pp 89-90.

[116] So, Witherington *Acts* 276.

[117] Acts 9:10-17.

[118] 2 Cor.12:7-9.

[119] 1 Cor.16:22; Rev.22:20.

[120] So, Hurtado *One* 106.

[121] Jn 14:13-14; 16:23-24.

[122] Hurtado 'Binitarian' 194-96.

[123] Gen.4:26; 12:8; 26:25; 1 Kgs.18:24; Zeph.3:9; Zech.13:9.

[124] Isa.12:4; Zeph.3:9; Zech.13:9.

[125] Hurtado 'Binitarian' 198-99 suggests it indicates that the early Christians 'intended' a direct association and analogy between their devotion to Jesus and OT cultic devotion to YHWH.

[126] Acts 9:13-14ff cf. discussion in section 'Prayer to Christ' above.

[127] cf. Acts 22:16; Rom.10:9-13; 1 Cor.1:2.

[128] cf. pp 85-86 section 'Delegation to his followers of authority over evil spirits and to perform miracles'for discussion of the significance of this delegation of authority in including Jesus within the unique divine identity.

[129] Acts 19:13-17.

[130] cf. p150.

[131] cf. Tob.6:4-7 and our earlier discussion of this on p 53f.

[132] 1 Kgs 8:33,35; 2 Chr.6:24 (and Heb. only 6:26).

[133] So, Hurtado *One* 113.

[134] Rom.10:9; 1 Cor.12:2-3; 1 Jn 2:23.

[135] Rom.10:9.

[136] Matt.10:32 (my translation).

[137] e.g. Acts 11:27-30; 13:1-4; 15:32; Rom.12:6; 1 Cor.12:7-11,27-31; 14:1-33,39-40; Eph.4:11.

[138] e.g. 2 Cor.12:8-9; Rev.1:1,9-19f; .2:1-7,8-11,12-17,18-29; 3:1-6,7-13,14-22; 16:15; 22:12-16,20 and probably Acts 18:9-10; 23:11; 1 Thess.4:15. Although NT prophecy was patterned after the form of OT prophecy, Paul clearly indicates that most prophecy in the early church did not have the authoritative status of scripture (1 Cor.14:29-32, 37-38; 1 Thess. 5:19-22). It therefore appears to have had a similar status to prophecy in the OT era that was not subsequently recorded in scripture (cf. 2 Kgs 2:3,5-7,15-18; 4:1,38;6:1-6; 9:1 etc.).

[139] Deut.18:20.

[140] So, Hurtado *Christ* 150-51.

[141] cf. e.g. its use in 1 Thess. 4:15-17.

[142] 2 Kgs.1:3-16.

[143] cf. discussion of 'The *malak YHWH*'pp 60-62.

[144] Acts 2:33 cf. :17-18.

[145] Matt.7:15-22; 10:40-42. The former also warns of similar copycat attempts to expel demons in Jesus' name, which Acts 19:13-16 records occurred during Paul's time at Ephesus.

[146] So, L. Hurtado *At the Origins of Christian Worship* [Carlisle:Paternoster,1999] 85-86, and 'Binitarian' cf. esp. 203. The latter emphasises most clearly that the only Jewish analogy for such a cultic role was God himself.

[147] 1 Cor.5:7.

[148] cf. 1 Cor.11:23-32.

[149] 1 Cor.5:7

[150] 1 Cor.11:20 cf. Ex.12:1-20.

[151] 1 Cor.10:18-22.

[152] cf. our earlier discussion in this chapter of the *Aqedath Isaac* pp 119-120.

[153] 1 Cor.8:6; Gal.3:19-20; Eph.4:5-6 (if 'Lord' means Jesus); 1 Tim.2:5 all affirming the beginning of the *shema* that God is one but designating Jesus as the mediator between God and man.

[154] So, F.F. Bruce *1 and 2 Corinthians* [London:Oliphants,1971] 80; Even Dunn *Christology* 179ff admits the formula contains elements of the Jewish *shema*.

[155] 1 Cor.8:4-6.

[156] Contra. Dunn *Christology* 179-83 who insists this must be the meaning as he assumes that the early church did not recognise Jesus' divinity in the pre-Pauline era. However, as Dunn's premise is also his thesis, this is a circular argument. For further discussion of Dunn's hypothesis cf. Appendix B.

[157] So, Conzelmann *1 Corinthians* 143. Similarly, Barrett *1 Corinthians* 192 notes that 1 Cor.8:6 parallels Deut.10:17 in putting 'gods' and 'lords' together.

[158] This argument appears to have originated with W. Bousset whose now largely abandoned theory of christological evolution argued that Christians first called Jesus 'Lord' in Hellenistic contexts.

[159] So, P. Ellingworth & H. Hatton *A Translators Handbook on Paul's First Letter to the Corinthians* [London:UBS,1985] 162.

[160] So, G.D. Fee *1 Corinthians* 374.

[161] cf. discussion on p 48 of the use of 'all things' as monotheistic rhetoric in 2TJ.

[162] So, Hengel 'Hymns' 82-83.

[163] cf. discussion of christological titles such as 'King of kings' (Rev.17:14; 19:16) pp 86-93.

[164] For a concise summary of possible second temple precedents cf. G.R. Beasley-Murray βαπτίζω *NIDNTT* 1:144-45, who notes the absence of any extant evidence of Jewish proselyte baptism at this time, although he does not exclude this possibility.

[165] cf. esp. Rev. 4:2-5; 5:1,6ff.

CHAPTER 5

MONOTHEISM IN THE ISLAMIC CONTEXT

The King upon His throne...[1]

Introduction

In this chapter we will survey important aspects of the Islamic context we are seeking to develop a contextualised christology for. In particular, we will examine the way in which monotheism is primarily conceived i.e. in bounded or unbounded, extrinsic or intrinsic terms; Islamic beliefs concerning theophany, epiphany and monolatry; and Islamic attitudes towards christological monotheism.

Although there are many local expressions of Islam, many aspects of Islamic belief are widespread across a range of Islamic contexts. In preparing this study it has been necessary to use Islamic texts drawn from an actual Islamic context, in order to avoid portraying an amalgam of various Islamic beliefs that does not necessarily occur in any Islamic society. However, although Islamic texts we have used in this chapter are drawn from one particular context, that of Sunni Islam in the Indo-Persian world, many of these texts are used widely across the Islamic world (*Qur'an*, *Ahadith*, classical *tafsir*), whilst others are representative of polarities and trends that are widely spread across the Islamic world, (mysticism, radical Islamism and traditional versus reformist interpretations of monolatry).

Although there are normally important differences between the various sectarian groupings that exist in most Islamic contexts, there are also frequently significant areas of commonality. All groups look to the *Qur'an* and *Ahadith* as sources of authority, and although the reformist movements typically reject various local practices such as saint veneration as *Bid'a* (innovation), both reformist and traditionalist groupings often follow the same *madrassa* curriculum. One of the clearest examples of this is the *Dars-i-Nizami* syllabus, which in the Indian subcontinent forms the basis of the *madrassa* curriculum for both the reformist (*Deobandi*) and traditionalist (*Barelvi*) *madrasas*. Consequently, the teaching in both reformist and traditionalist mosques is likely to reflect their *mullahs*[2] having both studied the same *tafsir* (commentaries). We will therefore examine the following texts, which constitute the key common elements of this curriculum: the *Qur'an*, *Ahadith* (*Mishkat al-Masabih*) and the classical *tafsir* of the Jalalain and Baidawi. Although we will make some reference to *kalam* (scholastic theology), as the latter is not easily understood outside of the *madrasa*, its impact on the beliefs of the majority of Muslims is somewhat constrained.[3] As our concern is to discover beliefs that are most widely held by Muslims,[4] we will also examine a number of other Islamic texts which are in use amongst the wider populace, including the radical Islamist *tafsir* of Mawdudi (*Tafhim al-Qur'an*) and Sayyid Qutb (*Fi Zilal al-Qur'an*); *Ta'wil al-Hadith* of Shah Wali Allah, to whom the various reform movements in the Indian subcontinent look for inspiration; *Qessas al-anbiya* ('Stories of the prophets'), whose easy narrative style has made its various editions one of the most widely circulated Islamic texts; and the mystical poetry of Rumi, Hafiz and Sa'di which are archetypical of much mystical poetry in the Indo-Persian world and beyond.[5] A more detailed description of these texts is included in Appendix C.

Our aim will be to determine how *Tawhid* is understood in popular Islam. By 'popular' we do not necessarily imply any opposition to 'orthodox' Islam,[6] but simply refer to the extent that a common perception of *Tawhid* exists across the different spheres of Islamic inculcation we examine.[7] This is important as contextualisation must insofar as possible be addressed to the community as a whole, rather than any particular segment of it.[8] For this reason, the beliefs of secularised liberal Muslims fall beyond the scope of this enquiry as in most Islamic countries they represent only a tiny urbanised element among the educated elite, rather than 'popular' Islam.

As in our study of the Jewish context in which early church christology was contextualised, we will here examine five issues: a) the main conceptual framework used to describe monotheism, in particular whether God is understood in bounded or unbounded, extrinsic or intrinsic terms; b) monolatry, can only God be legitimately worshipped, adored or invoked? Here we are not so much concerned with whether such practice occurs, but are using the texts outlined above as indicators of the degree of legitimacy with which such practices are viewed. For example various forms of malevolent witchcraft are practised in many Islamic countries, but are normally regarded as illegitimate;[9] c) Theophany, can mortal men ever see God? d) Epiphany, can God ever appear on earth? e) Attitudes towards christological monotheism. We will also briefly examine a number of broader cultural themes that any contextualisation of christology needs to engage with.

How Muslims Think About God: The Conceptual Framework used to Describe Monotheism

Bounded Extrinsic Monotheism

The *Qur'an* repeatedly describes God's unique identity in terms of bounded extrinsic monotheism. Time after time God is described by the use of exclusive terms such as the only God,[10] the one beyond comparison with others,[11] 'the Most High, Most Great'[12] and so forth, and a vigorous polemic against associating any created thing with God forms a central part of the *Qur'an*.[13]

A number of *Qur'an*ic references refer to God as *al-Hai* ('The Living') and *al-Qayyum* ('The Self-subsisting').[14] However, these simply acknowledge the existence of God, rather than giving any specific information concerning the internal 'nature' of God's oneness. In this respect, the Qur'anic conception of monotheism is no different from the OT's description of YHWH's self-existence revealed to Moses as 'I AM' (אֶהְיֶה אֲשֶׁר אֶהְיֶה), *al-Hai* interestingly being cognate with this.[15]

The famous light verse (Q24:35) could conceivably be understood to depict the essence of God pantheistically emanating out into the universe by varying degrees; i.e. unbounded monotheism, although it certainly does not require this interpretation. But however this verse is interpreted, throughout the rest of the *Qur'an* there is an insistent polemic concerning the absolute boundary between God and all else. It is therefore fair to say that the *Qur'an* at least primarily portrays God in terms of 'bounded monotheism'. The *Qur'an* also repeatedly describes God's unique identity in extrinsic terms.

Sole Creator, Ruler and Judge

The *Qur'an* describes God as the sole creator, who created all things by his divine fiat,[16] sustains it[17] and will eventually recreate it.[18] As such he is both the beginning and the ending of creation.[19] He alone is the giver of life and death, the inability of other beings to impart life except by God's permission being one of the boundaries that distinguishes God from all else.[20]

A variety of terms are also used to designate God as the sole ruler of all things. The title 'Lord' (*Rabb*), and its various combinations, occurs 151 times.[21] Particularly significant is the title *Rabb al-alamin* ('Lord of the worlds'),[22] which occurs forty two times including in the *Fatihah*, which is recited by many Muslims twice daily. Other similar descriptions include *Rabb al-'arsh* ('Lord of the throne'),[23] *al-Malk* ('the King'), *Malk al-mulk* ('King of kings')[24] and *Rabb kull shay* ('Lord of all things').[25] God is also repeatedly described in terms such as the one having dominion over the heavens and the earth,[26] the East and the West[27] and so forth.

The *Qur'an* repeatedly warns of the judgement of God, referring to God as the 'Master of the day of judgement' (*Malik Yaum al-din*), a divine title, which, amongst other places, occurs in the *Fatihah*.[28] The *Qur'an* describes God as the only judge,[29] and the only one who can forgive sins.[30] Both statements indicate that the designation of God as judge again functions as a boundary marker clearly distinguishing God from all else.

Significantly, these extrinsic descriptions of God equate quite closely with the conceptual framework of monotheism that we observed in the Jewish context, where God's identity was also known as the sole creator, ruler, final eschatological judge, and additionally in Judaism as the only saviour. It is noticeable however, that the *Qur'an* never once refers to God as 'the Saviour'. Although it does speak of God saving his people from Hell, this salvation appears solely to consist in issuing warnings, and involves no redemptive activity on the part of God.[31] Whilst God might occasionally answer prayers for deliverance from temporal calamity,[32] such protection appears to be by the action of an agent, rather than God himself ever acting to save his people.[33]

Both Mawdudi and Qutb use this extrinsic conception of God as the sole Creator and ruler to explain how God is active in the world. Mawdudi explains:

> The Lord of the universe did not retreat into retirement once the universe was created… He is not only the Creator of the universe, but also its sovereign and its actual ruler[34]

Interestingly, Qutb specifically argues that this view of God

> is diametrically opposite to the misguided view of Aristotle, the most eminent of the Greek philosophers, that God takes no interest in His creation, because He is too great to preoccupy Himself with anything else…The Islamic view of God…is…that God is actively and constantly sustaining all existence, and that the existence of everything emanates from his will and design.[35]

Qutb's comments here are particularly significant for us as they highlight the need in the Islamic context for a very different contextualisation of christology, from that developed by patristic creeds in contexts where Greek philosophy was a significant influence.

Ahadith narrate that there are ninety nine names of God, although no specific list of these is given.[36] After the *Shahada*,[37] the ninety nine names arguably represent the simplest and most widespread 'theology' of Islam. Their importance in forming popular conceptions of God is indicated by the common practice of addressing God by the name or attribute to which the worshipper wishes to appeal; e.g. *al-Tauwab*, 'the Receiver of repentance' is used when seeking pardon.[38] These names are particularly important in Muslim devotions involving the rosary (*tasbih*), which commonly consists of thirty three beads counted three times. Five of these names refer in some way to God as the Creator, thirteen as sole ruler of the universe, at least ten as the final eschatological judge and at least eleven refer in some form to God's benevolence and mercy towards mankind, although none specifically designate him as the saviour. Significantly, many of these names such as *al-Malik* ('the King'), *Malik al-Mulk* ('the King of kings'), *al-Awwal* ('the First') and *al-Akhir* ('the Last') are also titles applied with the definite article to Jesus in the NT, whilst others such as *al-Ghafer* ('the Forgiver') and *al-Mujib* ('The Answerer of prayer') are exclusively divine attributes ascribed to Jesus in the NT.

Boundary Markers Distinguishing God from All Else

A similarity to the Jewish context is that in both the *Qur'an* and *Ahadith* these extrinsic descriptions of God function as boundary markers between God and all else by means of subject/object distinctions; i.e. creator/created, ruler/ruled, judge/judged. This can be seen in the following *Hadith* relating a prayer of Muhammad:

> There is no god but Thee! Thou art my Lord, and I am Thy servant.[39]

These extrinsic descriptions of God are also often supplemented by the phrase 'all things', which forms part of the *Qur'an*'s monotheistic rhetoric indicating that God is the Creator of all things,[40] rules all things,[41] knows all things[42] and so forth. Surah *al-Hudud* for example begins:

> ...To Him belongs the dominion of the heavens and the earth; It is He Who gives life and death; and He has power over *all things*. He is the First and the Last, The Evident and the Immanent: And He has full knowledge of *all things*.

He it is Who created the heavens and the earth in six days, and is moreover firmly established on the Throne....[43]

This bounded extrinsic conception of God is also emphasised in Islamic *tafsir*. Baidawi for example accepts that God must have 'necessary existence',[44] but rejects any idea that the intrinsic nature of God can be known.[45] His comment on the throne verse, indicates that God's unique identity is primarily known by him being the sole creator and ruler of all:

> He is considered as exalted on account of his uniqueness as God and is to be praised *because he alone is Lord* (of the world)...God showed them that only one is worthy of being Lord, namely he, since it is *he to whom the act of creation and the command (amr) are suited.*[46]

A further boundary marker is the reservation of certain titles for God alone, for example a number of *Ahadith* prohibit the title 'King of kings' (*Malik al-mulk*) being applied to anyone other than God.[47]

Sufism

Historically, Sufism has conceived of God in two ways. *Wahdat al-wujud*, which was emphasised by the medieval Sufi Ibn Arabi,[48] focused so much on God's uniqueness that God was regarded as the only real existence. Some expressions of this even regarded the entire universe including man as a series of emanations from the divine light of God. The Sufi aim is therefore to merge the self with God, thereby achieving reunion with 'the Reality'; i.e. God.[49] This is therefore an extrinsic unbounded concept of God as creator, to which is added an intrinsic unbounded concept of God as restorer.

Shaikh Ahmad Sirhindi (1564-1624) saw the danger of *wahdat al-wujud* slipping into a pantheistic identity of substance between God and the world. He therefore sought to purify Sufism of unislamic elements by emphasising *wahdat al-shuhud*. This stressed the transcendence of God, teaching that union (*wasl*) with God consists of God witnessing to himself in the heart of the believer, rather than an actual merging of the self with God. It therefore maintained the bounded extrinsic understanding of God that we have seen in the *Qur'an* and *tafsir*. At least in the Indo-Persian world, Sirhindi's emphasis on *wahdat al-shuhud* has had a major impact on Islamic mysticism and was a formative influence on Islamic revivalists such as Shah Wali Allah (1702-62). The latter sought to reunite both streams of Sufism by asserting that both Ibn Arabi and Sirhindi taught complementary perspectives, the union claimed by *wahdat al-wujud* being reinterpreted in bounded terms as a subjective experience of illumination, rather than an ontological reality.[50]

This bounded conception of God can be seen in popular texts such as *Qessas al-anbiya* and Shah Wali Allah's *Ta'wil al-Hadith*, both which show the influence of Sufism. These primarily describe God's unique identity in bounded terms as the sole creator and ruler of all things,[51] Shah Wali Allah frequently speaking of God as the *mudaabbir* ('administrator') of the heavens and the earth.[52] The conception of creation in these books is somewhat different from that portrayed in the *Qur'an*. *Qessas al-anbiya* speaks of God creating first of all the light of Muhammad from which all else, including the divine throne and the pen, were subsequently created,[53] while *Ta'wil al-Hadith* speaks of God having first created the original soul from which all forms of creation were subsequently made.[54] However, in both texts this primeval being is specifically described as created, and therefore distinct from God.

The Persian mystical poetry of Sa'di, Hafiz and Rumi all similarly use an extrinsic description of God as creator and ruler of his creatures as a basic framework to portray God. This is most clearly seen in the titles of God used. Even Rumi's *Masnavi*, despite its evident Sufi influences, describes God with titles such as 'my Creator', 'Lord of the worlds' and 'King of kings'.[55]

Sa'di uses the subject/object distinctions of Lord/servant; Judge/judged and so forth to distinguish God from all else in the comparison between divine and human kingship that is a major theme of the *Gulistan*. In the following poem he reminds kings that though they may be lord and judge of the whole face of the earth, God alone is the creator of their subjects and they themselves are servants of God, who is their own Lord and Judge:

> A saint was passing by a Lord (*khudavand*),
> the latter who was punishing his ward,
> having bound him hand and foot with cord.
>
> and so to the Lord he gave this adage,
> 'oh my son, to thy slave be not so savage,
> on a creature of the King of glory, cease this ravage...
>
> ...you too have a greater Lord (*khudavand*),
> and ere Arslan and Aghosh be your ward,
> hasten to remember your own master and Lord'

The Hadith of God's judgement hath said
of the pure slave who to heaven is led
while for his master 'to hell' will be said.[56]

Intrinsic Conceptions of God

Although it is clear that in the Islamic context God is primarily conceived of in bounded extrinsic terms, other conceptions sometimes exist alongside this.

In *kalam*, which is taught to future *ulema* in *madrasas*, the name *Allah* is regarded as the name of the essential being of God (*Ism al-dhat*) while the ninety nine names are commonly considered to be the names of the attributes of God (*Ism al-sifat*).[57] Furthermore, the attributes themselves are sometimes divided into descriptions of essence (*sifat al-dhat*) and action (*sifat al-fi'l*).[58] This suggests that although the names such as al-*Khaliq* ('the Creator'), *Malik al-mulk* ('King of kings') and *al-Ghafur* ('the Forgiving') are clearly extrinsic descriptions of God, in *kalam* the bounded extrinsic conception of God is supplemented by a bounded intrinsic one.

Similarly, although Rumi speaks of God in extrinsic terms, he sometimes supplements this with Sufi imagery that approximates to an unbounded intrinsic concept of God. In particular, he speaks of the time before creation when the souls of men were immersed 'up to the neck in the sea of God's potency',[59] and of the light of God now being screened by 700 veils of light which the soul must pass through to become again immersed in the ocean of God.[60] However, it appears that this is an additional perspective that Rumi has added on to the bounded extrinsic concept of monotheism that is more evident in texts such as the *Qur'an* and *Ahadith*.

Summary

In summary, we may say that in the Islamic context God is primarily conceived of in bounded extrinsic terms, as the sole creator, ruler and judge of all things. Although this may at times be supplemented by other bounded intrinsic conceptions as in *Kalam*, or even unbounded intrinsic conceptions derived from *wahdat al-wujud* Sufism, the primary and most widespread conception of God appears to be a bounded extrinsic one.

Monolatry: Can Only God legitimately be Worshipped, Adored or Invoked?

Intercession

In the Islamic context the subject of monolatry is closely linked to belief in intercession. The idea that figures such as prophets might be able to request God to forgive others raises the question of whether such a person might be legitimately invoked to intercede on one's behalf.

In the early years of Islam the *Mu'tazila* denied the possibility of intercession.[61] However, within orthodox (Asharite) *kalam* a growing acceptance of intercession occurred. The *Wasiyat* creed attributed to Abu Hanifa explicitly affirmed the intercession of Muhammad, even for Muslims guilty of mortal sins,[62] a position now endorsed even by the Wahhabis.[63] The later *Fikh Akbar* 2 went further and affirmed the intercession of all the prophets to be a reality.[64] Significantly, it also affirmed the related issue of the existence of saints (*awliya*) and their miracles (*karamat*),[65] which the *Mu'tazila* had earlier denied.[66] Although this creed did not take the further step of formally justifying a doctrine of intercession by saints, who could then be appealed to or invoked for assistance, it is clear that its affirmations of both intercession by prophets and the existence of *awliya* and their *karamat* laid a foundation which could be developed in this direction by those who chose to.

Reformist and Traditionalist Beliefs

The subsequent developments in Islamic theology[67] need to be understood in the light of the religious history of the regions which Islam gradually penetrated. In areas such as India, wandering *fakirs* and *Sufis* appear to have played a significant role in the conversion of the masses, particularly in the fifteenth and sixteenth centuries, which ultimately resulted in a degree of fusion between Islam and various existing religious customs.[68] This has led to two quite opposite poles of Islamic theology emerging. We may characterise these as the traditionalist pole, which has legitimated the incorporation into Islam of various local religious practices, including the veneration and invocation of living and dead saints, the latter often centred around the saint's tomb;[69] and the reformist pole, which rejects all such 'local' religious practices as innovations.

The Indian subcontinent provides a good illustration of these two poles in the form of the *Deobandi* reform movement and the *Barelvi* movement, which seeks to justify traditional religious practice. Although neither movement formally emerged until the late nineteenth century, specific antecedents of both poles existed in earlier centuries in the region, as they did throughout the Islamic world.

The Roshaniyah sect that began among the Pushtuns during the sixteenth century represents the antetype of the *Barelvi* pole. The self-designated *Pir-i-Roshan*[70] claimed that all *pirs* were manifestations of divinity, in view of which he told his followers 'I am your Pir and your God' and therefore demanded absolute obedience to himself.[71] Although the Roshaniyah sect is a very extreme example of the exaltation of saints, the veneration of, and prayer to, living and dead saints is widespread both in the Indian subcontinent and in many other areas of the Islamic world. However, it is important to note that its devotees do not necessarily justify the practice theologically in the same way as the *Pir-i-Roshan*, or indeed with any formal theology at all.

The longstanding existence of such practices led to a series of reform movements affecting Sunni Islam. In Arabia, Muhammad Abd al-Wahhab (1703-1792) drew on the writings of the earlier Islamic revivalist Ibn Taymiyya (d.1328) in founding what in the west is generally termed 'the Wahhabi movement', but itself uses the designation *Muwahiddun* (Unitarians) i.e. those who uphold and practice monotheism. In the Indo-Persian region a similar movement was started by Shah Wali Allah of Delhi (1702-1763), which became the inspiration for a series of later reformers, and culminated in the *Deobandi* movement (1867-).[72] Although Abd al-Wahhab rejected all forms of Sufism, reform movements whether in India or the Arab world have not generally rejected Sufism *per se* but only sought to reform it of religious practices that they considered unislamic, including prayer to living and dead saints.[73]

In the Indian subcontinent reaction against the reformers was most clearly articulated by Maulana Ahmad Riza Khan of Barelvi (1856-1921). Riza Khan vigorously defended any custom that elevated the stature of Muhammad and the saints. He emphasised the Sufi doctrine of the *Noor-i-Muhammad*,[74] which regarded Muhammad as an emanation of God's light pre-existing at the beginning of creation. The saints were at once part of and aware of the light of Muhammad, and after death, were able to intercede with God on behalf of ordinary believers just as Muhammad himself could. One consequence of this has been the development of *na'at*, hymns venerating Muhammad that sometimes bear marked similarities to the Christian portrayal of the exalted Jesus.[75]

Although the *wahdat al-wujud* concept of the medieval Sufi writer Ibn 'Arabi almost certainly had a strong influence on the development of this theology, it did not start from that point. Rather, it was an attempt by Riza Khan to justify existing Islamic practice in the subcontinent, much of which was strongly linked to the intercession of Muslim saints. In fact, it is more accurate to characterise the *Barelvi* pole as the acceptance of a range of practices, rather than adherence to a particular theology, such as Riza Khan's, that seeks to justify these practices. This has resulted in a situation, even amongst *ulema*, where a large number characterise themselves as '*Barelvi*' simply because they practice what has become a traditional form of Islam that looks not only to the *Qur'an* and *Ahadith*, but also to the intercession of saints.[76]

The formal Islamic texts that we have so far examined, *Qur'an*, *Ahadith* and classical *tafsir*, have a certain degree of ambiguity on this subject, thereby allowing both traditionalist and reformist poles to appeal to them.

The *Qur'an* explicitly refers to God as the only one worthy of worship.[77] It prescribes monolatry, the exclusive worship of God precisely because God is the sole creator[78] and sole ruler[79] of his creation. Paradoxically however, the *Qur'an* on seven separate occasions ascribes the origin of Iblis's (Satan's) rebellion against God to his refusal to obey God's command for the angels to prostrate themselves before Adam in obeisance.[80] Interestingly, these Qur'anic accounts closely parallel the command for Satan to worship Adam in *Life of Adam and Eve*,[81] a Jewish text probably dating from the first century CE. This raises the possibility that the early church may have contextualised its christology against a background which included similar beliefs to these.

The Qur'anic teaching on intercession is equally ambiguous. Intercession is explicitly stated to be an exclusively divine prerogative.[82] Muhammad's earlier authorisation of invoking the pre-Islamic deities *al-Lat, al-Uzza* and *Manat* is ascribed to satanic deception[83] and it is forbidden to invoke beings to intercede with God.[84] However, other verses suggest that God might grant prophets, the Spirit and angels specific 'permission' to intercede on the day of judgement.[85] This understanding of heavenly intercession means that Christian teaching of Jesus' heavenly intercession will almost inevitably be interpreted as being 'by God's permission' and in no sense unique.[86]

Although the *Qur'an* merely hints at the intercession of prophets and angels, *Ahadith* very specifically relate that various prophets such as Abraham and

Jesus will be intercessors on the day of resurrection. However, Muhammad is singled out as the leader of intercession on that day.[87] Despite this, there is no suggestion that Muhammad himself is to be invoked before the day of resurrection. Furthermore, some *Ahadith* actually forbid visiting graves to venerate the dead,[88] although some interpret this as a temporary injunction that Muhammad later reversed.[89]

Similar ambiguity exists concerning the use of charms, some of which invoke the names of God's prophets such as Solomon and various angels.[90] Some *Ahadith* sanction the use of charms, particularly against the evil eye and snakebite.[91] It is even narrated that Muhammad himself specifically advised using a 'spell' to cure a girl of jaundice,[92] and specifically authorised the use of some pre-Islamic charms saying 'there's no harm in (the) charm, so long as there is no polytheism in it.'[93] However, other *Ahadith* narrate Muhammad describing charms as being 'from the actions of the devil',[94] and enjoin reliance solely on prayer to God.[95] Nonetheless, the sanctioning of charms by some *Ahadith*, together with the Qur'anic account of Solomon's power over evil spirits and jinn,[96] provides some legitimation for a range of prophylactic practices in the Islamic context such as the wearing of charms and burning of rue seeds, that are widely used to protect people and property against the jinn, evil spirits and the evil eye.[97]

Both Baidawi and the Jalalain add emphasis to the Qur'anic injunction that no one other than God is to be worshipped. For example, the Jalalain add the emphatic word 'alone' to the Qur'anic text of Q6:102:

> This God is your Lord. There is no God but He, the Creator of everything: therefore worship ye Him (*alone*).[98]

However, neither commentator is explicit as to whether it is legitimate to pray to, or invoke lesser beings or people. For example, Baidawi takes the injunction of Q3:64 against taking lords and patrons other than God, as a paradigm of polemic against Christian worship of Jesus and Jewish veneration of their rabbis,[99] and simply ignores the cult of saint veneration that had gained widespread acceptance among Muslims a century earlier.[100]

Mawdudi is less ambiguous, although he does avoid an explicit attack on *Barelvi* practice *per se*, probably due to his desire to appeal to the entire Muslim *ummah*. However, his commentary on the words of the *Fatihah* 'Praise be to Allah, the Lord of the entire universe' implies rejection of both saint veneration and hymns in praise of Muhammad (*na'at*):

> ...what is said here is not merely that praise be to God, but that *all* praise be to God *alone*...no human beings, angels, demigods, heavenly bodies - in short, no created beings - are possessed of an innate excellence...if there is anyone at all whom we ought to adore...it is the *Creator* of excellence rather than its *possessor*.[101]

He also makes a strong implicit attack on one of the key motivations behind the veneration of saints and Muhammad, the hope of intercession on the day of judgement. His commentary on Q2:255 'Who is there who might intercede with Him save with His leave?', ascribes such practices rather implausibly to 'polytheists':

> This is a refutation of the ideas of those polytheists who consider either *saints,* angels or other beings to be so influential with God that if they were adamant in demanding something of Him, their demand would prevail...none - *not even the greatest Prophets* and the most highly esteemed angels - will dare utter one word in the majestic court of the Lord unless they are expressly permitted to do so.[102]

This is quite a radical statement, as even Shah Wali Allah, who was in many respects the ancestor of the Indian reform movements, specifically affirmed the intercession of prophets, apostles and saints on the day of judgement, stating that Muhammad would be the greatest intercessor.[103]

Qessas al-anbiya is probably representative of a wide body of popular belief when it similarly accords 'the crown of intercession' to Muhammad, but specifically rejects worship of him, recording the words uttered by Abu Bakr when Muhammad died, that only God should be worshipped as he is 'the Ever Living', while Muhammad is dead.[104]

Summary

In summary we may say that the Islamic understanding of monolatry whilst ultimately focused on God, is varied and complex. Some sections of the Islamic community believe that prayer to, and veneration of historical and living persons such as Muhammad and saints is actually part of the worship of the one God, whilst others reject such practices as innovations. This means that in the Islamic context christological worship runs the risk of being interpreted as being akin to traditionalist veneration of other prophets, and so cannot convey quite so emphatically as it did in the Jewish context, that Jesus is on the God side of the God/non-god divide.

Theophany: Can God be seen?

The issue of theophany implicitly raises a number of questions in the Islamic context: whether God can locally manifest a form of his presence in a particular place; whether people, particularly mortals on earth, could see such a manifestation of God; and whether the possibility of seeing God implies that God could assume an anthropomorphic form, as indeed Qur'anic references to God's hands and feet and so forth could imply.

Local Manifestations of the Presence of God

This issue has been raised in Islamic debates about the statement of Q7:54 that God seated himself on the throne (*'arsh*). Baidawi finds this verse extremely difficult to interpret:

> Then his power (*amr*) was placed (on the Throne), or he took possession (of the Throne). According to our followers, the sitting upon the Throne is an attribute of God (which one accepts) 'without (asking) how' (*bi-la kaifa*). This means that when one says that God sits upon the Throne...in so doing one must keep free from (the idea) of residing or being settled in a place.[105]

Although Baidawi is cautious about the implication of specific locality, his suggestion that it was God's power that sat on the throne to some extent parallels the suggestion in some Jewish targums that it was the *shekinah* sitting on the throne.

However, the Islamist *tafsir* of Mawdudi is much clearer on the implication of specific locality and suggests that:

> After the creation of the universe God focused His effulgence at a particular point in His kingdom which is known as the Throne, from where He showers the blessings of life and power, and governs the whole universe.[106]

Mawdudi's thought here is extremely important, because it suggests the possibility that God could locally manifest his presence in a particular place, without that manifestation in any sense constituting or restricting the totality of God. At this point Mawdudi's thought closely parallels biblical concepts of theophany.

Visible Manifestations of God

A positive answer to the question of whether God can be seen is strongly implied by the *Qur'an's* repeated insistence that mankind will actually meet God on the day of judgement.[107] In fact, the unbelievers' denial of this meeting is one of the major grounds for Muhammad and earlier prophets condemning them.[108] It is stated that even backslidden Muslims will see God coming on canopies of clouds with his angels, and the faithful are promised that they will see God's angel-surrounded throne and be in the presence of a sovereign omnipotent.[109] Al-Ashari's reaction against the Mutazilite denial of this sight of God has resulted in a strong affirmation by Asharite *kalam* that this visible meeting with God is a reality, which should not be taken metaphorically, a position affirmed even by the Wahhabis.[110]

However, there is an apparent tension in the *Qur'an* as to whether God can be seen before this time. Two Qur'anic passages, including surah *Ya Sin*, considered by many Muslims as the heart of the *Qur'an* and frequently read to the dying, explicitly state that God is invisible to mortal men.[111] In a similar vein Q42:51 states that it is not fitting that God should speak to a man except 'from behind a veil', although the following clause 'or by sending a messenger (*rasul*)' creates a certain ambiguity. A number of *Ahadith* reinforce this by describing the seeming impossibility of any of God's creation, including even Gabriel, seeing God's face directly. It is stated that veils of light form an absolute boundary shielding God from all else, and if they did not do so, the brilliance of God's face would burn up all within his sight.[112]

However, despite this, Q53:1-18 appears to relate that Muhammad twice saw God, once during the *mi'raj* (ascension) and once when God apparently descended to earth at a distance of two bow lengths from him. The question of whether Muhammad actually saw God has generated a great controversy among *ulema*,[113] which has been fuelled by the existence of two distinct interpretative traditions within the *Ahadith*.

On the one hand traditions ascribed to Ayesha, Muhammad's favourite wife, and Ibn Mas'ud are categorical that Muhammad only saw Gabriel, not God, although they also make it clear that this question was hotly disputed in the earliest years of Islam. For example, an *Hadith* relating that Masruq asked Ayesha if Muhammad saw God, records her emphatically denying this:

> Did Muhammad see his Lord?...Then I read: *He has indeed seen of the greatest signs of his Lord* - Q53:18. She said: May the eye be lost to you! he was Gabriel....
>
> ...I asked Ayesha: Where is his saying - *Then he drew near, then he drew nearer. So he was of the measure of two bows or closer still* (Q53:8-9)? She said: He was Gabriel.[114]

However, on the other hand traditions ascribed to Ibn Abbas, Muhammad's cousin and regarded as the founder of Qur'anic exegesis, affirm that Muhammad did indeed see God:

> Ibn Abbas reported about "The heart could not be untrue of what he saw. And certainly he saw Him in another descent". He said: He saw Him twice with his heart. ...Muhammad saw his Lord...

When asked about the compatibility of this with the Qur'anic verse 'visions comprehend Him not' (Q6:103), Ibn Abbas continues:

> That is when He shines with His light which is His own light. And he saw his Lord twice.[115]

Here Ibn Abbas appears to be alluding to the Qur'anic reference to God speaking from behind a veil (Q42:51), but implying that Muhammad still saw a form of God. The implication is that God in some way veiled his glory so as to be seen by mortal eyes. This is significantly close to the Biblical concept of God locally manifesting a form of his presence to men that veils his glorious splendour.

Both Baidawi and the Jalalain reject the idea that Muhammad saw God. Baidawi assumes that the sight beyond description which Muhammad saw (Q53:18) was only the whole host of angels worshipping under the lote tree, while the Jalalain more imaginatively suggest that it was the birds which sit in the branches of the tree.   However, the existence of conflicting *Ahadith* traditions, and the claims of Ibn Ishaq in the earliest extant biography of Muhammad, that Gabriel took Muhammad to 'the seventh heaven and his Lord',[116] means that the issue is by no means settled among the *ulema*. It is significant however, that at the popular level *Qessas al-anbiya* explicitly states that on the *mi'raj* Muhammad was allowed to go beyond the lote tree and actually see God, a privilege that was not even permitted to Gabriel.[117]

However, even among the *ulema*, there is near unanimity that Moses actually did see God. Although we will deal with this at more length in our discussion of epiphany, here we will simply note that Moses' sight of God is found in a whole spectrum of Islamic texts ranging from the *Qur'an* to *Qessas al-anbiya*. Although the *Qur'an* records Israelites, who are portrayed as unbelievers, asking Moses to show them God but then being seized by thunder and lightning for their presumption,[118] it also relates a more positive response to Moses' own request to see God. The *Qur'an* narrates that God did manifest his presence to Moses, although Moses did not see God directly due to the overwhelming power of this 'theophany'.[119]

Moses' sight of God has led *kalam* to allow the possibility that mortals on earth might see God. Al-Ashari argued this on the basis that Moses saw God and being an apostle he could not have asked for something wrong,[120] although the Wahhabis dissent from this view.[121]

Divine Anthropomorphism

In the Islamic context, the issue of theophany is related to longstanding debates as to how various anthropomorphic descriptions of God in the *Qur'an* should be viewed. Clearly this issue is of particular importance to our study, as while we have so far established that there is a widely held concept that, at least in the case of Moses, God has in the past locally and visibly manifested a form of his presence to a mortal human being, this is still some way removed from the OT concept that God could appear in an anthropomorphic form.

As a whole *Ahadith* are generally less restrained than the *Qur'an* in their application of anthropomorphic language to God. The language of some *Ahadith* is not only more explicitly anthropomorphic, but also less clearly metaphorical, as in the *Hadith*:

> Allah created Adam and then rubbed his back with His right hand and took out a progeny from him...[122]

Similar anthropomorphic language occurs in *Ahadith* which affirm Muhammad's actual meeting with God during the *mi'raj*, for example Mu'az bin Jabal reported that Muhammad said:

> I was by the side of my Lord, the Blessed and the Glorious, in the best form... Then I saw Him placing His palm between my shoulders till I felt (sic) coldness of His fingers between my chests...[123]

Such anthropomorphisms become even more explicit following the resurrection day as *Ahadith* unequivocally affirm that every believer will see 'his Lord in his open form' and converse with him, and see his face.[124] In fact, several *Ahadith* seemingly bizarrely relate that God will uncover one of his legs before the believers:

> I heard the Messenger of Allah say: Our Lord will disclose His leg. Then every male believer and every female believer will fall down in prostration before Him...[125]

The teaching of *kalam* concerning the divine anthropomorphisms implied in the *Qur'an* goes back to al-Ashari who addressed this issue with the device of *bila kayfa wa la tashbih* i.e. accepting the Qur'anic statements concerning the sight of God without asking how or making comparisons.[126] This position has been adopted by subsequent creedal statements which affirm the sight of God as obligatory dogma, but admit uncertainty concerning the description of this,[127] sometimes adding clauses such as 'without body' and 'without limit' to avoid the opposite dangers of implying that God was limited to finite space.[128] However, it is not easy to see how such statements can be reconciled with the explicit anthropomorphisms in *Ahadith*.

Sufi Interpretations of Theophany

Within Sufism the vision of God is almost invariably interpreted in terms of the inward sight of the heart,[129] although this does not necessarily exclude physical vision. In fact, in the *Kashaf al-Mahjub*, the oldest Persian treatise on Sufism, al-Hujwiri implies that Muhammad first of all saw God with his bodily eyes, and then as he continued to look, with his spiritual eyes.[130] A similar position is taken by Shah Wali Allah who states that Muhammad did see God on the *mi'raj*, but implies that this should be understood in terms of *wahdat al-shuhud* i.e. reflection of God in the heart of the seeker.[131]

The Sufi longing for the sight of God's face sums up the endeavour for union with God *(wasl)* that is a major theme of mystical poetry. Hafiz speaks of the mystic whilst on earth, despite all his faults, reflecting God's face like a mirror:

> With dust my heart is thick, that should be clear,
> A glass to mirror forth the Great King's face.[132]

This imagery exhibits a degree of similarity to the NT portrayal of believers on earth with unveiled faces reflecting the Lord's glory by means of the Holy Spirit, but as yet only seeing him as a poor reflection in a mirror, while in heaven anticipating that he will be seen face to face.[133]

Summary

In summary, we may say that there is an existing concept of theophany in the Islamic context. The idea that God can locally manifest a visible form of his presence is implied in the Qur'anic descriptions of the throne and particularly in the strong emphasis in the *Qur'an* and *Ahadith* that believers will visibly see God in paradise. Furthermore, some *Ahadith* descriptions of this meeting depict God in unequivocally anthropomorphic form. However, most significantly, there is a very widely held belief that God visibly appeared to Moses, which raises the question of whether other mortals might similarly see him while still on earth.

Epiphany: Can God Appear on Earth?

The issue of theophany naturally leads on to the question of epiphany – can God visibly appear on earth?

The Last Day

One area of Islamic belief that at least implicitly touches on the issue of epiphany is that of 'the Last Day' (*Yaum al-akhir*). The *Qur'an* states that on the last day trumpet blasts will herald the coming of God on the clouds, accompanied by his angels.[134] Q14:48 does indicate that the heavens and the earth will in some manner be changed from their present form prior to the actual day of judgement when men will be assembled on earth before God. However, the *Qur'an* does make it clear that God will eschatologically come to earth in judgement. To this extent there is at least a partial parallel with the OT expectation that God will eschatologically come to earth as judge. In fact, the Qur'anic description of the 'Last Day' has many features in common with Biblical descriptions of the 'Day of the Lord', which is interpreted in NT christology as the second coming of Christ. Motifs common to both the Biblical and Islamic contexts include the designation 'the Great Day' (*Yaum azim*), the heavens being stripped away, the sun and moon being darkened, mountains rocked by a major earthquake, God bringing to life those who are in the tombs, and God coming on the clouds accompanied by his angels.[135]

Epiphany Prior to the Last Day

However, in order to assess how far Islamic beliefs move in the direction of God appearing on earth in known history, we must more particularly examine whether there is any concept that God can, or even has, appeared on earth prior to the last day.

We earlier observed how the OT speaks of God manifesting his presence on earth by his Spirit inspiring the prophets, by a local manifestation of his glory (כָּבוֹד) and by assuming an apparently anthropomorphic form that is redactionally dubbed the *malak YHWH*.[136] Interestingly, the *Qur'an* speaks of the Spirit only being sent at God's command.[137] However, it is presented as a created being and portrayed in such a way that it is commonly understood to be a synonym either for Gabriel or occasionally Jesus, although both Baidawi and the Jalalain accept Q40:15 and Q42:52 as referring instead to 'the Spirit of Prophecy'.[138]

However, two Qur'anic passages do raise the rather intriguing issue of whether God could locally manifest his presence so as to appear on earth to people. We have already discussed the interpretation of Q53:1-11, which has sometimes been interpreted as Muhammad seeing God descend at two bow length's distance to earth. However, the Qur'anic Moses narratives are less equivocal, as Moses is explicitly described as the prophet to whom God spoke directly.[139] The *Qur'an* appears to relate three incidents in which God appeared on earth to Moses.

Firstly, at the burning bush, which is related in three separate surahs, all of which record the voice speaking to Moses as specifically identifying itself as God himself.[140] Individual accounts record the hallowing of the ground, implicitly as a result of God's presence[141] and the specific terrestrial locality of the voice: 'a voice was heard from the right bank of the valley, from a tree in hallowed ground:'[142]

Secondly, surah *Ta Ha* records Moses ascending the mount for what appears to be a meeting with God at a specific locality on the top of the mountain. Surah *al-Araf* similarly records the 70 reaching the place of meeting. Both descriptions strikingly parallel the OT Sinai narratives.[143]

Thirdly, and most importantly, is the description of God's response to Moses' request to see him. *Al-Aaraf* records that 'his Lord manifested His glory on the Mount' and adds that this local manifestation of God's presence was so overpowering that the mountain crumbled to dust and Moses swooned.[144]

A number of *Ahadith* also relate in summary form that God spoke to Moses and took him close for secret talks, again implying a terrestrial context.[145]

The only hint given in either the *Qur'an* or *Ahadith* as to why God appeared to Moses, is that it was for Moses to receive the law and to commission him to warn Pharaoh to turn from his sin.[146] The burning bush narratives contain no hint of the revelation of God's character as the saviour that is emphasised in the equivalent OT narratives.

Nevertheless, these incidents are significant for our study as they describe God actually appearing on earth to Moses and are repeated in a wide range of Islamic texts.

Both Baidawi and the Jalalain not only accept that on all three occasions God directly spoke to Moses, but are emphatic that on Sinai Moses met personally with God 'without an intermediary',[147] his 30-40 day fast being necessary to prepare him for this privilege.[148] In fact, Baidawi interprets the simple statement of Q4:164 'The Lord spoke to him (i.e. Moses)' as meaning not only that God spoke to Moses, but that he spoke to him face to face, without the mediation of anyone else, in the same way that he speaks to the angels.[149]

Interestingly it is the radical Islamist commentator Mawdudi who is most insistent that God actually appeared on earth to Moses. He insists that God's communication to Moses at the burning bush was not simply hearing a voice as other prophets had, but was in a similar manner to that which Exodus 33:11 describes as 'The Lord would speak to Moses face to face, as a man speaks with his friend'.[150] He is equally emphatic that on Sinai Moses 'stood in God's presence',[151] although he does not attempt to explain what this means.

The concept of God actually appearing to Moses is also evident at the level of popular literature. *Qessas al-anbiya* implies that God was in some manner locally present in the tree when it narrates how Moses heard the voice calling him, and was then helped to the tree by an angel, where he heard the words 'I am thy Lord, take off thy shoe'.[152]

This widespread belief, that God actually appeared to Moses at the burning bush and on the mountain, suggests that Moses' request to actually see God implies that Moses was asking for something greater than this, possibly to see God in all his glory. The Jalalain interpret this greater sight of God that Q7:143 records Moses then saw, as being both glorious and anthropomorphic:

> That is, when there appeared, of His light, half of the tip of His little finger, as related in a tradition which El Hakim hath verified.[153]

Mawdudi who explains this appearance as God casting 'His effulgence on the mountain,' is somewhat more cautious about the anthropomorphism such divine manifestations imply. However, even he refuses to rule out the possibility that the tablets given to Moses on Sinai were written by God himself.[154]

One further aspect of the way the Moses narratives are related in the Islamic context is that a number of texts include extra Qur'anic material that partially parallels the OT narratives of the theophanic *malak*. However, where parallels to OT narratives occur, Baidawi, the Jalalain and Mawdudi all suggest that the actual figure appearing may have been Gabriel.[155] However, *Qessas al-anbiya* contains a closer parallel to the OT narratives when it refers to the cloud accompanying the Exodus and specifically relates this to the voice of God being heard both on Sinai and when Israel rejected the report of the twelve spies.[156]

Sufism and Epiphany

Within Sufism a different issue arises concerning the possibility of epiphany. Ikbal Ali Shah speaks of Sufism refusing to acknowledge the incarnation of the divine being and, by implication, his epiphany, because that would be to bring God down, whereas the Sufi aim is to bring man up towards God.[157] It is perhaps for this reason that Shah Wali Allah appears to interpret the result of Moses asking to see God, in terms of *wahdat al shuhud*, suggesting that Moses only saw God as a mirror in his own heart, and adds that Moses then realised that 'if God has manifested himself in His form' he would have been destroyed.[158]

However despite this, two of the images that are important in mystical poetry have an intriguing potential to become vehicles for expressing the concept of epiphany in a contextualised christology.

The first is that of 'the lover' and 'the beloved', the portrayal of which bears marked similarities to the Song of Solomon and the divine bridegroom imagery of the OT, except that the gender roles are reversed. In Persian mystical poetry 'the beloved', who represents God, is implicitly and occasionally explicitly female, a view that is almost inevitably in tension both with the otherwise masculine depiction of God (king, judge and so forth) and the characteristic view of male dominated societies that tends to view women as less than equal to men.[159] The female image occurs because the culture dictates that 'the lover', who represents the seeker pursuing and courting the presence of God, must be male. So for example Hafiz asks:

> When shall the bridegroom come to the couch of the bride?[160]

However, a simple reversal of the referents of the lover/beloved imagery to follow the Biblical pattern whereby God is the bridegroom who pursues his bride (the seeker), not only provides a vehicle for expressing epiphany that the NT already uses,[161] but has the added impetus of resolving an otherwise implacable tension in the existing indigenous portrayal of God.

The second related image is that of the warrior of love, who must forsake all and risk everything to win his beloved. This concept has marked affinities both to the depiction of the suffering servant in Isa.52:13-53:12 who must undergo suffering and humiliation before being vindicated as he wins his goal, and to the parallel depiction of Christ in Phil.2:5-11. The potential of these images as a vehicle to express epiphany can be seen by making this gender reversal whilst reading the poetry of Rahman Baba, the most renowned Pushtu mystical poet:

> A man who can't forsake
> For his beloved's sake
> His peace of mind, his heart and soul
> is nothing but a fake...

> ...When you will save your life,
> When you avoid the knife,
> How shall as a warrior of love
> You conquer in the strife?...

> ...You're no Majnun who stakes
> His all for Laila's sake.[162]
> Nor a Mansur who pays the price[163]
> Supreme upon the stake.'[164]

Summary

In summary, we may say that although the Islamic literature we have surveyed neither focuses on nor develops the concept of epiphany, this concept is strongly implied in the Moses narratives that are prominent in a range of Islamic texts including the *Qur'an*, *tafsir* and *Qessas al-anbiya*. The *tafsir* we have examined emphasise that Moses met with God on three separate occasions, and the Islamist *tafsir* of Mawdudi is emphatic that on Sinai Moses stood in the actual presence of God as a result of God locally manifesting his presence there. The idea that God could appear on earth in a form that is possible for mortals to see is one of the most significant points of contact for a contextualised christology to start from.

Attitudes to Christological Monotheism

Unlike the Jewish context in which the earliest christology emerged, the Islamic context not only contains little in the way of specific antecedents that could be said to prepare the way for understanding of christological monotheism, but also evidences strongly held beliefs that are antithetical to it.

Hints of Incipient Bifurcation?

In our earlier discussion of theophany and epiphany we observed an implicit, although relatively widespread assumption that God could locally manifest a form of his presence, without this constituting the totality of God. This appears to be the closest that any widely held Islamic belief comes to implying that there might be a degree of bifurcation within God.

Fatherhood of God

Although the texts such as the *Qur'an* and *Ahadith* that are most central to Islamic belief do not refer to God as 'Father', the concept of God acting in a fatherly way towards his creation finds a limited degree of expression in mystical poetry:

Sa'di narrates how a poor dervish asked Moses to pray that God would give him provision. However, when the prayer was answered he obtained wine and under its influence killed a man. Sa'di appears to refer to God as being like a wise father, when at the end of the poem he concludes:

> The Father has an abundance of honey
> but the son has become sick and ill
> The One who does not bestow on you wealth and money
> Knows more what for you is fitting, than you ever will.[165]

Rahman Baba is slightly more explicit in metaphorically portraying God as a loving father, although he is careful to refute any implication of this implying the existence of a son:

> God made this universe from love
> For Him to be the Father of
> There cannot be
> Another such as He.[166]

Titles and Descriptions of Jesus

Relative to other prophets the *Qur'an* gives a very high status to Jesus (*'Isa*). His virgin birth is affirmed,[167] and his mother Maryam is described as chosen and purified above the women of all nations.[168] He is described as 'strengthened by the Holy Spirit', a *rasul* like Moses, who alone God spoke directly to,[169] 'a Spirit (*Ruh*) proceeding from Him' (i.e. from God),[170] 'a Word' (*Kalimah*) from Him, the Messiah 'Isa. He is said to be 'held in honour in this world and the Hereafter and of (the company of) those nearest to God',[171] and 'a sign of the coming hour'.[172] *Ahadith* additionally speak of his return to earth prior to the last day.[173]

Baidawi and the Jalalain emphasise the high status of Jesus in their *tafsir*, the Jalalain specifically affirming the tradition that unlike all other prophets Jesus and his mother were uniquely sinless.[174] However, both commentators are careful to explain that the high titles given to Jesus in the *Qur'an* do not imply his divinity. 'Word of God' is explained as his creation by the divine fiat 'be' without a father, just as Adam was;[175] 'eminence in this world' is explained as his prophetic office; 'and in the hereafter' as his intercessions and high stations;[176] while 'near to God', according to Baidawi either refers to his being raised to heaven and the society of angels, or a high place in paradise.[177] Interestingly however, Baidawi says that Jesus is the 'spirit of God, because he gives life to the dead and to the hearts of men',[178] and he is

> possessed of a spirit proceeding from God, not mediately, but direct, both as to origin and essence.[179]

This relatively high view of Jesus is also reflected in mystical poetry, which, in the context of narrating Jesus raising the dead, describes him as 'the Lord of the water of life'.[180] The mysterious figure Khizr, who Baidawi and the Jalalain interpret as the figure that Q18:65-82 narrates briefly travelled with Moses, is depicted as having drunk from 'the water of life' and so gained immortality.[181] However, only Jesus is described as 'Lord of the water of life'. This is significant because, as we earlier demonstrated, the NT depiction of Jesus as the source of the water of life, which is symbolic of the Spirit, is one of the ways that Jesus is identified as God.[182]

This relatively 'high view' of Jesus contrasts with the 'minimalist view' of modern Islamist writers such as Mawdudi, who is clearly writing to counter Christian belief in the trinity, which he regards as both illogical and irreconcilable with belief in monotheism.[183] His *tafsir* makes no direct comment at all on the high titles of Jesus in Q3:45,[184] and in contrast to Baidawi understands the Qur'anic christological title 'spirit of God' to mean that God gave Jesus a pure soul. Mawdudi emphatically rejects the Christian view of Jesus, claiming that Christians exceeded the proper limits of 'veneration' for Jesus, as a result of which in Christian thinking,

> the 'spirit *from* God' became the 'spirit *of* God', and the 'spirit of holiness' was interpreted to mean God's own Spirit which became incarnate in Jesus.[185]

Mawdudi argues that this was the process by which the Christian doctrine of the trinity developed. This theory of Christian origins appears to echo early-mid twentieth century theories of 3-4 stage evolutionary christology in which the early church is supposed to have initially venerated Jesus and eventually (mis)understood him to be divine under the influence of pagan Greek thought.

However, if this is the case, Mawdudi makes no reference to either the source of this theory being western liberal scholarship, or to the denial of the possibility of miracles that is its cornerstone.[186]

Denial of Jesus' Divinity

Although Jesus is given high titles of honour in the *Qur'an* he is clearly distinguished from God himself by a series of subject/object distinctions: the creator/creature;[187] the lord (of all things)/servant;[188] and the judge/judged,[189] as is illustrated by Jesus' virgin birth being portrayed as a specific act of God's creation akin to his creation of the first man Adam.[190] Consequently, God is the one worshipped and Jesus the worshipper.[191] Both Baidawi and the Jalalain stress that Jesus' miracles merely confirm his prophethood. In fact, the Jalalain suggest that Jesus' first words in the cradle 'I am a servant of God' were put into his mouth to obviate any imagination that he might be divine on account of his speaking while still a baby.[192] Both commentators stress that his healing and raising the dead were solely by prayer to God and 'by God's permission'. Baidawi claims that the latter is emphasised in the Qur'anic reference to Jesus raising people from the dead,

> in order to refute the fancy of those who maintain his divinity. For raising to life does not belong to the class of human actions.[193]

Baidawi's latter point fully accords with both the OT and NT. His implicit assertion that only God can give permission to impart life is in fact potentially significant for the development of a contextualised christology, as the NT describes Jesus himself granting this authority to his disciples in his own name.[194] Interestingly, the Jalalain insert into their commentary on the companions of the city (Q36:13-32) a non-Qur'anic tradition that the 3 disciples of Jesus both cured the blind, lepers and sick and raised the dead in Antioch, yet do not ascribe individual prophethood to these disciples of Jesus.[195]

The *Qur'an* specifically denies Jesus' divine sonship, although this is essentially a denial of the pagan idea of God having a wife and procreating a son.[196] In a similar vein Christians are condemned for worshipping three gods, although the tritheism so condemned consists of God, Jesus and Mary.[197] More specific still is the assertion that God is not the Messiah the son of Mary,[198] which is widely interpreted as denying that Jesus is in any sense divine.

Denial of Jesus' Atonement

The Qur'anic portrayal of the crucifixion is not presented as a denial of the possibility that true prophets could be killed; in fact the *Qur'an* positively affirms this.[199] Rather, it is presented as God vindicating Jesus' honour in the face of Jewish rejection and slander by taking Jesus up to himself. To this extent it follows the pattern of NT teaching. However, the point of dissimilarity is the apparent denial of the crucifixion in the words 'but they killed him not, nor crucified him, but so it was made to appear to them'.[200]

Baidawi gives three possible interpretations of Q3:55 'I am going to receive you (*inn-i mutawaffi-ka*) and raise you to myself' all of which avoid the crucifixion.[201] His preferred interpretation is that God says:

> I am holding you back from being killed by the unbelievers and causing you to tarry until the term I have decreed for you and causing you to die by natural causes not by being killed at their hands.[202]

This is the only one of his three interpretations that in any measure gets around the fact that the normal Qur'anic usage of *tawaffa* refers to death.

In fact, both the Jalalain, Baidawi and Mawdudi interpret the apparent denial of the crucifixion in Q4:157 as meaning that someone else was crucified in Jesus' place.[203]

However, such interpretations have always had to contend with the reference in the earlier surah *Maryam* to Jesus' death. Although the issue of whether or not Jesus died was debated in classical *tafsir*, today the *ulema* almost invariably interpret Q19:33 as referring to Jesus' second coming, when it is anticipated he will die and then be raised, although there is no unequivocal Qur'anic reference to such a *parousia*.[204] However, intriguingly, *surah Mariyam* presents the lives of John the Baptist (*Yahya ibn Zakariya*) and Jesus in a parallel literary structure that concludes with blessings of peace on each for the day of their birth, death and resurrection.[205] As Zwemer observed, in relation to Jesus these dates represent the three most important Christian festivals, Christmas, Good Friday and Easter Sunday and so potentially provide a point of departure for the contextualisation of Christian theology.[206]

In modern Islamic writers rejection of the crucifixion is often linked to rejection of Christian belief in the atonement. Q6:164 is often cited as an argument 'disproving' Christian belief in the atonement,[207] although its statement that that no man can bear another's burden does little more than provide a close parallel to Ps.49:7 in pointing to the impossibility of any mere creature having surplus merit to pay another's debt. However, Mawdudi goes further than this, and perceptively observes that Christian claims for the atonement stand or fall on the question of Jesus' divinity, asserting that

> the doctrine of expiation automatically falls apart by repudiating the dogma that Jesus was the son of God.[208]

The depth of this Islamic antipathy to Jesus' crucifixion is further reinforced by *Ahadith* accounts that speak of Jesus destroying the very symbol of the cross when he eschatologically returns to earth.[209]

Denial of the Self-Humbling of God

In the light of the emphatic Qur'anic denial of Jesus' divinity, it is hardly surprising that its denial of the crucifixion is based on other grounds than the impossibility of God so humbling himself as to vicariously suffer and die. However, the absence from the *Qur'an* of any real suggestion that God is humble is combined with the positively antithetical description of God as *al-Mutakabbir* ('The Proud'),[210] a name widely accepted as one of the ninety nine names of God. As such it is likely that even were Jesus' divinity accepted by Muslims, this novel aspect of God's character would still be at least as much of a conceptual difficulty as it was to second temple Jews for whom it was largely unknown, although not scripturally denied.[211]

Denial of the Possibility of Incarnation

In the Islamic context a fundamental objection to incarnation is that this would involve mixing God with non-God. Illustrative of this is the Jalalain commentary on the exalted titles of Jesus in Q3:45 which interprets this passage as a polemic against Christian exaltation of Jesus. They state that Jesus is:

> a spirit (that is, a being possessing a spirit) from Him. (He is mentioned in conjunction with God, in order to show him honour, and is not, as ye assert, the son of God, or a God with Him, or the third of three; *for the being possessing a spirit is compound, and the Deity must be confessed to be pure from the imputation of composition and the relationship of a compound being to Him*).[212]

Despite such assertions, Sunni *kalam* has been unable entirely to avoid imputing a compound nature to God. In response to the Mu'tazilite claim that an eternally existent *Qur'an* implied that it was a second God, the Asharites had asserted that divine attributes such as speech were neither identical with

God's essence nor additional to it. They claimed that the *Qur'an* as divine speech was eternal and uncreated, but that its inscription and recitation were created. However, this formula itself implied that God (the divine attribute of speech) might be both united with, and even actually exist *in*, a created thing (i.e. the *Qur'an* as a book),[213] which is precisely the grounds on which *kalam* argues that incarnation is impossible.

A further objection to the incarnation raised by *kalam* is that although attributes such as life, knowledge, power, will, seeing, hearing and speech are found in both the creator and the creature, God is devoid of attributes relating to the inferiority of creatures. These are said to include fatigue, sleepfulness, death and weakness.[214] This assertion therefore excludes any possibility of incarnation and closely parallels the Qur'anic polemic that as Jesus ate food, he could not be God.[215]

Portrayal of Jesus as Surpassed by Muhammad

A further issue that a contextualised christology has to deal with is that in the Islamic context Muhammad is frequently portrayed as surpassing Jesus not merely because according to the *Qur'an* he is 'the seal of the prophets' i.e. the final prophet,[216] but also in the honour and exaltation that is believed to have been accorded him by God.

The relative status accorded Jesus and Muhammad can be seen in *Ahadith* narrating Muhammad's *mi'raj*: Jesus only appears in the second heaven, while Muhammad ascends beyond the seventh.[217]

Ahadith descriptions of Muhammad's eschatological role focus on his supreme importance next to God on the day of judgement itself, while those relating to that of Jesus' primarily relate to the period before then. It is narrated that before the hour of judgement Jesus will descend from heaven on the wings of angels,[218] destroy the symbol of the cross,[219] and kill the Antichrist (*Dajjal al-Masih*), a source of evil said to have existed since at least the time of Noah,[220] which will result in the conversion of almost all Jews and Christians to Islam.[221] However, on the day of judgement, believers are depicted as asking a series of prophets including Adam, Jesus and Moses to intercede for them. Each prophet, including Jesus, declares he is unfit to do so, except Muhammad, who alone is allowed to intercede.[222]

This exaltation of Muhammad in *Ahadith* forms one of the foundations for the widespread adulation of Muhammad. This includes the acclamation of him as the perfect man,[223] and the portrayal in Qessas al-anbiya of Muhammad rather than Jesus as the one whose coming was eagerly anticipated by all the prophets and holy books,[224] and the one who alone has gone into the presence of God to receive knowledge not granted to any other.[225] An analysis of titles of Muhammad clearly illustrates that Muhammad is seen as next only to God. God is *al-Rahim* ('the Merciful'), *al-Haq* ('the Truth'), *al-Wali* ('the Governor'), *al-Muqaddas* ('the Holy'), and so forth, while Muhammad is *rahim* ('a mercy'), *haq* ('truth'), *wali* ('a governor'), *ruh muqaddas* ('spirit of holiness') and so forth. Zwemer observed that the printed lists of 201 titles of Muhammad that are rote learnt in schools across the Islamic world contained many such implications of apotheosis.[226] Such observations led him to suggest that 'for all practical purposes Mohammed himself is the Moslem Christ'.[227] This is a slight overstatement as, when applied to God, the titles are almost invariably absolutised by the use of the definite article. However, amongst the *Barelvi*, as we earlier observed, the use of christological motifs in hymns adoring Muhammad does come close to deifying him.[228] Nevertheless, whatever the extent of the adulation of Muhammad, his displacement of Christ in popular Muslim perception is strongly rooted in *Ahadith* and clearly presents an additional difficulty that any contextualisation of christological monotheism must grapple with.

Cultural Themes

Our discussion so far has focused on conceptual categories and Islamic beliefs related to the identity of God. However, there are other important cultural themes and values that any contextualisation of christology must also engage with. Some of these are relatively widespread across a whole range of Islamic societies, whilst others will be more specific to individual cultures.

This book only attempts to set out a basic framework for the contextualisation of christology, as it is the task of the local church to adapt and refine its christology in relation to the particularities of the culture in which God has placed it. However, it will be helpful at this point in our study to briefly note the existence of a number of cultural themes that are relatively widespread in the Islamic world and which have some relevance to contextualisation of christology.[229] The following list is not in any sense intended to be exhaustive, but simply highlights a number of themes that have particular relevance to the contextualisation of christology. Significantly, we earlier demonstrated that the early church also drew on similar cultural themes in contextualising its christology in the context of Jewish monotheism.

Honour and Shame

In contrast to western cultures that tend to focus on law and guilt, Islamic cultures more typically focus on loyalty and shame. Whilst guilt is the violation of specific individual moral rules, shame is much more wholistic as it involves a loss of the honour that has been accumulated by a lifetime of living up to society's ideals of honourable behaviour. Failing to live up to these group ideals is an act of disloyalty to one's society that brings shame not only on the individual, but also on the family and to some extent the wider community.

The difference in focus between shame and guilt is an important one as it has profound implications for how we express the significance of what God has done for us in pardoning our sin. The western emphasis on guilt results in a view of jurisprudence that emphasises that each individual act of wrongdoing must be punished because it is intrinsically wrong in itself.[230] Consequently, western explanations of the atonement have often been couched in terms of Jesus having taken the 'punishment' for our sins, because sin is morally 'wrong' in itself, and therefore 'must' be punished. However, cultures that focus more on shame tend to have a more relational concept of jurisprudence that focuses on punishing the offender in order to restore the honour of the person who has suffered as a result of the offence. Interestingly, the Jewish context addressed by the early church appears to have similarly focused more on shame rather than guilt. There are therefore good grounds for supposing that the early church's emphasis on the vindication of Jesus' honour by his exaltation to the highest point of heaven may also be appropriate in an Islamic context.

Hospitality

Whilst western cultures tend to emphasise personal privacy, Islamic cultures more characteristically emphasise hospitality. As Musk observes whereas the phrase 'my home is your home' is on the lips of Arabs many times every day, the assumptions most westerners are brought up with are exemplified in the proverb 'an Englishman's home is his castle'.[231]

In many Islamic cultures the duty of hospitality includes an obligation to provide sanctuary to a fugitive. For example, among the Pushtun's who inhabit the north west frontier region of Pakistan one of the gravest violations of honour is to allow a guest to be either captured, or even worse handed over to his enemies to be killed. Sir Olaf Caroe, the last British governor of this region before Pakistan's independence in 1947, observed that Pushtuns still spoke with disdain of the Pushtun king Timur Shah (d.1793), because he handed over a fugitive to his enemies for execution, even though the event had occurred 150 years earlier.[232]

This emphasis on hospitality creates the potential for churches in Islamic societies to use the motif of violated hospitality codes to underline the seriousness and corporate shame that resulted from the rejection of Jesus, in a similar manner to that which we earlier observed in the early Jewish church. The Fourth Gospel for example speaks of the creator himself coming to his own creation, but his own people refused to receive him hospitably – and even conspiring to kill him.[233]

Jurisprudence

We have already referred to the relational concept of justice that tends to characterise Islamic cultures, in which the focus is on restoring the honour of the person who has been offended, rather than simply punishing the guilty.[234] Although the *Qur'an* and *Ahadith* set out specific penalties for certain crimes, which are termed *Hudud* offences (adultery, fornication, false accusation of adultery, drinking wine, theft and highway robbery) there is also a concept in *Shariah* known as *Qisas*, meaning 'retaliation'. This allows the person offended against to remit the punishment that has been fixed by law. Fazlul Karim in his commentary on the *Mishkat al-Masabih* contrasts this aspect of Islamic jurisprudence with the western jurisprudence that the British colonial authorities introduced to India:

> In the British law, the right of mercy and pardon goes to the head of government but it is otherwise in Islam. *Only the person wronged can forgive.*[235]

So for example, in the case of murder, the judge will typically ask the family of the murder victim whether they wish the execution to go ahead or whether they will 'forgive' the murderer.[236] In this context 'forgiveness' is not simply a private emotional decision in the heart, but involves releasing the person from the actual punishment that is due to them. The somewhat more narrowly constrained western concept of forgiveness, which can say 'I forgive you, but you must still take the punishment for your crime', is foreign to most Islamic cultures. This was forcibly brought home to me some years ago when a thief was caught trying to steal my bicycle from outside a church building in an Islamic country. The thief persistently pleaded with me to forgive him and not hand him over to the police. His meaning was clearly not a request that I avoid holding an attitude of bitterness towards him in my heart, but that I release him from the punishment, which I as the offended person had the right to demand.

The point is simply this, in relational justice only the party offended against can either demand punishment or grant forgiveness, because the emphasis is on restoring the honour of the offended party, rather than punishing an act because it is morally wrong in a more abstract sense. This has profound implications for the way that christology is presented in Islamic contexts, as it means that only God can forgive sins and act as the final eschatological judge, for he is the one that has ultimately been offended against and dishonoured by the sin of his servants. It is therefore conceivable that in Islamic contexts Gospel accounts of Jesus forgiving sins and references to him as the final eschatological judge may be more clearly understood to identify him as God, than they are by people in the western cultures.

A further aspect Islamic cultures is that there is often a far greater stress on corporate responsibility for the deeds of the kinship network than would be the case in western societies.[237] For this reason when someone has committed a serious crime there are often severe repercussions not only for the individual but also for their whole family.[238] This creates the possibility of human sin being presented in terms the creator visiting his own creation and mankind corporately bearing shame for men having conspired against him.

CONCLUSIONS

In this chapter we have seen that in the Islamic context God is primarily conceived of in bounded extrinsic terms. This similarity to the Jewish context means that the basic framework of the NT's contextualisation of christology can be reapplied in the Islamic context. However, a contextualised christology will need to expand the Islamic concept of God being the sole creator, ruler and judge of all, to additionally identify him as the only saviour.

We have also demonstrated that in the Islamic context there is an existing concept that God can locally manifest a form of his presence, without this being understood to be the totality of God. Moreover, it is widely accepted that God has a visible form, which will not only be seen eschatologically, but was actually seen by Moses when God appeared to him on earth. However, as this concept of epiphany is not as clearly defined as it was in the Jewish context, a contextualised christology will need to strengthen it and supplement it with the concept of God appearing in epiphany when he acts as saviour.

Other aspects of the Islamic context are more problematic for the contextualisation of christology. The widespread veneration of prophets and saints means that christological worship will not signal that Jesus is on the God side of the God/non-god divide as clearly as it did in the Jewish context. As such, devotional practices will need to very specifically emphasise that Jesus is worshipped because he is God, if they are not to be misunderstood as being akin to *Barelvi* saint veneration.

However, the greatest obstacle a contextualised christology must overcome is the strong antithesis to Jesus' divinity. This includes denial of the possibility of divine sonship, as well as the related concepts of the self-humbling of God, incarnation and atonement, and is further complicated by the displacement of Christ by Muhammad in popular Muslim perception. A contextualised christology must find appropriate apologetic responses to these, central to which must be the search for an alternative way of expressing the NT concept of Jesus' divine sonship and the Logos christology that lies behind it.

Endnotes

[1] 'The Hallelujah Chorus' of G.F. Handel's *The Messiah*.

[2] Here we follow A.S. Ahmed 'Islam and the District Paradigm: Emergent Trends in Contemporary Muslim Society' *CTIS* 17:2 (1983) 155-83 in using the term *mullah* simply to denote those involved in Islamic teaching and preaching who have been educated at a *madrasa*. Ahmed observes that the role of the mullah is both one of the most important influences in village and rural society and also one of the least studied.

[3] So, F. Rahman *Islam* [London:Weidenfeld & Nicolson,1966] 90 who speaks of it as having only 'a partial and indirect relationship to the living realities of the faith'.

[4] We follow this basic argument of A.S. Ahmed's *Towards an Islamic Anthropology* [Herndon:International Institute for Islamic Thought,1986] that there is a need to give greater focus to common elements in Islamic societies than many western studies have done. However, we cannot unquestioningly accept his further contention that debates between different schools of Islamic thought are 'merely academic exercises' (57). Ahmed's work is in fact open to many of the same criticisms which he makes of western anthropologists, particularly in respect of claimed 'academic neutrality'.

[5] In the Indo-Persian region Persian poetry has also frequently been included as an additional subject in the *madrasa* curriculum, for example N. Snider 'Mosque Education in Afghanistan' *MW* 58:1 (1968) 24-35 found that books such as Sa'di's *Gulistan* were taught in primary school level *madrasas* in Afghanistan.

[6] In this study we follow O. Roy *Islam and Resistance in Afghanistan* [Cambridge:CUP,2nd edn,1990] 31 ET from French of *L'Afghanistan: Islam et modernite politique*, in using 'Popular' Islam to denote those aspects of Islam that are derived from a world view common to a wide range of both social categories (*ulema*, Islamists and ordinary Muslims) etc. rather than necessarily meaning 'folk Islam'.

[7] This is somewhat akin to the argument of V. Das 'For a Folk-Theology and Theological Anthropology of Islam' *CTIS* 18:2 (1984) 293-300 for a 'folk theology' that deals with the meanings and use of scripture in the everyday life, rather than simply contrasting formal Islam with 'folk Islam'.

[8] cf. the observations of J. Ingleby 'Trickling Down or Shaking the Foundations: Is Contextualization Neutral?' *Missiology* 25:2 (1997) 183-87 that some past attempts at contextualisation in India directed only towards the most high status religious practitioners both distorted the Gospel and created barriers to its acceptance by the wider community.

[9] cf. E. Westermarck *Pagan Survivals in Mohammedan Civilisation* [London:Macmillan,1933} 6,10,99,136 who illustrates this in North Africa; B.A. Musk *The Unseen Face of Islam* [Speldhurst:MARC,1989] 103 similarly gives examples of malevolent witchcraft (*suhur*) from the Sudan and the Philippines, while Sirdar Iqbal Ali Shah *Afghanistan of the Afghans* [London:Diamond,1928] 78-100 speaks of malevolent witchcraft (*jadu*) being widespread in his native Afghanistan.

[10] e.g. Q2:255; 3:2; 4:87; 7:158.

[11] Q42:11; 112:4.

[12] e.g. Q34:23; 40:12.

[13] e.g. Q2:21-22; 4:48; 7:190; 112:1-4.

[14] e.g. Q2:255; 3:2; 20:111.

[15] Ex.3:14.

[16] e.g. Q2:117; 6:73; 36:81-82.

[17] Q13:2-3; 35:41.

[18] Q14:48.

[19] Q6:73; 10:4.

[20] Q2:258; 22:73; 53:44.

[21] In the following examples Yusuf Ali sometimes translates *Rabb* as 'Lord' and sometimes as 'Cherisher', e.g. 'the Lord and Cherisher of the Universe' (Q2:131). However, this does not significantly change the meaning beyond importing the suggestion that God's rule of the universe is benevolent.

[22] e.g. Q6:71; 7:104; 10:37.

[23] e.g. Q9:129; 17:42; 21:22.

[24] Q3:26 (Yusuf Ali translates the Arabic *Malk al-mulk* as 'Lord of Power'. However, the meaning is essentially the same); 20:114; 23:116 (Arabic *Malik*).

[25] Q6:164 (Arabic *Rabb kull Shay*).

[26] e.g. Q3;189; 4:170; 18:14.

[27] Q2:115; 55:17.

[28] Q1:4.

[29] Q6:114.

[30] Q3:135.

[31] e.g. Q3:103.

[32] e.g. Q4:75; 37:114-16; 133-35.

[33] Q6:61 'He sets guardians over you' (cf. 6:63).

[34] Sayyid Abdul A'la Mawdudi *Tafhim al-Qur'an* ET by Z.I. Ansari as *Towards Understanding Islam* [Leicester:Islamic Foundation,1988] (notice of intended 'fair use' given June 2005) (hereafter referred to as 'Mawdudi *Tafhim*') n.20:2 to Q20:4-5.

[35] Sayyid Qutb *Fi Zilal al-Qur'an* ET by M.A. Salahi & A.A. Shamis as *In the Shade of the Qur'an* [Leicester:Islamic Foundation,1979-99] (hereafter 'Qutb *Zilal*') 1:320 on Q2:255.

[36] MM38 Section 3 (Names-Allah) cf. esp. 38:52,53(Names-Allah).

[37] 'There is no God but Allah and Muhammad is his apostle' recited daily by many Muslims.

[38] So, T.P. Hughes *Dictionary of Islam* [London:Allen,1885: reprinted Calcutta:Rupa,1988] 142.

[39] MM34:214 (Takbir-Prayer).

[40] e.g. Q6:102; 13:16; 39:62.

[41] e.g. Q38:66; 64:1; 67:1.

[42] Q41:36; 42:12; 48:26.

[43] Q57:2-4.

[44] 'Abd Allah ibn 'Umar al-Baidawi (d.c.1286)'s Anwar al-Tanzil *wa Asrar al-Ta'wil*. on Q112 ET in K. Cragg *The Mind of the Qur'an* [London:Allen & Unwin,1973] (Hereafter 'ET Cragg') 62-64.

[45] Zwemer *God* 24 citing pp 1:5-6 of Baidawi's *tafsir*.

[46] on Q7:54 ET in H. Gatje *The Qur'an and its Exegesis* [Oxford:Oneworld,1996] 149 (emphasis added) ET of *Koran und Koranexegese*. (Notice given of intened 'fair use' June 2005) (Gatje's translations from Arabic are hereafter referred to as 'ET Gatje'). Bracketed English represents Gatje's interpolations.

[47] MM5:91,92,95,100 (Names).

[48] Muhyi' al-Din ibn al-'Arabi (d.1240).

[49] So, R.A. Nicholson *The Mystics of Islam* [1914 – reprinted Lahore:Islamic Book Service,1997] 15-16,28; L. Gardet 'Allah' *EI²* 1:406-17.

[50] So, Gardet 'Allah' and Roy *Resistance* 40,55-56.

[51] *Qissasul Anbiya* ET by B. Azimabadi [New Delhi:Saeed International,1994] (hereafter 'QA') 2-5,8,19-20,43,90, 122-23; Shah Waliyullah *Ta'wil al-Hadith* ET by G.N. Jalbani [Lahore:Sh. Muhammad Ashraf,1991], e.g. 8-9,17.

[52] *Ta'wil* 6,19,35,50,60,63,73-74, 88.

[53] *QA* 2-5.

[54] *Ta'wil* 73-74.

[55] *The Masnavi* by Jalalu'd-Din Rumi ET by C.E. Wilson [1910 reprinted Karachi:Indus,1976] (hereafter 'Rumi *Masnavi*') 214;286;100ff respectively.

[56] Musleh ud-Din Sa'di Shiraz (d.c.1291) Gulistan 7:16 (my translation from Persian of *Gulistan of Shaikh Sa'di* [Islamabad:Iran-Pakistan Institute of Persian Studies,1984]).

[57] So, Zwemer *God* 29.

[58] So, A.J. Wensinck *The Muslim Creed* [Cambridge:CUP,1932. 2nd edn. New Delhi:Oriental Books Reprint Corporation, 1979] 206 citing p 23 of the commentary to the *Fikh Akbar 1*.

[59] Rumi *Masnavi* 18.

[60] Rumi *Masnavi* 73-74.

[61] So, Wensinck *Creed* 182-83.

[62] Article 25 ET in Wensinck *Creed* 130. Although the widespread attribution of these creeds to Abu Hanifa is improbable, their importance for us lies not in their historical authenticity, but in the publication of these texts as '*akida* (creeds) along with commentaries (Hyderabad 1321AH) by *ulema* in the Indian sub-continent (*Creed* 2,185ff). Wensinck's ET of these has now been republished in the sub-continent.

[63] So, Wensinck *Creed* 183.

[64] Article 20 (ET in Wensinck *Creed* 194-195).

[65] Article 16 (ET in Wensinck *Creed* 193).

[66] So, Wensinck *Creed* 224ff.

[67] We here use the term 'theology' to denote Islamic theology in general and reserve *kalam* for the specific type of scholastic theology developed since the time of al-Ashari.

[68] So, M. Mujeeb *The Indian Muslims* [London:Allen & Unwin,1967] 21-25,116f who speaks of some being included within the Islamic fold 'among whom the doctrines of Islam had barely found a foothold' (24).

[69] So, P. Lewis *Pirs, Shrines and Pakistani Islam* [Rawalpindi:CSC,1985] passim.

[70] ET 'Saint of light' (Persian).

[71] For a concise summary of the doctrines of Pir-i-Roshan and the reputed Roshaniyah remnant amongst the Afridis of NWFP, cf. M. Titus *Indian Islam* [London:OUP,1930] 105-106. For a more detailed description cf. Caroe *Pathans* 199-204,226.

[72] For a concise summary of these movements cf. R. Geaves *Sectarian Influences within Islam in Britain* [Leeds:University of Leeds,1996] 130-158.

[73] This is true of all the Indian reform movements and is exemplified in the in Arab world by the Sanusi movement started by Muhammad Ali Ibn al-Sanusi (1787-1859) in Libya and the Mahdiyyah movement started by Muhammad Ahmad (1848-1885) in the Sudan.

[74] ET 'heavenly light of Muhammad' (Persian).

[75] cf. Geaves *Sectarian* Appendix C for an example of a Barelvi hymn of adoration of Muhammad (*na'at*) sung after Friday prayers by Barelvi Muslims. The hymn includes references to Muhammad as: the heavenly bridegroom (cf. Jn 3:29; Rev 21:2,9); the chosen One (cf. Lk. 9:35); God's fountain of wisdom (cf. Jn 4:14; 1 Cor.1:24); God's agent in creation (cf. Jn 1:1-3); the one given the universe as his possession (cf. Heb.1:2; Matt 28:18); the essence of Allah's mercy (cf. οὐσία in the Nicene Creed) and so forth.

[76] So, Geaves *Sectarian* 95-96 who notes the difficulty of assessing the extent to which Ahmad Riza Khan's theology was followed even by the Barelvi *ulema* who initially followed him.

[77] e.g. Q3:64; 6:56; 40:66.

[78] Q2:21-22; 6:95-102.

[79] Q2:116; 10:3; 19:65.

[80] Q2:34; 7:11-18; 15:28-35; 17:61-63; 18:50; 20:116-17; 38:71-85.

[81] LAE 12:1-16:3.

[82] Q39:43-45.

[83] Ibn Ishaq's *Sirat Rasul Allah* (c.120 AH) the earliest extant Muslim biography of Muhammad (ET by A. Guillaume as *The Life of Muhammad* [Karachi:OUP,1955,1996]), records that these 'Satanic verses' were initially added by Muhammad onto Q53:19-20, but retracted when news of this reached the companions who had fled to Abyssinia (239-240 on pp 165-67 in Guillaume's translation).

[84] Q34:22.

[85] Q2:255; 53:26; 78:38.

[86] cf. Rom.8:34; Heb.7:25; 1 Jn 2:1.

[87] MM44:3(Muhammad) cf. also 38:1(invocations).

[88] MM34:128,129,150(Mosques).

[89] So, e.g. al-Haj Maulana Fazlul Karim *al-Hadis: An English Translation & Commentary* [Calcutta,1939/ Lahore:Sh.Muhammad Ashraf,n.d.] (hereafter 'MMComm') 3:225 n.1662 to MM34:150(Mosques).

[90] cf. Musk *Unseen* 210-13 for a description of a popular amulet known as the 'Seven covenants of Suleiman' that invokes the names of Suleiman (Solomon) and various angels of God against demonic affliction.

[91] MM9:13,14(Diseases-Treatment).

[92] MM9:15(Diseases-Treatment).

[93] MM9:17(Diseases-Treatment).

[94] MM9:76a(Omens).

[95] MM9:37,39,40(Disease-Treatment).

[96] Q21:81-82; 34:12-14; 38:34-38.

[97] Musk *Unseen* 27 speaks of 'a vast world of prophylaxis' in Islamic context. The use of pungent smoke from such things as rue seeds is a common form of prophylaxis in a number of Islamic regions including North Africa (cf. Westermarck *Survivals* 9). Such practices provide potentially significant parallels to the belief of some second temple Jews that the burning of fish liver would drive away evil spirits cf. p 53f.

[98] *Tafsir al-Jalalain* by Jalaluddin Muhammad bin Ahmad al-Shafi'i al Mahalli (d.1459) and Jalaluddin 'Abdur Rahman bin Abu Bakr al-Suyuti (d.1505) ET from Arabic in S. Lane-Poole *Selections From the Kuran* [London:Trubner,1879] (Hereafter 'ET Lane-Poole') 9.

[99] ET from Arabic by D.S. Margoliouth as *Chrestomathia Baidawiana* [London:Luzac,1894] (Hereafter 'ET Margoliouth'. Qur'anic references are adjusted to the numbering system used throughout the present study) 45-46.

[100] A.D. Kynsh *Islamic Mysticism* [Leiden:Brill,1999] refers to popular veneration of individual saints starting even as early as the eighth and ninth centuries (19-20,49).

[101] Mawdudi *Tafhim* n.1:2 to Q1:1 (emphasis Mawdudi's).

[102] Mawdudi *Tafhim* Q2:255 n.2:281 (emphasis added).

[103] *T'awil* 80-81,83.

[104] *QA* 162.

[105] (ET Gatje 149).

[106] Mawdudi *Tafhim* n.7:41 to Q7:54.

[107] e.g. Q14:48-52; 18:105,110; 19:37-39, 77-80.

[108] e.g. Muhammad Q6:31; Earlier prophets Q23:33.

[109] Q2:210; 39:75; 54:54-55.

[110] cf. A.A.B. Philips *The Fundamentals of Tawheed* [Riyadh:Tawheed Publications,1990] 144-47.

[111] Q6:102-103; 36:11.

[112] e.g. MM32:10(Predestination); 34:475w(Mosques); 43:661w(Creation-Prophets).

[113] So, Fazul Karim MMComm.4:180-81(Vision-Allah) who notes a 'great controversy' on this point amongst Islamic jurists that originates from the time of the companions of Muhammad.

[114] MM42:50(Vision-Allah) (italics original to source text).

[115] MM42:49(Vision-Allah).

[116] Ibn Ishaq *Sirat* 272 ET in Guillaume *Muhammad* 186.

[117] *QA* 137-38.

[118] Q2:55; 4:153.

[119] Q7:143-45 cf. Ex.33:14-34:8.

[120] al-Ashari *Ibana 'an Usul al-Diyana*:13ff ET in Wensinck *Creed* 88-90.

[121] cf. Philips *Tawheed* 138-9.

[122] MM32:14(Predestination).

[123] MM34:155(Mosques) cf. also 34:474w(Mosques).

[124] e.g. MM42:35 (Paradise-Hell); 45,47,52 (Vision-Allah), citation 42:47(Vision-Allah).

[125] MM41:11(Resurrection) cf. also 41:39(Intercession-fountain).

[126] So, C. Glassé 'Bila Kayfa' *CEOI* 73-74, although in fact the device dates back at least as early as Ibn Hanbal (d. 855).

[127] cf. ad. art. 24 of the Wasiyat, and ad. art. 17 of *Fikh Akbar 2* ET in Wensinck *Creed* 179,229.

[128] e.g. Fikh Akbar 2 article 4 cf. also *Wasiyat* of Abu Hanifa article 8 (ET in Wensinck *Creed* 190,207-210; and 127,147-149 respectively).

[129] So, Nicholson *Mystics* 50.

[130] al-Hujwiri *The Kashaf al-Mahjub* (c.1042CE/435AH) ET by R.A. Nicholson [1936 - reprinted Karachi:Darul Ishaat,1990] 330.

[131] *Ta'wil* 71.

[132] Shams al-Din Muhammad Hafiz al-Shirazi (1320-1389) *Divan* ET by G.M. Bell as *Selected Sonnets From the Divan of Hafez* [1897, reprinted as Farsi/English diglot, Tehran:Eghbal,1985] 41.

[133] cf. 2 Cor.3:18; 1 Cor.13:12; Matt.5:8; Jn 17:24; 1 Jn 3:2.

[134] Q2:210; 36:49-53; 39:67-70.

[135] Q2:210; 22:1-7; 75:8-9; 81:1-11; 82:1-5; 83:4 (*Yaum azim*); 84:1-5.

[136] cf. pp 59-64.

[137] Q17:85; 40:15 ; 97:4.

[138] So, Hughes *Dictionary* 605 who also provides an analysis of how each Qur'anic spirit reference has been interpreted in *tafsir*.

[139] Q4:164.

[140] Q20:9-36; 27:7-12; 28:29-35,43-44. (Yusuf Ali n.2504,2505 sees Q19:51-52 as a further probable reference).

[141] Q20:12; 28:30.

[142] Q28:30.

[143] Q20:83-84 cf. Ex.24:12-32:1ff; Q7:155 cf. Ex.24:9-11.

[144] Q7:143.

[145] MM32:3(Predestination) cf. also 42:50(Vision-Allah).

[146] Q7:144-45; 20:24; 27:12-14; 28:32,46.

[147] Jalalain (ET Lane-Poole 117), Baidawi ET in G. Sale *The Koran* [1734,London:Warne,n.d. c.1936] (hereafter 'ET Sale') 157 n.4 both to Q7:143 (citation – Jalalain, similar wording in Baidawi).

[148] Jalalain (ET Lane-Poole 117), Baidawi (ET Sale 157 n.3) both to Q7:142ff.

[149] (ET Sale 157 n.4 on Q7:143).

[150] n.4:206 to Q4:164 in which he refers to Q20:11ff (the burning bush incident) as illustrative of this.

[151] n.20:62 to Q20:85.

[152] *QA* 75-76.

[153] (ET Lane-Poole 117), 'El Hakim' probably denotes the name of God as there is no known *Hadith* transmitter with this title.

[154] Mawdudi *Tafhim* n.20:62 to Q20:85 cf. n.101 to Q7:143-45.

[155] to Q20:86-96 Baidawi (ET Sale 312 n.3); Jalalain (ET Lane-Poole 119); Mawdudi *Tafhim* n.20:73 (Ex 23:20ff). cf. also similar references to Gabriel in *Ta'wil* 28-29, *QA* 43 (cf. Gen.18:1-15); 44 (cf. Gen.22:1-19).

[156] *QA* 82, 85-86 (cf. Num.14:10ff).

[157] Sirdar Ikbal Ali Shah *Islamic Sufism* [1933 - reprint Delhi:Idarah-i-Adabiyat-i-Delhi,1979] 50-51.

[158] *Ta'wil* 46-47.

[159] cf. the couplet of Rahman Baba's poem in Appendix D – 'If in this quest you fail, put up your pride for sale; Remove your turban and exchange it for a woman's veil' (J. Enevoldsen *The Nightingale of Peshawar* [Peshawar:InterLit,2nd edn.1993] 68-69).

[160] *Ghazzalat Hafiz Shirazi* Persian/English arranged by Mohsen Ramezani, ET by A.J. Arberry [Tehran: Padideh Publishing, 1367 AH{P}=1947CE] 99-100, used by kind permission of Mrs Anna Evans.

[161] i.e. Jesus as the Bridegroom. e.g. Matt.9:15; Jn 3:29; Rev.19:7.

[162] A popular folk story of a boy (Majnun), who fell in love with a nomad girl (Laila) and constantly wandered in search of her.

[163] A reference to the medieval Sufi al-Husayn bin Mansur al-Hallaj (d. 919)'s crucifixion for declaring 'I am the Truth'.

[164] Enevoldsen *Nightingale* 68-69.

[165] *Gulistan* 3:16 (my translation from Persian) cf. also the end of 7:20 for a further possible though less clear reference to God as 'Father'.

[166] Enevoldsen *Nightingale* 36-37.

[167] Q19:20-22.

[168] Q3:42.

[169] Q2:87,253.

[170] Q4:171.

[171] Q3:45.

[172] Baidawi on Q43:61 (ET Gatje 129), although Tabari's tafsir (Abu Ja'far Muhammad b. Jarir al-Tabari *Jami' al-Bayan fi Tafsir al-Qur'an*) states that some interpreters understood the reference to be to the *Qur'an*, rather than to Jesus. Tabari also noted three variant readings a)*'ilmun* i.e. 'knowledge' b) *'alamun* i.e. 'sign' - these variants being due to different vocalisations/vowel pointing of the consonantal text, and c) *dhikrun* meaning recollection or reminder – a textual variant which Tabari attributes to Ubaiy (ET Robinson 90-91).

[173] e.g. MM39:85 (Greater Signs).

[174] (ET Lane-Poole:149) to Q3:36.

[175] on Q3:39 Jalalain (ET Lane-Poole 150); Baidawi (ET Margoliouth 31).

[176] on Q3:45 Jalalain (ET Lane-Poole 152); Baidawi (ET Margoliouth 35).

[177] on Q3:45 (ET Margoliouth 35-36).

[178] on Q4:171 ET by W. Goldsack *The Testimony of the Qur'an to Christ* [Madras:Christian Literature Society,1905] (hereafter 'ET Goldsack') 21.

[179] On Q4:171 (ET Goldsack *Qur'an* 21).

[180] Rumi *Masnavi* 43-44.

[181] Baidawi and the Jalalain on Q18:65 cf. Hughes *Dictionary* 272-73 and (ET Sale 292 n.2); Hafiz cf. Eghbal *Divan* 24.

[182] cf. Jn 4:10-14; 7:37-39; Rev.7:17; 21:6; 22:1.

[183] cf. Mawdudi *Tafhim* n.4:215 to Q4:171.

[184] Although, elsewhere he gives identical interpretations of 'Word of God' to the classical commentators.

[185] Mawdudi *Tafhim* n.4:213 to Q4:171 also referring to Q2:87.

[186] cf. Mawdudi *Tafhim* n.5:101 to Q5:76.

[187] Q3:47,59 cf. also 5:19.

[188] Q4:171-72 cf. also 5:19.

[189] Q5:119-20.

[190] Q3:47,59 cf. also 5:19.

[191] Q5:75,119-20.

[192] (ET Lane-Poole 154 n.1 on Q19:30).

[193] Jalalain on Q3:49 (ET Lane-Poole 155); Baidawi on Q5:110 ET G. Parrinder *Jesus in the Qur'an* [London:Sheldon,1965,1977] 85; quotation on Q3:49 (ET Margoliouth 37-38 citation 38).

[194] cf. discussion of Jesus' Delegation to his followers of authority over evil spirits and to perform miracles on pp 85-86 and of the significance of these miracles as fulfilling OT prophecy of the signs that would accompany God himself coming to earth pp 112-13.

[195] (ET Lane-Poole 159-161 on Q36:13-32).

[196] Q9:30f; 72:3-5.

[197] Q4:171; 5:75-80,119-20.

[198] Q5:19,75.

[199] e.g. this is the basic message of surah *Hud*: Q11:25-49 (Noah), 50-60 (Hud), 61-68 (Salih), 69-83 (Lot), 84-95 (Shu'aib), 96-99 (Moses) cf. also 23:23-50 (all prophets rejected including Noah, Moses and Jesus). The only Qur'anic exception to the rejection of the prophets is Jonah, in whose case the whole town repented (Q10:98).

[200] Q4:157.

[201] Among the classical commentators only Razi (Fakhr al-Din al-Razi *Mafatih al-Ghaib*) and Tabari give a possible interpretation that Jesus did die ET in N. Robinson *Christ in Islam and Christianity* [Basingstoke: Macmillan,1991] (hereafter 'ET Robinson') 120-122.

[202] (ET Robinson 117-123, citation 123 on Q3:55).

[203] on Q4:157 Baidawi (ET Robinson 139); Jalalain (ET Lane-Poole 161); Mawdudi *Tafhim* n.4:193.

[204] A number of classical commentators report that Q4:159 'there is none of the People of the Book but must believe in him before his death' was so interpreted in early Islam, presumably as a means of resolving the apparent contradiction. However, Baidawi following Zamakhshari takes the reference as being to the believer's rather than Jesus' death (cf. Robinson *Christ* 78-105 for a full discussion).

[205] Q19:1-33 - parallel elements being: 'Relate!'(*zikur*) (:2/16); Zakariya/Mary in secret (:3/17); announcement of a son (:7/19); 'How shall I?' + two reasons (:8/20); 'That is easy for me' (:9/21); Yahya/'Isa kind to parent and not overbearing (:14/32); Peace on day of birth, death, resurrection (:15/33).

[206] So, Zwemer *Christ* 182.

[207] e.g. A. Yusuf Ali *The Holy Qur'an: Translation and Commentary* [Lahore:Sh. Muhammad Ashraf,1934 – reprinted 1967] n.987 to Q6:164.

[208] Mawdudi *Tafhim* n.4:216 to Q4:171.

[209] MM40:1,2(Descent-Jesus).

[210] Q59:23, although Yusuf Ali translates this as 'the Supreme'.

[211] cf. 1 Cor.1:21-23.

[212] (ET Lane-Poole 164-165 on Q3:45) (emphasis mine).

[213] Ibn Rushd's account in Sweetman *Theology* 2:2:108-109.

[214] So, Sweetman *Theology* 2:2:105.

[215] Q5:78.

[216] Q33:40.

[217] MM44:97(Mi'raj).

[218] MM39:95(Greater Signs).

[219] MM40:1,2(Descent-Jesus).

[220] MM39:42(Battles-Hour); 106(Greater-signs).

[221] MM40:1(Descent-Jesus) as interpreted in MMComm.4:80.

[222] MM41:64(Intercession-Fountain).

[223] cf. MMComm. Introduction (Muhammad) 4:235-315 for an example of acclamation of Muhammad as the perfect man, including ideal king and judge (250-253), although expressly rejecting adoration comparable to Christian worship of Jesus (4:283).

[224] *QA* 124ff (cf. this NT christological claim in Lk.24:27,44ff; Acts 3:18-24; 10:43). The extent to which these and other parallels with NT christology are a response to Christian mission is beyond the scope of this study, but clearly merits investigation. However, we will note that a form of this process of 'adoption for Muhammad of NT christology' is found in the 'Gospel of Barnabas', a purported gospel whose contents suggest it was written by a European Muslim sometime between approximately1300 and the first recorded reference to this text in 1634. The Gospel of Barnabas records Jesus denying that he is the Messiah (G.Barn 42, 96-97), claiming that this title belonged to Muhammad who would come after him. The origin of this process therefore dates back at least as early as the seventeenth century.

[225] *QA* 137-38.

[226] Zwemer *Christ* 155-173.

[227] Zwemer *Christ* 157.

[228] cf. n.75.

[229] From a missiological perspective one of the most useful studies of cultural themes that appear to transcend the boundaries of individual cultures is B.A. Musk *Touching the Soul of Islam* [Crowborough: MARC,1995]. Musk lists eight widespread cultural tensions that characterise a range of Islamic societies: male/female polarity; family and individual; honour and shame; hospitality and violence; time and space; language and silence; brotherhood and rivalry; resignation and manipulation.

[230] Regardless of whether the misdeed has actually hurt anyone. This is well illustrated by the prosecution of motorists in western countries for exceeding the speed limit, even when the 'offence' has been committed in the middle of the night on an otherwise empty road.

[231] Musk *Soul* 95.

[232] O. Caroe *The Pathans 550 BC – AD 1957* [Karachi:OUP,1958,1975] 262. Caroe also retrospectively observes that all the agreements the British government made with Pushtun tribes for the handing over of criminals were never implemented by the tribes precisely because it would have been an impossible breach of honour for the tribal leaders to hand over a fugitive who had claimed sanctuary (35-51).

[233] cf. Jn 1:10-11ff.

[234] cf section 'Honour and shame' above.

[235] MMComm.2:486 (underlining – emphasis added).

[236] A third option established in various *Ahadith* is the acceptance of blood money by the murder victim's relatives cf. MM25:11,14(murder).

[237] It is questionable as to whether this derives directly from Islam, as corporate responsibility is a characteristic feature of many tribal societies. However, most Islamic cultures are observably less individualistic than western cultures.

[238] cf. Musk *Soul* 49.

CHAPTER 6

CONTEXTUALISING CHRISTOLOGY
FOR ISLAMIC CULTURE

I did think I did see all Heaven before me, and the Great God Himself.[1]

Introduction

In this chapter, we present a framework for the contextualisation of christological monotheism in an Islamic culture, that in so far as is possible, uses conceptual categories, forms and symbolic motifs commonly used in that culture. The chapter will conclude with a concrete example of a form in which this contextualised christology could be expressed.

In chapter 1 we suggested that the use of western christologies in Islamic contexts over the last 200 years has been problematic as there has been insufficient recognition of the conceptual framework through which monotheism is primarily understood in Islamic environments. Two aspects stand out in this respect.

Firstly, some christologies used in Islamic contexts have not taken sufficient account of the emphatic stress on bounded monotheism that is central to the belief of most Muslims. Such christologies have reflected the tendency of the western theologians to develop christologies from below that begin from the earthly Jesus, and have concentrated on the similarities between the portraits of Jesus in the NT and in Islamic texts.[2] However, this approach has almost inevitably been seen by many Muslims as an attempt to make a man into God, thereby breaching the absolute gulf emphatically understood to distinguish God from all else. The christology we are proposing is therefore a 'christology from above'; i.e. one that starts by examining the degree of common understanding of the identity of God.

Secondly, in chapter 1 we saw that over the last 200 years christology in Islamic contexts has been interpreted through the filter of western christological formulations that often attempt to identify Jesus as divine using conceptual categories different from those commonly used by Muslims.[3] Much western theology, including patristic creedal formulations, speaks of God in *intrinsic* terms; i.e. focusing on God's internal nature.[4] However, in chapters 2 and 5 we demonstrated that in both the Jewish context in which the early church developed its christology, and in Islamic contexts, God is typically conceived of primarily in *extrinsic* terms; i.e. focusing on God's identity that is revealed as he relates to all else.

One particularly problematic consequence of defining God in intrinsic terms is that the trinity is described by focusing on internal relationships within the Godhead, rather than on how God as Father, Son and Holy Spirit relates externally to his people as creator, saviour and so forth. This focus on internal relationships within the Godhead results in the Father, the Son and the Holy Spirit being spoken of as three divine 'persons', a doctrinal expression that has been repeatedly misunderstood in Islamic contexts as tri-theism.

The christology that we propose therefore goes back behind western and patristic formulations to the christology of the early Jewish church expressed in the final form of the NT.[5]

The Proposed Christology:

A Christology From Above that Starts from the Unique Identity of God

The widespread emphasis in the Islamic context on the absolute boundary between God and all else[6] necessitates a contextualised christology being a christology from above. This does not mean that the portrait of Jesus in the *Qur'an* and other Islamic texts will be entirely ignored. Certain aspects of the proposed christology will create a positive resonance with miracles and high titles ascribed to Jesus in the Islamic context.[7] However, this Islamic portrait of Jesus does not form a *foundation* on which a divine christology can be built. Even the miracles of Jesus do not in themselves identify Jesus as being more than a powerful prophet, unless either a) they are shown to be specific fulfilments of earlier prophecies of what would happen when God himself visibly came to earth, or b) it is shown that Jesus delegated authority to his disciples to perform similar miracles in his name, thereby indicating that he himself had the power and authority to perform miracles such as raising the dead, rather than merely performing such miracles by God's permission.[8]

Using Islamic Concepts

The degree of commonality in the way that the Jewish and Islamic contexts have conceived of God's unique identity will determine the extent to which the contextualisation of christology developed by the early Jewish church can be used as a foundation for developing a contextualised christology for an Islamic culture. Conversely, differences between Jewish and Islamic concepts of monotheism will require us to make appropriate adjustments and modifications to the early church's contextualisation of christology.

Extrinsic Concept of Monotheism

In chapters 2 and 5 we saw that both the Jewish context in which the early church contextualised its christology, and Islamic contexts, characteristically conceive of God primarily in extrinsic terms.[9] In fact, in neither the Jewish nor Islamic contexts have we found any unambiguous examples of intrinsic descriptions of God in the texts that appear to be regarded as most authoritative; i.e. the OT and LXX, and the *Qur'an* and *Ahadith*, respectively. Even where alternative conceptions do occur in Islamic *Kalam* and some Sufi texts, these appear to be complementary perspectives overlaid on a more widely held, bounded extrinsic conception of God.[10]

The form that this extrinsic description of God takes is similar, though not identical, in both contexts. In Judaism, God was repeatedly referred to as the sole creator and ruler of all things, ultimate judge, and only saviour. In Islam, God is *al-Khaliq*, the only creator who alone can allow life to be imparted; he is designated as the absolute ruler of all things by titles such as *Rabb al-'alamin*, 'the Lord of the worlds', *Rabb kull shay* 'the Lord of all things'; he is also the only judge, *Malik Yaum al-din*, 'the Master of the Day of Judgement', who alone can forgive sins.[11] There is, however, no Islamic equivalent to the Jewish understanding that God himself is also the saviour who personally comes down to save his people.[12] This constitutes one of the major differences between Jewish and Islamic monotheism.

Emphasis on Bounded Monotheism

Both second temple Judaism and Sunni Islam primarily conceive of God in bounded terms.[13] Although some Sufi texts do also speak of God in unbounded intrinsic terms, the dominant emphasis is clearly a bounded extrinsic concept.[14] This emphasis on bounded monotheism is expressed in similar ways in both contexts.

a) The extrinsic descriptions of God that we noted above function as identity markers, defining God in distinction from all else by means of:

- The subject/object distinctions inherent in them: God is the creator – all else is his creation; he is the ruler – all else is ruled by him; he is the judge - all else is judged by him.

- Their use in combination with various aspects of monotheistic rhetoric such as the words 'only' or 'one' to emphasise that God is the 'only' creator, the 'only' ruler, the 'one' judge and so forth; the use of 'all things' or equivalent phrases such as 'the heaven, the earth, the sea and all that is in them', to indicate that God created 'all things', rules 'all things' and so forth.[15]

b) Certain names are reserved exclusively for God. Many of these names are common to both contexts, with some even being cognates.[16]

Name	Islamic name	Hebrew (where name is cognate)
'the Living One'	al-Hai	אֶהְיֶה ('I AM')[17]
'the Merciful'	al-Rahim	רַחוּם
'the Compassionate'	al-Rahman	-
'the First'	al-Awwal	-
'the Last'	al-Akhir	אַחֲרוֹן
'the King'	al-Malik	מֶלֶךְ
'King of kings'	Malik al-mulk	-
'the Holy One'	al-Quddus	קָדוֹשׁ
'the Mighty One'	al-Aziz	-
'the Creator'	al-Khaliq	-
'the Maker'	al-Bari	בּוֹרֵא
'the Lord of all'	Rabb kull shay[18]	-

In Judaism these names are never applied to any heavenly being other than God, a situation paralleled in the Islamic context where, when prefaced by the definite article, they are used exclusively for God. Similarly, in both contexts formulaic descriptions such as 'King of kings' and 'our Great God' are used exclusively for God. Islamic *Ahadith* in fact prohibit the former being applied to anyone other than God.[19]

The existence of this degree of similarity is significant. It suggests that a contextualised christology will be able to maintain significant continuity with the Islamic emphasis on bounded monotheism in a similar manner to that adopted by the early Jewish church in relation to Jewish monotheism.

Expanding Islamic Concepts

Despite the evident similarities of the conceptual frameworks used to describe monotheism in the Jewish and Islamic contexts, they are not entirely identical. It will be necessary for a contextualised christology to expand the existing Islamic conception of God as sole creator, ruler of all things and final eschatological judge, to also refer to God as the only saviour, who is the only source of salvation for men.

This expansion of the existing extrinsic conception of God is necessary in order to set a contextualised christology in the context of the biblical story of God, who on occasions has locally and visibly manifested his presence on earth when he acted as the saviour of his people. Although this concept does not occur in the Islamic scriptures, there is in fact little that could be said to contradict this concept in principle.

In chapter 3 we demonstrated how the early Jewish church used this bounded extrinsic concept of monotheism to include Jesus within the unique identity of the one God by identifying him as the creator, ruler, judge of all things and the only saviour.[20] The existence of a substantially similar concept of monotheism in the Islamic context gives validity to a christology contextualised for Islamic culture following a similar pattern.

The Biblical Story of God's Self-Revelation

Theophany and Epiphany: Similarities and Differences Between the Jewish and Islamic Contexts

In chapters 2 and 5 we saw that although both the OT and the Islamic scriptures claim that mortals cannot see God and live, both sets of scriptures suggest that God can in some way veil his appearance in order to reveal a local manifestation of himself. The clearest examples of this, occurring in both the Jewish and Islamic scriptures, are the appearances of God to Moses at the burning bush and on Sinai, it being widely accepted in both contexts that Moses actually saw God.[21]

Both the OT and the Islamic scriptures also speak of God eschatologically, visibly coming to earth on the clouds accompanied by his angels, although the *Qur'an* states that the earth and heavens will have been changed in some way before this happens. Significantly, in both contexts it appears to be accepted that this appearance of God will be in some measure anthropomorphic.[22] These parallels are potentially significant as we earlier demonstrated that the early Jewish church identified Christ's return as judge as this anticipated eschatological epiphany, which the OT terms 'the Day of the Lord'.[23]

In both the Jewish and Islamic contexts, descriptions of God being in a particular locality have been perceived to require a layer of interpretation in order to avoid the inference that the totality of God could be said to be confined to a finite space. Consequently, the Jewish targums began to interpret OT throne theophanies as God's glory or *shekinah* sitting on the throne, while the Islamic *tafsir* similarly suggested that perhaps it was God's power that was seated on the throne, or that the divine throne represents a particular point in the universe, where God cast his effulgence in order to govern the universe.[24]

These parallels are potentially significant for the development of a contextualised christology as they point to at least a degree of common belief that God can locally manifest his presence, without such a manifestation constituting the totality of God, and that God can even locally manifest a form of his presence on earth that is sufficiently veiled so as to be seen by mortals.

Although this concept is widely disseminated in the Islamic context,[25] in the following respects it is not as clearly developed as the concept of epiphany was in second temple Judaism.

1. In the Islamic context there is nothing that in any way equates with the OT 'theology of epiphany', that portrays the purpose of epiphany as God himself acting as saviour-deliverer and judge. Indeed, the former divine role is almost entirely absent in Islam to the extent that in the Qur'anic narratives even the Moses epiphanies are not related to God acting in any salvific way. Moreover, although an eschatological vision of God is anticipated in the Islamic context, the Islamic scriptures do not imply that this is in any sense the restoration of the presence of God that was lost as a result of sin at the fall.[26]

2. In so far as there is an Islamic concept of epiphany, this does not normally extend beyond the recognition of Moses, and possibly Muhammad, having actually seen God on earth.[27]

3. The Islamic scriptures contain no equivalent of the OT narratives of God being seen in anthropomorphic form in theophanic visions and epiphanies. It is therefore perhaps unsurprising that in the Islamic context there is a greater degree of hesitancy concerning the concept of God being seen in anthropomorphic form.[28]

4. Although, the Qur'anic account of Moses' request to see God implies that the theophanies Moses saw on other occasions must have been a somewhat veiled form of God, the concept of God assuming a veiled form of his presence so as to be seen by mortals on earth is not developed in the way that it is in the OT, but remains implicit.[29]

The underlying reasons for the greater clarity of the concepts if theophany and epiphany in the Jewish context can be seen by comparing the concepts introduced in OT with those in the Islamic scriptures:

	Jewish context	Islamic context
God cannot be seen by mortals.	X	X
God can assume a veiled form so as to be seen.	X	X
Moses epiphanies	X	X
Epiphanies experienced by other prophets	X	--
Anthropomorphic description of God		
- in eschatological visions of God.	X	X
- descriptions of God's throne.	X	(Debated)
- malak YHWH epiphanies.	X	--
God reveals himself in epiphany to act as saviour.	X	--
Immediate presence of God lost due to sin.	X	--

However, it is important to note that the more limited development of the concept of epiphany in the Islamic context is not simply due to the absence of parallels to certain biblical narratives, but is also due to the presence of a number of antithetical ideas that were not present in the Jewish context.

1. In the Islamic context the specific repudiation of any doctrine of incarnation itself creates at least a degree of hesitancy towards the related concept of epiphany.[30] In the Jewish context, incarnation was certainly unexpected, but it was in no sense inconsistent with what were recognised as its authoritative scriptures. However, the same cannot be said of the Islamic context.[31] To this

extent, the Islamic context more closely resembles rabbinical Judaism with its reaction against Christian theology, than second temple Judaism.

2. A number of Islamic texts contain narratives that parallel OT *malak YHWH* narratives, but replace the *malak YHWH* by Gabriel, who is emphatically understood to be a created being.[32] This potentially means that any reference to *malak YHWH* epiphanies in an Islamic context will require additional clarification to emphasise that it is God, rather than Gabriel, who is being referred to.

3. Some Sufis have also evinced a degree of antipathy to the concept of epiphany on the grounds that by bringing God down to earth, epiphany appears to do the exact opposite of the Sufi aim, which is to bring man up to God.[33]

Whilst a christology contextualised for Islamic culture may be able to strengthen the concept of epiphany by the inclusion of narrative material that is otherwise absent, the presence of antithetical ideas will require a more specific apologetic response.

However, even with the caveats we have noted above, the concept of epiphany that occurs in a range of Islamic texts is potentially one of the most important conceptual bridges to the explanation of the Christian understanding of incarnation. Strangely, as we saw in chapter 1, it is also one that has received very little attention in the christologies that have to date been used by the Christian church in the Islamic world.[34]

Laying the Foundations for Christology: OT Theophany and Epiphany Narratives

In order to take account of these differences between the Jewish context in which the early church contextualised its christology and the Islamic context, it will be necessary to strengthen the existing Islamic concepts of theophany and epiphany. Discussion of the incarnation needs to be prefaced by at least a summary reference to key OT theophany and epiphany narratives. These give added emphasis to the concept that God can locally manifest his presence, even on earth, without that manifestation constituting the totality of God.

The following constitute key OT passages that could be used to preface any explanation of the incarnation in a contextualised christology:

1.   The throne theophanies such as Isaiah 6:1-13, Ezekiel 1:1-28 and Daniel 7:1-14. These closely correspond to the existing Islamic concept of God having seated himself on the throne. However, they develop this slightly by providing

actual narrative descriptions of the throne and, in the case of Ezekiel and Daniel, provide restrained, though apparently anthropomorphic, descriptions of the figure on the throne. Narration of these theophanic visions therefore affirms the existing concept that God can locally manifest his presence, as implied by the Qur'anic throne verse. It also strengthens the rather more weakly held idea that God can assume an anthropomorphic form.

2. The pre-fall Eden narratives of God walking with man and woman in the garden and their banishment from God's presence as a result of sin (Genesis 1:1-3:24). This element of the christology builds on the widely held Islamic concept that believers will see God in the gardens of paradise, by introducing the idea that God previously walked with mankind in the garden, but mankind was banished, losing this immediate presence of God as a result of sin. This sets later epiphanies in a salvation historical context, which is otherwise absent from the Islamic context. The introduction of the Biblical concept of sin also lays an important foundation for comprehension of God as saviour, and humanity's need for salvation.

3. Other OT epiphany narratives:

a) The visitations to Abraham announcing the covenant of circumcision, the promise of Isaac and the judgement of Sodom (Genesis 17:1-18:33). This epiphany forms an important stage in the Biblical narrative of salvation history, as well as introducing the concept that God comes in epiphany to act as judge. The Biblical account of this epiphany is likely to have resonance in the Islamic context, as the story is related in more general terms in the *Qur'an* (Q11:69-83) and *Ahadith*.

b) The Moses epiphanies. These are likely to have a significant resonance in the Islamic context, as each of these incidents is referred to in the *Qur'an* and a range of other Islamic texts, often with implicit hints of epiphany. It is widely accepted that God revealed himself on earth to Moses:

i) God's appearance to Moses at the burning bush announcing that he has come down to rescue his people from the Egyptians and bring them into the promised land (Exodus 3:1-4:17). This introduces the concept of God appearing in epiphany to act as saviour of his people. This OT narrative is also likely to have a strong resonance in the Islamic context, as the *Qur'an* narrates this incident four times, and includes implications of epiphany such as God's voice coming from a specific terrestrial locality, and the hallowing of the ground.

ii) The subsequent Exodus deliverance in which God himself went ahead of the Israelites in a pillar of cloud by day and fire by night (Exodus 13:17-14:31). The Exodus deliverance, including the crossing of the Red Sea, is also narrated in the *Qur'an* and other Islamic texts. However, it is important to counter the Islamic tradition that the figure in the cloud was Gabriel. This can be done in a similar fashion to the LXX's counter to created angel traditions, by an emphatic assertion that 'not an ambassador, nor an angel, but God himself saved them'.[35]

iii) God coming to Moses in a dense cloud on top of Sinai and delivering the Torah (Exodus 19:1ff). This is also echoed in the *Qur'an* and other Islamic texts, although there the focus tends to be on the Israelites' sin of making the golden calf, rather than on the epiphany experienced by Moses.

iv) Moses and the 70 elders meeting with God on Sinai and eating and drinking in his presence (Exodus 24:1-18). This incident, which is also referred to in the *Qur'an*, establishes that God's appearances to men on earth were not just limited to Moses.

v) Moses' request to see God (Exodus 33:12-34:9). This narrative is important because it introduces the idea that even Moses could not see God in his glorious form, but in other epiphanies God evidently assumed a more veiled form that could be seen by mortals. This lays an important conceptual foundation for an understanding of the incarnation.

These epiphany narratives raise the conundrum for Muslims that Stephen implied in his Sanhedrin speech: 'you believe God himself appeared to Moses on Sinai; how can that be when creation itself cannot contain him?' As such they may similarly prepare the way for a fuller explanation of christology.[36]

4. OT prophecies of God eschatologically appearing as saviour:

a) The prophecy of Isaiah 35:4ff, 'Your God will come...He will come to save you,' which results in the eyes of the blind being opened, the deaf hearing, the lame walking and the dumb speaking. This prophecy forms the foundation of Matthew 11:1-15's recognition of who Jesus is; John the Baptist ending the era of the law and the prophets; and the coming of Jesus bringing in the long awaited kingdom of God. At least some aspects of Isaiah 35 and Matthew 11 are likely to have a positive resonance in the Islamic context, as the *Qur'an* twice refers to Jesus having healed the blind and lepers and raised the dead. Moreover, this text counters the Qur'anic assertion that Jesus only raised the dead 'by God's permission', by demonstrating that Jesus' performance of these miracles was the fulfilment of an OT prophecy of what would happen when God himself came to earth as saviour.

b)   The prophecy of Isaiah 9:1-7. This builds on the concept of God eschatologically coming to earth as saviour by stating that one whose name was 'Mighty God' would be born as a child on earth, resulting in the land of Galilee seeing a 'great light'. This is an important foundation for the concept of incarnation.

c)   The prophecy of Malachi 3:1 and 4:5 that God will send his messenger who would prepare the way before him, after which he himself will come. This prophecy lays the foundation for Matthew 11:1-15's recognition that John the Baptist is the messenger and Jesus is the one for whom he has prepared the way. This prophecy is an important foundation for the explanation of who Jesus is, as the *Qur'an* explicitly links John (*Yahya ibn Zakariya*) and Jesus, portraying John as having been sent to announce the coming of Jesus.

5.   OT prophecies of God eschatologically appearing as judge on 'the Day of the Lord'. The christology implicit in the NT asserts that God had come once as saviour and would return again as judge. Although this belief was consistent with the OT, it was an interpretation that had not been anticipated and was therefore unexpected in second temple Judaism. However, with the benefit of hindsight, the christology we are proposing can specifically demonstrate that earlier prophets spoke of God eschatologically coming both as saviour and as judge:

Zechariah 14:1-7's description of the Day of the Lord when 'the Lord my God will come with all his holy ones with him' is the clearest expression of this in the OT. This lays a foundation for the NT's identification of the 'Day of the Lord' as the second coming of Jesus as judge, which is described in language directly paralleling Zechariah 14. Zechariah 14 also describes the Day of the Lord using a number of motifs that are commonly used in the Islamic context to describe 'the Last Day' (*Yaum al-akhir*), such as an earthquake, the absence of sunlight and God himself coming with his angels.

This strengthening of the existing concept of epiphany lays a foundation for the subsequent explanation of God appearing in the incarnation when he acted as universal saviour, and returning a second time as universal judge on the 'Day of the Lord'.

Explaining Christological Monotheism Without Describing God as '3 persons'

This strengthening of existing concepts of theophany and epiphany lays part of the foundation for a contextualised christology, by emphasising that God can locally manifest a visible form of his presence, even on earth. However, this raises the question of whether these local manifestations of God's presence are merely temporary forms adopted by him for the purposes of relating to his creation or whether they are in fact permanent aspects of the unique identity of God.

We earlier demonstrated that the early church's contextualisation of christology emphasised that God has related to his creation in various ways, as the Spirit who came upon the prophets and in particular as Jesus, through whom God undertook the acts of creation and salvation.[37] However, the NT also makes it clear that the early church understood christological monotheism as more than simply *modalism*; i.e. God manifesting himself in different modes.[38] The prologue to the Fourth Gospel begins by declaring that in the beginning the Word was both with God and yet also was God, clearly implying the existence of permanent relationships within the unique identity of the one God. Although NT christology does not focus on this issue,[39] the NT's affirmation of it made it vital that we assessed whether there were any specific Jewish antecedents of christological monotheism in the Jewish background which the early church related to. We must compare these findings with the antecedent attitudes to christological monotheism[40] in the Islamic context that we discussed in chapter 5 in order to assess what modifications will be needed for the early Jewish church's contextualisation of christology to be applied in the Islamic context.

Jewish and Islamic Attitudes Towards Christological Monotheism

In our discussion of second temple Judaism we observed a number of features, which could in some manner be said to be antecedents of christological monotheism. These included divine attributes such as God's word, wisdom, name and glory which were described in ways that implied they were both God's agent and also God; the Spirit, who was widely understood by Jews to be the real and actual presence of God; and the *malak YHWH*, a form in which God appeared in theophanic visions and epiphanies. The latter is particularly significant, as it appears to have led many Jews to accept that God could appear on earth in anthropomorphic form. The *malak YHWH* motif was also used to interpret a small number of OT prophecies as implying a divine messiah, although the most widely held messianic expectations were clearly of a non-divine messiah.

To some extent all of these implied that there might perhaps be some form of bifurcation within the Godhead. However, they were largely capable of being explained in terms of God revealing himself in different forms (i.e. *modalism*), rather than implying the existence of permanent relationships within the Godhead. Indeed, the attempts to reinterpret some OT texts to remove any suggestion that there might be two simultaneous local manifestations of the divine being suggests that forms such as the *malak YHWH* were understood as merely temporary manifestations of God.[41]

In the Islamic context, we have already noted that there is no equivalent of the *malak YHWH*, and the Spirit is most commonly understood as a created being, often identified with Gabriel. The discussion of divine attributes within *kalam* does provide at least a partial parallel to the Jewish context, with divine attributes such as speech being described as neither identical with God's essence, nor additional to it. However, these hints of bifurcation are not as widespread as in the Jewish context, being largely confined to the somewhat philosophical discussions of *kalam*.[42]

We therefore have a situation where although there are more hints of bifurcation within the Jewish context, in neither the Jewish nor Islamic contexts does there appear to be any concept that local manifestations of the presence of God might imply some form of permanent relationships within the Godhead. Both contexts may in this sense be described as *modalist*. This common starting point means that the contextualisation of christological monotheism used by the early church in the context of Jewish monotheism can form the basis for a similar articulation in the Islamic context.

However, the most significant differences between the Jewish and Islamic contexts lie not in the existence of antecedent hints of bifurcation in the Jewish context, but in the specific denials of Jesus' divinity and incarnation in the Islamic context. Although the concept of permanent relationships within the unique identity of the one God was unexpected in the Jewish context, there was nothing in the sacred scriptures to deny it. However, in the Islamic context the *Qur'an* contains very specific denials that God is the Messiah and that Jesus is the Son of God, and condemns Christians for worshipping three gods.[43] These denials will inevitably mean that any expression of christology consistent with the NT will face a path of greater resistance in the Islamic context than the early church's christology faced in the Jewish context, and will require a contextualised theology that will find new expressions for concepts such as Jesus' divine sonship.

Expanding the Islamic Concept of God

The NT depiction of christological monotheism goes substantially further than simply identifying Jesus as God; it includes Jesus within the unique identity of the one God, thereby disclosing a significant new aspect of the identity of God. This expansion of the theology of God is expressed in a new name of God, 'the name (singular) of the Father, the Son and the Holy Spirit'.[44] This name appears to reflect a belief that just as God had revealed a new name expressing the salvific aspect of his character when he came down at the Exodus to act as saviour, so too the coming of Jesus as saviour had revealed a new aspect of the character of God, expressed in this newly revealed name of God.[45]

It is therefore essential that any contextualised christology should include an explanation of the relationship between the Father and Jesus, if it is to avoid implying that Jesus represents the totality of God. Moreover, in an Islamic context it is particularly important that the relationship between the Father and Jesus is clearly explained in view of the Islamic denial and misunderstanding of Jesus' divine sonship.

The concept that God can locally manifest his presence in order to reveal himself to men needs to be expanded to form the basis of a Logos christology which is foundational for understanding Jesus' divine sonship. This Logos christology depicts God as impossible for men to approach, dwelling in unapproachable light, but who locally manifests a veiled form of his presence, in order to have personal contact with his creation. The NT describes Jesus' divine sonship in these terms. It is as the Son that God relates to creation as creator, ruler, judge and saviour. The Son is therefore one with the Father from whom he has come, yet also has life in himself.[46] This concept is expressed in Jesus' title 'the Word of God' in the prologue to the Fourth Gospel, and by other NT writers in terms such as 'the image of the invisible God', and 'the radiance of God's glory, the exact representation of his being'.[47]

The extrinsic description of God that we earlier demonstrated will be used to articulate this divine agency relationship between the Father and Jesus:

Creator

The Father and Jesus are together the one Creator (*al-Khaliq*).[48] The NT describes the purpose of creation as being both for the Father 'for whom we live', and Jesus 'for whom all things were created'.[49]

However, the Father is the source of creation 'from whom all things came', while Jesus 'through whom he made the world' is the agent who carried out the actual activity of creation, and is its sustainer 'who sustains all things by his powerful word'.[50] Jesus is also the means by which all creation will be brought back into a union of harmony (*wasl*) with the Creator.[51]

Ruler of All Things

The Father and Jesus are together the only sovereign ruler of all things (*Rabb al-'alamin*), King of kings (*Malik al-mulk*) and Lord of lords.[52] However, elements of God's creation have rebelled against his sovereign rule.

The Father has therefore put all things under Jesus, in order that Jesus may reign as Lord over all creation (*Rabb kull shay*), until he has put all hostile forces including death beneath his feet.[53] When the power of these forces is completely destroyed Jesus will hand the kingdom back to the Father,[54] and God's rule will be exercised unchallenged in all things from the throne (singular) of God and Jesus.[55]

Final Eschatological Judge

The Father and Jesus are together the one final eschatological Judge (*Malik Yaum al-din*).[56] However, the Father himself judges no one directly, but exercises all judgement through Jesus who became man.[57]

Saviour

The Father and Jesus are together God the Saviour.[58]

The Father sent Jesus to save men and women from their sins and reconcile them to himself.[59] Jesus added human nature to himself, so that by his death he could be the means of reconciling men and women to the Father, and free them from the powers of evil and death.[60]

The Father saves those who repent of their sins and believe in Jesus, making them alive with new spiritual birth.[61]

Jesus is the Lord 'of the water of life' (*ab-i-hayat*), who pours out the Holy Spirit on those who experience new spiritual birth in order to renew them.[62]

Advantages of this Description of God

This contextualisation explains Jesus' relationship to the Father in terms of the extrinsic description by which God is primarily thought of in the Islamic context (i.e. God's identity in relation to all else). It avoids the notion of 'personhood' derived from the intrinsic description of God (i.e. God's internal nature) used in the patristic creedal formulations that have heavily influenced western theology. By expressing the relationship between Jesus and the Father in other terms, Christian claims for Jesus' divinity are more likely to be comprehensible in an Islamic culture, and less liable to be misunderstood as part of a belief in tri-theism.

A 'Dynamic Equivalent' for NT Terms Expressing Christological Monotheism

It is clear from our discussion so far that it will be appropriate to use the Islamic title *al-Batin* ('the Hidden'), one of the ninety nine names of God, to refer to God the Father, who is invisible. However, the clarity with which a contextualised christology can express the relationship between Jesus and the Father will be significantly enhanced if at least a partial 'dynamic equivalent'[63] can also be found for the NT christological designations such as 'Son of God', 'Word of God', 'image of the invisible God', and the 'radiance of God's glory, the exact representation of his being', that express this theology.[64]

It is essential that any such designation both be able to identify Jesus as God,[65] and also express the concept of God himself acting as divine agent that is at the heart of the Logos christology. An identification of Jesus as God without clearly expressing the latter would be liable to be misunderstood as implying two gods. We will therefore examine a number of designations currently used in the Islamic context to assess their potential suitability in the light of these criteria.

Islamic Names of God as Possible Dynamic Equivalents
Word of God

At first sight, it appears that the most obvious possibility is the title 'Word of God' (*Kalimat Allah*) given to Jesus in the *Qur'an*.[66] The meaning is certainly not identical to that of the Johannine 'Word of God', as the Qur'anic reference gives no hint of the meaning of this title as expounded in the Fourth Gospel's prologue. The weakness of the title is that it is not an Islamic name of God. Moreover, its potential to identify Jesus as God has been weakened by the extensive arguments of Islamic scholars that this Qur'anic christological title does not identify Jesus as divine. However, despite this, the assertion of Islamic *kalam* that the *Qur'an*, as dictated divine speech, is also the word of God gives a limited potential to expand the title *Kalimat Allah* to identify Jesus with the divine attribute of speech. However, the potential of this title is limited both because only a minority of Muslims are familiar with the arguments of *kalam*, and because the title *Kalimat Allah* cannot easily be used to identify Jesus with other areas of God's identity such as his activity in creation, sovereign rule of all things and eschatological judgement.

A number of possible alternatives occur in the lists of the ninety nine names of God, which are widely circulated among Muslims. As accepted names of God, these at least potentially identify Jesus as God.

Al-Wakil

We earlier observed that W.H.T. Gairdner suggested that in an Islamic context *al-Wakil* might be a suitable title for Christ. However, he did not develop this beyond a cursory mention, and did not use it to identify Jesus as God.[67] As an Islamic name of God *al-Wakil* has a range of meanings including 'the Guardian' and 'the Advocate'. However, in Farsi *wakil* is also commonly used to denote an 'agent', such as an ambassador or an attorney. As an accepted divine title that occurs in lists of the 99 names of God it has the potential to directly identify Jesus as God, and if the meaning of 'agent' could be emphasised, it could also express the concept of divine agency that is central to the Logos christology. It would be necessary however to give a much more carefully nuanced meaning of 'the agent' than the divine title is commonly understood to have, especially as its common meaning in Urdu is simply 'attorney', rather than 'agent'. Although *wakil* does have a wider range of meaning in Farsi, the divine title is still primarily understood to mean 'the Advocate'. Whilst 'advocate' is a NT christological title (παράκλητος), its meaning there relates to Jesus' speaking to the Father on behalf of believers.[68] Thus, whilst it admirably expresses this aspect of christology, it does not so easily express how Jesus relates to creation on behalf of God, which is the predominant aspect of christological monotheism that we need to express. In the NT 'Advocate' (ὁ παράκλητος) is also a designation for the wide-ranging work of the Holy Spirit as he brings the presence of God to the world.[69] As such the title *al-Wakil* may be a more suitable designation for the Holy Spirit, and merits being reserved for this reference in a more complete contextualisation of Christian monotheism.

Al-Wali

A further possibility is the title *al-Wali* ('The Governor'). However, whilst this clearly encompasses God's activity of universal rule and potentially even eschatological judgement, it is less clear how easily it could embrace God's activity of creation. A further difficulty with this title is that the title *Wali* is commonly used to designate Sufi saints. There is therefore a danger that even with the use of the definite article, this title might be understood as identifying Jesus as no more than a very senior Sufi saint, rather than directly identifying him as God.

Al-Malik and Malik al-mulk

The Islamic titles *al-Malik* ('The King') and *Malik al-mulk* ('The King of kings') present further possibilities and have the advantage of partially paralleling the NT christological title 'King of kings and Lord of lords'.[70] The title *Malik al-mulk* is in fact a particularly emphatic divine designation, as some *Ahadith* forbid its application to anyone other than God. However, these titles are limited in that they cannot easily be expanded to encompass the work of creation. This particular problem could be overcome by a minor modification of these titles to 'the King of kings and Lord of creation' or in a shorter form simply as 'the King of creation'[71]. However, the most fundamental limitation of these titles is that on their own they do not clearly express the concept of divine agency, and as such could imply belief in two gods; i.e. 'God' and the *Malik al-mulk*.

Summary

It therefore appears that within the Islamic context there are no existing designations that are in themselves adequate to express a Logos christology. The title with the greatest potential appears to be *al-Wakil*. However, even this would need very careful nuancing as its primary meaning at the moment is that of 'advocate' rather than 'agent'.

The Appropriateness of NT Christological Titles in Islamic Contexts

As the existing designations that are already embedded in the context cannot easily express the theology of christological monotheism, we will now examine the contextual suitability of NT expressions that do adequately convey this theology.

Word of God

We have already seen that the NT title 'Word of God' (*Kalimat Allah*) is problematic because in the Islamic context it has a meaning somewhat different from that in the NT, and it is not commonly understood to refer to God.[72]

The Radiance of God's Glory

A further possibility is the designation used in the epistle to the Hebrews 'the radiance of God's glory, the exact representation of his being'.[73] This has the merit of focusing on God's glory, which is an existing motif on the Islamic context. However, the existence of *wahdat al-wujud* Sufi claims that Muhammad and Islamic saints are an emanation of divine light means that Christian use of this title runs the risk of being misunderstood as making the same claims for Jesus as *Barelvi* Islam makes for Muhammad and Islamic saints. Therefore in the Islamic context it does not clearly convey the theology that it conveyed in the Jewish context addressed by Hebrews.

The Image of the Invisible God

The NT christological titles 'the image of the invisible God', and 'the image of God'[74] as they stand are extremely problematic in the Islamic context, as 'image' has the connotation of 'idol'. However, if this could be replaced by a less problematic synonym, this title could potentially be appropriate as it is based on the normal 'invisibility' of God, which we earlier demonstrated was a significant motif in the Islamic context. It also directly addresses the unresolved tension created in the Islamic context by the combined emphasis on God's invisibility and his visible appearance to Moses. We therefore propose that the title 'the visible manifestation/form of the invisible God' and the shortened form 'the visible manifestation/form of God' be used. We have already demonstrated that the Islamic context has an existing, if ill-defined, concept of God manifesting a form of his presence. There are three main possibilities as to how this might be expressed: a) 'manifestation': a century ago St Clair Tisdall briefly drew attention to the Arabic word *mazhar* as a means of expressing this concept, although it did not form a significant part of his theology. This word is cognate with the Urdu and Farsi word *zohur* meaning 'appearance' or 'manifestation'; b) 'form': such as the word *surat* which is used in the main Urdu and Farsi Bible translations for the christological title in both Col.1:15 and 2 Cor.4:4;[75] c) 'face' or 'countenance': such as the word *chahar*[76] used for these verses by the recently published Farsi Contemporary Bible[77] which utilises a lower register vocabulary than the standard Farsi NT.[78] The word 'face' has the advantage of being an existing Qur'anic description of God.[79] However, it has the theological disadvantage that certain Biblical texts also speak of the face of the Father.[80] Other things being equal, it is preferable to maintain continuity with the existing Bible translations. However, where the distinction between terms is primarily linguistic rather than theological, it is imperative that the contextual theologian should defer to the judgement of the indigenous church as to which word should be used.

Directly Identifying Jesus as the One God - In the Context of Christological Monotheism

Applying Bounded Extrinsic Descriptions of God to Jesus

Earlier in the study we demonstrated that according to the NT the early Jewish church directly identified Jesus as the visible manifestation of the invisible God, by applying to him the OT's extrinsic conception of God as the sole creator, ruler of all things, final eschatological judge and only saviour.[81] As the first three of these are common to the primary way that God is conceived of in the Islamic culture under study,[82] the same process can be used to directly identify Jesus as the one God. The contextualised christology can therefore directly identify Jesus as the one God by referring to him as:

a)   'the Creator' (*al-Khaliq*); 'the Maker' (*al-Bari*); 'the Fashioner' (*al-Musawir*); and 'the Beginner' (*al-Mubdi*).

b) 'the Lord of all things' (*Rabb kull shay*); 'the Lord of the worlds' (*Rabb al-'alamin*); 'the Lord of the throne' (*Rabb al-'arsh*); 'the King' (*al-Malik*); 'the King of kings' (*Malik al-mulk*).

c) 'the Master of the Day of Judgement' (*Malik Yaum al-din*); 'the Judge' (*al-Hakim*); 'the Judge of judges' (*al-Hakim al-hakimin*).

It will be necessary to expand significantly the concept of God's rule of all things to take in the biblical teaching on the kingdom of God, as this formed the central aspect of both Jesus' own teaching and that of the early church. This needs to include the following: the arrival of the kingdom in the personal presence of Jesus, who called people to enter the kingdom by repentance and submitting to his kingly rule in their lives; Jesus' defeat of all the powers of evil on the cross; the full consummation of the kingdom following Jesus' *parousia*, when he exercises final eschatological judgement on the powers of darkness; God's rule then extending unchallenged over all things, resulting in sin, sickness, suffering and death being abolished.

In order to counter Islamic concepts of the kingdom of God being a political concept, it will be particularly important to emphasise that the kingdom is entered by individual repentance and involves submission of the individual's will to the kingly rule of God in terms of daily conduct and the battle against one's own sin.[83]

In addition to these Jesus will also be identified as:

d) The only saviour – who is the only source of salvation for men.

We earlier observed that in both second temple Judaism and the Islamic context being studied, these extrinsic descriptions of God emphasise the absolute boundary that exists between God and all else, by means of a series of subject/object distinctions: God is the Creator – all else his creation; he is the Lord – all else his creatures; he is the final eschatological Judge – all others are judged by him.[84] The effect of applying these extrinsic descriptions of God to Jesus in the Islamic context therefore communicates in a similar way to the early church's application of them in the context of Jewish monotheism, i.e. it emphasises the claim that Jesus is on the God side of the God/non-god divide.

Identifying Jesus' Parousia as the Last Day (Yaum al-akhir)

In the Islamic context 'the Last Day' (*Yaum al-akhir*) is depicted in terms strikingly similar to Biblical descriptions of 'the Day of the Lord', which the NT portrays as Jesus' eschatological return as judge.[85] These similarities include a mountain-shaking earthquake, the emergence of the antichrist (*al-Dajal al-Masih*)/beast, the heavens being split asunder and the sun darkened. These events culminate in the blast of the trumpet, subsequent to which God himself visibly comes to earth on the clouds, accompanied by his angels for the Day of Judgement (*Yaum al-din*).[86] These similarities allow us to use the Islamic concepts of 'the Last Day' and 'the Day of Judgement' as dynamic equivalents of the OT concept of 'the Day of the Lord'. A contextualised christology can therefore portray Jesus' *parousia* as 'the Last Day' (*Yaum al-akhir*), when he visibly arrives on the clouds accompanied by his angels, before later acting as the final eschatological judge (*Malik Yaum al-din*) on the Day of Judgement (*Yaum al-din*). It will however be necessary to emphasise that he came once as saviour, and will return only once again with his angels on the clouds as *Malik Yaum al-din*, in order to counter the Islamic belief that Jesus will return to earth before the Last Day.[87]

Ascribing Divine Prerogatives to Jesus:

Eschatological Forgiveness of Sins

The notion of justice, indigenous to Palestinian Judaism and also commonly found in Islamic cultures is a relational one that primarily focuses on the satisfaction of the aggrieved party's honour rather than, as in western jurisprudence, on the punishment of the wrongdoer because the deed is morally wrong in a more abstract sense. This focus on the injury suffered by the aggrieved party means that only the aggrieved can forgive or require judicial satisfaction from the malefactor.[88] The NT's claim that Jesus is able to grant eschatological forgiveness of sins therefore potentially carries the same significance in the Islamic context as it did in Palestinian Judaism; i.e. it implicitly claims that Jesus is God, as only God can forgive sins – as he is the one sinned against.[89]

Sending the Spirit

In the OT and other second temple Jewish texts the Spirit is consistently portrayed as God himself, particularly as he relates to his creation. The NT's claim that Jesus sends the Spirit therefore implicitly identifies Jesus as the one

God. Although the *Qur'an* depicts the Spirit as a created being, it is sent only at God's command.[90] Therefore, the assertion that Jesus sends the Spirit also implies that Jesus is being identified as the one God, although not quite as strongly as it did in the second temple context.

Delegation to His Followers of Authority Over Diseases and Evil Spirits in His Own Name:

i)   Miracles

Although the OT records prophets performing miracles including raising the dead by prayer to God, Jesus not only enacted such miracles, but also delegated authority to enable his disciples to do so 'in the name of Jesus'. He told his disciples that through prayer 'in my name' they would do even greater things than he had done, which presumably included raising the dead. Jesus' instruction for his disciples to pray in his name, so that they would do mighty works, clearly indicated that he himself had this authority, rather than merely doing such mighty acts by prayer to God as other prophets had done.[91] This provides an apologetic response to the Qur'anic insistence that Jesus' miracles, including raising the dead, were done merely 'by God's permission'.[92]

ii) Authority over evil spirits

The NT also portrays Jesus as having authority in himself over evil spirits. Although certain second temple texts speak of various prophylactic practices, and calling on angels believed to have been divinely matched in power against specific demons, God alone was believed to have authority in himself over the demonic realm. The NT portrayal of Jesus as delegating authority to his disciples in his own name; i.e. 'in the name of Jesus', over all demonic powers, clearly indicated that he himself had this authority, rather than it having been delegated to him. As such it implicitly identified him as God.[93]

The Islamic context mirrors the Jewish context to some extent, in that some *Ahadith* enjoin reliance solely on prayer to God for deliverance from demonic affliction, although others allow the use of various prophylaxes such as charms against evil spirits.[94] The parallels between the Jewish context in which Jesus ministered and some Islamic beliefs makes Jesus' authority over powers of darkness a potentially important aspect of a christology contextualised for the Islamic context. Illustrative of this is the fear many Muslims have of curses and demonisation. This results in a widespread practice of burning of seeds such as rue in a prophylactic attempt to ward off evil spirits, which closely parallels a similar Jewish practice described in *Tobit*.[95] It is therefore conceivable that deliverance from demonic activity by using the name of Jesus rather than prophylactic rituals might result in similar reactions to those which greeted Jesus' deliverance of people from evil spirits.

The NT's portrayal of the early church exercising authority over sickness and the demonic alongside its christological proclamation suggests that at this point, contextualisation of christology for an Islamic culture needs to move beyond articulation of theological concepts to actual praxis.[96]

Applying Islamic Names of God to Jesus

In the NT, a number of OT names of God are applied to Jesus. Frequently, these are names such as 'the Holy One' that are exclusively applied to God in the OT, and often occur in the most polemically monotheistic sections of the OT such as Isa.40-55.[97] A number of these NT christological titles are identical to some of the 99 names used to refer to God in Islamic contexts. As such, in a contextualised christology these can function as dynamic equivalents of the early church's application of OT titles of God to Jesus. This is particularly significant as the 99 names of God are an important part of popular Islamic practice, the name of God used in prayer often relating to the nature of the request being made; e.g. God is often addressed as *al-Ghaffur* ('the Forgiving') when seeking forgiveness, while many Muslims regularly recite all 99 names of God using the rosary.[98] Interestingly however, although most of the 99 names occur in the *Qur'an*, the Qur'anic context does not always make clear their actual meaning in the way that the Biblical narratives do.[99] There is therefore the potential for the application to Christ of these Islamic divine titles to show how God is *al-Mum'in* 'the Faithful', *al-Salam* 'the Peace', *al-Hadi* 'the Guide' etc.[100] In order to emphasise that Jesus is on the God side of the God/non god divide, it is important that these Islamic names of God should be applied to Jesus with the definite article, as they are sometimes applied anarthously to Muhammad.[101] The following divine titles, which the NT applies with the definite article to Jesus, also occur in Islamic lists of the 99 names of God and may therefore be used directly to include Jesus within the unique identity of the one God:

'the First' (*al-Awwal*)[102]

'the Last' (*al-Akhir*)[104]

'the King' (*al-Malik*)[106]

'the King of kings' (*Malik al-mulk*)[108]

'the Light' (*al-Nur*)[110]

'the Peace' (*al-Salam*)[112]

'the Heir of all things' (*al-Warith*)[114]

'the Faithful' (*al-Mu'min*)[103]

'the Wise' (*al-Hakim*)[105]

'the Just' (*al-'Adl*)[107]

'the Witness' (*al-Shahid*)[109]

'the Truth' (*al-Haq*)[111]

'the Living One' (*al-Hai*)[113]

'the Holy One' (*al-Quddus*)[115]

A number of other Islamic names of God may also be applied to Jesus, as they are roles ascribed to Jesus in the NT, even though they do not occur as actual titles there:

'the Forgiver' (*al-Ghafir*)[116]

'the Forgiving' (*al-Ghafur*)[118]

'the Pardoner' (*al-Afuw*)[120]

'the Bestower' (*al-Wahab*)[122]

'the Opener' (*al-Fattah*)[124]

'the Knowing One' (*al-'Alim*)[126]

'the Exalted' (*al-'Ali*)[128]

'the Reckoner' (*al-Hasib*)[117]

'the Majestic' (*al-Jalil*)[119]

'the Possessor of Majesty' (*Dhu al-jalil*)[121]

'the Glorious' (*al-Majid*)[123]

'the Answerer of Prayer' (*al-Mujib*)[125]

'the Advocate' (*al-Wakil*)[127]

Expressing Christology: Worship of Jesus that Emphasises Monolatry

We earlier demonstrated that one way in which the early church expressed its inclusion of Jesus within the unique divine identity was by making him the object of various devotional practices. Many of these acts of devotion were contemporary Jewish practices that at least the majority of Jews appear to have believed could only legitimately be directed towards God. Such devotional acts therefore clearly expressed the early church's conviction that Jesus was on the God side of the God/non-god divide.[129] In order to determine whether such practices could likewise express similar beliefs in an Islamic context, we must first compare the Jewish context in which the early church contextualised its christology with attitudes to monolatry in the Islamic context.

Key Differences Between Jewish and Islamic Attitudes to Monolatry

In our earlier discussion of monolatry in the Jewish and Islamic contexts we raised the question of whether representatives of God such as prophets, saints or angels could legitimately be addressed in prayer, praise or even adoration, if that veneration was ultimately directed towards God.[130]

This question receives a variety of responses in both contexts. However, it appears that the most conservative concepts of monolatry in the Islamic context broadly equate with the most liberal concepts in the Jewish context. This can be illustrated in a number of respects.

i)   Prayer to saints and departed figures

In the Islamic context it is widely, although not universally, regarded as legitimate to pray to saints. The practice is closely linked to belief in the intercession of saints on the Day of Judgement, belief in both saints and intercession being regarded as one of the orthodox articles of belief in Islamic creeds. This contrasts sharply with the Jewish context, where there is no evidence that any Jews regarded the invocation of saints as legitimate or any texts legitimating belief in eschatological intercession.

ii)   Legitimation of the use of charms

The use of charms that invoke the names of angels for protection against evil spirits does occur in both contexts. In the Islamic context various *Ahadith* specifically legitimate this. However, in the Jewish context although at least some Jews do appear to have regarded it as legitimate to use various invocations against demonic affliction, there was no equivalent scriptural justification for such practices.[131]

iii)   Acts of veneration directed towards figures other than God

In chapter 5 we saw that in the Islamic context saint veneration and hymns sung in praise of Muhammad, although not universally accepted, have for many centuries been widely regarded as legitimate. However, our examination of the evidence from the Jewish context found no conclusive evidence that *any* second temple Jews regarded it as legitimate to accord similar veneration to departed human or heavenly figures.[132]

Summary

It is therefore fair to say that as far as monolatry is concerned, the Islamic context both appears to tolerate a wider definition of what is legitimate and, almost certainly, has a more widespread participation in devotional practices that include figures other than God.[133] The differing attitudes to monolatry between the Islamic and Jewish contexts can probably be explained to a certain extent by the parallels we have found, being not between the two sacred texts of the *Qur'an* and the OT, but between the *Qur'an* and Jewish texts somewhat removed from the OT. This is well illustrated by the presence in the *Qur'an* of seven separate narratives describing the fall of Satan for refusing to obey God's command to bow before Adam. However, there is no OT parallel whatsoever for heavenly beings bowing before anyone other than God. The closest Jewish parallel to the Qur'anic narratives is in fact an almost identical account that occurs in a single Jewish apocryphal text: the *Life of Adam and Eve.*[134]

Implications for Christological Worship

This relatively less constrained attitude to monolatry in the Islamic context has implications for the development of a contextualised christology.

It appears likely that the expression of divine christology in devotional practices may be a path of relatively lesser resistance than other expressions.

However, conversely, this also means that devotional practices focused on Jesus cannot communicate that Jesus is on the God side of the God/non-god divide as clearly as they did in the Jewish context from which the early church emerged. In the NT Christ is not a figure somehow less than God, but able to receive adoration because he either stands close to God, or reflects God in some way. Revelation 5 in fact depicts him as the central object of heavenly worship. This distinguishes the type of worship he receives from that offered to saints in *Barelvi* expressions of Islam.

This means that christological devotional practices must build in additional affirmations to emphasise that the one to whom they are directed is himself God, so that Jesus is not understood as being in the same category as other prophets or saints who are objects of devotional acts performed by many Muslims. In particular, it must be emphasised that devotional practices are a response to *who* God is, and so may be directed to no one else. In the early Jewish church this was done by maintaining the Jewish 'refusal tradition' of refusing to bow or adore any figure other than God, whilst at the same time making Jesus the object of devotional practices such as prayer and hymns of adoration.[135] This twin emphasis, on worshipping Jesus, yet also emphasising that God alone may be worshipped, invoked and adored, will be necessary to prevent christological devotion being misunderstood as being similar to *Barelvi* devotional practices.

Devotional Practices that Express Christological Worship

However, despite these caveats, devotional practices can be used to express christological monotheism, provided that it is emphasised that Jesus is worshipped because he is God, and that God alone is worthy of worship. Moreover, Jesus is worshipped because of the new aspect of the identity of God that has been revealed in Jesus.[136]

As in the early Jewish church, it will be the collective impact of various devotional practices that will be most important, rather than any individual element.[137] It is not essential that all devotional practices are necessarily based on those already existing in the Islamic context. Indeed, even some aspects of early Christian devotion, such as baptism, appear to have had no clear precedent in the Jewish context.[138] However, the following devotional practices used by the early church can be used to express christological monotheism in the Islamic context:

Prayer to Jesus

The NT records three aspects of prayer to Jesus: a) Prayer directly and specifically addressed to Jesus, as in the case of Stephen's final prayer. Although this identifies Jesus as God, in the Islamic context the existence of prayer to other figures weakens the potential impact of this; b) Prayer to God in the name of Jesus, which occurs relatively more frequently in the NT; c) The Fourth Gospel also records Jesus stating that he himself will grant whatever prayers are asked in his name.

This is significant as one of the 99 names by which God is popularly known in the Islamic context is *al-Mujib* 'the Answerer of Prayer'. These last two aspects of NT prayer emphasise that Jesus is the means of access to God and the way in which God relates to men. This is therefore a potentially important way of expressing the Logos christology on which the contextualised christology is based.[139]

Hymns

The NT provides evidence of hymns of worship both celebrating Christ and specifically directed to Christ. In fact there is more evidence of hymns to Christ than hymns less specifically addressed to 'God'. One of the main reasons for this is that these hymns appear to presuppose a Logos type christology that understands Christ as the way God has related to creation as creator, saviour and judge. They therefore celebrate the work of Christ through whom all things were created, his earthly obedience and redemptive suffering through which God brought salvation to men, and his eschatological triumph over hostile powers who have usurped God's rule over creation. More specifically, they also celebrate a new revelation of God's identity in terms of Jesus' self-humbling to the point of death in order to become the universal saviour. Illustrative of the latter is the heavenly hymn of Revelation 5, which specifically speaks of Christ being worthy to receive universal worship because of this new aspect of God's identity that his salvific work has revealed.

This hymnic celebration of what Christ has done in creation, salvation and eschatological triumph can therefore form an important part of the way that a contextualised christology is expressed. However, in view of the *Barelvi* practice of singing hymns (*na'at*) to figures such as Muhammad, it will be necessary carefully to distinguish the type of worship Christians offer to Jesus from such Islamic practices. One important way that this could be achieved would be by following the example of NT christological hymns which emphasise that it is as Christ that God created all things, acts as saviour and triumphs over hostile powers i.e. emphasising a christology from above.[140]

The Name of Jesus

The early church used the name of Jesus in ways similar to that in which Judaism used the name of God, such as calling on the name of Jesus and gathering in the name of Jesus. They also used the name of Jesus to take authority over evil spirits and heal the sick. We have already discussed the significance of Jesus' delegation of authority over sickness and the demonic, as indicating that he himself had authority in these areas rather than merely healing by God's permission. The early church expressed their belief that Jesus was able to delegate this authority to them by using the name of Jesus to expel demonic influence and heal the sick.[141] We earlier observed certain similarities between second temple Jewish and Islamic beliefs and practices relating to protection against demonic influence and sickness.[142] This suggests that the early church's use of the name of Jesus in this way may also be an appropriate expression of christology in the Islamic context. For example, whereas many homes in the Islamic context invoke the name of God with inscriptions such as *Mashallah*, Christian belief could be expressed by the use of the name of Jesus to cleanse houses that are perceived to be 'haunted' or have demonic influence in them.[143] As Musk observes, this is an area that non-western Christians tend to be much more aware of the need for, and effectiveness of, than westerners.[144]

In the Islamic context the widespread practice of visiting saints to obtain healing means that prayer for healing in Jesus' name will not demonstrate his divinity quite so clearly. However, in such contexts prayer in the name of Jesus for healing is essential if Christ is not to be viewed as less powerful than Muslim saints. Indeed, the failure to provide such ministry has often resulted in syncretism as first generation Christians continue to visit saints for healing.[145] However, as Hiebert observes, such prayer must be taught to be a relational request to God and not be allowed to default to a mechanical-magical formula or chant that aims to force God to do one's will.[146]

Confessing Jesus and the Shema

The early Jewish church confessed the name of Jesus in a similar manner to that in which Jews confessed the name of God. One expression of this was the Jewish *shema*, affirming the oneness of God, which came to be recited twice daily by pious Jews.[147] The early church appears to have adapted the Jewish *shema* to include Jesus within the unique identity of the one God. Although the only NT example of such a christianised *shema* is one addressed to Christians from a pagan background, its very existence makes it probable that a similar contextualisation existed amongst Christians from a Jewish background.[148] In the Islamic context the *shahadah* plays a similar role to the Jewish *shema* in daily affirming belief in *tawhid* (monotheism). This creates the potential to create a dynamic equivalent of the christianised *shema* used by the early church.[149] The following shows a possible form that this could take:[150]

There is but one God,

(The opening affirmation of both the Jewish *shema* and the Islamic *shahadah*).[151]

Whom alone we worship.

(Reflecting the second section of the *shema*, monolatry is an appropriate response to monotheism; and the 'refusal tradition' that is necessary to avoid confusion with *Barelvi* concepts of monolatry).[152]

We know Him as Father, al-Batin, *who dwells in unapproachable light,*

(a NT teaching paralleled by Islamic belief that veils of light surround God, designation of the Father with the Islamic name of God *al-Batin* 'the Hidden').[153]

yet tenderly cares for us, planned our creation and salvation.

(The NT teaching that the Father planned creation and salvation, and acts in a fatherly way towards us, the latter receiving very occasional expression in the Islamic context).[154]

And we know Him as 'Isa, the visible form of the invisible God, who comes to us from the Father

(Jesus is the visible form of the invisible God, and the way that God relates to his creation as creator, ruler, judge and saviour).[155]

Who created, rules and will judge all things and became our Saviour.

And we know Him as the Holy Spirit,

Whom 'Isa sends to us from the Father,

(sending of the Spirit by Jesus from the Father prevents the *shema* being understood in *modalist* terms).[157]

Who breathed life into creation,

(role of the Spirit in creation).[158]

is the all-seeing presence of God throughout creation,

(role of the Spirit in universal rule).[159]

Who inspired the prophets,

(role of the Spirit in revelation).[160]

convicts the world of sin,

(role of the Spirit in judgement).[161]

and whose presence unites us with God,

(role of the Spirit as God's presence).[162]

sanctifying our sinful hearts and empowering us to serve Him.[156]

(role of the Spirit in salvation). [163]

This is the one God we worship.

He alone is the Creator (al-Khaliq) *of all things,*

Lord of all things (Rabb kull shay),

Master of the Day of Judgement (Malik Yaum al-din),

and the only Saviour.

It is also important to note that other devotional practices not found in the early church context, but presently used in the Islamic context, may also be adapted as expressions of christology. Forms which are currently only used for the worship of God are most likely to express the fact that the Jesus who is being worshipped is on the God side of the God/non-god divide. One possible example of such a devotional form may be Islamic recitation of the names of God. This could potentially be adapted into a liturgical recitation of the Islamic names of God that we earlier identified as NT titles and attributes of Christ.[164]

Prophecy

We earlier observed that in the early church the origin of prophecies was ascribed both to the Father and Jesus, or simply delivered in the name of Jesus.[165] The Islamic understanding that it is God who inspires the prophets[166] means that this is one of the clearer ways that devotional practices can publicly state that Jesus is on the God side of the God/non god divide.

Other Specific Issues Raised by the Islamic Context

Sufism

In addition to Islamic practices and beliefs derived from the *Qur'an* and *Ahadith*, many Muslims are involved in various forms of mysticism, which are often referred to under the umbrella term of *Sufism*. Most Sufis aim at achieving a spiritual union (*wasl*) with God. However, in Sufi theology there is a diversity of thought as to how this might be achieved. Two schools of thought are particularly noteworthy in this respect. The *wahdat al-wujud* Sufi theology developed by Ibn 'Arabi understands this union as seeking to return the divine spark believed to be in man back to submersion and annihilation in God, its original source. In contrast, *wahdat al-shuhud* Sufism, which does not have these pantheistic tendencies, aims to achieve a mystical reflection of God's presence, which is often expressed as seeing God's face in the mirror of the believer's heart. This form of Sufism is widely reflected in a range of mystical poetry in the Islamic context.[167]

This desire for union with God gives an opportunity for a contextualised christology to present:

1.   Sin as the cause of man's separation from God. Before sin entered the world God walked with man and woman in the garden. It was as a result of sin that they were expelled from the immediate presence of God in the garden. Men and women are therefore in need of a saviour who can deal with the problem of sin.[168]

2.   Union with God is possible through the work of the saviour Jesus, who reconciled people to God by dealing with the sin that separated them from God.[169]

3.   Jesus sends the Spirit of God into believers' hearts.[170] The Spirit unites them with God, bringing God's presence to the believer's heart.[171]

4.   The *wahdat al-shuhud* aspiration of achieving a mirror-like reflection of God in the believer's heart is fulfilled in the mirror-like vision of Christ's glory in believers' hearts, transforming them into Christ-likeness with ever increasing glory.[172]

5.   When Christ has finally and completely defeated all hostile spiritual powers that have rebelled against God, universal *wasl* will be achieved, as God's rule is exercised unchallenged over all things from the throne (singular) of God and Jesus.[173]

Denial of the Self-Humbling and Suffering of God

Appearance as an Actual Human Being

Our earlier discussion of the *malak YHWH* demonstrated that in the Jewish context it was widely believed that God could appear on earth in human-like form.[174] However, this is significantly different from him appearing as an actual human being engaging in normal human functions, such as eating and sleeping. In fact, Jews appear to have believed that even angels, who also appeared in human-like form, only 'appeared' to undertake human functions such as eating and drinking. We find no suggestion anywhere in the second temple literature that there was any expectation that God would appear and live on earth for a number of years as an actual contemporary human being. The most that can be said is that there was nothing in the Jewish scriptures that specifically repudiated such a possibility.[175] To this extent there is a parallel between the Jewish and Islamic contexts, although, as we shall see, in the Islamic context there are also specific denials of this possibility.[176]

Suffering and Death

The sufferings and even violent death of God's prophets is a significant theme in second temple literature. Moreover, whilst the OT does imply that God suffers emotionally from the waywardness of people he loves, there is no indication that any Jews considered the possibility that God himself might physically suffer either in the way that many of the prophets had, or to effect redemption. Indeed, the LXX rephrasing of the only OT text that appeared to point in this direction illustrates the great difficulty that Jews had with even beginning to comprehend the idea that God might physically suffer. The most that could be said is that the idea was not commonly denied because the possibility was rarely even considered.[177]

Interestingly, the concept of prophets suffering and being killed is developed in the *Qur'an* to an even greater extent than in the OT.[178] It therefore appears that in neither the Jewish nor Islamic contexts is an assertion that God must deliver his prophets the *major* impediment to belief in Jesus' incarnation and death.

Specific Obstacles in the Islamic Context

In the Islamic context there are also certain additional antithetical features, which make it somewhat more hostile to the idea of God suffering than the Jewish context was.

Rejection of Divine Humility

The divine title 'the Proud' (*al-Mutakabbir*) which is commonly included in lists of the 99 names of God, means that the concept of God voluntarily humbling himself may be even more difficult for Muslims to comprehend than it was for second temple Jews, for whom it was unexpected, though not scripturally denied.[179]

Rejection of the Possibility that God can be Joined to Anything Else

The Christian doctrine of God humbling himself to become incarnate as a man faces the more specific Islamic objection that God cannot be said to be a compound of both God and non-God. However, despite such assertions we earlier saw how even *kalam* has been unable to avoid asserting that the *Qur'an* itself is a compound of the uncreated divine attribute of speech and an inscription and recitation that is created. Even so, the assertion of *kalam* that God is devoid of all attributes of creatures which make them inferior to him, such as fatigue, sleepfulness and death, means that the Islamic context starts from a position of antithesis in relation to the self-humbling of God to become a man.[180]

Denial of the Historicity of the Crucifixion

The *Qur'an* appears to deny the historical actuality of Jesus' death in Q4:158. This undoubtedly constitutes the primary Islamic objection to Jesus' crucifixion.

Rejection of the Possibility of Atonement

In modern Islamic writers, rejection of the crucifixion is often linked to rejection of the possibility of atonement on the grounds that the *Qur'an* asserts that no man can bear the burden of another. However, Mawdudi at least recognised that the Christian doctrine of expiation requires the assumption of Jesus' divinity, which the *Qur'an* also emphatically denies.[181]

Summary

We therefore have a situation in respect of the self-humbling and suffering of God, where although NT christology is in discontinuity with the expectations of both the Jewish and Islamic contexts, there are significantly greater impediments to this belief in the latter. However, this shared discontinuity does mean that the manner in which the early Jewish church addressed this aspect of christology can potentially be utilised in the Islamic context, provided due account is taken of the additional objections raised there.

An Apologetic Response

The following aspects of the early church's contextualisation of christology are capable of being re-applied in the Islamic context:

Suffering as the Normative Experience of the Prophets

When the early church articulated its christology, particularly to those outside their own Christian community, they claimed that suffering and rejection was the normative experience of all the prophets. This motif also occurs in the *Qur'an*, which repeatedly describes the rejection of God's prophets by those they were sent to.[182] This suffering and rejection motif therefore needs to be emphasised in a contextualised christology.

Jesus' Sufferings Prophesied by All the Prophets

The early church also claimed that Jesus' sufferings were prophesied by 'all the prophets'.[183] This is an important apologetic in an Islamic context that stresses the importance of honour and shame, as it asserts that Jesus' death was not weakness and defeat, but fully in accord with the plan of God.

Combining Titles with Clearly Divine and Human Referents

The unprecedented idea of God becoming an actual human being engaging in normal human functions, such as eating and drinking, was addressed in the NT by referring to Jesus with a combination of messianic and divine titles, such as 'both Lord and Messiah'.[184] In the Islamic context the title 'Messiah' (*al-Masih*) can similarly be applied to Jesus. However, because Jesus is widely and emphatically understood by Muslims to be human, a similar apologetic can potentially be achieved by simply combining the name Jesus (*'Isa*) with divine titles and designations.

Emphasis on the Vindication of Jesus' Honour

Western christology has often tended to view the significance of Jesus' death primarily in terms of substitutionary atonement, a concept that is particularly meaningful in western cultures due to their predominant focus being on guilt rather than shame, an emphasis partly derived from Roman law. However, Islamic cultures tend to focus much more on honour and shame, a situation that at least partially appears to parallel second temple Judaism.[185] This honour-shame focus makes substitutionary atonement relatively harder to comprehend than it would be in a culture that focused more on guilt. It may therefore be significant that, at least in its apologetics addressed to outsiders, the early Jewish church placed a major emphasis on the vindication of Jesus' honour, with evangelistic speeches frequently expressing the vindication motif as 'men killed…but God raised'.[186]

The frequent NT references to Jesus that allude to the suffering servant of Isa.52:13-53:12 in which both the servant's substitutionary work and his vindication by God are equally prominent, suggests that both of these were important aspects of the early church's christology.[187] However, it is noteworthy that the sections of the NT that express the significance of the cross in terms of substitutionary atonement are addressed to Christians who have already received initial teaching, and so presumably build on an earlier foundation in which the cross was presented as God vindicating Jesus in the face of men's sinful rejection.[188] Contextualisation of christology needs to follow this example, with initial communication of Christian belief giving prominence to God's vindication of Jesus by his resurrection from the dead and ascension to the throne of God in highest heaven. This can lay a foundation for subsequent communication of the significance of the cross in terms of substitutionary atonement.

Use of the Concept of 'Sacrifice'

The concept of sacrifice can be used to introduce the idea of Christ's death as the means of reconciling men to God and prepare the way for understanding of atonement. Although in the Islamic context there is no equivalent to the OT sacrificial system, the concept of sacrifice is found in the Qur'anic story of Abraham's willingness to sacrifice his son.[189] This is celebrated in the feast of *'id al-azha*, sometimes known in the Persian speaking world as the *'id al-quorban* ('feast of sacrifice). In most parts of the islamic world this is regarded as the most important annual festival, and is sometimes referred to as the *'id al-kabir* ('the great festival').[190] We earlier saw how the NT portrays the binding of Isaac as the ante-type of Christ's sacrifice, designating Jesus as the one foretold in the promise to Abraham of a lamb to be provided by God himself, his sacrifice reconciling people to God.[191] In this context, John the Baptist's designation of Jesus as 'the Lamb of God, who takes away the sin of the world'[192] is particularly significant as the *Qur'an* portrays him as the forerunner and herald of Jesus.[193] Significantly, the *Qur'an* states that God ransomed Abraham's son with a momentous (*azim*) sacrifice.[194] This description is not easily understandable in the context of the Qur'anic narrative, but in Christian usage would clearly be an appropriate description of Christ's sacrifice, particularly as *al-Azim* is one of the 99 Islamic names of God. The fact that it is God himself who suffers can be further reinforced by narration of John's theophanic vision in which he saw Christ symbolised as 'a Lamb, looking as if it had been slain', standing in the centre of God's throne;[195] and by Revelation's description of him as the Lamb slain before the foundation of the world,[196] indicating that his death had significance beyond the earthly chronology in which it occurred. The 'slain appearance of the Lamb in heaven' motif is likely to particularly resonate in the Islamic context as many Muslims hold that after death the resurrected body will have the wounds and disfigurements of the earthly body,[197] and an *Hadith* states that after death the body experiences suffering in the same way as before.[198]

The NT's typological identification of Christ's sacrifice with both the binding of Isaac and the Passover lamb raises the possibility that similar typology may appropriately be used in Christian celebrations of Christ's death. A contextualisation of the 'Lord's supper' could focus on Abraham's attempted sacrifice of his son as the ante-type of Jesus' sacrifice, which fulfilled the OT prophecy of God himself providing a sacrifice.[199] In this context, Christ's sacrifice could appropriately be described as a momentous (*azim*) sacrifice. Similar typological motifs can be used in the Christian celebration of 'Good Friday', which could then be designated as *'id al-Azim* ('the feast of *al-Azim*'), or more fully *'id al-Qorban al-Azim* ('the feast of the sacrifice of *al-Azim*'). This contextualisation could be given particular resonance if 'Easter' is celebrated as two distinct festivals; i.e. 'Good Friday' and 'Easter Sunday', so that there are three major Christian festivals each year corresponding to the days Jesus was born, died and was raised to life.[200] Celebration of the *'id* of Christ's death can also draw on much of the imagery, and even forms, used in the Islamic remembrance of Abraham's attempted sacrifice in the annual festival of *'id al-Azha*. Although the *Qur'an* describes the animal sacrifice during this festival as a 'symbol', it is not clear exactly what the sacrifice is supposed to symbolise, although it has sometimes been viewed as having some redemptive value.[201] Christian adaptation can therefore fill this existing symbolism with a degree of meaning that it currently lacks.

The *Christus Victor* Motif

A further development of the vindication motif in the NT is the *Christus victor* motif. Christ's self-humbling was in order to triumph over the hostile spiritual powers, thereby releasing captive men and women.[202] The widespread fear of evil powers in Islamic culture makes Christ's victory over them an appropriate emphasis in a christology contextualised for an Islamic context. However, it cannot be the most prominent aspect, as the NT emphasises that people are primarily sinners responsible for their own actions, rather than simply victims of hostile spiritual powers.[203]

Use of Local Cultural Themes

The early church also used prominent cultural themes to highlight key aspects of their christology. As a number of similar cultural themes also occur in many Islamic cultures, there is the potential to similarly use these to further embed a contextualised christology in local culture.

i) Hospitality and corporate responsibility for wrongdoing

The early church used prominent cultural values such as hospitality to underline the seriousness and corporate shame that the rejection of Jesus brought on mankind. This can be seen in the Synoptic Gospel's narration of the parable of the tenants who refuse to receive their lord's envoys hospitably and actually kill the son. Luke's account of Peter's temple colonnade speech also narrates the added indictment that Jesus was handed over to those who would kill him, something that in many Islamic cultures would be a most serious violation of hospitality and sanctuary codes.[204]

The strong value that Islamic cultures tend to place on hospitality and corporate responsibility for the misdeeds of one's kin,[205] creates the possibility for a contextualised christology similarly to use these prominent cultural values to present the biblical teaching that all people are sinners in need of a saviour, concepts that are not widely accepted in Islamic contexts.

In some Islamic cultures the duty of hospitality includes the offering of sanctuary, even to an enemy who asks for it. In such cases it is a grave violation of honour is to allow such a guest to be either captured or, even worse, handed over to his enemies to be killed.

Islamic cultures also characteristically tend to have at least some sense of corporate responsibility for the misdeeds of others in the kinship network. Indeed the emphasis that Islamic cultures typically have on honour and shame may often mean that serious misdemeanours bring shame on the family, and even on the whole community for generations to come.

This combination of cultural values allows the possibility of turning the rejection of Christ into a means of pointing to people's need of a saviour in a similar manner to the prologue to the Fourth Gospel; i.e. the creator visited his own creation, but mankind brought shame on themselves by refusing to receive him hospitably and even violated their own sanctuary codes by working with his enemies (Satan's kingdom) against him.

ii) 'The Lover/Beloved imagery'

One of the OT divine titles that the early church applied to Jesus was 'the Bridegroom'.[206] Although this is not an Islamic name of God, the Lover/Beloved imagery is a widespread theme in mystical poetry, where it is used to depict the quest of the Sufi to find God. The Sufi is portrayed as the (male) lover who heroically forsakes all and endures suffering in order to reach the (female) beloved; i.e. God. The motif of suffering is often highlighted by the Lover being depicted as a nightingale enduring bloodshed from thorns in order to reach the beloved who is portrayed as a rose.

There is therefore the potential for a simple reversal of gender roles to depict God as the bridegroom, who endures thorns and bloodshed as he comes to seek out his bride. This depiction of God as the (male) suitor who actively seeks out his bride, is not only in accord with the biblical portrayal of God himself coming to earth to seek out his bride, but also resolves the 'problem' of poetry appearing to portray of God as female, which is generally in tension with Islamic culture, which typically perceives women to be weaker than men.[207] This simple reversal of gender roles means that many existing mystical poems can be used to depict God himself coming to seek and search for the lost. (See Appendix D for examples of such poetry).[208]

iii) The 'ideal man' and 'ideal woman' images

Many cultures have a concept of the 'ideal man' and 'ideal woman',[209] which can sometimes be utilised in the contextualisation of Christian beliefs.[210] Although the form that these images take will vary from culture to culture, there may be broad similarities across a range of Islamic cultures. We can illustrate the potential that such themes have for the contextualisation of christology with reference to the Pushtuns of Pakistan.

a)   The *Christus victor* motif we earlier referred to can be developed further by the portrayal of Jesus as the ultimate fulfilment of the 'ideal Pushtun man' image of the warrior-king-mystic which is exemplified in the life of Ahmad Shah Abdali (d.1773), founder of modern Afghanistan, who as 'Sufi by temperament, warrior-king by profession' is viewed as the prototype Pushtun leader.[211]

b)   The 'ideal Pushtun woman' image can be used to highlight the significance that the biblical portrayal of Christ has for women. The 'ideal Pushtun woman' is largely defined by the ability to retell stories of *gham* (grief and sadness).[212] The highlighting of this prominent cultural theme in 'faith stories' that tell 'how much Jesus suffered for me' is therefore likely to create a certain resonance with female listeners.[213] This theme can be further developed by the reversal of the poetic bride/bridegroom imagery that we earlier referred to.[214] This highlights the supreme bride-price paid for the believer, which Christ as the divine bridegroom has paid not with perishable things such as silver or gold, but with his own blood.[215]

Relationships Within the Godhead

We earlier saw that in neither the second temple Jewish nor Islamic contexts is there any commonly accepted notion of there being relationships within the Godhead. To this extent, the antecedent conditions faced by the early church, when they developed their contextualisation of christology, parallel those faced by the church in Islamic contexts. In both contexts local manifestations of the presence of God, such as God sitting on the throne or appearing on earth to Moses, could be seen in terms of '*modalism*', i.e. God manifesting himself in different modes.[216]

This similarity of context suggests that in the Islamic context this issue might be addressed in a fashion similar to that used by the early church in the context of Jewish monotheism. Earlier in this chapter we therefore spelt out various aspects of the early church's contextualisation of christology that could be utilised in the Islamic context.[217] However, the Islamic context does present additional problems not faced by the early church, as here the concept of there being relationships within the Godhead is not only unprecedented, but also widely understood to be specifically denied in the *Qur'an*.[218] We will here discuss how a contextualised christology might additionally address this specific denial.

The Revelation of The Great Name of God (Ism al-Azim)

We earlier drew attention to the newly revealed name of God in the NT: the name (singular) of the Father, the Son and the Holy Spirit. This appears to represent a newly revealed aspect of God's character that has been disclosed by Jesus, which parallels the revealing of the name 'YHWH' to Moses at the burning bush. This had disclosed a new aspect of God's character that he was the saviour who had personally come down to save his people from Egypt.[219]

The prominence of the burning bush narratives in the *Qur'an* and other Islamic texts[220] creates the potential for a contextualised christology to introduce the revelation of a name of God at this point, reflecting the disclosure that God is the saviour who personally comes down to save his people. This creates a foundation for subsequently introducing the concept that when God himself came down to act as the universal saviour, he revealed a new name reflecting a further hitherto undisclosed aspect of his identity, 'the name (singular) of the Father, the Son and the Holy Spirit'.[221]

The concept of a previously unknown name of God is itself not without precedent in the Islamic context, as there is a tradition that a great name of God (*Ism al-Azim*) exists. There are conflicting *Ahadith* accounts as to what this name is, although a tradition traced to Ayesha relates that it is known only to the prophets and other saintly persons.[222] There is, however, agreement that God will answer whoever calls on this name.[223] This creates the potential for a contextualised christology to speak of the *Ism al-Azim* which the OT prophets looked forward to being revealed,[224] 'the name (singular) of the Father, the Messiah and the Holy Spirit'. In using this form of the name we have retained 'Father' as there is a limited acceptance in the Islamic context of the idea that God acts like a father towards his creation. However, the combination of 'Father' and 'Son' is so widely misunderstood that it is appropriate to replace 'the Son' by 'the Messiah', as this remains as close as possible to the Biblical form,[225] yet avoids the misunderstandings that arise from the use of 'Son' in the Islamic context.[226]

Jesus Not Muhammad is the Culmination of God's Revelation

The *Qur'an* describes Jesus as a prophet (*rasul*) and the Messiah (*al-Masih*), but gives a superior prophetic status to Muhammad describing him as 'the seal of the prophets'; i.e. the final prophet. It is therefore taken as axiomatic by Muslims that just as the *Qur'an* has superseded the Gospel (*Injil*), so Muhammad is superior to Christ. This tendency to exalt Muhammad at the expense of Christ is exacerbated by the tendency of the *Barelvi* pole of Islam to exalt Muhammad well beyond the status ascribed to him in the *Qur'an*. The titles and roles ascribed to him, such as the heavenly bridegroom, the fountain of God's wisdom, the one given the world as his possession, often bear marked similarities to NT descriptions of Christ.[227]

In many respects we have been addressing this issue throughout this chapter, as directly identifying Jesus as God places him in a position immeasurably superior to the highest status any Muslims accord to Muhammad. We have also referred to the claim repeatedly made by the early church that all the prophets looked forward to the coming of the Messiah. As such, Jesus is the culmination of all the prophets and the climax of the story of God's dealings with mankind.[228] This climax of the 'God-story' approach also has the merit of potentially resolving the tension created by the Qur'anic recitation of a series of narratives concerning Biblical characters without providing an overarching meta-narrative that historically links them together.

However, it is also appropriate to make at least some more specific responses to Islamic claims for Muhammad. In dealing with this issue in a contextualised christology care is needed to avoid directly refuting Islamic claims concerning Muhammad. In many Islamic contexts this is likely to be important both in order to avoid creating unnecessary offence, and because in many Islamic countries denigration of Muhammad constitutes a serious legal offence.[229]

However, the NT suggests a number of specific avenues of approach to positively expressing the superior status of Christ:

Refutation by Allusion

We earlier observed the parallels between Jewish traditions of heavenly ascent journeys by various OT patriarchs and *Ahadith* accounts of Muhammad's *mi'raj* to the highest heaven.[230] The NT portrays Jesus implicitly refuting such traditions by stating that 'no-one has ever gone into heaven *except* the one who came from heaven – the Son of Man'.[231] Peter's Day of Pentecost speech similarly follows the literary structure of ascent traditions, but has an implicit polemic against such traditions, asserting that it is Jesus, rather than any patriarch, who has truly ascended to the throne of God in highest heaven, The parallels with Muhammad's *mi'raj* create the potential for a similar contextualisation by stating that it is only Jesus who has truly ascended to the immediate presence of God, where he now permanently sits on the divine throne. Moreover, he has received not a book but the Spirit of God himself, and only Jesus' bestowal of this Spirit can unite believers in mystical union (*wasl*) with God.

This approach of 'refutation by allusion' therefore constitutes a way that Christians can express their own perspective on Islamic claims for Muhammad, without directly focusing on Muhammad himself.

John the Baptist the Last Prophet

Jesus' claims in Matthew 11 can be reiterated: The age of the law and the prophets were until *Yayha ibn Zakariya* (John the Baptist) Jesus' forerunner, after which Jesus as the *Malik al-mulk* brought in the long awaited kingdom of God. This reinforces the reference earlier made to this NT passage, which demonstrated that Jesus fulfilled OT prophecy of the events that would happen when God himself eschatologically came to earth.[232]

Expressing a Contextualised Christology in Concrete Form

So far in this chapter, although we have dealt with the issue of monolatry, we have been primarily concerned with the theological content of a contextualised christology. However, a christology must have a concrete form if it is to become meaningful communication.[233] There are many forms through which christology might be expressed. These include creeds, hymnody, theological curricula, church sermon series, chronological Bible storying,[234] drama[235] and poetry.[236] Discussion of the merits of particular forms is beyond the scope of this study. However, it is important to note that the contextualised christology must be expressed in a form which is both accessible to, and transmittable by, a wide spectrum of people within the community, not simply those who have either studied theology or are significantly more educated than the majority. In a culture where communication is primarily oral, the christology must be expressed in a form that is capable of oral transmission if it is to become part of the church's expression of its faith.[237]

Although limitations of space prevent us illustrating the shape this christology might take in a diversity of forms, we will here give one concrete example of how this christology might be expressed. This first is in the form of a confessional recitation.

Example: A Confessional Recitation

In order to facilitate oral learning and transmission the confessional recitation is divided into a number of cantos and has a largely narrative and versified structure. This study can only point towards the ultimate form that this structure and versification might take in any given culture.[238] However, it is important that a form of versification be adopted which is accessible to the widest spectrum of the population, rather than necessarily following the style and conventions of classical poetry.[239] The discourse structures that typically characterise oral literature will require this confessional recitation to use a far greater degree of repetition than the written texts that predominate in the West. Indeed, a large body of scholarship suggests that repetition is the key feature of oral literature.[240] This use of narrative and repetition will inevitably make this expression of christology significantly longer than the more systematic expressions of theology appropriate to other contexts.[241] However, these features of oral discourse will facilitate a greater comprehensibility of theology in many non-western contexts.[242] Indeed, it is precisely the concise expressions of systematic theology that non western theologians have criticised as being too abstract to be easily comprehensible in the non western world.[243]

First Canto

There is but one God	(*Tawhid* – affirmation of monotheism).
Whom alone we worship	(Monolatry – which needs to be emphasised so that christological devotion is not misunderstood as being akin to *Barelvi* veneration of Muhammad and saints).
The Creator (al-Khaliq) *of all things*	(Extrinsic descriptions of God which are used in the Islamic context).
The Lord of all things (Rabb kull shay) *The Master of the Day of Judgement* (Malik Yaum al-din) *And the only Saviour.*	
Heaven, even the highest heaven cannot contain Him,[244]	(This counters the subsequent affirmation of God locally manifesting his presence, being misunderstood as constituting the totality of God).[245]
Yet He manifested His presence on the throne of heaven, when He unveiled visions of Himself to the prophets Isaiah, Ezekiel and Daniel,	(The concept accepted by many Islamic writers that God locally manifested his presence when he seated himself on the throne of the universe).[246]
who saw Him surrounded by His angels high above all else.	(Alluding to the Qur'anic description of God as the 'Most High').[247]

He walked in the garden with Adam and Eve, before He banished mankind from His presence on account of their sin.

(This introduces the concept of epiphany and sets it in the context of mankind corporately having lost intimacy with God's presence as a result of sin. It also uses important Islamic symbolism – Paradise being pictured as both a meeting with God and a garden).[248]

But He veiled His glory and appeared on earth to Abraham, announcing his covenant and the gift of a son.

(Introduces the concept of God assuming a veiled form of his presence. The promise of a son to Abraham is a well-known Islamic story).[249]

And He appeared on earth to Moses at the burning bush and on the Mount, when He revealed that He was the Saviour who would rescue His people from Egypt, and revealed the name YHWH expressing this revelation of His identity as the Saviour.

(Introduces the concept of God appearing on earth to act as saviour. Both stories occur in the *Qur'an* and in a wide range of other Islamic literature; introduces the concept of a name of God being revealed to express a previously undisclosed aspect of God's identity – which lays a foundation for the new name of God in Matt.28:19).[250]

He veiled Himself in the cloud and went before His people to rescue them from Egypt. Not an angel, nor an ambassador, but He Himself became their Saviour.

(This reinforces the concept of God appearing in epiphany as saviour. Islamic assertions that Gabriel accompanied the Exodus are countered by following the example of the LXX which appears to be refuting similar ideas that the Exodus was accompanied by a created angel rather than God himself).[251]

The prophets foretold that He would come to earth again, as Saviour and Judge. They told of the blind seeing, the deaf hearing, the dumb speaking and lame walking, when God Himself came to earth.

(OT prophecies of God eschatologically appearing as saviour and judge; the signs that would accompany this – laying a foundation for Matt.11/Lk 7's identification of Jesus as performing these signs, which the *Qur'an* also narrates he did).[252]

Isaiah spoke of a child to be born, Who would be called 'Mighty God'.

(Introducing the concept of God not just appearing in epiphany, but also being born as an actual human being).[253]

Malachi foretold how God would send His messenger to prepare the way, before He Himself would come to earth.	(Introduces the concept of God sending a messenger before he himself comes to earth, this lays a foundation for understanding John the Baptist as preparing the way for the coming of God to earth. The *Qur'an* also links John with the coming of Jesus).[254]
Yahya ibn Zakariya was that messenger who prepared the way for God's own coming, calling all to repent for the kingdom of God was at hand.	(Introduces the concept of the kingdom of God).[255]
For all the law and the prophets were only until Yahya.	(Presents the Christian perspective that there would be no prophets after John, thereby indirectly presenting a Christian perspective on Muhammad's claim to prophethood).[256]
For all the law and the prophets spoke of the coming of al-Masih, Who came to earth to rescue men and women from obedience to Satan and restore them to rule of God their King.	(The Messiah as the climax of God's revelation, anticipated by all former prophets, bringing the kingdom of God).[257]
And when He came to earth, by His own authority He healed the blind and lepers, brought the dead to life; the dumb spoke, the deaf heard and demons left the afflicted.	(Affirmation of the Qur'anic claim that Jesus healed the blind and lepers and raised the dead, but stating that he did this by his own authority to counter Islamic claims that Jesus only did this as a prophet 'by God's permission').[258]
He also gave this authority to His disciples, in His name to heal the sick and over all the powers of darkness.	(Jesus' delegation of this authority to his disciples reinforces the assertion that Jesus had authority in himself to do these things. Baidawi's *tafsir* refers to Jesus' disciples being able to heal the sick, blind and lepers).[259]
And yet when He the Creator (al-Khaliq) God came to earth, men and women - his own creatures refused to receive Him hospitably, and brought shame, guilt and dishonour on the family of man by working with Satan to crucify Him.	(Use of the prominent cultural values of hospitality, protection of guests and corporate responsibility for the wrongdoing of one's kin to emphasise human sinfulness and need for a saviour).[260]

But by His death on the cross, He defeated Satan and demons, He dealt with our sin that had separated us from God. He alone could forgive us our sins, for it was Him we had sinned against.

(Introduces the concept that the cross was a defeat of Satan's kingdom and enabled men and women to be reconciled to God. The local concept of relational justice is used to demonstrate that only God can forgive sins, as it is he who has been sinned against).[261]

He fulfilled all that the prophets had spoken, as they prophesied the sufferings of al-Masih and the glories to follow.

(Jesus' suffering and death was by the plan of God, prophesied by all the prophets, and resulted in vindication).[262]

Therefore He was raised back to life for death could not hold Him and He was exalted back to the very throne of God in heaven.

(The vindication motif – Jesus' death was a triumph not defeat. The explicit statement of the resurrection counters Islamic claims that Jesus ascended without first dying).[263]

From there He poured out the very Spirit of God, on those who submitted to his kingly rule in their lives.

(From the throne in heaven Jesus sends the Spirit of God – which the *Qur'an* asserts is sent by and proceeds from God; Jesus is the King of the kingdom of God).[264]

There the angels and all the host of heaven worship Him, declaring that He is worthy to receive honour and glory and praise, for with his blood He redeemed men from every tribe and language, people and nation to worship God.

(Jesus is worshipped because he suffered to redeem all peoples on earth).[265]

From there 'Isa will come again in glory on the Last Day (Yaum al-akhir), accompanied by His angels to take those in His kingdom to the place prepared for them in heaven.

(Identification of Jesus' *parousia* as 'the Last Day' when God comes with his angels).[266]

On that day He alone will sit as Judge, the Master of the Day of Judgement (Malik Yaum al-din). He will burn in the lake of fire those who rejected His kingship, along with Satan and his demons.

(Identification of Jesus as the final eschatological Judge – a divine title and prerogative).[267]

But those in His kingdom will see His face, they will serve day and night before His throne. Never again will they hunger, never again will they thirst, the sun will not beat upon them, nor any scorching heat and He will wipe away every tear from their eyes.

(The widely-held Islamic hope of seeing God in paradise).[268]

Behold He is coming soon!

This is our God, the only true God.

(Repeated affirmation of *tawhid* – monotheism).

We worship Him alone.

(Repeated affirmation of monolatry to counter worship of Jesus being misunderstood as akin to *Barelvi* veneration of Muhammad and saints).

Second Canto

He alone is the one Creator (al-Khaliq) *of all things,*

(Extrinsic description of God, widely used in the Islamic context).

The Father who dwells in unapproachable light is the source of creation from whom all things came.

(Introduction of distinctions within the Godhead – different roles of the Father dwelling in unapproachable light and Jesus, the visible form of the invisible God).[269]

From all eternity 'Isa, the visible form of the invisible God was with God, and was God. All things were created through Him, without him nothing was made that has been made.

(Jesus, the visible form of the invisible God, is the way that God relates to his creation; application to Jesus of the Islamic monotheistic rhetoric 'all things' to indicate that he is the sole creator).[270]

He is the Creator (al-Khaliq), *the Maker* (al-Bari), *the Fashioner* (al-Musawir) *and the Beginner* (al-Mubdi) *of all things. We are His creatures.*

(Islamic names of God and the subject/object distinction applied to Jesus to indicate that he is the sole creator of all things).

He is the one Creator God, the Self-subsisting One (al-Qayum) *who alone has life in Himself, and has imparted life to His creation through His Spirit who alone is the Quickener* (al-Muhyi), *the giver of life.*

(Distinctions within the Godhead: Jesus has life in himself; distinction between Jesus and the Spirit – all things were created through Jesus, but life is imparted by the Spirit).[271]

This is our God, the only true God.

(Repeated affirmation of *tawhid* – monotheism)

We worship Him alone.

(Repeated affirmation of monolatry to counter worship of Jesus being misunderstood as akin to *Barelvi* veneration of Muhammad etc.).

Third canto

He alone is Ruler of all things (**Rabb kull shay**), *the Lord of the worlds* (**Rabb al-'alamin**), *the King of kings* (**Malik al-mulk**) *and Lord of lords, who created all things and rules all things.*

(Extrinsic description of God, widely used in the Islamic context, used to identify Jesus as God the ruler of all things).

When Satan and his demons rebelled against God, they were thrown out of heaven down to earth, where they seek to deceive the children of men, bringing rebellion, death and destruction with them.

(The cause of sin and rebellion in the world).[272]

Therefore the Father, Who dwells in unapproachable light, put all things under 'Isa, the visible form of the invisible God, in order that He may reign as Lord over all creation until he has put all the powers of darkness beneath his feet. He is the Lord of all things (**Rabb kull shay**) *to whom all creatures must submit.*

(God deals with the problem of sin and rebellion in the world by acting through Jesus, his visible form, to defeat the hostile spiritual powers that have rebelled against God).[273]

He defeated the proud rebellion of Satan, by laying aside his heavenly glory, clothing himself, the visible form of the invisible God, with humble human nature, becoming a man as we are. And being found in appearance as a man,

He defeated Satan's proud rebellion by humbling himself to the point of death on the cross, where he disarmed Satan and all the powers of darkness, triumphing over them, redeeming men and women from their bondage to Satan's kingdom.

(The self-humbling and suffering of God seen in the incarnation and the cross were God's own means of defeating Satan and all the powers of darkness, and redeeming men and women out of Satan's kingdom into the kingdom of God. Jesus' incarnation and suffering was a temporary and voluntary

Therefore, He was raised from the dead, and not only raised, but also exalted back to the highest place in heaven, that every knee in heaven and earth should bow before Him, and confess that He is Lord of lords and King of kings (Malik al-mulk).

humiliation, which climaxed in vindication and glorification. The resurrection is again explicitly affirmed to counter Islamic claims of Jesus ascending without first dying).[274]

From heaven He has sent the Spirit of God to His church, that through His church, His kingdom might spread throughout the earth, among every tribe, language, people and nation that His death redeemed for God.

(From heaven Jesus sends the Spirit of God, which in the *Qur'an* God sends. The Spirit empowers the church to continue the work of Jesus in extending the reign of kingdom of God to all peoples on earth).[275]

He will then come once more to earth as Judge. He will finally destroy all the powers of darkness that have rebelled against God.

(Jesus' defeat of the hostile spiritual powers that rebelled against God results in him executing final eschatological judgement on them).[276]

When He has finally destroyed all rebellion against God, 'Isa, the visible form of the invisible God will hand the kingdom back to the Father Who dwells in unapproachable light, and sit with Him on

(Jesus' defeat of all rebellion against God completes his mission and God's rule extends unchallenged through the entire creation. The Father and Jesus sit on one throne).[277]

His throne, the one Lord of the one throne (Rabb al-'arsh).

There will be no more suffering, no more sickness, no more sin.

(The results of Jesus' defeat of the powers of darkness and sin).[278]

For God's rule will reign unchallenged in all things from the one throne in heaven of the one God,

(Affirmation of the oneness of God – one throne of one God).[279]

This is our God, the only true God,

(Repeated affirmation of *tawhid* – monotheism).

We worship Him alone.

(Repeated affirmation of monolatry to counter worship of Jesus being misunderstood as akin to *Barelvi* veneration of Muhammad and saints).

Fourth canto

He alone is the Saviour,

(Expansion of the extrinsic framework by which God's identity is known in the Islamic context: creator, ruler, judge – to additionally include saviour).

He alone can forgive us our sins, for it is He that we have sinned against.

No-one else could save us from our sin.

He is the Ruler and King of all things, all creatures whether angels or men owe Him perfect, absolute and undivided obedience.

No mere man could redeem the life of another, or give to God a ransom for him.

Even the most perfect of His creatures could have no surplus merit to pay the debt of another.

Only God Himself could pay the debt we owe, only He could save us.

(Demonstration that only God can forgive sins: a) by using the relational concept of justice, whereby only the one who has been sinned against can forgive;[280] b) by the use of Ps.49 to turn Islamic use of Q6:164 from an argument against the atonement to demonstration of the necessity of God himself paying the price. All creatures are mere servants owing a duty of perfect obedience to their Lord, no servant can therefore have any surplus merit to pay the debt of another – so only God himself could deal with sin;[281] c) subject/object distinctions used to identify Jesus as being on the God side of the God/non-god divide).

He, al-Azim became the momentous (azim) sacrifice promised to Abraham, the only sacrifice that could ransom us.

(Islamic name of God *al-Azim*; typological allusion to the Qur'anic account of God ransoming Abraham's son with a momentous (*azim*) sacrifice).[282]

He the Compassionate (al-Rahim) and the

Merciful (al-Rahman) became our Saviour.

(Expansion of the Islamic concept of God being the Merciful and the Compassionate, to him acting in mercy and compassion by becoming the saviour).

The Father who dwells in unapproachable light, al-Batin, whom no-one has seen or can see, sent 'Isa, the visible form of the invisible God to save us from our sins and reconcile us to Himself.

(Distinctions within the Godhead – different roles in enacting salvation of the Father and Jesus. The Islamic name of God *al-Batin* 'the Hidden' applied to the Father; Jesus the visible form of the invisible God is the way that God acts towards his people as their saviour).[283]

He added human nature to Himself; the immortal visible form of God clothed Himself with mortal flesh like ours, and became a man. Man could not be united with God, only God could unite Himself with man.

(Jesus was fully God and fully man. Counter to a) the Islamic assumption that Christian belief in Jesus' divinity is claiming that a man is God; b) the Islamic assumption that God cannot be united with man, by implicitly stating that God is not limited in this way).[284]

As a nightingale suffers thorns and bloodshed to reach the rose it loves, so God our saviour, laid aside his heavenly glory and humbled Himself, suffered thorns and bloodshed to save us. Out of His great love, He endured the cross for us to free us from the powers of evil, sin and death and reconcile us to Himself.

(Use of common symbolism from Persian mystical poetry with the gender roles reversed, so that God becomes the seeker enduring thorns and bloodshed to reach the object of his love; i.e. men and women. The gender reversal removes an otherwise unresolved tension in the culture, created by mystical poetry, portraying God as passive and female).[285]

By His death and resurrection He paid the penalty for our sin, only He could do it.

(The purpose of Christ's suffering, building on the earlier foundation that only God could pay the debt and forgive people's sin. The resurrection is again explicitly affirmed to counter Islamic claims that Jesus ascended without first dying).

He freed us from the power of sin and death, delivered us from the kingdom of Satan, and transferred us to His own glorious kingdom.

(The purpose of the cross – redemption out of the dominion of Satan into the kingdom of God).[286]

This was solely an act of his grace. We did not earn it, we could not earn it.

(Counter to the common Islamic belief that various acts may sway God's mind on the Day of Judgement).[287]

Therefore He was exalted back to the highest place in heaven. Now all the host of heaven worship Him because He is the Lamb who was slain to purchase men for God from every tribe, and language and people and nation.

(Jesus' death and resurrection portrayed as the vindication of his honour – exemplified in him being the central focus of the worship of heaven because he redeemed men and women for God in this way).[288]

Because 'Isa did this the Father saves all who repent of their sins and believe in Him, making them alive with new spiritual birth.

(The role of the Father in the salvation of people).[289]

And 'Isa, the Lord of the water of life (ab-i-hayat), *has poured out the Spirit of God, the Giver of life* (al-Muhyi) *on those who repent, making them alive with new spiritual birth and renewing them.*

(The role of Jesus – sending the Spirit, and the role of the Spirit in salvation, expressed by the motif used in mystical poetry of Jesus being the 'Lord of the water of life'.)[290]

We who were formerly spiritually dead in our sins, He has made alive, and by His Spirit united us (wasl) *to Him.*

(God has acted as the saviour by making us spiritually alive and uniting us with him by his Spirit – this fulfils the aspiration for *wasl* – union with God that is the subject of much mystical poetry).[291]

When He Himself acted to save us from our sin He revealed that He, Father, Messiah and Holy Spirit, was the Saviour of all men. And so He has revealed to us His great name (Ism al-azim), *'the name of the Father, the Messiah and the Holy Spirit'.*

(The new name of God revealing this new aspect of the character of God, just as God had earlier revealed his name YHWH to Moses at the burning bush. Identification of this name as the *Ism al-Azim* whose identity is the subject of speculation in *Ahadith*).[292]

This is our God, the only true God, the only Saviour.

(Repeated affirmation of *tawhid* – monotheism).

We worship Him alone.

(Repeated affirmation of monolatry to counter worship of Jesus being misunderstood as akin to *Barelvi* veneration of Muhammad and Muslim saints).

Fifth canto

He alone is the final Judge. Every creature in heaven and on earth must appear before Him.

(Extrinsic description of God used in the Islamic context).

The Father who dwells in unapproachable light has given all judgement to 'Isa, the visible form of God, Who became man.

(The Father relates to his creation as judge through Jesus, the visible form of God, who became man).[293]

He is the Master of the Day of Judgement (Malik Yaum al-din), *the Judge of judges* (al-Hakim al-hakimin), *all things will be judged by Him.*

(Jesus described using common Islamic names of God, and the subject/object distinction indicating that he is God, the final judge).

He is the Just One (al-'Adl) *who will judge with perfect righteousness and justice.*

(Counter to commonly held ideas of God being unpredictable on the Day of Judgement).[294]

He has sent the Spirit of God, al-Wakil, *into the world to convict men and women of sin, righteousness and judgement.*

(Role of the Spirit in judgement).[295]

Those who refuse to follow Him, who refuse to repent and accept His sacrifice for their sin, He will throw into the lake of fire prepared for the devil and His angels.

(God's judgement on the Day of Judgement will divide people into two groups on the basis of how they responded to Jesus).

But those who repent of their sins and follow Him, He will welcome into the very presence of God in heaven. His perfect sacrifice has cleansed them from their sin.

(God's judgement is therefore perfectly predictable because it is based on grace i.e. Jesus' forgiveness, not human merit).[296]

They shall dwell with God.

(The Islamic aspiration of seeing God in paradise is more than fulfilled by actually dwelling with God.

This also fulfils the mystical aspiration of *wasl* – union with God).[297]

They will be His people,

And God will wipe every tear from their eye, there will be no more death, or mourning, or crying or pain.

For God will make everything new.

(God's new creation – a theme mentioned, but not described in the *Qur'an*).[298]

Sixth canto
There is but One God,

(The contextualised *shema/shahada* earlier referred to).

Who alone we worship.

We know Him as Father, **al-Batin,**
who dwells in unapproachable light,

*Yet tenderly cares for us, planned our
creation and salvation.*

*We know Him as 'Isa, the visible form
of the invisible God,*

*Who created, rules and will judge all
things, and became our Saviour.*

And we know Him as the Holy Spirit,

Who breathed life into creation,

*is the all-seeing presence of God
throughout creation,*

Who inspired the prophets,

convicts the world of sin,

and whose presence unites us with God,

*sanctifying our sinful hearts and
empowering us to serve Him.*

This is the one God we worship.

He alone is the Creator (**al-Khaliq**) *of
all things,*

Lord of all things (**Rabb kull shay**),

Master of the Day of Judgement
(**Malik Yaum al-din**),

And the only Saviour.

Endnotes

[1] Reputed comment by G.F. Handel while writing *The Messiah* (Christian History Institute web site *www.gospelcom.net/chi/GLIMPSEF/Glimpses/glmps147.shtml*).

[2] In chapter 1 we discussed a number of christologies such as that of Zwemer, which advocated starting from Qur'anic christological titles.

[3] cf. Introduction Fig.1.

[4] cf. Introduction esp. Fig. 3 for explication of the difference between intrinsic and extrinsic conceptions of God.

[5] cf. Introduction Fig.2.

[6] cf. discussion pp 141-144.

[7] cf. section 'Titles and descriptions of Jesus' pp 163-164.

[8] Both of which we demonstrated were the case in the Jewish context cf. pp 62-64, 85-86, 112-113.

[9] cf. pp 48-51, 141-144.

[10] cf. pp 144-46.

[11] cf. pp 48-51, 141-144.

[12] This is not to say that there is no concept of 'salvation'. However, in Sunni Islam this has a predominantly contemporary political meaning, as can be seen in the use of *nejat* ('salvation') in the names of political parties such as *Jabha-yi nejat-i milli* (cf. Roy *Resistance* 235). We will also note that in Shi'a Islam, which is beyond the limits of this study, the deaths of Ali and his sons is sometimes seen as having salvific significance. However, in neither Sunni nor Shi'a Islam is there any thought of God himself personally acting as the saviour-deliverer.

[13] cf. pp 48-51, 141-144.

[14] cf. discussion of 'Sufism' pp 144-146.'

[15] cf. pp 47-48, 143-144.

[16] In the following examples cognates are indicated by the inclusion of the Hebrew name.

[17] Although the semantic domain of 'the Living One' is almost certainly included within the meaning of the divine name 'I AM' (אֶהְיֶה), the OT context implies that the name 'I AM' means somewhat more than simply 'living existence'.

[18] Semantically this equates with the OT 'Lord of all the earth' (cf. Josh.3:11,13; Ps.97:5; Mic.4:13; Zech.4:14).

[19] cf. pp 47-48, 143-144.

[20] cf. pp 78-84.

[21] cf. pp 55-64, 152-162.

[22] cf. pp 62-64, 157.

[23] cf. pp 113-114.

[24] cf. pp 56-58, 152.

[25] cf. pp 152-162 particularly in respect of the Islamic Moses traditions.

[26] cf. discussion of the Garden of Eden and Sinai theophanies and anticipated eschatological epiphany pp 59-64.

[27] cf. pp 157-160.

[28] cf. pp 155-156 for discussion of the Islamic debate on this subject.

[29] cf. pp 55-58, 157-160.

[30] cf. p 167.

[31] pp 68, 114-118.

[32] cf. discussion of Gabriel p 160.

[33] cf. discussion of Sufism pp 160-161.

[34] Even one of the most recent suggestions for explanation of the trinity, J.J. Yoder 'The Trinity and Christian Witness to Muslims' *Missiology* 22:3 (1994) 339-46, claims that the Qur'anic portrayal of Allah is one of absolute omnipotence with 'no face to face encounter' (343).

[35] cf. discussion of this pp 60-62.

[36] cf. discussion of this pp 114-118.

[37] cf. pp 78-84, 93-94 cf. also p 64.

[38] For a concise summary of early church debates concerning *modalism* cf. J.N.D. Kelly *Early Christian Doctrines* [London:A&C Black,5th edn,1977] 119-26.

[39] Even the Johannine prologue moves swiftly on to speak of 'the Word' as the way in which God has created all things.

[40] Although the term 'antecedent attitudes' may appear somewhat unwieldy, it represents the best possibility of comparing the specific antecedents to christological monotheism found both in pre-Christian Judaism which the early church had to relate to, with those that already exist in the Islamic context and which any contextualisation of christology has similarly to engage with.

[41] cf. discussion of the malak YHWH pp 67-78.

[42] cf. pp 162-68 esp. 167.

[43] cf. pp 65-68, 163-165'.

[44] So, Bauckham *Crucified* 75-76 referring to Matt.28:19.

[45] ibid.

[46] Jn 5:21-27; 10:30.

[47] Jn 1:1-18; Col.1:15; Hebs.1:3.

[48] The Islamic names of God are familiar to many Muslims from the use of the 'rosary'.

[49] 1 Cor.8:6; Col.1:16.

[50] 1 Cor.8:6; Col.1:16; Heb.1:2; Jn 1:1-3,10.

[51] 1 Cor.15:24-28 cf. the *wahdat al-shuhud* Sufi hope of achieving union (*wasl*) in harmony with the creator based on Q53:42; 96:8 that we outlined in our discussion of 'Sufism' pp 144-146.

[52] Eph.1:22; 1 Tim.6:15; Rev.17:14;19:16.

[53] 1 Cor.15:24-28; Rev.3:14.

[54] 1 Cor.15:24-28 cf. discussion of this pp 80-81.

[55] Eph.1:10; Rev. 22:1,3 note the singular ὁ θρόνος τοῦ θεοῦ καὶ τοῦ ἀρνίου.

[56] James 4:12; 5:7-9; 2 Tim.4:1; 1 Pet.1:17; 2:23.

[57] Jn 5:22ff; Acts 10:42; 17:31; Rom.2:16.

[58] Tit.2:13; 3:4; 2 Pet.1:1; Jude:25.

[59] 2 Cor.5:18-19; 1 Tim.1:15; 1 Jn 4:14.

[60] Rom.5:9-11; 2 Cor.5:18-19; Col..2:15; 2 Tim.1:10; Heb.2:14; 1 Jn 3:8.

[61] Eph.2:4-5; Tit.3:4-6; cf. also Jn 3:16-18; Acts 2:38; 3:19; 16:31; Rom.10:9-10.

[62] Jn 4:13-14; 7:37-40; Rev.22:1; cf. also Tit.3:5-6. The imagery of 'the water of life' occurs in a variety of Islamic literature, esp. in Persian mystical poetry. It is generally portrayed as giving eternal life to those who drink it. We observed on p 163 that some mystical poetry portrays Jesus as the lord of the water of life. This therefore forms a link with similar imagery used of Jesus' gift of the Spirit in John's Gospel.

[63] i.e. one intended to produce a similar impact on the hearers as the original word did in its context. The use of 'dynamic (or 'functional') equivalents' in contextualisation was originally developed by C. Kraft (*Christianity* passim but cf. esp. 261-312) by analogy with E. Nida's theory of dynamic equivalence Bible translation. However, its use to contextualise theology and other aspects of church life is neither dependent on the validity of Nida's approach to Bible translation, nor limited by precisely the same constraints. A precedent for Kraft's argument in this respect can be found in the NT. Paul's *theology* replaces the term 'Son of Man' with alternatives such as 'Lord' (e.g. 1 Thess.4:16-17 cf. Matt.16:27; Mk 13:26f) and possibly 'the man from heaven' (1 Cor.15:47-49). I.H. Marshall 'Culture and the New Testament' 17-31 in Stott & Coote (eds) *Lausanne* notes that this was necessary because 'Son of Man' as a term 'had no pre-history outside Jewish circles and the Greek form of the phrase was grotesque' (25). Conversely however, Mark who was writing a *Gospel* rather than *theology*, felt constrained to retain the form 'Son of Man' despite addressing a similar Greek audience. A comparable distinction between 'translation principles' and 'language for evangelization' is made by L.O. Sanneh 'Jesus, Son of God – a Translation Problem – Further Comments' *BT* 28:4 (1977) 241-44.

[64] cf. discussion of the christological titles 'Word of God', 'Visible manifestation of the invisible God' and 'the Glory of God' pp 89, 91-92, 92-93.

[65] For this reason the term 'Servant of God', which A. de Kuiper & B. Newman 'Jesus, Son of God – a Translation Problem' *BT* 28:4 (1977) 432-38 suggested as a functional equivalent in Bible translation for the NT term 'Son of God', is wholly inadequate.

[66] Q3:45; 4:171.

[67] cf. chapter 1 section 'W.H.T. (Temple) Gairdner'.

[68] 1 Jn 2:1 cf. also Rom.8:34; Heb.7:25; 9:24.

[69] Jn 14:16,26; 15:26; 16:7.

[70] cf. our earlier discussion of this as a NT christological title pp 87-88, 88-89.

[71] This title is of course already familiar to western Christians through its use in the hymn 'Praise to the Lord the Almighty, the King of creation' by Joachim Neander (1650-80) translated into English by Catherine Winkworth (1829-78).

[72] cf. earlier section of this chapter 'Islamic names of God as possible dynamic equivalents'.

[73] cf. our earlier discussion of this NT christological title pp 92-93.

[74] cf. our earlier discussion of these NT christological titles pp 91-92.

[75] *Kitab Maqadus* (Urdu Revised Version) [Lahore:Pakistan Bible Society, n.d.]; *Kitab Maqadus* (Persian Bible Standard Version – new edition,1996) [Godalming:Elam Ministries,1996].

[76] Cognate with the Urdu word *chahara* which has a similar meaning.

[77] *Farsi Contemporary Bible* [Colorado Springs:IBS,1995].

[78] The standard Persian NT is a revision of the original Henry Martyn translation whose language register gives it a degree of inaccessibility to some sections of society.

[79] Q55:27.

[80] Matt.18:10; Rev.6:16 and as we noted in chapter 3 n.151 Christian interpretation has often understood texts such a Ex.19:20ff/23:20ff and Dan.7:9 in this way. However, conversely, Rev.22:3-4 could be understood to speak of believers eschatologically seeing the one face of the Father and Jesus.

[81] cf. pp 78-84.

[82] cf. pp 141-143.

[83] So, B.J. Nichols 'New Theological Approaches in Muslim Evangelism' 155-163 in McCurry *Compendium* cf. esp. 158. S. Schlorff 'Muslim Ideology and Christian Apologetics' *Missiology* 21:2 (1993)

173-85 similarly stresses the need to emphasise the kingdom of God in apologetics to counter Muslim misunderstanding of Christianity as equating with western politics.

[84] cf. pp 47-48, 143-144.

[85] cf. pp 113-114.

[86] cf. pp 157-160.

[87] cf. pp 163-164, 167-168.

[88] cf. pp 81-83, 169-172.

[89] cf. pp 81-83.

[90] cf. discussion of this pp 157-160.

[91] cf. pp 85-86.

[92] cf. discussion of this in pp 164-165.

[93] cf. pp 85-86.

[94] cf. discussion of this aspect of monolatry pp 147-151.

[95] cf. pp 53-55, 147-151.

[96] The NT clearly indicates that both Jesus and the early church saw healing as a sign of the kingdom of God, that should happen alongside proclamation (cf. Lk.7:18-23; 9:1-2; 10:9; Jn 20:30-31; Acts 2:22; 4:29-30; 14:3; Rom.15:18-19; Heb.2:3-4). The NT also records deliverance from evil spirits happening alongside preaching, although it does not suggest that either Jesus or the early church understood deliverance as being *primarily* a means of convincing people of Christian beliefs, which probably reflects deliverance from evil spirits being linked to repentance and entry to the kingdom of God (Lk.9:1-2; 11:14-26). However, the NT does indicate that reports of people being set free by mere word of command led to news about Jesus spreading and questioning as to his identity (cf. Matt.9:32-33; Mk 1:21-28; Lk.11:14ff).

[97] cf. pp 86-93.

[98] cf. discussion of the 99 names p 143

[99] So, Sweetman *Theology* 1:1:18-20.

[100] cf. G.L. Cockerill 'To the Hebrews/To the Muslims: Islamic Pilgrimage as a Key to Interpretation' *Missiology* 22:3 (1994) 347-59 and *Guidebook for Pilgrims to the Heavenly City* [Pasadena: William Carey, 2002] passim which together are a noteworthy study by a NT scholar of how the pilgrimage motif in Hebrews may be used in Islamic contexts to portray Christ as the pilgrim 'guide'.

[101] cf. pp 167-168.

[102] Rev.1:17; 2:8; 22:13.

[103] Rev.1:5; 3:14; 19:11.

[104] Rev.1:17; 2:8; 22:13.

[105] 1 Cor.1:24 (θεοῦ σοφία).

[106] Matt.25:31-34.

[107] Acts 7:52; 22:14; 1 Jn 2:1 (ὁ δίκαιος); 2 Tim.4:8 (ὁ δίκαιος κριτής).

[108] Rev.17:14; 19:16.

[109] Rev.1:5; 3:14.

[110] Jn 1:8-9; 8:12.

[111] Jn 14:6.

[112] Eph.2:14.

[113] Rev.1:18.

[114] Heb.1:2.

[115] Acts 3:14.

[116] Matt.9:2-6/Mk 2:3-10/Lk.5:18-24.

[117] Jn. 5:22-23,27; Acts 10:42; 17:31.

[118] Matt.9:2-6/Mk. 2:3-10/Lk.5:18-24.

[119] 2 Pet.1:16.

[120] Matt.9:2-6/Mk. 2:3-10/Lk.5:18-24.

[121] 2 Pet.1:16.

[122] Jn. 14:13-14; 14:16; Acts 2:33.

[123] Jn. 1:14; 1 Cor.2:8 ('The Lord of glory'); Heb.1:3.

[124] Rev. 3:7-8; 5:2-9 (the Lamb who was slain is the only one in heaven and on earth worthy to open the scroll).

[125] Jn 14:13-14.

[126] Matt.11:27 (Jesus is the only one who knows the Father and so is able to reveal him to others).

[127] Heb.7:25; 1 Jn 2:1.

[128] Acts 2:33; 5:31; Phil. 2:9; Heb.7:26.

[129] cf. pp 121-130.

[130] cf. pp 52-55, 147-151

[131] cf. discussion of this pp 53-55, 147-151.

[132] cf. discussion of this on pp 52-53, 147-151.

[133] This comparative analysis provides some incidental support for the contention of Hurtado *Christ* 31-32 and Bauckham *Crucified* 15 that the reservation of various devotional acts for God alone was held by Jews to be particularly important and one of the ways that Jews emphasised the uniqueness of God.

[134] cf. pp 52-53, 147-151.

[135] cf. p 121.

[136] cf. discussion of this aspect of NT christology pp 114-120.

[137] cf. pp 128-129.

[138] cf. pp 129-130.

[139] cf. pp 123-124.

[140] cf. p 122.

[141] cf. pp 85-86, 124-125.

[142] cf. discussion on pp 53-55, 147-151.

[143] W. McClintock 'Demons and Ghosts in Indian Folklore' *Missiology* 18:1 (1990) 37-47 lists 29 categories of malignant spiritual beings that are widely feared in the Indian sub continent. He argues that it is incumbent on those contextualising the Gospel to grapple seriously with a worldview that perceives the misfortunes of life to be attributable to such supernatural beings. This theme is developed in practical terms in R. Love *Muslims, Magic and the Kingdom of God* [Pasadena: William Carey Library,2000] passim and with particular reference to women in J. Colgate 'Muslim Women and the Occult: Seeing Jesus Set the Captives Free' 33-63 in F. Love and J. Eckheart (eds) *Ministry to Muslim Women* [Pasadena: William Carey Library,2000].

[144] Musk *Unseen* 170-71 mentions the need for Christians to reclaim in the name of Jesus places such as toilets, graveyards and sorceresses' homes that are seen by Muslims as residences of jinn and other places polluted by evil spirits and human rebellion against God. Musk only speaks of deliverance of places in this respect, which accords with the caveat we made in n.96 above.

[145] So, P. Hiebert 'The Flaw of the Excluded Middle' *Missiology* 10:1 (1982) 37-47.

[146] Hiebert 'Flaw'. V. Stacey *Christ Supreme over Satan* [Lahore:MIK,1986] 81-82 similarly warns of situations in Pakistan where Bible verses are continuously repeated in a similar manner to the repetition of Qur'anic verses in order to secure blessing, protection, healing or revenge.

[147] cf. pp 125-126.

[148] cf. pp 128-129.

[149] M. Brislen 'A Model for a Muslim-Culture Church' *Missiology* 24:3 (1996) 355-67 presents such a dynamic equivalent, which he envisages could be used by a *muezzin* in an 'Isa mosque'. Although this proposal has much to commend it, the format he suggests relies on Qur'anic titles of Jesus such as 'Word of God' and 'Messiah' that are not commonly understood by Muslims to be divine titles. Only his statement that Jesus sends the Spirit hints at Jesus' divine status. We will therefore propose a dynamic equivalent of the *Shahada* that does directly include Jesus within the unique divine identity.

[150] In both this and the subsequent confessional recitation we follow the normal syntactical practice in the Islamic context of capitalising English pronouns which refer to God.

[151] Deut.6:4.

[152] Deut.6:5; 11:13 cf. Ex.20:3-6.

[153] Jn 1:18; 1 Tim.5:16 cf. Q6:103; MM32:10(Predestination).

[154] 1 Cor.8:6; 2 Tim.1:8-10; Tit.3:4-6.

[155] cf. our discussion earlier in this chapter section 'A 'dynamic equivalent' for NT terms expressing christological monotheism'.

[156] This contextualised *shema* only focuses on how God relates to all else, which is the dominant emphasis of NT christology. Although this does refer to distinctions within the Godhead, a fuller expression of christology such as the confessional recitation proposed at the end of this chapter will affirm this more explicitly whilst maintaining its central focus on how God relates to his creation. However, it may be significant that the christianised *shema* in 1 Cor.8:6, as a summary statement of monotheistic belief, does not deal with the question of distinctions in the Godhead, although elsewhere in the NT this is clearly affirmed.

[157] Jn 14:16; 16:7; Acts 2:33.

[158] Rom.8:11 (cf. Job 33:4; Ps.104:29-30).

[159] Ps.139:7-10; Zech.4:1-10 cf. 2 Chron.16:9; Rev.5:6.

[160] 1 Pet.1:10-12.

[161] Jn 16:8-11.

[162] Jn 14:18; Rom.8:9-11.

[163] Rom.15:16; 1 Cor.6:11; Tit.3:5; 1 Pet.1:2; Acts 1:8.

[164] Some progress in this direction has been made by L. Vander Werff 'The Names of Christ in Worship' 175-194 in Woodberry *Emmaus*, who advocates a litany in which the Messiah is identified by the christological titles in the Fourth Gospel. Although this has some merit it does not relate these titles to Islamic names of God, or take account of the differences in meaning between the Jewish and Islamic contexts. It is important that a contextualised christology does both of these.

[165] cf. pp 126-127.

[166] cf the Qur'anic affirmation that the spirit is only sent at God's command Q17:85; 40:15; 97:4.

[167] cf. discussion of 'Sufism' pp 144-146.

[168] Gen.3:1-24.

[169] Rom.5:11; 6:5.

[170] It is appropriate to maintain the biblical metaphor of God sending the Spirit to the 'heart' (Rom.5:5; 2 Cor.1:22; Gal.4:6 etc.) as it resonates with the *wahdat al-shuhud* hope of a mystical reflection of God's presence in the believer's 'heart'.

[171] Jn 14:16-20; Phil.2:1.

[172] 1 Cor.13:12; 2 Cor.3:17-18 cf. the goal of *wahdat al-shuhud* Sufism which we discussed on pp 144-146.

[173] 1 Cor.15:22-28; Rev.22:1,3.

[174] cf. our earlier discussion pp 60-62.

[175] cf. pp 114-118.

[176] cf. following section 'Specific obstacles in the Islamic context'.

[177] cf. pp 117-120.

[178] cf. pp 165-166 esp. n. 199.

[179] cf. p 166.

[180] cf. p167.

[181] cf. our discussion of this pp 165-166 and the argument that we observed in chapter 1 was advanced by St. Clair Tisdall that only God can make atonement, as every creature owes a duty of absolute obedience to God, and cannot therefore have any surplus merit to pay the debt of another creature.

[182] cf. pp 117-120 and 165 esp. n.199.

[183] cf. pp 117-120.

[184] cf. pp 114-118.

[185] So, B. Musk *Touching the Soul of Islam* [Crowborough:MARC,1995] 67-88 ,who contends on this basis that a christology of honour may be an appropriate apologetic in Islamic contexts. Musk suggests that this honour-shame focus is found across a range of Islamic contexts.

[186] cf. discussion of this on pp 117-120.

[187] cf. discussion of this on pp 117-120.

[188] cf. discussion of this on pp 117-120.

[189] Q37:99-110.

[190] So, Hughes 'Idu'l-Azha' *Dictionary* 192.

[191] cf. discussion of this on pp 117-120.

[192] Jn 1:29.

[193] Q3:39 (cf. Yusuf Ali n.381); 19:1-33.

[194] Q37:107.

[195] Rev.5:6.

[196] Rev.13:8.

[197] Hence Islamic aversion to cremation cf. Hughes 'Burning the Dead' *Dictionary* 47.

[198] MM30:96(Burial).

[199] Gen.22:8,14.

[200] cf. the words Q19:33 ascribes to Jesus, and Zwemer's comment on these that we noted in chapter 1.

[201] Hughes 'Idu'l-Azha' *Dictionary* 192-4 cites a *Khutbah* (mosque sermon) given on *'id al-azha* which states 'If you sacrifice a fat animal it will serve you well, and carry you across the Sirat' (the razor sharp bridge over the fire that has to be crossed to enter paradise) (194).

[202] cf. discussion of this on p 119.

[203] So, K. Ferdinando *The Triumph of Christ in African Perspective: A Study of Demonology and Redemption in the African Context* [Carlisle:Paternoster,1999] 397. Ferdinando clearly elucidates this in the context

of African traditional religions (396-407). However, his comments have a more general validity as well as some specific relevance to the Islamic context. Illustrative of this is the observation of I.J. Glaser 'Qur'anic Challenges for Genesis' *JSOT* 75 (1997) 3-19 that the Qur'anic Adam narratives imply that the responsibility for human wrongdoing lies primarily with Satan seeking to deceive people, in contrast to the OT emphasis on human responsibility (cf. esp. 12), an implication which parallels the African context addressed by Ferdinando.

[204] cf. discussion of violated hospitality codes on pp 117-120.

[205] cf. discussion of this on pp 165-172. Musk *Soul* 44-66, 89-110 suggests that such cultural values occur in a range of Islamic contexts.

[206] cf. p 88.

[207] The point is simply that this depiction of God as female is an existing tension within Islamic cultures. This aspect of the christology neither affirms, nor makes any statement on male attitudes towards women in the Islamic context, beyond semiotically identifying all people, both male and female, as symbolically 'female' in relation to God.

[208] cf. p 88 esp. n.104 for discussion of the NT expansion of the OT imagery to portray Christ as paying the bride price for his bride with his own blood.

[209] cf. the OT chronicler's portrayal of David in this way (2 Chron.17:3; 28:1; 29:2; 34:2) and the idealised portrait of the wife of noble character in Prov. 31:10-31.

[210] cf. T.A. Steffan *Reconnecting God's Story to Ministry* [La Habra:COMD,1996] 95, who highlights this with respect to the Pushtuns of Pakistan, a case study which we will follow in the following illustration.

[211] A. Ahmed *Millennium and Charisma Among the Pathans* [London:RKP,1980] 53.

[212] So, B. Grima *The Performance of Emotion Amongst Paxtun Women* [Austin:University of Texas Press,1992] 11ff.

[213] So, Steffan *God's* 95, who cites this aspect of Pushtun culture as an example of cultural themes that are likely to increase the receptivity of women to the Christian message.

[214] cf. discussion of the 'Lover/Beloved imagery' above and the NT bridegroom motif p 88.

[215] 1 Pet.1:18-19 cf. 1 Cor.7:23.

[216] cf. our discussion earlier in this chapter in section 'Attitudes towards christological monotheism'.

[217] cf. section 'Contextualisation of christological monotheism: expansion of existing categories' earlier in this chapter.

[218] The conclusion we earlier reached in section 'Attitudes to christological monotheism' of this chapter, cf. chapter 5 sections 'Titles and descriptions of Jesus' pp 163-164 and 'Denial of Jesus' divinity' pp 164-165 for specific details.

[219] cf. discussion of this in relation to Matt.28:19 on p 96.

[220] cf. discussion of this on 157-160.

[221] cf. p 96.

[222] cf. Hughes *Dictionary* 142 for discussion of conflicting traditions.

[223] MM38:54,55(Names-Allah).

[224] cf. 1 Pet.1:10-12.

[225] Because the revelation of a specific divine name is an historical event as well as 'theology', it cannot be so easily recontextualised in the way that theological expressions can, but must stay as faithful as possible both to the original 'form' and 'meaning'. As the meaning of 'Son' is widely misunderstood in the Islamic context, it is necessary to replace it, but to do so in a way that stays as close as possible to the historical form of the name 'of the Father, the Son and the Holy Spirit'.

[226] There is an interesting historical parallel for the form we have suggested above that was used in the context of pre-Islamic Arabian polytheism, where the terms 'the Father' and 'the Son' were similarly liable to be misunderstood. The Sirwah inscription in Mareb, the Sabean capital, detailing the suppression of a revolt against Ethiopia in 542CE begins 'In the power of the All Merciful, and His Messiah and the Holy Ghost'. Zwemer *God* 27,90 and *Challenge* 21 attributes the inscription's discovery to Edward Glasser in 1888. Zwemer gives an incorrect reference to a further secondary source, however the dates and details he gives in respect of Glasser give a reasonable degree of confidence that this part of his citation is accurate.

[227] cf. pp 147-151, 167-168.

[228] cf. pp 114-118.

[229] e.g. in Pakistan this carries a mandatory death sentence, which P. Sookhdeo *A People Betrayed* [Fearn: Christian Focus,2002] 239-43 observes has been given to a number of Pakistanis, both Muslim and Christian, who have been accused of 'blaspheming Prophet Muhammad' by a Muslim acquaintance.

[230] cf. pp 114-118.

[231] Jn 3:13.

[232] Matt.11:1-15 cf. our earlier reference in this chapter (pp 192-193) to this NT passage in relation to strengthening the existing concept of epiphany.

[233] As R. Bauckham *Mission* observes, whilst a mission hermeneutic, including contextualisation, may be situated within what he terms 'the academic guild of biblical scholars', it must also 'transcend' this and 'address the church in its mission to the world' (3 cf. also 16-17).

[234] This approach was pioneered by New Tribes Mission. For an academic analysis and advocacy of this approach cf. T.A. Steffan *Passing the Baton* [La Habra:COMD,1993] passim and at a slightly more popular level *Reconnecting God's Story to Ministry* (*op cit.*) passim.

[235] As we observed on p 17 this approach was used by Gairdner in Cairo. It has more recently been advocated by K.E. Bailey *The Cross and the Prodigal* [St Louis:Concordia,1973 – reprinted Melbourne: Acorn Press,2000] passim.

[236] One of the clearest examples of this within the English-speaking world is John Milton's *Paradise Lost*, whose *epic* genre approximates to the Persian *masnavi* genre that we examined in Chapter 5.

[237] So, Steffan, *Baton* 115-30, who concludes that the use of oral communication both assists the internalisation of supracultural truth and enables effective propagation of it. Steffan's work is illustrative of a body of recent scholarship that has refuted earlier notions exemplified in the comments of D.A. McGavran *Understanding Church Growth* [1970 – 3rd edn. revised and edited by C.P. Wagner, Grand Rapids:Eerdmans,1990] that classes to enable the illiterate to read the Bible are 'an essential part of redemption.' (215).

[238] Both because discourse structures vary between different linguistic and cultural groups and because the final form in which a contextualised christology is expressed is rightly the domain of local Christians, both in respect of ownership and intuitive knowledge of the culture.

[239] The experience of W.H.T. Gairdner may be instructive here. In developing versified Gospel stories in early twentieth century Cairo, Gairdner found that merely simplifying classical (in his case Arabic) metres was 'useless' for uneducated sections of the population, such as street children. He found it necessary to adopt 'purely colloquial verse' using metres for which popular (Arabic) tunes were available (Gairdner's own written comments cited in Padwick, *Gairdner* 313-14).

[240] So, R. Finnegan *Oral Poetry* [Bloomington & Indianapolis:Indiana University Press,1992] who in discussing oral literature in general presents a concise summary of scholarship concluding this (126-33). Finnegan also notes the wide use of repetition of units from syllables and single lines to whole verses and lengthy passages in oral poetry including religious liturgy (102-03).

[241] However, as Bosch, *Mission*, observes 'in the Bible and earliest Christian literature any form of systematisation was virtually absent' (206). Bosch goes on to affirm the earlier observation of A. Harnack that 'Dogma in its conception and development is a work of the Greek spirit on the soil of the Gospel.' (206).

[242] Finnegan *Oral* 129 observes that oral composition gravitates towards repetition precisely because it is 'more easily understandable and retainable'.

[243] This was the view of the 55 theologians from Africa, Asia and Latin America who drew up the 1982 'Seoul Declaration'. This implicitly criticised the western emphasis on systematic theology as having often reduced the Christian faith to abstract concepts. For discussion of this cf. B.R. Ro & R. Eshenaur *The Bible and Theology in Asian Contexts* [Taichung:Asia Theological Association,1984] 21-27. Bauckham *Mission* 2-3,16-17 similarly affirms that the hermeneutical context for contextualisation is ultimately the church itself and relates this to the position of L. Newbiggin *The Gospel in a Pluralist Society* [London:SPCK,1989] 222-33 that the local congregation must be the primary hermeneutical context in which the Gospel is worked out.

[244] In the confessional recitation itself we follow the normal syntactical practice in the Islamic context of capitalising English pronouns used for God.

[245] 1Kgs 8:27.

[246] Isa.6:1ff; Ezek.1:26-28; Dan.7:9-10 cf. Q7:54.

[247] e.g. Q2:255; 34:23.

[248] Gen.3:8-24 cf. Q10:9.

[249] Gen.17:1-22 cf. Q11:69-73.

[250] Ex.3:2-15 cf. Q20:9-36; 27:7-12; 28:29-35.

[251] LXX Isa.63:9. cf. p 160 for discussion of Islamic suggestions that Gabriel accompanied the Exodus.

[252] Isa.35:4ff; Matt.11:2-6/Lk.7:18-23 cf. Q3:49.

[253] Isa.9:1-7.

[254] Mal.3:1-3; 4:1-6; Matt.11:7-14 cf. Q3:39,45; 19:1-33.

[255] Matt.3:1-12.

[256] Matt.11:11-13.

[257] Lk.24:44-49; Acts 3:21-24.

[258] Lk.7:21-23 cf. Q3:49.

[259] Lk.9:1-6; 10:1-17 cf. Q3:49 and Baidawi's *tafsir* on Q36:13-32 (ET Sale n.30).

[260] cf. Jn 1:10-12.

[261] Col.1:13-14; 2:13-15.

[262] Acts 2:23-36; 1 Pet.1:10-12,20.

[263] Acts 2:24,33 cf. discussion of Q3:55 p 165.

[264] Acts 2:33 (cf. Q17:85; 40:15); Matt.25:31-34.

[265] Rev.5:8-14.

[266] 1 Thes.4:15-5:3 cf. Q20:102-08.

[267] Jn 5:22; James 5:7-9 cf. Q1:4; 95:7-8.

[269] Rev.7:9-17 cf. Q39:75; 54:54-55.

[269] 1 Cor.8:6; Heb.1:2.

[270] Jn 1:1-3; 1 Cor.8:6.

[271] Jn 5:26; 6:63; Rom.8:11; 2 Cor.3:6.

[272] Jn 8:44; Rev.12:7-9.

[273] 1 Cor.15:24-28.

[274] Eph.1:20; Phil.2:5-11; Col.1:13, 2:13-15.

[275] Acts 2:33 (cf. Q17:85; 40:15); Lk.24:46-49; Jn 20:21-23; Acts 1:1-5.

[276] Jn 5:22; Rev.19:15-20:15.

[277] 1 Cor.15:24-28; Rev.22:1,3.

[278] Rev.7:14-17; 21:3-8.

[279] Rev.22:1,3.

[280] cf. discussion of this in respect of the Islamic context pp 169-172.

[281] cf. chapter 1 for discussion of this argument put forward by St. Clair Tisdall. The claim of Q6:164, that no one can bear the burden of another before God, has often been used by Muslims to refute Christian belief in the atonement. Here it is alluded to by quoting the similar words of Ps.49:7 that no man can redeem the life of another, to show the necessity of God himself redeeming man.

[282] Q37:107.

[283] Gal.4:4-5; Col.1:15; 1 Jn 4:14.

[284] Rom.1:1-3; Gal.4:4-5 cf. p 167 for discussion of these Islamic arguments.

[285] cf. discussion of 'Sufism' pp 160-161 and Appendix D for an example of such mystical poetry.

[286] Col.1:13-14.

[287] Eph.2:8-9; 2 Tim.1:9.

[288] Phil.2:9-11; Rev.5:9-14.

[289] Tit.3:5-6.

[290] Jn 4:14; Tit.3:5-6; Rev.7:17; 22:1,17 cf. discussion of 'the water of life' in the Islamic context p 163.

[291] Eph.2:1-7.

[292] cf. earlier section of this chapter 'The revelation of 'the great name of God' (Ism al-Azim).

[293] Jn 5:21-27; Rom.2:16.

[294] 1 Jn 2:1; Rev.19:11 cf. also Isa.11:3-5.

[295] Jn 16:7-11.

[296] 1 Jn 1:7-2:2; Rev.20:10-15 cf. Acts 15:11; Eph.2:5-9; 2 Tim.1:9-10.

[297] 1 Cor.13:12; Rev.21:3 cf. pp 152-162 for discussion of this Islamic aspiration.

[298] Rev.21:1-5 cf. Q13:5; 14:48.

CONCLUSIONS

In this study, we have established a basic framework for the contextualisation of christological monotheism in an Islamic context that starts directly from the final form of the NT, rather than being interpreted through the filter of western christological formulations as other christologies that have been.

We have demonstrated that in the Islamic context the *emic* conceptual category primarily used to conceive of monotheism is a bounded extrinsic one. In this God's unique identity is principally known by him being the sole creator, universal ruler and judge of all things.

The NT's use of a similar bounded extrinsic framework gives validity to following the basic structure of the early church's direct inclusion of Jesus within the unique identity of the one God.

However, the differences between the Jewish and Islamic context have required certain adjustments to be made to the early church's contextualisation of christology. These include expanding the extrinsic conceptual framework to identify God as not merely creator, ruler and judge but also as the only saviour; and strengthening of the concept of epiphany, which although present in the Islamic context is not clearly defined.

We have also applied to Jesus various Islamic forms and symbolic motifs relating to God's unique identity, such as the titles 'Lord of the worlds' (*Rabb al-alamin*) and 'Master of the day of judgement' (*Malik Yaum al-Din*); Islamic names of God that occur in the NT as christological titles; and symbolic motifs such as the 'Lord of the water of life' and 'the Bridegroom' who endures thorns and bloodshed to reach his beloved.

The contextualised christology starts from the concept of God dwelling in unapproachable light, that is common to both the Bible and the Qur'an. It builds on widely held Islamic beliefs to present the concept that God can locally manifest a veiled form of his presence in order to relate to his creation, including visibly appearing to human beings on earth. Jesus is then identified as this visible form of the invisible God, through whom the Father created the world, restores his sovereignty over it that has been usurped by hostile powers, judges the world and enacts salvation for mankind.

We have used this bounded extrinsic concept of monotheism to develop an expression of Christian monotheism that clearly distinguishes between the Father, Jesus, and the Spirit without resorting to the concept of 'three divine persons' that has commonly been misunderstood in the Islamic context as implying belief in tri-theism This has been done by focusing on the differing roles of the Father, Jesus and the Spirit in carrying out the actions of creation, universal rule, salvation and eschatological judgement. The Father planning salvation, Jesus being sent to carry out the actual act of salvation and the Holy Spirit being sent to renew those who repent of their sins, and so forth.

This study has had a number of qualitative limitations. Firstly, the metacultural grid we have used has allowed us to obtain an approximation to the *emic* conceptual categories in the second temple and Islamic contexts. However, as the conceptual categories in this metacultural grid are based on generalisations derived from a range of cultures, they are still ultimately *etic* categories that at best only approximate to *emic* categories.

Secondly, the need to compare an ancient context, that of second temple Judaism, with a contemporary one, that of Islamic monotheism, has necessitated the use of texts as indicators of beliefs. However, although texts both inculcate beliefs and provide a degree of legitimation for them, they only provide a direct window into the beliefs of the authors themselves and any groups that the authors are directly representative of. Whilst the circulation of texts is likely to imply that readers have at least a degree of sympathy with the beliefs they contain, the texts do not in themselves provide a direct window into the beliefs of the community as a whole.

Thirdly, in the second temple context this situation is complicated still further by the absence of any extant texts from groups such as the Sadducees and Zealots and the destruction of many MSS considered 'unorthodox' by post-Christian rabbinical leaders. As the latter almost certainly included a number of pre-Christian texts with interpretations favourable to later Christian claims, it is difficult to assess accurately the extent to which there were specific Jewish antecedents for subsequent Christian claims.

This study has also had certain limitations in respect of its scope: firstly it has only sought to establish a basic framework for the development of a contextualised christology, based on the conceptual categories commonly used in the Islamic context, together with some indicators of forms and symbolic motifs that may appropriately be used in such a contextualisation. Although the final form of any contextualisation is rightly the domain of the local church, it is to be hoped that this study will provide a basis for this development; secondly, this study has focused on the question of how christological monotheism may be contextualised, as this has frequently been the aspect of Christian belief that Muslims have found most difficult to comprehend. However, we have made only passing reference to other aspects of christology, such as Jesus' humanity, or indeed to other aspects of the Christian doctrine of God, such as the Spirit. These areas clearly merit further research in the development of a full contextualisation of Christian monotheism.

GLOSSARY OF KEY ISLAMIC TERMS

All words are Arabic unless indicated otherwise by the letters {P} Persian or {U} Urdu.

Ab-i-hayat – 'the water of life', which according to Persian mystical poetry is supposed to impart eternal life to whoever drinks it {P}.

Adab – custom.

Ahadith – plural of *Hadith* (q.v.). *Ahadith* together with the *Qur'an* form the Islamic scriptures.

Ahl-i-Hadith – Islamic reform movement in the Indian sub-continent stressing reliance on the *Qur'an* and *Ahadith*, rather than Islamic tradition. Adherents profess to hold the views of the early Islamic group known as the *Ahl al-Hadith* who opposed the *Mu'tazila* {P/U}.

'Alim – Islamic teacher who has completed the most advanced course at a *madrasa* (q.v.).

al-Ashari – Scholastic theologian (d.c.930) who led the reaction against the rationalism of the *Mu'tazila* (q.v.), which came to be regarded as 'orthodox' kalam by many Muslims.

Awliya – plural of *wali* (q.v.).

Azan – the public call to prayer announced by the *muezzin* (q.v.).

al-Baidawi – (d. c.1283-91) author of a classical commentary on the *Qur'an* that forms part of the *Dars-i-Nizami* curriculum.

Barelvi – movement in the Indian subcontinent that originated in opposition to the *Deobandis* (q.v.) that stressed the legitimacy of existing religious practices {U}.

Bid'a – innovation in religion.

Bila kayfa wa la tashbih – aspect of *Kalam* proposed by al-Ashari stating that one should accept the Qur'anic statements concerning the sight of God without asking how, or making comparisons.

al-Dajjal al-Masih – the antichrist who according to *Ahadith* Jesus will kill on his return to earth. This figure is not referred to in the *Qur'an*, only in *Ahadith*.

Dars-i-Nizami - the curriculum used in most Sunni *madrasas* in the Indo-Persian world {P/U}.

Deobandi – Islamic reform movement originating in nineteenth century India that rejects many indigenous practices as 'unislamic' {U}.

Dhat – the essence or inner being of God (*Sufism and Kalam*).

Fakir – wandering Islamic mystic, sometimes used synonymously with *pir* (q.v.).

al-Fatihah – the opening *surah* of the *Qur'an*, recited daily by many Muslims.

Fikh – Islamic jurisprudence.

Fikh Akbar 1,2 – Islamic creeds.

Ghazzal – love poems based on court praise. The term is used in both the Urdu and Persian Bibles for the 'Song of Solomon' {P/U}.

Gulistan – literally 'the rose garden', a renowned collection of poems by Sa'di stressing the need to prepare oneself for the next life by appropriate actions in this life {P}.

Hadith – tradition relating a saying of or aspect of the life of Muhammad (plural is *Ahadith*).

Hafiz – 1. 'The Guardian' - one of the 99 Islamic names of God; 2. One who has memorised the entire *Qur'an*; 3. Renowned Persian poet famous for his *ghazzals*.

al-Hallaj – renowned medieval Sufi (also popularly known as *Mansur*) who was crucified for heresy after claiming 'I am the Truth'.

Hikmat – wisdom.

Ijtehad – interpretation of the *Qur'an*.

'Isa – Qur'anic name for Jesus.

Ism al-Dhat – the name of the essence of God in *Kalam*.

Ism al-Sifat – the names of the attributes of God in *Kalam*.

al-Jalalain – al-Mahalli (d.1495) and al-Suyuti (d.1505) authors of a classical commentary/paraphrase of the *Qur'an* that forms part of the *Dars-i-Nizami* curriculum.

Kalam – Islamic systematic theology.

Kashf al-Mahjub – the oldest Persian work on Sufism, written by al-Hujwiri (c.1042) {P}.

Karamat – miracles of the saints.

Khizr – figure in Islamic tradition supposed to have drunk from the water of life and gained immortality. Some classical commentators including Baidawi identified him with the mysterious figure who, the *Qur'an* narrates, accompanied Moses in the desert (Q18:60-82).

Laila – cf. *Majnun* {P/U}.

Madrasa – Islamic theological college.

Majnun – popular story of a boy (*Majnun*) who fell in love with a nomad girl (*Laila*) and wandered constantly in search of her. Often used as a poetic metaphor of the soul's search for God {P/U}.

Malang – Sufi follower of Zindu Shah Madar, but often used for any wandering mendicant {P/U}.

Masnavi – any epic Persian poem, but commonly used to refer specifically to the *Masnavi* of Rumi, a highly revered work of Persian poetry that shows significant influences of Sufism {P}.

Mawdudi – (1903-79), widely regarded in the Indian subcontinent as the leading twentieth century islamist writer, author of a commentary on the *Qur'an*.

Mi'raj – Muhammad's reputed night ascension to the highest heaven, reported in the *Qur'an* and *Ahadith*.

Mishkat al-Masabih – collection of *Ahadith* used in the *Dars-i-Nizami* curriculum.

al-Mudabbir – designation of God as the 'administrator' of the heavens and the earth, used by Shah Wali Allah.

Muezzin – the announcer of the public call to prayer (*azan*).

Mujtahid – Literally 'One who strives' to achieve a high position of learning and scholarship, the highest title of learning among the *ulema* (q.v.).

Mullah – Islamic teacher {P/U}.

Murid – disciple who has made a commitment to obeying the *tariqa* of a particular *pir*.

Mu'tazila – early Islamic group who from the second century of the Islamic era applied reason to the interpretation of the *Qur'an* and claimed that the *Qur'an* was created and not co-eternal with God.

Muwahiddun – 'Unitarians', self designation of the Wahhabi movement (q.v.) founded in Arabia by Muhammad Abd al-Wahhab (1703-1792), that emphasises strict monotheism and rejects all forms of saint veneration.

Na'at – hymns venerating Muhammad {U}.

Noor-i-Muhammad – 'Light of Muhammad', doctrine associated with *wahdat al-wujud* Sufism that claims Muhammad was an emanation of the light of God. The doctrine was vigorously defended by Ahmad Riza Khan in opposition to the *Deobandi* movement {P}.

Pir – Muslim saint {P/U}.

Qazi – publicly appointed Islamic judge.

Qessas al-anbiya – 'Stories of the prophets', non canonical collection of stories about prophets including Adam, Moses, Jesus and Muhammad.

(Sayyid) Qutb – (1906-66) author of a radical islamist commentary on the *Qur'an* .

Rabb – Lord, used in in the *Qur'an* in combinations such as *Rabb al-alamin* ('Lord of the worlds'), *Rabb al-'arsh* ('Lord of the Throne'), *Rabb kull shay* ('Lord of all things' etc.).

Riwaj – Custom {U}.

Rumi - renowned Persian poet famous for his *Masnavi*, which has sometimes been called 'the *Qur'an* of Persia'.

Sa'di – renowned Persian poet, whose Persian poems are contained in the *Gulistan*. Also reputed to have been the first to compose Urdu poetry.

Salat – ritual prayers supposed to be performed five times daily.

Shahada – the confession 'There is no God but Allah and Muhammad is his apostle'.

Sifat al-Dhat – the essence of God (*Kalam*).

Sifat al-fi'l - description of the actions of God (*Kalam*).

Sufi – practitioner of Sufism (q.v.), *murid* ('disciple') of a *pir* who follows a *tariqa* ('path') with the aim of achieving wasl ('union') with the divine.

Sufism – Islamic mysticism and in a narrower sense, the following of a spiritual guide along a *tariqa* ('path') with the aim of achieving *wasl* ('union') with the divine.

Suliman – Qur'anic name for Solomon.

Surah – one of the 114 chapters of the *Qur'an*.

Tafsir – commentary on the *Qur'an*.

Takbir – the expression *Allahu Akbar* ('God is great') which forms part of the *salat*.

Taqlid – conformity to traditional *ijtedhad* (q.v.).

Tariqa – path of spiritual exercises and disciplines followed by a *Sufi* to achieve *wasl* ('union') with God.

Tasbih – rosary.

Tawhid – monotheism.

Ta'wil al-Hadith – summary lives of the prophets written by the Indian Islamic reformer Shah Wali Allah.

Ulema – Plural of *'alim* (q.v.).

Wahhabi - Islamic reform movement originating in Arabia that rejects many religious practices including *Sufism* as unislamic.

Wahdat al-wujud - concept of *tawhid* associated with the Sufism of Ibn al-'Arabi that understands all things to be an emanation of the being of God (cf. *wahdat al-shuhud* for an alternative *Sufi* view of *tawhid*).

Wahdat al-shuhud – *Sufi* concept of *tawhid* that sharply distinguishes God from all else and understands *wasl* ('union') with God in terms of a reflection of God in the believer's heart (cf. *wahdat al-wujud* for an alternative *Sufi* view of *tawhid*).

Wali – saint, Arabic equivalent of *pir* (q.v.).

Wasl – mystical union with God {P}.

Yahya ibn Zakariya - Qur'anic name for John the Baptist.

APPENDIX A

Evolutionary Christology

'Evolutionary Christology' refers to various hypotheses claiming that as Christianity moved out of its monotheistic Jewish origins into the Gentile world, its christology gradually evolved until ultimately Jesus was regarded as divine, which was something wholly inconsistent with what he himself had intended.

The theory can be traced back to the 'Deism' of seventeenth century writers such as Reimarus (1694-1768), which sought to replace traditional views of religion with rationalistic ones. Although deists did not reject the concept of God *per se*, they did reject the idea of God revealing himself in history. As such they discarded any doctrine based on claims that the scriptures were divinely inspired. This led to the assumption that Jesus himself never taught that he was divine, or even intended his followers to believe him to be so.

In the nineteenth century D.F. Strauss' *The Life of Jesus* (1835) developed the evolutionary theory using the historical-critical method. Strauss' christology was based on a denial of the possibility of the supernatural. This presupposition logically led him to assume that there could be no such thing as miracles. Therefore the miracle stories in the NT could not be authentic, but must have been created by the early church. Strauss claimed that the Gospels were basically myths invented by pious followers of Jesus who wanted to claim that he had been the messiah spoken of in the OT. However, as the OT spoke of the coming messiah performing miracles, the Gospel writers had to invent miracle stories such as Jesus healing the blind and raising the dead in order to prove that he was the messiah. Struass' *Life of Jesus* led to what became known as 'the Quest for the historical Jesus' which was based on the application to the Gospels of the historical critical method, frequently combined with the anti-supernatural assumptions.

In the twentieth century, the evolutionary theory came to prominence with W. Bousset's *Kyrios Christos* [1913], the fifth edition of which was published as late as 1964 with an English translation in 1970.[1] Bousset's theory claimed that when Christianity moved into places such as Antioch in the gentile world, it became open to influences from pagan Hellenistic religion. This was the form of Christianity that Paul received and developed further to speak of Christ as a mystical spiritual power. An important refinement of Bousset's ideas appeared in F. Hahn's 1963 *The Titles of Jesus in Christology*, which appeared in English in 1969. Hahn argued that the various christological titles found in the NT evolved as Christianity moved through various stages, beginning with the Aramaic speaking Jerusalem church, then a Hellenistic Jewish Church, and finally a Hellenistic Gentile Church, which was influenced by pagan concepts of apotheosis. According to Hahn, in the first stage Jesus was only viewed as a coming apocalyptic figure, first called 'Lord' in the second stage to indicate his role as coming judge, and only in the third stage did the designation 'Lord', begin to express the divinity of Jesus. It is claimed that the final form of the NT text represents the reworking of earlier traditions to incorporate third stage beliefs about Jesus, in the narratives about Jesus and the early Church. The evidence cited in support of such a hypothesis primarily derives from the application of the 'criterion of dissimilarity', which states that any teaching of Jesus which distinguishes him from both the Judaism of his day and the early Church may be regarded as authentic. The negative application of this criterion made many NT scholars reluctant to accept the authenticity of any Gospel traditions of Jesus' sayings that were in continuity with the later beliefs of the early Church.[2]

Although in recent years P.M. Casey has produced a more nuanced version of the evolutionary hypothesis in his book *From Jewish Prophet to Gentile God*, [3] evolutionary christology no longer enjoys widespread acceptance among NT scholars.

In the Islamic world the use of evolutionary christology can be traced back to the translation into English of Strauss' *Life of Jesus* in 1846. This made it accessible to a number of Muslims in North India who were seeking to find new material, which could improve the effectiveness of the attacks they had for some time been making on the teachings of Christian missionaries. Their use of Strauss' writings in the 1853 Agra debate they initiated with Pfander and French resulted in them in achieving at least the semblance of public success. The main Muslim protagonist at this debate, Rahmat Allah Kairanawi, subsequently included the evolutionary theory he had learned from Strauss in his *Izhar al-Haq*, which he claimed was a response to Pfander's *Mizan al-Haq*. Rahmat Allah's work marked the beginning of a continuous use of evolutionary christology by Muslim writers of anti-Christian polemical literature.

On first acquaintance evolutionary christology could appear to present a Jesus similar to Islamic claims, in that he is not divine. However, evolutionary theories such as those of Strauss cannot validly be claimed to support the Islamic view of Jesus as they are based on a denial that Jesus was the messiah and performed miracles, both of which the *Qur'an* affirms. Furthermore, it will be clear from the above outline of the origins of evolutionary christology, that historically the theory has been underpinned by that the denial of the very possibility of supernatural events such as divine revelation and the possibility of miracles. Clearly any acceptance of such presuppositions would refute Islamic belief in the 'miracle' of the *Qur'an* and Muhammad's prophethood every bit as much as it does Christian belief. Therefore the Muslim use of the evolutionary theory, which began at the Agra debate, was in no sense challenging the missionaries 'on their own ground' as some scholars have asserted.[4] In fact, it was not until the publication of St. Clair Tisdall's *The Sources of Islam* nearly half a century later (1900) that Christian missionaries even began to write books for Muslims which used the historical-critical method to critique Islam.[5] Significantly, even Tisdall was extremely careful to use this method only in a way that was consistent with belief in the supernatural. Had Rahmat Allah Kairanawi half a century earlier followed a similar careful and critical appraisal of Strauss' theory of evolutionary christology, then the animosity inculcated by a considerable volume of polemical literature might conceivably have been somewhat lessened.

APPENDIX B

Second Temple Jewish Monotheism and the Origins of NT Christology: The Scholarly Debate

In this study we have used a series of anthropological categories in order to help determine the conceptual categories (bounded/unbounded; extrinsic/intrinsic) by which God's unique identity was conceived by Jews in the second temple era, and in the present day by Sunni Muslims in the Islamic context, respectively. The use of these categories as a metacultural grid, enables us to move beyond the conceptual categories used in our own culture, and is therefore an important tool in understanding how the earliest Jewish christology developed in relation to its Jewish context. This is particularly important in assessing the various paths of christological development that in recent years have been proposed by NT scholars. In fact, the primary difference between these hypotheses lies in their understanding of how second temple Jews conceived of monotheism, and the scope that this allowed the early Church to develop its christology, without being perceived to have breached the limits of Jewish monotheism.

A hypothesis that may be termed 'strict monotheist', is based on the implicit assumption that second temple Jews conceived of the identity of God in 'bounded intrinsic' terms. This means that Jews believed that an absolute boundary existed between God and all else. The strict monotheist position also implicitly assumes that God could be known in his ontological nature, so that there would have been no possibility of confusing another figure merely exercising divine functions on God's behalf, with God himself. Scholars holding to the strict monotheist position, argue that although the early church might have ascribed functional divinity to Jesus whilst remaining within the bounds of Judaism, it could not have conceived of him as being ontologically God without breaching the limits of Jewish monotheism. Such an understanding of second temple monotheism, therefore leads to the conclusion that this theological development must have happened very late, after the parting of the ways between Christianity and Judaism. Dunn for example, argues that the earliest church understood Jesus to be the climactic embodiment of God's power and purpose. He claims that although the early Church initially understood Jesus to have been designated the 'Son of God' at the resurrection, the Church progressively understood this appointment to have occurred at earlier and earlier times. However, it was only in the post Pauline era that this led to Jesus being understood to have been pre-existent in heaven, and not until the writing of the Fourth Gospel with its full blown Logos christology, that the early Church claimed that Jesus was on the God side of the God/non-God divide, speaking of him as God-incarnate.[6] In essence, Dunn is arguing that before the break with Judaism, Jesus was only understood to have carried out divine functions on behalf of God, not to be God himself. Consequently, during the Pauline era Jesus was never worshipped, as this would have been incompatible with Judaism. He was merely venerated.

The strict monotheist position therefore makes an important, though only implicit assumption, that Jews believed that God could be known in his ontological inner being or nature, rather than merely by how he acted. In fact, the assertion that Jews would have clearly understood that the ascription to Jesus of divine functions, including rule of the entire cosmos, did not imply a claim to divine ontology, requires the assumption that second temple Jews *primarily* conceived of God's identity in terms of his inner being i.e. in intrinsic terms.[7] Somewhat surprisingly, strict monotheist scholars such as Dunn, simply assume this conceptual understanding of monotheism, rather than substantiating it. However, whilst our earlier analysis of a range of second temple texts clearly demonstrated that God was primarily conceived of in bounded terms, we failed to find any unequivocal evidence that God was conceived of in intrinsic terms.

A further implicit assumption commonly made by scholars holding to the strict monotheist position, is that not only did second temple Jews draw the boundary between God and non-God very sharply i.e. 'bounded monotheism', but that boundary excluded the possibility of God appearing on earth in human form.[8] However our analysis of second temple Judaism in chapter 2, has demonstrated that although Jews of this period normally did draw an absolute boundary between God and all else, this did not preclude the possibility of God visibly appearing on earth in an apparently anthropomorphic form. Indeed for many Jews this was something that according to the OT, God had done in the past when he had appeared on earth to enact salvation on behalf of his people, most notably at the exodus. Moreover, they expected him to do so in the future when he appeared as eschatological judge on the 'Day of YHWH'. Whilst this certainly does not mean that that most, or indeed any second temple Jews expected God to appear as an actual contemporary human being, it does mean that there was considerably greater room for the development of divine christology within Judaism than strict monotheist scholars such as Dunn have allowed for.

A response to the strict monotheist position is what may be termed a 'revisionist' reading of the Jewish context of early christological development. This position also assumes that Jews conceived of God in 'intrinsic' terms, but suggests that at least some Jews believed that the boundary between God and all else was considerably more flexible than strict monotheist scholars allow. Revisionist scholars contend that some Jews believed in semi-divine beings with degrees of divinity.[9] They have argued that figures such as personified divine attributes, certain exalted patriarchs and principal angels acted as YHWH's grand vizier in relation to his creation. They were therefore regarded as functionally, though not ontologically divine.[10] According to the revisionist hypothesis, this conceptual category of 'functional divinity' enabled the early Church to develop a high christology while remaining within the bounds of Judaism and was the conceptual stepping stone that eventually enabled full ontological divinity to be ascribed to Jesus.

Although, like the strict monotheist position, the revisionist hypothesis requires the assumption that second temple Jews conceived of God in 'intrinsic' terms, it is distinguished from the strict monotheist position by its assumption that at least some Jews understood the boundary between God and all else to have a degree of permeability i.e. it assumes '(partly) unbounded intrinsic monotheism'. The revisionist hypothesis does at least have the advantage over the strict monotheist position of claiming that there were second temple precedents for the early Church's supposed initial ascription of functional, but not ontological divinity to Jesus. However, a closer examination of these claimed precedents, gives no unequivocal evidence of second temple Jews believing that heavenly beings could be functionally but not ontologically divine. Apart from divine attributes, which we earlier argued were never seen as distinct from YHWH himself, the case for semi-divine intermediary beings rests largely on contested interpretations of a very small number of marginal Judeo-Hellenistic texts.[11]

The revisionist hypothesis can only explain the NT's clear ascription of divine functions to Jesus, if it is assumed that this '(partly) unbounded intrinsic' conception of monotheism, was sufficiently widespread within second temple Judaism for it to be clearly understood that the church was ascribing functional but not ontological divinity to Jesus. However, our survey of the second temple evidence suggests that even if any Jews did believe in semi divine beings, this was a very marginal belief that was not at all widespread in second temple Judaism. Hence, had the early Jewish Church really used such ideas as conceptual stepping-stones in its articulation of who Jesus was, it would have contextualised its christology to only one marginal segment of Judaism, rather than to Judaism as a whole. This scarcely fits the phenomenal growth of the early Jewish Church, which does not appear to have been even largely confined to such marginal groups. Indeed Luke's account appears to stress the appeal of Christianity to Jews of all backgrounds.[12]

Our analysis of second temple texts by means of an anthropological grid of conceptual categories, has in fact demonstrated that most Jews appear to have at least *primarily* conceived of God in 'bounded extrinsic' terms i.e. as emphatically distinct from everything else and whose identity was primarily known by how he related to all else, as for example, the sole creator, ruler of all things, final eschatological judge and only saviour. Therefore, had the early Church ascribed similar divine titles and roles to the heavenly Jesus, but only intended thereby to describe Jesus as being functionally but not ontologically divine, it is likely that considerable confusion would have resulted, not least in its evangelism. Such descriptions would have been understood by many Jews as a claim that Jesus was the supreme God.

Our analysis of Jewish monotheism as being primarily conceived in 'bounded extrinsic' terms, is supported by the work of Hiebert, who as an anthropologist and missiologist applied this framework to OT monotheism.[13] It is also supported by the work of Bauckham who has drawn similar conclusions from a theological analysis of a much wider range of second temple literature.[14] Bauckham, who is unusually both an historical theologian and NT scholar, implicitly criticises a number of NT scholars, for imposing the conceptual categories commonly used in western theology back onto the Biblical and second temple evidence. He argues that the intrinsic conception of monotheism familiar to western Christians from patristic creeds,[15] was a conceptual category that simply did not exist in second temple Judaism, but was later used in Nicene theology to resist the Platonic understandings of Jesus' divinity inherent in Arianism.[16] He further, and for our purposes most significantly, argues that this bounded extrinsic understanding of monotheism, enabled the early Jewish Church to maintain continuity with second temple monotheism. According to Bauckham, the early church deliberately used the extrinsic framework of second temple monotheism, God being understood as sole creator and unique sovereign over all things, in order to include Jesus within the unique identity of YHWH. Bauckham's application of this framework to the NT has so far concentrated on the Pauline Epistles, the Fourth Gospel and Revelation. However, in chapter 3 we demonstrate that in all the major sections of the NT that have a Jewish *Sitz im Leben*, this framework is directly and consistently used to include Jesus within the unique identity of YHWH the only God, whilst maintaining significant continuity with the way that second temple Jews understood monotheism.

APPENDIX C

Profile of Islamic Texts

1. *Qur'an*

For the purposes of this study unless otherwise indicated we have used the English translation of the *Qur'an* made in Lahore by A. Yusuf Ali as this represents a Muslim understanding of the *Qur'an*.

2. *Ahadith*

The *Mishkat al-Masabih* which is a selection of *Ahadith* drawn from the canonical collections.[17] As the main *Ahadith* text of the *Dars-i-Nizami*, this is taught in *madrasas* across the Indian subcontinent and is thus likely to be the main source of *Ahadith* which the *ulema* trained in such *madrasas* transmit in their teaching.

3. Classical *Tafsir*

The *tafsir* of the Jalalain and Baidawi, which form a central part of the *Dars-i-Nizami* curriculum.[18]

We have also examined a number of texts, which although not having the same degree of universal acceptance, do to some extent cut across sectarian divides. These are:

4. The Islamist *tafsir*

We have principally examined *Tafhim al-Qur'an* of Sayyid Abdul A'la Mawdudi (1903-1979CE),[19] who is widely regarded in the Indian subcontinent as the leading Islamist writer of the past century.[20] However, we have also make occasional reference to the *Fi Zilal al-Qur'an* of the Egyptian Islamist Sayyid Qutb (1906-1966CE).[21]

5. *Kalam*

Although this study would have been incomplete without some discussion of *kalam* (systematic theology), its importance is limited. Once one moves significantly beyond the simple statements of the *shahada*, *kalam* becomes increasingly inaccessible to the populace and largely confined to the domain of the educated *ulema*. Indeed, Fazlur Rahman speaks of the development of *kalam* as Islam being launched 'on a career where its dogmatic formulations had only a partial and indirect relationship to the living realities of the faith'.[22]

As well as the scholastic theology represented by *kalam* we have also referred to other aspects of Islamic theology that are specific to individual groupings, including Sufism, where these are relevant to our study.

We have also examined a number of popular Islamic texts:

6. *Qessas al-anbiya*

This non-canonical collection of stories about the prophets has achieved great popularity. This is almost certainly due to its narrative style being much more accessible than other Islamic texts in a society where oral transmission is still the major means of communication, and the vast majority have not attained written literacy.[23]

7. *Ta'wil al-Hadith*

This work in many ways mirrors *Qessas al-anbiya*, but was produced by the reformer and populariser of Indian Islam Shah Wali Allah, whose work is viewed with great respect by many Muslims who look to the reformist pole of Islam.[24]

8. Mystical poetry

The oral transmission of poetry forms an important part of many Islamic cultures and much of this poetry is of a mystical character. The works of Persian poets such as Rumi, Hafiz and Sa'di are not only significant in themselves, but also form the archetype on which mystical poetry in many other languages is modelled.[25] We have therefore examined the *Masnavi* of Rumi, whose importance is such that it has been called 'the *Qur'an* of Persia'.[26] This is the only poetry we have examined which contains explicitly Sufi statements; The *Ghazzals* of Hafiz, love poems based on court praise, a poetic form Hafiz is popularly regarded as the perfector of; and the *Gulistan* of Sa'di, a form of poetry which focus on the need to prepare oneself for the next life by appropriate actions in the present. Sa'di is reputed to be have been the first to compose Urdu poetry,[27] and is claimed by Browne to enjoy the greatest reputation of any Persian poet.[28]

APPENDIX D

The Effect of Gender Reversal Reading on the Lover/Beloved Imagery in mystical Poetry

Examples of the poetry of Hafiz and Rahman Baba (1653-1711) the most renowned Pushtu poet which illustrate how when reading existing poetry, a simple reversal of gender roles can result in God being portrayed as the (male) lover, who endures bloodshed from thorns in order to reach the (female) beloved:

Rose and Nightingale (Hafiz)[29]

I walked within a garden fair
At dawn, to gather roses there;
When suddenly sounded in the dale
The singing of a nightingale.

Alas, he loved a rose, like me,
And he, too, loved in agony;
Tumbling upon the mead he sent
The cataract of his lament.

With sad and meditative pace
I wandered in that flowery place,
And thought upon the tragic tale
Of love, and rose, and nightingale.

The rose was lovely, as I tell;
The nightingale he loved her well;
He with no other love could live,
And she no kindly word would give.

It moved me strangely, as I heard
The singing of that passionate bird;
So much it moved me, I could not
Endure the burden of his throat.

Full many a fair and fragrant rose
Within the garden freshly blows,
Yet not a bloom was ever torn
Without the wounding of the thorn...

Either –or (Rahman Baba)[30]

A man who can't forsake
For his beloved's sake
His peace of mind, his heart and soul
Is nothing but a fake...

If in this quest you fail,
Put up your pride for sale;
Remove your turban and exchange
It for a woman's veil

A million there may be
Of your calamities –
What matter? Quantity does not
Add up to quality

When you will save your life,
When you avoid the knife,
How shall as a warrior of love
You conquer in the strife?

A moth that never came
Close to the candle flame –
A nightingale that missed the rose –
My brother, what a shame!

You're no Majnun who stakes
His all for Laila's sake.[31]
Nor a Mansur who pays the price[32]
Supreme upon the stake.

Obey the silent voice,
Rahman, and make your choice:
You either shall frustrate your life
Or in the friend rejoice.

Endnotes

[1] W. Bousset *Kyrios Christos: A History of the Belief in Christ from the Beginnings of Christianity to Irenaeus* ET by J.E. Steely from German 5th edn (1964*)* [Nashville:Abingdon,1970] passim. L. Hurtado has recently produced a monumental refutation of Boussett's *Kyrios Christos* in his magnum opus *Lord Jesus Christ* [Cambridge:Eerdmans.2003].

[2] For concise overviews of the development of this theory a) from Reimarus to Strauss cf. S.N. Williams 'Deism' *NDT* 190 and H. Harris 'Strauss, David Friedrich' *NDT* 663 b) from Bousset to Hahn cf. I.H. Marshall *The Origins of New Testament Christology* [Leicester:Apollos,2nd edn,1990] 15-26.

[3] P.M. Casey *From Jewish Prophet to Gentile God* [Cambridge:James Clarke,1991] passim.

[4] e.g. H. Goddard *Muslim Perceptions of Christianity* [London:Grey Seal,1996] 50.

[5] As we demonstrated in Chapter 1, what missionaries such as Martyn and Pfander primarily did was to respond to the five standard proofs of the truth of Islam, which the *ulema* presented as an argument against Christianity.

[6] This is developed in a number of Dunn's works, but particularly in *Christology in the Making* [London: SCM,2nd edn.1989] passim and *The Partings of the Ways* [London:SCM,1991] passim.

[7] Dunn *Christology* 42-43 claims that Paul could not have introduced a doctrine of incarnation in his epistles *because* this would have created confusion and misunderstanding concerning the nature of Christ's lordship.

[8] Dunn *Christology* 149-62 acknowledges that in the OT it is frequently impossible to distinguish the angel of the Lord from YHWH himself, but dismisses it as simply a literary figure for God's active concern for man 'whatever the historical actuality behind these narratives' (150). However, he fails to provide any evidence that second temple Jews understood OT *malak YHWH* narratives in this way.

[9] cf. the title of a recent Ph.D. thesis that developed this hypothesis: K.S. Ellis *'Degrees of Divinity': The Importance of the Role of Mediatorial Figures for an Understanding of Jewish Monotheism and the Development of Christological Beliefs* [unpublished Ph.D. thesis London Bible College/Brunel University,1996].

[10] L.W. Hurtado has particularly developed this hypothesis in *One God, One Lord* [1988, 2nd rev'd edn Edinburgh:T&T Clark,1998] passim, However, he does not focus on this in his more recent works such as *At the Origins of Christian Worship* [Carlisle:Paternoster,1999]; 'The Binitarian Shape of Early Christian Worship' 187-213 in C.C. Newman, J.R. Davila & G.S Lewis (eds) *The Jewish Roots of Christological Monotheism* [Brill:Leiden,1999] and his magnum opus *Lord Jesus Christ* [Cambridge:Eerdmans.2003]. He has however consistently argued that only divine functions and not divine worship could be shared in this way.

[11] Principally, *Orphica* and *The Exagoge* both of which we earlier argued do not depict beings who are functionally but not ontologically divine cf. pp 50-51.

[12] e.g. Acts.2:5-12 cf. :41 (Diaspora Jews); 4:34ff (landowners and poor); 5:14 (men and women); 6:1 (Hebraic and Hellenistic Jews); 6:5 (ethnic Jews and proselytes); 6:7 (Priests); 8:26-40;10:1-48 (Gentile godfearers); 9:31 (Galileans and Samarians); 15:5 (Pharisees); 9:35 (*all* who lived in Lydda and Sharon) cf. also 5:13.

[13] P. Hiebert *Anthropological Reflections on Missiological Issues* [Grand Rapids:Baker,1994] 124-25.

[14] Although R. Bauckham in his *The Theology of the Book of Revelation* [Cambridge:CUP,1993] 62-63 cautiously appeared to accept that the early Jewish Church may for a brief period have accorded Jesus functional but not ontological divinity, his latest work on christology *God Crucified* [Carlisle:Paternoster,1998] passim clearly enunciates the view that most Jews of that time simply did not think in such conceptual categories (cf. esp. 1-22).

[15] cf. for example the intrinsic statements of the Creed of Nicea (325CE), the Nicene (381CE) and Athanasian (c.500CE) creeds that Jesus is of one 'substance' with the Father.

[16] Bauckham *Crucified* passim but cf. esp. 77-79. Bauckham does not himself use extrinsic/intrinsic terminology. However, his contrast of Jewish categories of 'identity' i.e. who God is in relation to all else, with Greek categories of 'nature' i.e. what God is in his inner being, is essentially synonymous with these terms.

[17] In view of the existence of a number of different editions of the *Mishkat al-Masabih* with minor variations in arrangement, we have attached subject headings to numerical references to facilitate access by the reader. The edition used here is the Arabic/English diglot *Al-Hadis: An English Translation and Commentary of Mishkat-ul-Masabih* by al-Haj Maulana Fazlul Karim 4 vols [Lahore:Sh.Mhd.Ashraf, n.d. but first published 1938] (referred to in footnotes as 'MM'). A concise summary of the *Mishkat al-Masabih* can be found in W. Goldsack *Selections from Muhammadan Traditions* [Madras:Christian Literature Society for India,1923] passim which draws exclusively on this collection.

[18] *Tafsir al-Jalalain* by Jalaluddin Muhammad bin Ahmad al-Shafi'i al Mahalli (d.1459) and Jalaluddin 'Abdur Rahman bin Abu Bakr al-Suyiti (d.1505CE) (referred to in the text as 'the Jalalain *tafsir*'); *Anwar al-Tanzil wa Asrar al-Ta'awil* by Qadi Nasriruddin Abu Sa'id 'Abdullah bin 'Umar al-Baidawi (d.c.1282-1291). cf. 'Bibliography' for a list of English translations from Arabic of these *tafsir*.

[19] Sayyid Abul A'la Mawdudi *Tafhim al-Qur'an* ET by Zafar Ishaq Ansari as *Towards Understanding the Qur'an* [Leicester:The Islamic Foundation,1988] (referred to in the text as 'Mawdudi *Tafhim*').

[20] 'Islamist' denotes one seeking to create an Islamic political ideology, not to be confused with 'Islamicist' denoting one engaged in scholarly study of Islam.

[21] Sayyid Qutb *Fi Zilal al-Qur'an* ET by M.A. Salahi & A.A. Shamis as *In the Shade of the Qur'an* [Leicester:The Islamic Foundation,1979-99] (referred to in the text as 'Qutb *Zilal*').

[22] F. Rahman *Islam* [London:Weidenfeld & Nicolson,1966] 90.

[23] There are numerous editions of *Qessas al-anbiya*. The edition we refer to is *Qissasul Anbiya: Stories of the Holy Prophets* ET by Badr Azimabadi [New Dehli:Saeed International,1984].

[24] Shah Waliullah *Ta'awil al-Hadith* ET by G.N. Jalbani [Lahore:Sh.Muhmmad Ashraf,1991].

[25] So, J.T.P. de Bruijn *Persian Sufi Poetry* [Richmond:Curzon,1977] 1-2.

[26] So, R.A. Nicholson *The Mystics of Islam* [1914 - reprint Lahore:Islamic Book Service,1997] 96.

[27] So, E.G. Browne *Literary History of Persia* [1906 - reprint New Dehli:Munshiram Manoharlal,1997] 2:532.

[28] Browne *Literary* 2:525,533.

[29] ET by A.J. Arberry in Ramezani (ed) *Hafiz* 173, used by kind permission of Mrs Anna Evans.

[30] ET by J. Enevoldsen in *The Nightingale of Peshawar* [Peshawar:InterLit,1993] 69 used by kind permission of InterLit Foundation.

[31] A popular folk story of a boy (Majnun) who fell in love with a nomad girl (Laila) and constantly wandered in search of her.

[32] A reference to the medieval Sufi al-Hallaj's crucifixion for declaring 'I am The Truth'.

Bibliography

Primary Sources
a) Second Temple Judaism

-   Hebrew OT: *Biblia Hebraica Stuttgartensia* ed. K. Ellinger & W. Rudoph [Stuttgart:Deutsche Bibelgesellschaft, 4th corrected edn,1990].
-   LXX: *LXX Septuaginta* ed. A. Rahlfs [Stuttgart: Deutsche Bibelgesellschaft,1935].
-   *Greek New Testament* ed. K. Aland, M. Black, C.M. Martini, B.M. Metzger & A. Wikgren [Stuttgart:United Bible Societies/Deutsche Bibelgesellschaft, 4th edn, 1994].
-   OT Apocrypha: in *The Revised English Bible* [Cambridge:CUP,1989,1996].
-   Pseudepigrapha: *The Old Testament Pseudepigrapha* ed. J.H. Charlesworth:
    -   *Volume 1 Apocalyptic Literature and Testaments* [New York: Doubleday,1983].
    -   *Volume 2 Expansions of the 'Old Testament' and Legends, Wisdom and Philosophical Literature, Prayers, Psalms and Odes, Fragments of Lost Judeo-Hellenistic Works* [New York:Doubleday,1985].
-   *The Complete Dead Sea Scrolls* ET by G. Vermes [London:Penguin,1998].
-   *Philo with an English Translation* by F.H. Colson and G.H. Whitaker [London:Heinemann,1929 – reprinted 1971] (Greek/English diglot) 12 vols.
-   *Josephus with an English Translation* by H.St.J. Thackeray [London: Heinemann,1926 reprinted 1966] (Greek/English diglot) 10 vols.
-   *Targum Neofiti 1: Genesis: Translated, with Apparatus and Notes* by M. McNamara *TAB* [Edinburgh:T&T Clark,1992].
-   *Targum Neofiti 1: Exodus: Translated, with Introduction and Apparatus* by M. McNamara and Notes by R. Hayward *TAB* [Edinburgh:T&T Clark,1994].
-   *The Targum Onqelos to Genesis: Translated, with a Critical Introduction, Apparatus, and Notes* by B. Grossfeld *TAB* [Edinburgh:T&T Clark,1988].
-   *The Targum Onqelos to Exodus: Translated, with Apparatus and Notes* by B.

Grossfeld *TAB* [Edinburgh:T&T Clark,1988].
- *The Targum of Chronicles: Translated, with Introduction, Apparatus, and Notes* by J.S. McIvor *TAB* [Edinburgh:T&T Clark,1994].
- *The Targum of the Minor Prophets: Translated, with a Critical Introduction, Apparatus, and Notes by K.J. Cathcart and R.P. Gordon TAB* [Edinburgh:T&T Clark,1989].
- *The Isaiah Targum: Introduction, Translation, Apparatus and Notes* by B. D. Chilton *TAB* [Edinburgh:T&T Clark,1987].
- *The Targum of Ezekiel: Translated, with a Critical Introduction, Apparatus, and Notes TAB* by S.H. Levey [Edinburgh:T&T Clark,1987].
- *The Babylonian Talmud: Translated into English with Notes, Glossary and Indices under the Editorship of* I. Epstein (ed). [London:Soncino Press,1935-61] 18 vols.
- *Mishnayoth: Pointed Hebrew Text, English Translation, Introductions, Notes, Supplement, Appendix, Indexes, Addenda, Corrigenda* by P. Blackman [Gateshead:Judaica, 2ⁿᵈ edn,1977].
- *The Midrash Rabbah: Translated into English with Notes, Glossary and Indices under the editorship of* H. Freeman and S. Maurice (eds.) [London:Soncino Press,1977] 5 vols.

b) Early Church
- *Ante-Nicene Christian Library: Translations of the Writings of the Fathers Down to 325CE* ed. A. Roberts & J. Donaldson [Edinburgh:T&T Clark,1867-69].
- *The Creeds of Christendom: With A History and Critical Notes* ed. P. Schaff, Revised D.S. Schaff [Grand Rapids:Baker, revised edn 1983].

c) Islamic Context
- A. Yusuf Ali *The Holy Qur'an: Translation and Commentary* [1934, reprinted Lahore:Sh. Muhammad Ashraf,1967].
- A.J. Arberry *The Koran Interpreted* [1930 – reprinted Oxford:OUP,1982].
- M.M. Pickthall *The Meanings of the Glorious Qur'an* [1930 – reprinted New Delhi:Kitab Bhavan,1993].
- *Mishkat al-Masabih* ET by al-Haj Maulana Fazlul Karim as *al-Hadis: An English Translation & Commentary* [Calcutta,1939/Lahore:Sh.Muhammad Ashraf,n.d.].
- 'Abd Allah ibn 'Umar al-Baidawi (d.c.1286) *Anwar al-Tanzil wa Asrar al-Ta'wil* ET by:
  - K. Cragg in *The Mind of the Qur'an.*
  - D.S. Margoliouth as *Chrestomathia Baidawiana* [London:Luzac,1894].
  - N. Robinson in *Christ in Islam and Christianity.*
  - S. Zwemer in *The Moslem Doctrine of God.*
  - W. Goldsack in *The Testimony of the Qur'an to Christ.*
  - G. Parrinder in *Jesus in the Qur'an.*

- Jalaluddin Muhammad bin Ahmad al-Shafi'i al-Mahalli (d.1454) and
  Jalaluddin 'Abdur Rahman bin Abu Bakr al-Suyuti (d.1505) *Tafsir al-Jalalain*
  ET from Arabic by:
    - S. Lane-Poole as *Selections From the Kuran* [London:Trubner,1879].
    - G. Sale in *The Koran* [1734,London:Warne,n.d. c.1936].
- Fakhr al-Din al-Razi (d.1209) *Mafatih al-Ghaib* ET from Arabic in N.
  Robinson *Christ in Islam and Christianity*.
- Abu Ja'far Muhammad bin Jarir al-Tabari (d. 923) *Jami' al-Bayan fi Tafsir al-
  Qur'an* ET from Arabic in N. Robinson *Christ in Islam and Christianity*.
- Sayyid Abdul A'la Mawdudi *Tafhim al-Qur'an* ET by Z.I. Ansari as *Towards
  Understanding Islam* 7 vols. [Leicester:Islamic Foundation,1988-2000].
- Sayyid Qutb *Fi Zilal al-Qur'an* ET from Arabic by M.A. Salahi &
  A.A. Shamis as *In the Shade of the Qur'an* vol.1 [Leicester:Islamic
  Foundation,1999].
- *Qessas al-Anbiya* ET by B. Azimabadi as *Qissasul Anbiya: Stories of the
  Prophets* [New Delhi:Saeed International,1994].
- Shah Waliyullah *Ta'wil al-Hadith* ET by G.N. Jalbani [Lahore:Sh.
  Muhammad Ashraf,1991].
- *The Masnavi* by Jalalu'd-Din Rumi ET by C.E. Wilson [1910 - reprinted
  Karachi:Indus,1976].
- Shams al-Din Muhammad Hafiz al-Shirazi *Divan* ET by:
    - G.M. Bell *Selected Sonnets From the Divan of Hafez* [1897, reprinted as
      Farsi/English diglot Tehran:Eghbal,1985].
    - *Ghazzalat Hafiz Shirazi* Persian/English diglot arranged by Mohsen
      Ramezani, based on original arrangement by A.J. Arberry with a Farsi
      introduction by Muhammad Ali Janab [Tehran:Padideh Publishing,
      1367 AH{P} =1947CE].
- Musleh ud-Din Sa'di Shiraz *Gulistan*. Published as *Gulistan of Shaikh Sa'di*
  [Islamabad:Iran-Pakistan Institute of Persian Studies,1984].
- J. Enevoldsen *The Nightingale of Peshawar Selections From Rahman Baba*
  [Peshawar InterLit,2nd edn,1993] (Pushtu/English diglot).
- Ibn Ishaq *Sirat Rasul Allah* (c.120 AH) ET by A. Guillaume as *The Life of
  Muhammad* [Karachi:OUP,1955,1996].
- *The Wasiyat Creed* attributed to Abu Hanifa and commentary ET in
  Wensinck *The Muslim Creed* 125-85.
- *Fikh Akbar 1 and Commentary* ET in Wensinck *The Muslim Creed* 103-17.
- *Fikh Akbar 2 and Commentary* ET in Wensinck *The Muslim Creed* 188-244.
- al-Ashari *Ibana 'an Usul al-Diyana* ET in Wensinck *The Muslim Creed* 88-90.
- al-Hujwiri *The Kashaf al-Mahjub* ET by R.A. Nicholson [1936- reprinted
  Karachi:Darul Ishaat,1990].

- A.A.B. Philips *The Fundamentals of Tawheed* [Riyadh:Tawheed Publications,1990] (Wahhabi text).
- M.A. Yusseff *The Gospel of Barnabas: Notes and Commentary* [Lahore:Muslim Educational Trust,n.d.].
- *Kitab Muqaddus* (Urdu Revised Version) [Lahore:Pakistan Bible Society,n.d.].
- *Kitab Muqadus* (Persian Bible Standard Version new edition,1996) [Godalming:Elam Ministries,1996].
- *Injil 'Isa Masih* (Farsi Contemporary Bible) [Colorado Springs:IBS,1995].
- *Kitab da Nui Ahed* (= Pushtu NT) [London:B&FBS,1890].
- *Kalam Allah* (= Pushtu Pentateuch) [London:B&FBS,1890].

Secondary Sources

Aalen, S.
- 'Glory, Honour: δόξα ' *NIDNTT* 2:44-48.

Ahmed, A.S.
- *Millennium and Charisma Among the Pathans: A Critical Essay in Social Anthropology* [London:RKP,1980].
- 'Islam and the District Paradigm: Emergent Trends in Contemporary Muslim Society' *CTIS* 17:2 (1983) 155-83.
- *Towards an Islamic Anthropology* [Herndon:International Institute for Islamic Thought,1986].
- *Islam Today* [London:Taurus,1999].

Anderson, G.H. (ed)
- *Biographical Dictionary of Christian Mission* [Cambridge:Eerdmans,1998].

Anderson, G.H., Coote, R.T., Horner, N.A. & Phillips, J.M. (eds)
- *Mission Legacies* [Maryknoll:Orbis,1994].

Bailey, K.E.
- *The Cross and the Prodigal* [St Louis:Concordia,1973 – reprinted Melbourne: Acorn Press,2000].

Barth, M.
- *Ephesians: Translation and Commentary on Chapters 4-6* AB [New York: Doubleday,1974].

Barrett, C.K.
- *A Commentary on the First Epistle to the Corinthians* [London:A&C Black, 2nd edn,1971].
- *A Critical and Exegetical Commentary on the Acts of the Apostles* ICC vol. 2 [Edinburgh:T&T Clark,1998].

Bauckham, R.
- *Jude, 2 Peter* WBC [Waco:Word,1983].
- *The Theology of the Book of Revelation* [Cambridge:CUP,1993].
- 'The Worship of Jesus' 118-149 in Bauckham *The Climax of Prophecy.*
- *The Climax of Prophecy: Studies on the Book of Revelation* [Edinburgh:T&T Clark,1993].
- *God Crucified: Monotheism and Christology in the New Testament* [Carlisle: Paternoster,1998].
- *Mission as a Hermeneutic for Scriptural Interpretation* CWC Position Paper 106 [Cambridge: Faculty of Divinity, University of Cambridge,1999].

Bavinck, J.H.
- *An Introduction to the Science of Missions* [Phillipsburg:Presbyterian & Reformed Publishing Co.,1960] ET from Dutch by D.H.Freeman of *Inleiding in de Zendingswetenschap* [Kampen:J.H.Kok,1954].

Beasley-Murray, G.R.
- βαπτίζω *NIDNTT* 1:144-45.

Bennett, C
- *Victorian Images of Islam* [London:Grey Seal,1992].
- 'Lewis Bevan Jones 1880-1960 Striving to Touch Muslim Hearts' *ML* 283-89.
- 'Henry Martyn 1781-1812 Scholarship in the Service of Mission'*ML* 264-70.
- 'Henry Martyn' *BDCM* 438.
- 'Tisdall, William St Clair' *BDCM* 673.
- 'Jones, Lewis Bevan' in *BDCM* 342.

Bevans, S.
- 'Models of Contextual Theology' *Missiology* 13:2 (1985) 185-202.

Birks, H.
- *The Life and Correspondence of Thomas Valpy French* [London:Murray,1895] 2 vols.

Blincoe, R
- *Ethnic Realities and the Church: Lessons from Kurdistan* [Pasadena: Presbyterian Centre for Mission Studies,1998].

Block, D.I.
- *The Book of Ezekiel: Chapters 1-24* [Grand Rapids:Eerdmans,1997].

Bosch, D.J.
- *Transforming Mission: Paradigm Shifts in Theology of Mission* [Maryknoll: Orbis,1991].

Botterweck, G.J., Ringgren, H. & Fabry, H-J. (eds)
- *Theological Dictionary of the Old Testament* [Grand Rapids; Eerdmans,1997] 8:308-325 ET from German by D.W. Stott of *Theologische Wörterbuch zum Alten Testament.*

Bousset, W.
- *Kyrios Christos: A History of the Belief in Christ from the Beginnings of Christianity to Irenaeus* ET by J. Steely from German 5th edn (1964) [Nashville:Abingdon,1970].

Brislen, M.
- 'A Model for a Muslim-Culture Church' *Missiology* 24:3 (1996) 355-67.

Brown, C. (ed)
- *New International Dictionary of New Testament Theology* [Carlisle: Paternoster,1986] 4 vols.

Brown, R.
- 'Forsyth, Peter Taylor' *NDT* 260-61.

Browne, E.G.
- *Literary History of Persia* [1906 - reprint New Delhi:Munshiram Manoharlal,1997].

Bruce, F.F.
- *1 and 2 Corinthians* [London:Oliphants,1971].
- *The Epistles to the Colossians, to Philemon and to the Ephesians NICNT* [Grand Rapids:Eerdmans,1984].
- *The Acts of the Apostles: The Greek Text with Introduction and Commentary* [Leicester:Apollos, 3rd rev'd. (edn,1990].

de Bruijn, J.T.P.
- *Persian Sufi Poetry: An Introduction to the Mystical Use of Classical Poems* [Richmond:Curzon,1977].

Burnett, D.
- *Unearthly Powers: A Christian Perspective on Primal and Folk Religions* [Eastbourne:MARC,1988].

Caroe, O.
- *The Pathans: 550 B.C.-A.D. 1957* [Karachi:OUP,1958,1983].

Carson, D.A.
- *The Gospel According to John* [Leicester:IVP,1991].

Casey, P.M.
- *From Jewish Prophet to Gentile God: The Origins and Development of New Testament Christology* [Cambridge:James Clarke,1991].

Catchpole, D.R.
- 'The Answer of Jesus to Caiaphas (Matt. XXV1.64)' *NTS* 17 (1970-71) 213-226.

Chapman, C.
- 'Rethinking the Gospel for Muslims' 107-125 in J.D. Woodberry (ed) *Muslims and Christians on the Emmaus Road* [Monrovia:MARC,1989].

Cheater, A.P.
- *Social Anthropology: An Alternative Introduction* [London Routledge,1986,1989].

Chester, A.
- 'Jewish Messianic Expectation and Mediatorial figures and Pauline christology' 17-89 in M. Hengel and U. Heckel (eds) *Paulus und das antike Judentum.*

Chilton, B.D.
- 'Rabbinic Literature:Targumim' *DNTB* 902-909.

Christensen, J.
- *The Practical Approach to Muslims* [Marseille:NAM,1977].

Cockerill, G.L.
- 'To the Hebrews/To the Muslims: Islamic Pilgrimage as a Key to Interpretation' *Missiology* 22:3 (1994) 347-59.
- *Guidebook for Pilgrims to the Heavenly City* [Pasadena:William Carey Library,2002].

Colgate, J.
- 'Muslim Women and the Occult: Seeing Jesus Set the Captives Free' 33-63 in F. Love and J. Eckheart (eds) *Ministry to Muslim Women.*

Cole, A.
- *Exodus: An Introduction and Commentary* [Leicester:IVP,1973].

Conzelmann, H.
- *1 Corinthians* [Philadephia:Fortress,1978] ET by J.W. Leitch of *Der erste Brief an die Korinther.*

Cotterell, P.
- *Mission and Meaninglessness* [London:SPCK,1990].

Cragg, K.
- *Christianity in World Perspective* [London:Lutterworth, 1968].
- *The Mind of the Qur'an* [London:Allen & Unwin, 1973].
- 'Temple Gairdner's Legacy' *IBMR*:5:4 (1981) 164-67.
- *Jesus and the Muslim: An Exploration* [London:Allen & Unwin,1985/Oxford].
- *The Christ and the Faiths: Theology in Cross-Reference* [London: SPCK, 1986].
- 'Gairdner, W(illiam) H(enry) Temple' *BDCM* 233-34.

Das, V.
- 'For a Folk-Theology and Theological Anthropology of Islam' *CTIS* 18:2 (1984) 293-300.

Dibelius, M. & Conzelmann, H.
- *A Commentary on the Pastoral Epistles* [Philadelphia:Fortress,1972] ET by P. Buttolph & A. Yarbro of M. Dibelius *Die Pastoralbriefe* 4th rev'd edn by H. Conzelmann.

Dodd, C.H.
- *The Interpretation of the Fourth Gospel* [Cambridge:CUP,1953].

Douglas, J.D.
- 'Mackintosh, Hugh Ross' *NDT* 409.

Douglas, J.D., Hillyer, N., Bruce, F.F., Guthrie, D., Millard, AR., Packer, J.I. & Wiseman, D.J. (eds)
- *New Bible Dictionary* [Leicester:IVP, 2nd edn,1982].

Dretke, J.P.
- *A Christian Approach to Muslims: Reflections from West Africa* [Pasadena: William Carey Library,1979].

D'Souza, A.
- 'Christian Approaches to the Study of Islam. An Analysis of the Writings of Watt and Cragg' *Bull.HMI* 11:2 (1992) 33-80.

Dunn, J.D.G.
- *Christology in the Making: A New Testament Inquiry into the Origins of the Doctrine of the Incarnation* [London:SCM,1980].
- *Romans 9-16* WBC [Dallas:Word,1988].
- *The Partings of the Ways: Between Christianity and Judaism and their Significance for the Character of Christianity* [London:SCM,1991].

Durham, J.I.
- *Exodus* WBC [Waco:Word,1987].

Dye, T.W.
- 'Towards a Cross-Cultural Definition of Sin' 439-54 in C.H. Kraft & T.N. Wisley (eds) *Readings in Dynamic Indigeneity*.

Edwards, D. (Pseudonym)
- '200 Years of Missions to Muslims Part 2. Claudius Buchanan and the Great Experiment' *CISN* 7 (1999) 8-9.

Ellicott, C.J.
- *The Pastoral Epistles of St. Paul: With a Critical and Grammatical Commentary, and a Revised Translation* [London:Longmans,Green,Reader & Dyer,1869].

Ellingworth, P. & Hatton, H.
- *A Translators Handbook on Paul's First Letter to the Corinthians* [London:UBS,1985].

Ellis, K.S.
- *'Degrees of Divinity': The Importance of the Role of Mediatorial Figures for an Understanding of Jewish Monotheism and the Development of Christological Beliefs* [unpublished Ph.D. thesis, London Bible College/Brunel University,1996].

Evans, C.A. & Porter, S.E. (eds)
- *Dictionary of New Testament Background* [Leicester:IVP,2000].

Fabry, H-J., Freedman, D.N. & Willoughby, B.E.
- *mal'ak* 8:308-25 in G.J. Botterweck, H. Ringgren & H.-J. Fabry (eds) *Theological Dictionary of the Old Testament*.

Fatehi, M.
- *The Spirit's Relation to the Risen Lord in Paul* [Tubingen:Mohr Siebeck,2000].

Fee, G.
- *The First Epistle to the Corinthians* [Grand Rapids:Eerdmans,1987].

Ferdinando, K.
- *The Triumph of Christ in African Perspective: A Study of Demonology and Redemption in the African Context* [Carlisle:Paternoster,1999].

Ferguson, S.B., Wright, D.F. & Packer, J.I. (eds)
- *New Dictionary of Theology* [Leicester:IVP,1988].

R. Finnegan
- *Oral Poetry: Its Nature, Significance and Social Context* [Bloomington & Indianapolis:Indiana University Press,1992].

Fitzmeyer, J.A.
- *The Gospel According to Luke (X-XXIV): Introduction, Translation, and Notes* AB [New York:Doubleday,1985].

Fohrer, G.
- 'σωτήρ in the OT' *TDNT* 7 1012-1013.
- 'σωτήρ in Later Judaism' *TDNT* 7 1013-1015.

Foster, B.E.
- 'Kenoticism' *NDT* 364.

France, R.T.
- *Jesus and the Old Testament: His Application of Old Testament Passages to Himself and His Mission* [London:Tyndale,1971].
- *The Gospel According to Matthew: An Introduction and Commentary* TNTC [Leiceter:IVP, 1985].

Gairdner, W.H.T.
- *The Reproach of Islam* [Edinburgh:Church of Scotland/United Free Church,1909]. Subsequently reprinted in its 5th edition (1920) as *The Rebuke of Islam.*
- *The Muslim Idea of God* [London:The Christian Literature Society,1909].
- 'The Doctrine of the Trinity in Unity' *MW* 1 (1911) 381-407.
- *God as Triune, Creator Incarnate, Atoner* [Madras:Christian Literature Society for India,1916].
- 'Christianity and Islam' in *The Christian Life and Message in Relation to Non-Christian Systems – Report of the Jerusalem Meeting of the International Missionary Council March 24th - April 8th 1928* [London:OUP,1928]:1:235-83.
- 'The Essentiality of the Cross' *MW* 33:3 (1933) 230-51.

Gardet, L.
- 'Allah' 406-17 in H.A.R. Gibb et al (eds) *Encyclopaedia of Islam,* (2nd revised edn) vol. 1.

Gatje, H.
- *The Qur'an and its Exegesis: Selected Texts with Classical and Modern Muslim Interpretations* [Oxford:Oneworld,1996] ET from German *Koran und Koranexegese* by A.T. Welch.

Geaves, R.
- *Sectarian Influences within Islam in Britain with Reference to the Concepts of 'Ummah' and 'Community'* [Leeds:University of Leeds,1996].

Gellner, E.
- 'A Pendulum Swing Theory of Islam' 128-38 in Robertson (ed) *Sociology of Religion.*

Gibb, H.A.R. et al (initial editorial committee)
- *Encyclopaedia of Islam* (revised edition) [Leiden:Brill,1979-].

Gieschen, C.
-   *Angelomorphic Christology: Antecedents and Early Evidence* [Leiden: Brill,1998].

Gilliland, D.
-   'Contextualisation' *EDWM* 225-27.

Glaser, I.J.
-   'Qur'anic Challenges for Genesis' *JSOT* 75 (1997) 3-19.

Glassé, C.
-   *Concise Encyclopaedia of Islam* [San Francisco:Harper & Row,1989].
-   'Bila Kayfa' *CEOI* 73-74.

Goddard, H.
-   *Muslim Perceptions of Christianity* [London:Grey Seal,1996].

Goldsack, W.
-   *The Testimony of the Qur'an to Christ* [Madras:Christian Literature Society,1905].
-   *Selections from Muhammadan Traditions* [Madras:Christian Literature Society for India,1923].

Green, J.B. & McKnight, S. (eds)
-   *Dictionary of Jesus and the Gospels* [Leicester:IVP,1992].

Green, J.B. & Turner, M. (eds)
-   *Jesus of Nazareth Lord and Christ: Essays on the Historical Jesus and New Testament Christology* [Carlisle:Paternoster:1994].

Grima, B.
-   *The Performance of Emotion Amongst Paxtun Women: "The Misfortunes Which Have Befallen Me"* [Austin:University of Texas Press,1992].

Hancock, C.D.
-   'Gore, Charles' *NDT* 278.

Hanson, A.T.
-   *Jesus Christ in the Old Testament* [London:SPCK,1965].

Harris, H.
-   'Strauss, David Friedrich' *NDT* 663.

Harris, M.J.
-   *Jesus as God: The New Testament use of Theos in Reference to Jesus* [Grand Rapids:Baker,1992].
-   *Colossians & Philemon* EGGNT [Grand Rapids:Eerdmans,1991]

Hengel, M.
-   'Hymns and Christology' 78-96 in M. Hengel *Between Jesus and Paul.*

- *Between Jesus and Paul: Studies in the Earliest History of Christianity* [London: SCM,1983].
- *Studies in Early Christology* [Edinburgh:T&T Clark,1995].

Hengel, M. and Heckel, U. (eds)
- *Paulus und das antike Judentum* [Tubingen:Mohr,1991].

Hiebert, P.G.
- *Cultural Anthropology* [Grand Rapids:Baker,1976,1983].
- 'The Flaw of the Excluded Middle' *Missiology* 10:1 (1982) 37-47.
- *Anthropological Reflections on Missiological Issues* [Grand Rapids:Baker,1994].

Hillyer, P.N.
- 'Ritschl, Albrecht' *NDT* 595-6.

Horbury, W.
- *Jewish Messianism and the Cult of Christ* [London:SCM,1998].

Hughes, T.P.
- *Dictionary of Islam* [London:Allen,1885: reprinted Calcutta:Rupa,1988].

Hurst, L.D.
- 'Re-enter the Pre-existent Christ in Philippians 2:5-11?' *NTS* 32 (1986) 449-557.

Hurtado, L.W.
- *One God, One Lord: Early Christian Devotion and Ancient Jewish Monotheism* [Edinburgh:T&T Clark,1988,1998].
- *At the Origins of Christian Worship: The Context and Character of Earliest Christian Devotion* [Carlisle:Paternoster,1999].
- 'The Binitarian Shape of Early Christian Worship' 187-213 in C.C. Newman et al (eds) *The Jewish Roots of Christological Monotheism.*
- *Lord Jesus Christ: Devotion to Jesus in Earliest Christianity* [Cambridge: Eerdmans.2003].

Ingleby, J.
- 'Trickling Down or Shaking the Foundations: Is Contextualization Neutral?' *Missiology* 25:2 (1997) 183-87.

Jeremias, J.
- *The Prayers of Jesus* [London:SCM,1967] ET from German of *Abba, Studien zue Neutestamentlichen Theologie und Zeitgeschichte.*

Jones, L.B.
- *Christianity Explained to Muslims: A Manual for Christian Workers* [Calcutta: YMCA,1938].

- *From Islam to Christ: How a Sufi found His Lord: Life of Bishop J. Subhan* [Brighton:FFM,1952].
- *The People of the Mosque: An Introduction to the Study of Islam with Special Reference to India* [London:SCM,1932, 3rd rev'd edn,1959].

Kasemann, E.
- 'An Apologia for Primitive Christian Eschatology' 169-195 in *Essays on New Testament Themes*, [London:SCM,1964] ET by W.J. Montague from German *Exegetische Versuche und Besinnungen*.

Kelly, J.N.D.
- *Early Christian Doctrines* [London:A&C Black,5th edn,1977].

Kerr, D.A.
- 'The Problem of Christianity in Muslim Perspective: Implications for Christian Mission' *IBMR* 5:4 (1981) 152-62.
- 'Abdul Masih, Salih' *BDCM* 1.
- 'Calverley, Edwin Elliot' *BDCM* 110.
- 'Cragg, Albert Kenneth' *BDCM* 157.
- 'French, Thomas Valpy' *BDCM* 227.
- 'Imad ud-Din' *BDCM* 317-18.

Kitchen, K.
- 'Some Egyptian Background to the Old Testament' *TynBul* 5-6 (1960) 4-18.
- *Ancient Orient and Old Testament* [London:Tyndale,1966].

Kittel, G. & Friedrich, G. (eds)
- *Theological Dictionary of the New Testament* [Grand Rapids:Eerdmans,1964-76] 10 vols. ET from German by G.W. Bromiley of *Theologische Wörterbuch zum Neun Testament*.

Knight, G.W.
- *The Pastoral Epistles* NIGTC [Carlisle:Paternoster,1992].

Koester, C.R.
- *Hebrews: A New Translation with Introduction and Commentary* AB [New York:Doubleday,2001].

Koyama, K.
- 'The Asian Approach to Christ' *Missiology* 12:4 (1984) 435-47.

Kraft, C.H.
- *Christianity in Culture: A Study in Dynamic Biblical Theologizing in Cross-Cultural Perspective* [Maryknoll:Orbis,1979].
- 'Dynamic Equivalence Churches: An Ethnological Approach to Indigenity' 87-111 in C.H. Kraft and T.N. Wisley (eds) *Readings in Dynamic Indigeneity*.

Kraft, C.H. & Wisley, T.N. (eds)
- *Readings in Dynamic Indigeneity* [Pasadena:William Carey Library,1979].

Kreitzer, L.J.
- *Jesus and God in Paul's Eschatology* JSNT Supp. Series 19 [Sheffield: JSOT,1987].

de Kuiper, A & Newman, B.
- 'Jesus, Son of God – a Translation Problem' *BT* 28:4 (1977) 432-38.

Kynsh, A.D.
- *Islamic Mysticism: A Short History* [Leiden:Brill,1999].

Lamb, C.
- *The Call to Retrieval: Kenneth Cragg's Christian Vocation to Islam.* [London: Grey Seal,1997].

Lane, (T) A.N.S.
- *The Lion Book of Christian Thought* [Oxford:Lion,2nd edn1992].

Lane-Poole, S.
- *Selections From the Kuran* [London:Trubner,1879].

Larson, W.F.
- *Islamic Ideology and Fundamentalism in Pakistan: Climate for Conversion to Christianity?* [Lanhan:University Press of America,1998].

Latourette, K.S.
- *A History of the Expansion of Christianity* [New York:Harper & Row,1937,1965,1970 – reprinted Exeter:Paternoster,1971] 7 vols.

Lee, S.
- *Controversial Tracts on Christianity and Mohammedanism by the Late Rev. Henry Martyn,B.D.* [Cambridge:no publisher cited in book,1824].

Lewis, P.
- *Pirs, Shrines and Pakistani Islam* [Rawalpindi:CSC,1985].

Lindars, B.
- *The Gospel of John NCB* [London:Oliphants,1972].

Loewenthal, I.
- *The Name 'Isa* - paper read at the American (Presbyterian) Mission meeting at Subathu, November 1860 and subsequently published [Calcutta:Baptist Mission Press,1861] later reprinted in *MW* 1:3 (1911) 265-82 with an introduction by S.M. Zwemer.

Longenecker, R.N.
- *The Christology of Early Jewish Christianity* [London:SCM,1970].

Love, F. & Eckheart, J. (eds)
- *Ministry to Muslim Women: Longing to Call Them Sisters* [Pasadena: William Carey Library,2000].

Love, R.
- *Muslims, Magic and the Kingdom of God* [Pasadena: William Carey Library,2000].

Margoliouth, D.S.
- *Chrestomathia Baidawiana* [London:Luzac,1894].

Marshall, I.H.
- *The Gospel of Luke: A Commentary on the Greek Text* NIGTC [Exeter: Paternoster,1978].
- 'Culture and the New Testament' 17-31 in J.R.W. Stott & R. Coote (eds) *Down to Earth, Studies in Christianity and Culture: The Papers of the Lausanne Consultation on Gospel and Culture.*
- *The Origins of New Testament Christology* [Leicester:Apollos,2nd edn 1990].
- *A Critical and Exegetical Commentary on The Pastoral Epistles* ICC [Edinburgh:T&T Clark,1999].

Martyn, H(enry)
- 'In Reply to Mirza Ibrahim' (Martyn's second Persian tract) ET by S. Lee in *Controversial Tracts on Christianity and Mohammedanism* 102-23.
- 'On the Vanity of the Sofee System, and on the Truth of the Religion of Moses and Jesus' (Martyn's third Persian tract) ET by S. Lee in *Controversial Tracts on Christianity and Mohammedanism* 139-60.

McClintock, W.
- 'Demons and Ghosts in Indian Folklore' *Missiology* 18:1 (1990) 37-47.

McCurry, D.M. (ed)
- *The Gospel and Islam: A 1978 Compendium* [Monrovia:MARC,1979].

McGavran, D.A.
- *Understanding Church Growth* [1970 – 3rd edn revised and edited by C.P. Wagner,Grand Rapids:Eerdmans,1990].

McIvor, J.S.
- *The Targum of Chronicles: Translated, with Introduction, Apparatus, and Notes* by J.S. McIvor *TAB* [Edinburgh:T&T Clark,1994].

Meyer, B.F.
- *Critical Realism and the New Testament* [Alison Park:Pickwick,1989].

Moo, D.J.
- *The Letter of James: An Introduction and Commentary* TNTC [Leicester:IVP,1985].

Moreau, A.S., Netland, H. & Van Engen, C. (eds)
- *Evangelical Dictionary of World Missions* [Carlisle:Paternoster,2000].

Morris, L.
- *The Gospel According to St. Luke: An Introduction and Commentary* TNTC [Leicester:IVP,1974].
- *The Gospel According to John: The English Text with Introduction, Exposition and Notes NICNT* [Grand Rapids:Eerdmans,1971].

Motyer, J.A.
- *The Revelation of the Divine Name* [London:Tyndale,1959].

Mounce, W.D.
- *Pastoral Epistles* WBC [Nashville:Nelson,2000].
- *The Book of Revelation* NICNT [Grand Rapids:Eerdmans, 2nd rev'd edn,1998].

Muir, W.(Sir)
- The Life of Mahomet and History of Islam to the Era of the Hegira [London:Smith Elder,1858].

Mujeeb, M.
- *The Indian Muslims* [London:Allen & Unwin,1967].

Musk, B.A.
- *The Unseen Face of Islam: Sharing the Gospel with Ordinary Muslims* [Speldhurst:MARC,1989].
- *Touching the Soul of Islam: Sharing the Gospel in Muslim Cultures* [Crowborough:MARC,1995].

J. Napper
- 'The Divine Liturgy: The Heart of Worship in the Orthodox Church' 46-54 in D.P. Teague (ed) *Turning Over a New Leaf: Protestant Missions and the Orthodox Churches of the Middle East*.

Nazir Ali, M.
- *Islam: A Christian Perspective* [Exeter:Paternoster,1983].
- 'Directions in Mission: Christian Worship, Witness and Work in Islamic Contexts' *IRM* 76:1 (1987) 33-37.
- *Frontiers in Muslim-Christian Encounter* [Oxford:Regnum,1987].

Neely, A.
-   'Zwemer, Samuel Marinus' *BDCM* 763.

Newman, B.M. & Nida, E.A.
-   *A Translator's Handbook on the Gospel of John* [London:UBS,1980].

Newman, C.C., Davila, J.R. & Lewis, G.S. (eds)
-   *The Jewish Roots of Christological Monotheism: Papers from the St. Andrews Conference on the Historical Origins of the Worship of Jesus* [Brill:Leiden,1999].

Neusner, J., Green, W.S. & Frerichs, E. (eds)
-   *Judaisms and Their Messiahs at the Turn of the Christian Era* [Cambridge: CUP,1987].

Newbigin, L.
-   *Trinitarian Doctrine for Today's Mission* [1963 – reprinted Carlisle: Paternoster,1998].
-   *The Gospel in a Pluralist Society* [London:SPCK,1989].

Nichols, B.J.
-   'New Theological Approaches in Muslim Evangelism' 155-163 in D. McCurry (ed) *The Gospel and Islam: A 1978 Compendium.*

Nicholson, R.A.
-   *The Mystics of Islam* [1914, reprinted Lahore:Islamic Book Service,1997].

Nida, E.
-   'Are We Really Monotheists?' *PA* 6:2 (1959) 49-54 reprinted in W.A. Smalley *Readings in Missionary Anthropology*:223-28.

Niehaus, J.
-   *God at Sinai: Covenant and Theophany in the Bible and Ancient Near East* [Carlisle:Paternoster,1995].
-   'Theophany, Theology of' *NIDOTTE* 1247-50.

Packer, J.I.
-   'The Gospel: Its content and Communication – a Theological Perspective' 97-114 in J.R.W. Stott & R.T. Coote (eds) *Down to Earth.*

Padwick, C.E.
-   *Temple Gairdner of Cairo* [London:SPCK,1929].

Parrinder, G.
-   *Jesus in the Qur'an* [London:Sheldon,1965,1977].

Parshall, P.
-   *The Fortress and the Fire: Jesus Christ and the Challenge of Islam* [Bombay: Gospel Literature Service,1975].

- *New Paths in Muslim Evangelism: Evangelical Approaches to Contextualisation* [Grand Rapids:Baker,1980].
- *Bridges to Islam: A Christian Perspective on Folk Islam* [Grand Rapids: Baker,1983].
- *Beyond the Mosque: Christians within Muslim Community* [Grand Rapids Baker,1985].
- *The Cross and the Crescent: Understanding the Muslim Mind and Heart* [Wheaton:Tyndale House,1989/Amersham:Scripture Press,1990].
- *Inside the Community: Understanding Muslims through Their Traditions* [Grand Rapids:Baker,1994].

Pfander, K.G.
- *Tariq al-Hayat* (= 'The Path of Life') [Lahore:Punjab Religious Book Society,1847] (Urdu).
- *Hal al-Ishkal da Jawab Kashf al-Astar wa Kitab Istifsar* (= 'Solution of difficulties in answer to the 'Kashf al-Astar' and the 'Kitab Istifsar') [Agra:no publisher stated,1847] (Persian).
- *Kitab Mizan al-Haqq* (= 'The Balance of Truth) [Agra:no publisher stated, 3rd rev'd edn, 1849] (Persian).
- *Kitab Mizan al-Haqq* [Agra:Agra Religious Tract Society, 2nd rev'd edn,1850] (Urdu).
- *The Mizan ul Haqq or, Balance of Truth by Rev C.G. Pfander, D.D.* ET by R.H. Weakley [London:CMS,1867].
- *Miftah al-Asrar* (= 'The Key of Mysteries') [Agra: no publisher stated,1850] (Persian).
- *Miftah al-Asrar* [Agra:Agra Religious Tract Society, 2nd rev'd edn,1850] (Urdu).

Poston, L.
- 'Gairdner, William Henry Temple' *EDWM* 383-84.

Powell, A.A.
- *Muslims and Missionaries in Pre-Mutiny India* [Richmond:Curzon,1993].

Von Rad, G.
- *Genesis: A Commentary* [London: SCM, 1972] ET by J.H. Marks from German. *Das erste Buch Mose, Genesis.*

Rahbar, D.
- 'Christian Apologetic to Muslims' *IRM* 54:3 (1965) 353-59.

Rahman, F.
- *Islam* [London:Weidenfeld & Nicolson,1966].

Rice, W.A.
- *Crusaders of the Twentieth Century, or The Christian Missionary and the Muslim* [Published by author – but supplied London:CMS,1910].

Ro, B.R. & Eshenaur, R.
- *The Bible and Theology in Asian Contexts: An Evangelical Perspective on Asian Theology* [Taichung:Asia Theological Association,1984].

Robinson, N.
- *Christ in Islam and Christianity* [Basingstoke:Macmillan,1991].

Rowden, H.H. (ed)
- *Christ The Lord: Studies in Christology Presented to Donald Guthrie* [Leicester: IVP,1982].

Rowland, C.
- 'The Vision of the Risen Christ in Rev.1:13ff.: The Debt of an Early Christology to an Aspect of Jewish Angelology' *JTS* 31 (1980) 1-11.
- *The Open Heaven: A Study of Apocalyptic in Judaism and Early Christianity* [London:SPCK,1982].

Roy, O.
- *Islam and Resistance in Afghanistan* [Cambridge:CUP,2nd edn, 1990] ET from French of *L'Afghanistan: Islam et modernite politique*.

Rudwin, A.
- 'Islam – An Absolutely Different Ethos?' *IRM* 71:1 (1987) 59-65.

Sanneh, L.O.
- 'Jesus, Son of God – a Translation Problem – Further Comments' *BT* 28:4 (1977) 241-44.

Sargent, J.
- *The Life and Letters of Henry Martyn* [1819,1862 – reprinted Edinburgh: Banner of Truth,1985].

Schirrmacher, C.
- 'Muslim Apologetics and the Agra Debates of 1854: A Nineteenth Century Turning Point' *Bull.HMI* 13:1 (1994) 74-84.

Schlorff, S.
- 'Muslim Ideology and Christian Apologetics' *Missiology* 21:2 (1993) 173-85.

Schnackenburg, R.
- *The Gospel According to St. John* [London:Burns & Oates,1980] ET by C. Hastings, F. McDonagh, D. Smith & R. Foley of *Das Johannesevangelium*.

Schneider, J. & Brown, C.
-   'σωτήρ' *NIDNTT* 3:216-223.

Schoeps, H.J.
-   *Paul: The Theology of the Apostle in the Light of Jewish Religious History*
    [London:Lutterworth,1961] ET by H. Knight of *Paulus: Die Theologie des
    Apostels im Lichte der Judischen Religionsgeschichte.*

Scott, M.
-   *Sophia and the Johannine Jesus* JSNT Supp. series 71 [Sheffield:JSOT,1992].

Segal, A.
-   *Two Powers in Heaven: Early Rabbinic Reports about Christianity and
    Gnosticism* [Leiden:Brill,1977].

Shah, Sirdar Iqbal Ali
-   *Afghanistan of the Afghans* [London:Diamond,1928].
-   *Islamic Sufism* [1933 - reprint Delhi:Idarah-i-Adabiyat-i-Delhi,1979].

Shenk, W.
-   'Claudius Buchanan 1766-1815 - Laying the Foundation for an Indian
    Church' *ML* 255-263.

Smalley, S.
-   *John – Evangelist and Interpreter* [Carlisle:Paternoster,1978,rev'd edn,1998].

Smalley, W.A.
-   *Readings in Missionary Anthropology* [New York:Practical
    Anthropology,1967].

Smith, G.
-   *Henry Martyn, Saint and Scholar: First Modern Missionary to the
    Mohammedans,1781-1812* [London:RTS,1892].

Sookhdeo, P.
-   *A People Betrayed: The Impact of Islamization on the Christian Community in
    Pakistan* [Fearn:Christian Focus,2002].

Snider, N.
-   'Mosque Education in Afghanistan' *MW* 58:1 (1968) 24-35.

Speight, R.M.
-   'Some Bases for a Christian Apologetic to Islam' *IRM* 54:2 (1965) 193-205.

Stacey, V.
-   *Life of Henry Martyn* [Hyderabad:Henry Martyn Institute,1980].
-   *Christ Supreme over Satan: Spiritual Warfare, Folk Religion and the Occult*
    [Lahore:MIK,1986].

- *Thomas Valpy French First Bishop of Lahore* [Rawalpindi:Christian Study Centre, 2nd edn,1993].
- 'The Legacy of Thomas Valpy French' French *ML* 277-282.

Steffan, T.A.
- *Passing the Baton: Church Planting that Empowers* [La Habra:COMD,1993].
- *Reconnecting God's Story to Ministry: Crosscultural Storytelling at Home and Abroad* [La Habra:COMD,1996].

Stewart, R.A.
- 'Shekinah' *NBD²* 1101-1102.

Stock, E.
- *The History of the Church Missionary Society* 4 vols [London:CMS,1899-1916].

Stott, J.R.W. & Coote, R.T. (eds)
- *Down to Earth: Studies in Christianity and Culture: The Papers of the Lausanne Consultation on Gospel and Culture* [London:Hodder & Stoughton,1980].

Stowe, D.M.
- 'Barton, James Levi' *BDCM* 46.

Stuckenbruck, L.T.
- *Angel Veneration and Christology: A Study in Early Judaism and in the Christology of the Apocalypse of John* [Tubingen:Mohr,1995].

Sweetman, J.W.
- *Islam and Christian Theology: A Study in the Interpretation of the Theological Ideas in the Two Religions* 2 vols each of 2 parts [London:Lutterworth,1945-67].

Taber, C.
- 'Contextualisation: Indiginization and/or Transformation' 143-54 in D.M. McCurry (ed) *The Gospel and Islam: a 1978 Compendium.*

Teague, D.P.
- *Turning Over A New Leaf: Protestant Missions and the Orthodox Churches of the Middle East: The Final Report of the Multi-Mission Study Group on Orthodoxy* [London:Interserve/Lynnwood:Middle East Media,2nd edn 1992].

Tisdall, W. St Clair
- *The Sources of Islam* [1900] ET from Persian by Sir W. Muir [Edinburgh: T&T Clark,1905].
- *A Manual of the Leading Mohammadanian Objections to Christianity* [London: SPCK,1904] subsequently republished under the title *Christian Reply to Muslim Objections* [Villach:Light of Life,1980].
- Revision and expansion of C.(K.)G. Pfander's *Mizan ul Haqq* [London:1910

- – reprinted Villach:Light of Life,1986].
-   Revision of K.G. Pfander's *Miftah al-Asrar* [London:Christian Literature Society for India,1912].

Titus, M.
-   *Indian Islam* [London:OUP,1930].

Turner, M.M.B.
-   'The Spirit of Christ and Christology' 168-90 in H.H. Rowden (ed) *Christ The Lord: Studies in Christology Presented to Donald Guthrie.*
-   'The Spirit of Christ and "Divine" Christology' 413-436 in J.B. Green & M. Turner (eds) *Jesus of Nazareth Lord and Christ.*

Vander Werff, L.L.
-   *Christian Mission to Muslims: The Record, Anglican and Reformed Approaches in India and the Near East 1800-1938* [Pasadena:Wiliam Carey,1977].
-   'Our Muslim Neighbours: The Contribution of Samuel M. Zwemer to Christian Mission' *Missiology* 10:2 (1982) 185-97.
-   'The Names of Christ in Worship' 175-194 in J.D. Woodberry (ed) *Muslims and Christians on the Emmaus Road.*

VanGemeren, W.A. (ed)
-   *New International Dictionary of Old Testament Theology and Exegesis* [Carlisle: Paternoster,1997].

Weakley, R.H.
-   (ET of) *The Mizan ul Haqq* or, Balance of Truth by Rev C.(K.)G. Pfander [London:CMS,1867].

Webster, J.B.
-   'Barth, Karl' *NDT* 76-80.

Wensinck, A.J.
-   *The Muslim Creed: Its Genesis and Historical Development* [Cambridge: CUP,1932. 2nd edn New Delhi:Oriental Books Reprint Corporation,1979].

Westermarck, E.
-   *Pagan Survivals in Mohammedan Civilisation* [London:Macmillan,1933].

Wherry, E.M.
-   *The Muslim Controversy* [London:The Christian Literature Society,1905].

Williams, D.J.
-   *Acts* NIBC [Carlisle:Paternoster,1990].

Williams, S.N.
- 'Deism' *NDT* 190.

Wilson, J.C. (Snr)
- *Apostle to Islam: A Biography of Samuel M. Zwemer* [Grand Rapids: Baker,1952].

Witherington, B. (iii)
- 'Lord' *DJG* 484-92.
- *The Acts of the Apostles: A Socio-Rhetorical Commentary* [Grand Rapids: Eerdmans,1998].

Woodberry, J.D. (ed)
- Muslims and Christians on the Emmaus Road [Monrovia:MARC,1989].

Wright, D.F.
- 'Platonism' *NDT* 517-19.

Wright, N.T.
- *The New Testament and the People of God* [London:SPCK,1992].

Yoder, J.J.
- 'The Trinity and Christian Witness to Muslims' *Missiology* 22:3 (1994) 339-46.

Zwemer, S.M.
- *The Moslem Doctrine of God: An Essay on the Character and Attributes of Allah According to Koran and Orthodox Tradition* [Boston:American Tract Society,1905 – reprinted Moseley:The Message for Muslims Trust,1981].
- *Islam: A Challenge to Faith: Studies on the Mohammedan Religion and the Needs and Opportunities of the Mohammedan World from the Standpoint of Christian Missions* [New York:SVM,1907].
- 'The Name 'Isa' Introduction to I. Loewenethal's paper 'The Name 'Isa' in *MW* 1:3 (1911) 265-82.
- *The Moslem Christ: An Essay on the Life, Character, and Teachings of Jesus Christ According to the Koran and Orthodox Tradition* [Edinburgh: Oliphant, Anderson & Ferrier,1912] – reprinted as *The Muslim Christ* [Moseley,Birmingham:The Message for Muslims Trust,n.d.].
- *Dynamic Christianity and the World Today* [London:IVF,1939].
- 'Karl Gottlieb Pfander 1841-1941' *MW* 31:3 (1941) 217-26.

Sources not Ascribed to Specific Authors

- *The Christian Life and Message in Relation to Non-Christian Systems – Report of the Jerusalem Meeting of the International Missionary Council March 24ᵗʰ-April 8ᵗʰ 1928* [London:OUP,1928].
- *First Report of the Church Missionary Society's Mission to the Afghans at Peshawur for the years 1855 and 1856* [Agra,1857].
- Report of the 1981 Pattaya consultation *Christian Witness to Muslims* Lausanne Occasional Paper No.13. LCWE web site 1ˢᵗ March 2004: www.gospelcom.net/lcwe/LOP/lop13.htm

Supplementary Citations

- Hymns Ancient and Modern [London:Clowes,1916].
- Philo 'On the Embassy to Gaius' in *Philo with an English Translation* by F.H. Colson and G.H. Whitaker [London:Heinemann,1929 – reprinted 1971].
- *Handel Messiah Highlights* (CD) Chicago Symphony Orchestra & Chorus, Sir George Solti [London:Penguin/Decca,1998].
- Christian History Institute web site 15ᵗʰ April 2004: http://www.gospelcom.net/chi/GLIMPSEF/Glimpses//glmps147.shtml.

Index of Modern Scholars

Index of Primary Sources

Primary Sources: Second Temple Judaism and Early Christianity

Old Testament

New Testament

Matthew

10:9	242
10:17-19	102
10:20	73
10:22	101, 105
11:13	102
11:14-26	242
11:14ff	242
11:19	71
11:20	85
11:47-48	71
18:31-33	135
20:9-19	135
20:37	133
22:70	105
22:29-30	101
23:46	123
24:25-27	135, 135, 135
24:27	180
24:37-43	134
24:40-47	135
24:44-49	135, 248
24:44ff	180
24:45ff	135
24:46-49	249

John

1:1	90, 91
1:1-3	78, 79, 89, 100, 104, 122, 176, 240, 249
1:1-11	135
1:1-18	74, 103, 133, 240
1:8-9	242
1:10	78, 79, 100, 104, 240
1:10-11ff	181
1:10-12	248
1:14	89, 104, 105, 135, 243
1:18	90, 91, 104, 107-108, 108, 133, 133, 244
1:29	120, 245
1:33	102
1:36	120
3:11-13	116
3:13	71, 247
3:16-18	105, 240
3:28-29	103
3:29	176, 178
3:35	105, 105
3:35f	101
4:10-14	179
4:13-14	240
4:14	38, 176, 249
5:20	105, 105
5:21-27	240, 249

8:9-11	244
8:11	100, 102, 244, 249
8:14-17	105
8:17	104
8:32	120, 135
8:34	176, 241
9:5	90, 91
9:20	100
9:26	103
10:9	125, 137, 137
10:9-10	240
10:9-13	137
11:33-36	80
11:36	79.81, 100
12:6	137
15:16	244
15:18-19	242
16:27	136

1 Corinthians

1:2	137
1:8	134
1:18	135
1:21-23	180
1:23	135
1:24	176, 242
2:2	135
2:8	104, 243

3:13	134
5:5	134
5:7	137, 137
5:13	100
6:2-3	70, 101
6:11	244
7:23	246
8:4-6	138
8:6	78, 79, 79, 79, 79, 100, 100, 100, 100, 104, 104, 128-29, 138, 240, 240, 244, 248, 249
10:1-10	111
10:18-22	137
11:20	127, 137
11:23-32	137
12:2-3	137
12:3	20
12:7-11	137
12:27-31	137
13:12	109, 133, 177, 245, 249
14:1-33	137
14:29-52	137
14:37-38	137
14:39-40	137

OT Apocrypha and Pseudepigrapha

Additions to Esther

Apocalypse of Abraham

Apocalypse of Zephaniah (A)

Apocalypse of Zephaniah (B)

2 Baruch

Works of Philo

De Agricultura

| 50-51 | 70 |

De Confusione Linguarum

| 62-63 | 65, 74 |

De Decalogo

| 60-64 | 70, 71, 71 |

De Fuga et Inventione

| 161-162 | 61, 73 |
| 164-65 | 70, 73 |

De Legatione ad Gaium

| 118 | 75, 100 |

Legum Allegoriarum

| 3:206 | 70 |

De Opificio Mundi

| 25 | 92, 104 |

De Posteritate Caini

| 167 | 70.70 |

Quod Deus sit Immutabilis

| 51-68 | 70, 72 |

De Vita Contemplatiea

| 6 | 70, 71, 71 |

Works of Josephus

Jewish Antiquities

4:212	136
8:45-49	71
12:22	xxxvii
18:14-16	73
18:16	73
18:17	73

Qumran Texts

1QS 10:9-10	136
1QH Hymn 16:27	70
1QH Hymn 16:33	70
1QH Hymn 19:1ff	70
1QH Hymn 23:10	70
1QM8:5-10	73
1QapGen passim	104
1QapGen 2:13	70
1QapGen 6:4	70
1QapGen 7:5	70
1QapGen 12:17	70
1QapGen 21:8	72
1Q36	136
4Q88	136
4Q119-122	
4Q163:1	70
4Q196-200	71

Targums

Targum of Chronicles

Targum of Isaiah

Targum of Ezekiel

Targum of the Minor Prophets

Targum Neofiti

Targum Onqelos

Other Rabbinical Texts

Mishnah

Midrash Rabbah

Q3:55	165, 248
Q3:59	179, 179
Q3:64	176
Q3:81	xxxvii
Q3:103	174
Q3:135	174
Q3:181-184	135
Q3:189	174
Q4:48	173
Q4:75	174
Q4:87	173
Q4:153	177
Q4:155-58	135
Q4:157	180
Q4:158	217
Q4:164	159, 178
Q4:170	174
Q4:171	179, 179, 241
Q4:171-72	179
Q5:19	179, 179, 179
Q5:72	104
Q5:72-77	134
Q5:75	134, 179, 179
Q5:75-80	179
Q5:78	180
Q5:110	102
Q5:119-20	179, 179, 179

Q6:31	177
Q6:56	176
Q6:61	174
Q6:63	174
Q6:71	174
Q6:73	173, 174
Q6:95-102	176
Q6:102	174
Q6:102-103	177
Q6:103	154, 244
Q6:114	174
Q6:164	166, 174, 234
Q7:11-18	176
Q7:11ff	71
Q7:54	174, 248
Q7:104	174
Q7:143	159, 178
Q7:143-45	177
Q7:144-45	178
Q7:155	178
Q7:158	173
Q7:190	173
Q9:30f	179
Q9:129	174
Q10:3	176
Q10:4	174
Q10:9	248
Q10:37	174
Q10:98	180

Ahadith
(Mishkat al-Masabih)

Names

Diseases-Treatment

Omens

Burial

Predestination

Mosques

Prayer-Takbir

Invocations

Names-Allah

Tafsir

Other Islamic Texts

The Gospel of Barnabas

passim   41

Ibn Ishaq: Sirat Rasul Allah

239-40   176

272   177

Philips: Tawheed* (Wahhabi)

                        177, 177

Bible Translations

Farsi: Kitab Muqaddus

2 Cor.4:4   202

Col.1:15   202

Farsi Contemporary NT: Injil 'Isa Masih

2 Cor.4:4   202

Col.1:15   202

Urdu: Kitab Muqaddas

passim

2 Cor.4:4   202

Col.1:15   202

Notes

Texts marked with an asterisk (*) are not versified and are therefore simply referred to on the page in which they are cited in this study.

Islamic *tafsir* are referred to according to the verse of the Qur'an/Ahadith commented on, except in introductory sections where page numbers are used.

Islamic creeds are cited according to their commonly used article numbers.

SUBJECT INDEX

Abba 26, 44 n.207

Agra debate (1853) 6, 10, 21-22, 262-263

Ahadith xxvi, 140, 269

Ahmadiyya 10-11, 21

Angel of the Lord (see *Malak YHWH*)

Anthropological categories xxxii-xxxv, 264-268

Apocrypha xxvi

Apologetics (early Church) 115-116, 117-120

Apologetic response to Islamic denials

- Christus victor motif 220

- Combining titles with divine and human referents 218

- Concept of sacrifice 219-220

- Jesus sufferings prophesied by all the prophets 218

- Suffering as normative experience of prophets 218

- Use of local cultural themes (Hospitality; corporate responsibility for wrongdoing; Lover/Beloved imagery; ideal man/ideal woman images) 221-223

- Vindication of Jesus' honour 218-219

Aqedath Isaac, 233